MW01076032

UNSHACKLING INDIA

Praise for *Unshackling India*

'Ajay Chhibber and Salman Anees Soz have written a truly wonderful book on India's current economic predicament and the way forward to achieving shared prosperity by 2047. It's a big book, but every page is lucidly written and worth reading. Packed with a wealth of information and clear, persuasive analysis backed by thorough research, this book is a must read for anyone interested in the future that India deserves, be they scholars, policymakers, students or thinking citizens.'

—Shankar Acharya, former Chief Economic Adviser to the Government of India, author of *An Economist at Home and Abroad*

'If you want to understand why India's economy, lauded only a decade ago as one of the most dynamic in the world, is now ailing, and what it will take to fix it, *Unshackling India* is the book to read. In clear and direct language, without resorting to economic jargon, Ajay Chhibber and Salman Anees Soz present a sweeping agenda of reforms to reinvigorate growth and share the benefits more equitably—in their words to make the country both more prosperous and happier.'

—Liaquat Ahamed, Pulitzer Prize-winning author of *Lords of Finance: Bankers Who Broke the World*

'Ajay Chhibber and Salman Soz make an urgent and pressing case for India's policymakers to fully and frontally confront long ignored realities about the Indian economy—its fragility, structural inequality, low levels of state capacity which have been made especially visible in the ravages of COVID-19. In this rigorously argued yet accessible book the authors place a much-needed spotlight on the challenge and offer important and often provocative policy prescriptions. Engaging with these provocations is crucial if India is to find her way back to sustainable growth. A must read for all those committed to the idea of a growing, resilient India and especially for those in the corridors of policymaking.'

—Yamini Aiyar, President, Center for Policy Research

'In *Unshackling India*, economists Ajay Chhibber and Salman Soz provide a highly readable, wide-ranging, and thorough overview of the reforms needed for the Indian economy to reach its full potential and deliver greater prosperity for its 1.4 billion citizens. Ranging from second generation reforms, to concerns about gender, climate, health, education, state capacity and other challenges, Chhibber and Soz offer practical steps that can be taken now to spur growth and more inclusive development. They notably highlight the urgency of the present moment, in the wake of COVID-19, against a worsening global climate, and at a time when a manufacturing-led pathway to prosperity can no longer be taken for granted. A must-read for all who care about India's future.'

—Alyssa Ayres, Dean, Elliott School of International Affairs, George Washington University

'This book is outstanding because it does not just present a vision of a happier, more inclusive and prosperous society by the hundredth anniversary of independence but also a very specific roadmap to attain it. Besides relying on a wide range of studies and data sources it also enriches the discussion with very relevant international comparisons. An old timer like me learnt a lot from it and one hopes that it will be read by all who influence India's development policy.'

—Nitin Desai, former Under-Secretary General for Economic and Social Affairs, United Nations

'Can India have the largest economy in the world? Yes, it can! Yet, success is never easy. Ajay Chhibber and Salman Soz have done India a huge service by documenting comprehensively the reforms—both painful and painless—India should undertake. India should set aside its partisan divides and heed their wise advice. India should not rely only on its US$2.7 trillion market when a global market of US$80 trillion beckons. If overseas Indians can compete successfully in global markets, so can India. And if India bravely jumps into global markets, India's economy could explode. Seize the moment.'

—Kishore Mahbubani, Founding Dean, Lee Kuan Yew School of Public Policy, National University of Singapore, author of *Has China Won?*

'In *Unshackling India*, Chhibber and Soz, draw on their experiences across the world and their intimate knowledge of India to paint a vision of the economy that India deserves. This is an extremely readable primer to the key challenges that the Indian economy will face in the post-pandemic world, and the bold policy reforms it needs to address them. It will be an important contribution to the political momentum for change.'

—Raghuram Rajan, Professor, University of Chicago Booth School

'Big picture, colourfully detailed, hugely ambitious. Ajay Chhibber and Salman Anees Soz offer a bold blueprint for how India could become a much higher income nation in twenty-five years.'

—Ruchir Sharma, global investor and author of *Rise and Fall of Nations* and *Break-out Nations*

'The Chibber-Soz book illuminates the pathway that our country needs to take for realizing the tryst in the centennial year 2047. Jawaharlal Nehru, our first prime minister, eloquently evoked it on the dawn of our independence and this wonderful book persuasively shows: Yes, we can! In the various chapters, authors highlight the needed structural reforms and social policy measures in the shadow of the unfolding global technological trends. Perhaps this is also one the first well-researched books that bring out the new possibilities of high quality growth by successfully tackling the climate change challenges. I particularly applaud their emphasis on the urgency of mobilizing the latent economic growth potential of our women with the needed policy measures for their empowerment. This is a must-read for the policymakers as well as for all those who deeply care about our country.'

—Vijay Kelkar, Chairman, 13th Finance Commission and former Finance Secretary

UNSHACKLING INDIA

HARD TRUTHS AND CLEAR CHOICES FOR ECONOMIC REVIVAL

AJAY CHHIBBER

SALMAN ANEES SOZ

HarperCollins *Publishers* India

First published in India by
HarperCollins *Publishers* 2021
A-75, Sector 57, Noida, Uttar Pradesh 201301, India
www.harpercollins.co.in

2 4 6 8 10 9 7 5 3 1

P-ISBN: 978-93-5489-334-6
E-ISBN: 978-93-5489-005-5

Cover design: Saurav Das

Typeset in 11.5/16 Sabon LT Pro
Manipal Technologies Limited, Manipal

Printed and bound at
Thomson Press (India) Ltd

HarperCollinsIn

To Rita, love of my life and my pole star
– Ajay Chhibber

To Asia, who is integral to whatever I do
– Salman Anees Soz

Contents

Part III
Freeing Markets and Unleashing Competitiveness

Part IV
Re-engineering the Economy

Part V
Preparing for the Future

1

India and the World in the Twenty-first Century

The secret of change is to focus all of your energy, not on fighting the old, but on building the new.

—Socrates (not that Socrates)[1]

A world in turmoil

In 2021, the United Nations (UN) declared code-red for humanity. The 2021 *Report of the Intergovernmental Panel on Climate Change* (IPCC) says the world will breach the 1.5°C —an upper target of the 2015 Paris Agreement—temperature rise by 2040. Forest fires, floods, rising sea levels, melting glaciers, more intense tornadoes and cyclones are already threatening human settlements all over the world. To add to these, the

COVID-19 pandemic has thrown developed and developing countries alike into crisis. On 15 August 2021, as India marked its 75th Independence Day, over 200 million cases were reported and about 4.5 million people had died worldwide—but the real number is likely much higher as there was ample evidence of under-reporting of infections and deaths in many parts of the world.

India was relatively less affected by the first COVID-19 wave—but nevertheless resorted unexplainably to a drastic lockdown, which upturned livelihoods with millions of migrant workers desperately streaming back to villages—a sight not seen in India since the Partition of 1947. Subsequently, it let its guard down and India's ruling party even declared victory in the fight against COVID-19 in February 2021.[2] But as the virus mutated to what is now called the Delta variant, India was hit with a massive second wave in March 2021. Daily reported cases breached the 4,00,000 mark and more than 4,000 people died daily for many days. Due to differences in virus-testing regimes and uneven record-keeping, the actual number of cases and deaths could be far higher. The virus exposed dangerous weaknesses in health and social safety systems, and the capacity of the state to handle such threats especially in India and other developing countries.

Compounding the health crisis are simultaneous economic and financial shocks that are growing in size and severity—with no clear or immediate end in sight. The International Monetary Fund (IMF) reported that the pandemic caused the global economy to contract sharply by 3.3 per cent in 2020. This was much worse than during the 2008-09 Global Financial Crisis (GFC), and similar in magnitude to the Great Depression.[3] Globalization is in retreat and may fracture further. Global trade as a share of gross domestic product (GDP) had already peaked at around 60 per cent due to the GFC and before this pandemic. This will surely come down further because of rising protectionism in key countries as well as disruptions to international trade. Recovery is underway in the United States (US) and China and some other developed countries but it is a very uneven two-track recovery.

New vaccines to counter COVID-19 have been developed in record times. In many developed countries, rapid vaccination programmes appeared to be a huge success—and more than 50 per cent of their populations have been vaccinated. But, as the United Nations Development Programme (UNDP) reports, only 1 per cent of the developing world had been vaccinated by July 2021.[4] 'Vaccine inequity is the world's biggest obstacle to ending this pandemic and recovering from COVID-19,' said Dr Tedros Adhanom Ghebreyesus, Director-General of the World Health Organization (WHO). 'Economically, epidemiologically and morally, it is in all countries' best interest to use the latest available data to make lifesaving vaccines available to all.'[5] Without much greater efforts to vaccinate the world, new variants even more deadly than the Delta variant, which now is running rampant in many developing countries and even amongst the non-vaccinated parts of the developed world, could emerge.

Complicating matters further, the crisis hit all countries almost simultaneously. While there are considerable variations to the containment of the virus itself, most developed countries, based on some painful lessons from the 2008-09 GFC, have acted relatively quickly. By November 2020, the Group of Twenty (G20) countries collectively committed $11 trillion to help their economies recover from the crisis. But many developing economies, with much less fiscal space, were unable to provide the same magnitude of support to their recoveries. And unlike after the GFC, there is very limited coordination globally to deal with the crisis. The Group of Two (G2), US and China, are at loggerheads, earlier on trade and now on the pandemic. The World Trade Organization (WTO) and WHO appear to be in disarray and the UN and the Group of Twenty (G20) appear powerless. Other than an agreement to delay debt payments to low-income countries until the end of 2021, and Special Drawing Rights (SDR) issued by the IMF, of which the poorer countries get a very small share, there is limited support to developing countries. It is a shocking failure of global coordination—and so short-sighted. Unless the pandemic is contained everywhere, it will not be contained anywhere. But this is where we are and at least for the foreseeable future, countries are on their own. India, in any case, must chart its own course.

For India, a crisis like no other

The socio-economic impacts of the COVID-19 pandemic will likely be devastating for India. Due to an unnecessary and much too drastic lockdown, India's GDP contracted by a massive 7.3 per cent in FY20-21. This was the worst GDP growth performance in almost four decades. But this was to be followed by a sharp recovery in FY21-22 to get India's GDP back to where it was in FY19-20. However, this is now highly improbable due to the impact of a severe second wave and a looming third wave.

The recovery in the Indian economy is, in any case, K-shaped—the better off recover quickly and the less well off see a decline in incomes, just as is the case in many other countries. But in the developed world and even in many upper-middle-income countries, social assistance payments have helped the poor and unemployed cope with this uneven recovery. In India, the fiscal space for such assistance is limited and free food rations and the Mahatma Gandhi National Rural Employment Guarantee Act (MGNREGA) have become the fallback option—but this is not enough. Corporate profits have risen as companies saved costs by laying off workers and reducing office and travel costs. The Micro, Small and Medium Enterprise (MSME) sector has been devastated despite efforts to provide liquidity support to MSMEs. According to Piketty (2020),[6] India was already one of the world's most unequal countries—now it is even more so (figure 1.1). An already-beleaguered banking sector will most likely weaken further. Government finances are highly constrained, a reflection of a slowing economy, and limit the government's ability to mitigate the impacts of the crisis.

Near-term firefighting

Slowing the disease and saving lives is a precondition to mitigating COVID-19's adverse impact on livelihoods. There are a series of measures that governments, including in India, are taking to reduce the risk of an economic collapse and the threat to weakest sections of society. The sudden and severe lockdown to contain the first wave of the pandemic hurt internal migrant workers the most. As the first wave receded, the country began to open and it appeared for a moment that the worst was behind India. However, that respite was short-lived as a second wave dealt a crushing blow to the national psyche. Unimaginable scenes of desperate people flocking to hospitals to save themselves or their loved ones became a common feature in India. Dead bodies began piling up in crematoriums and graveyards. Rivers swelled with dead bodies, as people ran out of space or firewood for the dead. The Indian state had failed to prepare after the first wave. So little had changed, despite all the attention the crisis received in India and around the world.

India faltered in other ways as well. It was considered before the pandemic to be the vaccine factory of the world. Everyone thought it would not only be able to produce enough vaccines for its own people but would emerge as the vaccine supplier to much of the developing world. But instead of ensuring this would happen, Indian policymakers at one stage even considered vaccines unnecessary and as a result India's vaccine production slumped. India was unable to vaccinate its own people and defaulted on vaccine contracts with many others. It is now gearing up its vaccine production, but it's a costly catch-up for lives and livelihoods.

As expected, and in the absence of a good health system, governments across India resorted to the only tool at their disposal. New lockdowns ensued, guaranteeing a slowdown in economic activity and prospects of further misery for the poorest and most vulnerable sections of society. When the government released the GDP data for the FY20-21, it also noted that the final January–March quarter saw a growth rate of 1.5 per cent. That was good news, but it was tempered by the realization that the second wave of the virus would snuff out that incipient recovery. The IMF had predicted that India would grow by 12.5 per cent in 2021. That is unlikely to happen. But even if we accept IMF's projections, that will mean India growing at an average rate of less than 3 per cent in the three years of 2020, 2021 and 2022. For a poor, emerging country, that is extremely low and ruinous, at least in the short-run.

The National Council of Applied Economic Research (NCAER) developed scenarios to assess long-term implications of the COVID-19 crisis. In the 'optimistic' scenario, 'the economy catches up with the "no pandemic" growth path only by 2029-30.'[7] As Sudipto Mundle at the NCAER notes, 'This is also the year when our low demographic dependency ratio will bottom out, implying that the narrow window for India's so-called demographic dividend will start closing.'[8] It is a gloomy picture. However, acknowledging this grim reality can help focus the minds of policymakers on what is likely to come India's way in the years ahead.

A long-term opportunity

India faces an intriguing future. At the turn of the century, based on the liberalization of its economy following the 1991 crisis, India was a rising economic power that could sustain growth at about 6-7 per cent or even higher. After the GFC, and especially since demonetization, sustaining high growth rates has looked challenging, with India struggling to sustain growth at 4-5 per cent. This is partly because of deep-rooted structural issues that remain intractable in the absence of meaningful reforms. The momentum to India's economy that came from the first set of economic reforms started in 1991 on the back of a balance of payments crisis has now dissipated.

A new set of reforms and measures—which this book lays out—are needed. In the meantime, the global environment has become more difficult. With the global economy getting reshaped, fractures in global supply chains and prospects of a prolonged recovery period, India will have to navigate its way forward strategically. India is no longer a closed economy. It must come to grips with the implications of a slowing global economy as it deals with the fallout of the pandemic. Does this crisis present an opportunity to push ahead with genuine structural reforms that the economy desperately needs? We believe so.

This point about the impact of the pandemic on India's growth potential merits further attention. In 2018, the Federal Reserve Bank of San Francisco reviewed the recovery post-GFC. The report found that a 'decade after the last financial crisis and recession, the US economy remains significantly smaller than it should be based on its pre-crisis growth trend'. It went on to add that the 'size of those losses suggests that the level of output is unlikely to revert to its pre-crisis trend level'.[9] A cross-country study of 190 economies found that 'all types of recessions—including those arising from external shocks and small domestic macroeconomic policy mistakes—lead to permanent losses in output and welfare'.[10] In poor countries, recessions tend to be more frequent and deeper. Poorer economies lose more ground to richer countries, and even when GDP and stock markets show quick recovery, the social and economic impacts on the lives of the poor and vulnerable last much longer.[11]

India's development so far has been lopsided. Unlike many successful East Asian economies and most of the developed world, India has not succeeded in industrialization—its growth has been fuelled largely by services. As a result, it has not created enough employment to get people off the farm. One big reason why India's structural transformation is so lopsided is the lack of second-generation reforms—this is the term economists use for reforms in labour, land and financial sectors.[12] India's labour laws restrict the use of its most plentiful supply—labour—and waste its most scarce resources—land and capital. It all springs from haphazard laws and regulations, and excessive overlapping roles of the government.

India improved its global rank in the World Bank's Ease of Doing Business Index (EDBI) by 79 positions from 142nd in 2014 when the Modi government came to power to 63rd in 2019. But despite a massive jump in its EDBI rankings, India's GDP growth rate fell more than 4 percentage points between 2016 and 2019 and private investment as a share of GDP fell by over 3 percentage points, from 25 per cent of GDP in 2004–13 to under 22 per cent of GDP in 2016–19.

The problem with EDBI is that it is easy to game it to show better results—without it having much meaningful impact on competitiveness. It is worth noting that India was able to attract considerable investment—both domestic and foreign—from 2004–13 even when its EDBI score was low.

Independent reviews show that the EDBI has many flaws, both in what it measures and how it is measured. An index that is built on the principle that less regulation is always better—is downright dangerous—as shown by the experience of the GFC in 2008-09. The EDBI does not include any labour or environmental regulations—quite shocking in today's world of rising inequality and threats from climate change. It encourages a race to the bottom.[*13]

Despite improvements in its EDBI rank, India's industry, with some exceptions, is not competitive. India has faced premature deindustrialization because the costs of doing business are much higher than its competitors. On paper, labour costs appear to be lower in India, but not when you compare it to labour productivity. Only 4 per cent of India's labour force is classified as skilled. In addition, labour laws encourage firms to stay small—at under ten employees to avoid a visit by a labour or

* On 16 September 2021, the World Bank Group discontinued the Doing Business Report after investigating reports of data irregularities on Doing Business 2018 and 2020.

tax inspector—whose raj runs rampant. More than 70 per cent of manufacturing employment is in firms with size smaller than ten—which cannot compete globally.

The costs of capital remain very high because the banking system is very inefficient. The spread between lending and deposit rates exceeds 500 basis points—amongst the highest in the world and much higher than its competitors. Rising non-performing loans, directed lending requirements and Statutory Liquidity Ratio (SLR) requirements explain these inefficiencies. As a result, India's credit to GDP ratio has stagnated at around 50 per cent for the last decade—whereas that of Vietnam, China, Malaysia, and Thailand is well over 100 per cent. India also ranks very low on financial inclusion—despite the spread of Jan Dhan accounts as their usage remains low.

India has a huge infrastructure deficit which has improved somewhat in recent years. India's rank on the World Bank's Logistics Performance Index (LPI) has improved to 44th place—yet, it remains behind major competitors such as China, Malaysia, Thailand, but is ahead of Indonesia and Vietnam.

While physical infrastructure has improved, the cost of infrastructure to business remains high as India cross-subsidizes consumers at the expense of producers. For example, electricity prices in India are cheap for consumers at 8.6 cents/kWh, but very high for industry at 11.7 cents/kWh much higher than in China, Indonesia, Thailand and Malaysia. Rail fares also cross-subsidize passengers relative to freight and while road transport infrastructure has improved, petrol and diesel prices in India are higher than all other emerging economies.

Petrol is 20 per cent and diesel 50 per cent more costly in India than in China—another energy-importing country. The government's fuel policy captures the benefits of lower crude prices by maintaining high taxes and not allowing lower pump prices, thereby making business more uncompetitive as fuel prices fall elsewhere. With petrol prices now crossing Rs 100 per litre, it's affecting India's inflation-targeting regime.

India prides itself on being an information technology (IT) leader—but the reality is that IT access in India is low around 55 per cent—on par with Pakistan, and below China, Vietnam, Malaysia, and Indonesia, which are 80 per cent or higher. Mobile telephony has expanded hugely but at the cost of data download speeds—which at around 8 Mbit/second, are again the same as in Pakistan but below all our East Asian competitors. India is also falling behind other competitors as its research and development (R&D) expenditures at 0.6 per cent of GDP, which compares very unfavourably with China at well over 2 per cent of GDP.

The outlook is extremely grim when we think about other challenges that were looming before the virus struck. There are dire predictions of devastating climate change, a technology revolution that threatens to leave poor countries behind and persistent shortfalls in human capital because of chronic underinvestment in health, education and social protection. Climate change and the COVID-19 pandemic illustrate this point well. A World Bank study found that fifty million people in India could fall back into poverty by 2030 due to climate change.

Don't think that such reversals are not possible. According to Azim Premji University surveys, over 230 million people have fallen into poverty due to the pandemic—almost as many as came out of poverty in the previous thirty years—highlighting the weak state of India's social safety nets (SSNs).[14] Hopefully, some of these people will come out of poverty as the economy recovers but nevertheless it shows that a very large part of India's population already lives under precarious conditions. But even so, today's focus on the immediate crisis obscures a future fraught with serious and even deeper challenges.

Figure 1.1: The rise of global inequality—COVID-19 will worsen it.

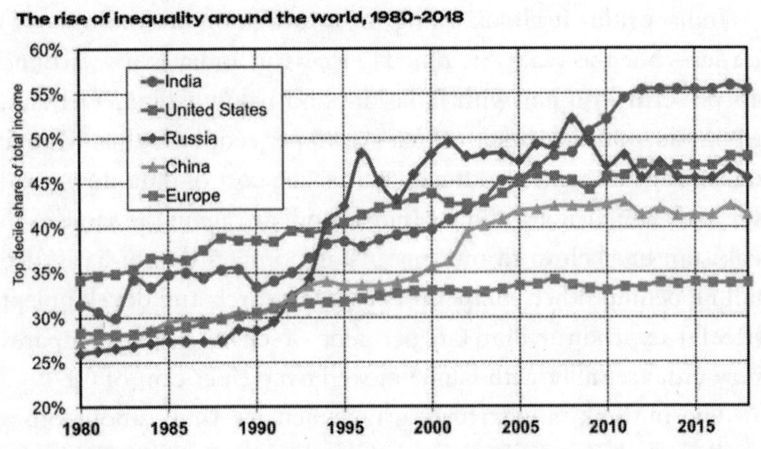

Source: Thomas Piketty—*Capital and Ideology* (Harvard University Press, 2020).

A reset for the twenty-first century

India's second COVID-19 wave was so powerful that it also swept away many of the debates around the future of India's economy. The country was engulfed by the virus, and survival was at the top of the agenda. Discussing the economy or the future did not seem like a priority. However, we know that there is no escaping difficult conversations about the pandemic and its human and economic toll. Not talking about the economy won't make future challenges disappear. And it isn't as if these challenges are far into the future. India is likely to face a humanitarian crisis in the near future, as livelihoods shrink and hunger grows. But we do believe that there will be life beyond the pandemic and that India must not be in its current situation again. For that to happen, we need ideas and debates on what shape the future ought to take, specifically India's economic future.

India has been forced to reset by the COVID-19 crisis. Perhaps that is how India reforms—in response to crises. While COVID-19 may have set us back by several years (or longer), India could convert this into an opportunity to revitalize and structure our economic system for the future. The political economy of reform has changed. India's goal of becoming a $5 trillion economy has been set back by at least five and possibly even ten years. If India does not turn inwards and instead focuses on making India globally competitive, it may ramp up growth to 6-7 per cent and thereby reach $5 trillion by 2030. But while a $5 trillion GDP maybe a useful target, India must reimagine its economy and society in more fundamental ways to ensure inclusion, dignity and trust for all its citizens. It goes beyond just GDP targets.

As India enters its 75th year of independence, questions pertaining even to its status as a democracy have arisen in India and across the world. India was exceptional in being a relatively poor democratic country—it was a beacon of hope. But that exceptionalism is fading, and fading fast. India holds elections—but appears to have lost its democratic traditions and norms. The last few years have seen an escalation in social conflicts in India. Unfortunately, this is often driven by political impulses that are short-sighted and, frankly, destructive. However, we believe that social conflict in India is not just about caste, religion or other identities. It is an economic issue. And majoritarianism, as a dominant identity wedge, is creating conditions for deepening rifts that may be difficult to overcome. Whether this dangerous lurch towards majoritarianism will be corrected will partly determine how successful India's economic transformation will be. At independence, many predicted that a poor and diverse

India with many languages and creeds would not survive as a unified, democratic country. But despite many challenges, India's leadership ensured that it remained not only intact but a surprisingly vibrant democracy. All that is now under threat—the COVID-19 crisis will come and go but if the cancer of intolerance and growing inequality—and climate change—are not addressed, India will not be a happy country and certainly not an economic superpower.

Conventional policy is unlikely to be able to combat the breadth of India's challenges. It may no longer be sufficient to enact reforms that many experts have unsuccessfully been pushing for. Across a range of areas—human capital, technology, agriculture, finance, trade, public service delivery and more—new ideas from around the world, adaptable to India's context, must now be on the table. The pandemic has also exposed the huge weaknesses in state capacity and its overreach. India has a weak state which tries to control too much—and ends up stifling the economy and the inherent energies of its young population.

This is also an opportunity to build back greener and cleaner, which is critical for India's future generations. This is one crisis that presents an opportunity of a lifetime. Can India use the next 25 years—when it will reach the 100th year of independence—to restructure not only the economy but rejuvenate its democratic energy and unshackle its potential—especially for its young and its women—in much more meaningful ways to become a genuinely prosperous economy by 2047? That would help achieve the destiny India was promised at its independence.

In that spirit, we present a book titled *Unshackling India*, written in five distinct but interconnected parts.

We begin in Part I by recommending a wholesale change in the role of the state. Without reforms to public sector institutions, other reforms are unlikely to come to fruition. We also recognize in Part II the critical need to focus on human capital development. For far too long, we have not properly focused on health, education, social protection and women's economic empowerment. This must change. In Part III, we shift focus to a discussion on unleashing India's factors of production as well as unclogging the all-important financial sector. Part IV focuses on reforming key sectors and promoting the idea that openness to trade remains vital to India's progress. Finally, in Part V, we discuss opportunities to preserve India's progress, something we failed to do during COVID-19, but also to find ways to convert a long-term crisis like climate change into a big opportunity for India.

We have tried as much as possible to assess India's performance in a global context. Often people in India compare with where they were ten or twenty years ago and feel quite satisfied with India's performance. But the world does not stand still and others have moved ahead much faster than India. India's performance must also therefore be assessed on a global yardstick, and we must ask why have others done even better? This is what this book has tried to do.

Often when you suggest solutions that have been tried elsewhere, a common response, especially in government circles, is that it will not work in India. But time and time again, and eventually, with considerable delays India is forced to come around to the same solutions. India is not sui generis. It is different in many cultural and social ways and proudly so, but people in India respond to the same incentives as anywhere else. They also are world-beaters when they compete and in fact do so well in other climes when they migrate. As Kishore Mahbubani[15] in the recent K.R. Narayan lecture suggests, India could become the world's largest economy—ahead of the US and China—but as he says, 'Many want to invest in India for geopolitical reasons.

However, as soon as they arrive in India and encounter Indian bureaucracy, they get discouraged.' We hope these ideas in our book *Unshackling India* will not only generate interest and discussion in the best traditions of 'argumentative' Indians, but also spur action and a thrust forward to achieve India's destiny in the world, in this century.

PART I

Changing the Role of the State

2

India's Interventionist State: Reduce Its Scope, Increase Its Effectiveness

Institutions, not armies, determine the destinies of nations.
—Napoleon Bonaparte, French Emperor

COVID-19 has exposed not just how weak India's health system is but more broadly how insufficient India's state capacity remains to manage and coordinate, and to deliver responses to such shocks. While India's economy suffered during the first wave due to an unnecessarily drastic and sudden lockdown where migrants suffered hugely, India appeared to recover quickly with, reportedly,[1] lower incidence rates and death rates per capita compared to most western countries. But the second wave hit a complacent India like a tsunami, with the prime minister more focused on elections and allowing religious festivals like the Kumbh Mela than on the pandemic. With weakened institutions, the system was unable to provide proper warning or have coordinated systems of response. The health system collapsed and the Indian government was overwhelmed by the severity of the crisis. The state withered away and India's citizens were left to fend for themselves, through personal and civil-society initiatives. But these weaknesses were there well before the pandemic hit. They were hidden by the trappings of government which tries to intervene everywhere but does it mostly very badly. When the tide went out, it became evident that the emperor had no clothes.

A reform of the state to reduce its scope and increase its effectiveness at all levels is badly needed to reset India for the twenty-first century. Its urgency has now been brought to the fore. This chapter lays out the broad contours of that reform, what it would entail and how to prioritize in such an ambitious undertaking.

1. What kind of state does India have?

There is a saying on the front of the Vidhan Soudha (state legislature) of Karnataka in the city of Bengaluru: 'Government Work Is God's Work'. This was meant to be a positive motivator—but now usually elicits a laugh—as the government is seen as overbearing and omnipotent in a not-so-positive manner and corruption-ridden. Sarkari raj permeates all aspects of life in India.

India's state is more welfarist than developmental. But it does not even do welfare very well. That is why the term 'welfarist'—that the intent is welfare but not the outcome—is more appropriate than 'welfare state'. India also aspires to be a developmental state but spends so little on basics like education, health and infrastructure that it can hardly be called one.

The size of the government, even adding in sub-national governments, is not too large but its scope is very wide.[2] As a result, it ends up trying to do too much and ends up doing things badly. Some have called it the 'flailing' state—suggesting that the head and its limbs are not well coordinated.[3] It has a penchant for grand schemes and plans—whose execution is weak. Some even argue that India has developed despite the state and that India grows at night when the government sleeps.[4]

The intent of India's Constitution was the achievement of socialist goals through democratic, evolutionary and non-violent means but was amended in 1976 to add the word 'socialist'. Since the 1991 liberalization, India has become more capitalist, but its larger capitalists have heavy influence on the state apparatus and regulatory system, while the bulk of them remain highly dependent on the state. The Modi government which came to power in 2014 said, 'the business of government is not business'. But getting the government out of business has not yet seen much success and the state remains omnipotent—perhaps even more than before. It remains a mixed economy, but with a strong nexus between large capitalists and politicians. Arvind Subramanian has called it 'stigmatized capitalism', but that suggests the capitalists are unfairly treated or that only the capitalists are at fault; perhaps a better term might be 'state-dependent pseudo-capitalism' or 'ersatz capitalism'.

Because India is a democracy, it cannot be an overly predatory state like kleptocracies such as Congo.[5] The poor are the vote banks and are doled out larger and larger promises of programmes and subsidies—which are then poorly distributed and subject to huge leakages. The voters keep the government from becoming too predatory by throwing out the government ever so often. It is a form of populism exercised every time there is an election. The electoral cycle doles out more and more handouts; what people need are steady hands-up to help them stand on their own feet through better education, health, electricity, roads and decent jobs. Some say India is not a democracy but an 'electocracy'—it holds elections with great gusto but is missing robust participatory democratic attributes.

Mehta and Walton (2014) pose these dilemmas of the Indian state by presenting three positive attributes of the Indian state—its stated objectives—but then show that these have not fructified as was intended.[6] They argue that the Indian state wants to be seen as a provider of services and protector of the disadvantaged, as a social welfare state built on the rights of citizens, as well as a handmaiden of capitalist development to make India an economically great nation in the world, and that different parts of the political system and the bureaucracy espouse these objectives. But the reality is quite different from those laudable objectives. The state has become more a mechanism of distributing privileges to individuals and groups, it has become more populist and has been captured by capitalist interest groups, increasing inequalities and damaging the environment.[7]

This constant and continuous struggle between these aspects of the state has played out but increasingly the negative outcomes are winning out in various ways and unless a major reset is undertaken, it will hold back India in the twenty-first century. This nexus between India's capitalists and the state, the growing illiberalism of the state—towards dissent, towards minorities—and the destruction of independent institutions are documented very well in a recent book by Ravinder Kaur (2020). This worrying condition is not unique to India.[8]

2. Some history: How did we get here?

The principles of good governance and state administration were laid out by Kautilya in the *Arthashastra* as early as 300 BCE—but were then forgotten for centuries after the Gupta Empire crumbled around 600 CE. In amazing detail, the principles of public administration were laid out and explained—from taxation, tax administration, judicial administration, activities of various departments and foreign policy, to dealing with epidemics, famines and catastrophes like fires and floods. With such attention to the conduct of the state, it is not surprising that India flourished during the Mauryan empire.

Another golden period was the rule of Akbar the Great during the Mughal Empire around 1600 when taxation was tempered, wars were contained and trade and commerce flourished—but all this soon disappeared as infighting and wars exacted huge pressures for greater taxation, and by the time Aurangzeb's rule ended around 1700, the empire was already in decline.

Pre-independence, most Indians were used to a colonial-style government that provided rudimentary security but not much else.[9] Even at times of extreme catastrophe—such as the 1918 Spanish flu pandemic, or during massive famines in 1944—the government did very little to help people.[10] Whatever help came, it came largely as a by-product of colonial interests. The railway system was not designed to develop India but to carry products needed by England to the ports and for military logistics. The plunder of India by the British was well-documented early on by eminent scholars like Dadabhai Naoroji and one of the best accounts recently is by Tharoor (2016).

As a result, between 1900 and 1950, India's GDP did not grow at all and at independence, almost 80 per cent of the population were in extreme poverty. Dr Manmohan Singh summarized it well:

> There is no doubt that our grievances against the British Empire had a sound basis. As the painstaking statistical work of the Cambridge historian Angus Maddison has shown, India's share of world income collapsed from 22.6% in 1700, almost equal to Europe's share of 23.3% at that time, to as low as 3.8% in 1952. Indeed, at the beginning of the 20th century, 'the brightest jewel in the British Crown' was the poorest country in the world in terms of per capita income.[11]

With independence, India swung from a minimalist extractive colonial state to the other extreme. Enamoured of the industrial success of the Union of Soviet Socialist Republics (USSR), Prime Minister Nehru espoused a state-led development model where the 'commanding heights of the Indian economy' would be in state hands. In 1956, with the Industrial Policy Resolution, India restricted key sectors of the economy to the state and nationalized some companies which were considered strategic, like airlines and shipbuilding. Subsequently, India nationalized large parts of its financial system, as well as some sectors such as coal and steel.

Figure 2.1: Degrees of state intervention

Degree of intervention	Addressing market failures			Improving equity
Minimal functions	Providing pure public goods: Defence Law and order Property rights Macroeconomic management Public health			Protecting the poor: Antipoverty programmes Disaster relief
Intermediate functions	Addressing externalities Basic education Environmental protection	Regulating monopoly Utility regulation Antitrust policy	Overcoming imperfect information Insurance (health, life, pension) Financial regulation Consumer protection	Providing social insurance Redistributive pensions Family allowances Unemployment insurance
Activist functions	Coordinating private activity Fostering markets Cluster initiatives State-owned enterprises and banks			Redistribution Asset redistribution

Source: Adapted from *World Development Report 1997,* World Bank.

Figure 2.1, adapted from the 1997 *World Development Report*, shows degrees of state intervention.[12] Based on this, India covered pretty much all the possibilities of state intervention. India's interventionist state started with the Industrial Policy Resolution of 1956.[13] The key goals of the Industrial Policy Resolution of 1956 were: (i) to build infrastructure and promote industrialization; (ii) to promote employment and balanced regional development; (iii) to create a self-reliant economy through import substitution and promote exports; (iv) to generate surplus for economic development; and (v) to prevent concentration of economic power. During this period, public sector investment reached over 50 per cent of total investment. Many new public sector companies were established and private companies in sectors such as coal, airlines, banking and insurance were nationalized.

Import substitution and state-led planned development became the model across much of the developing world. Industrial licensing was introduced—prescribing what the public and the private sector could produce.[14] India was not the only country in the developing world that went down this path after the Second World War (WWII). Most post-colonial countries did so, across Africa and Asia, as well as countries like China and others in Latin America. In India, this involved not only setting up state-owned enterprises but also efforts to control and plan private sector development. An entire apparatus—often referred to as the 'licence raj'—was established to make decisions on the number and types of licences.

The licence raj, combined with public sector enterprises, nurtured inefficiency, and corruption, producing a bevy of intermediaries whose main function was to grab these licences and sell them off to the highest bidder. Prof. Raj Krishna called the licence raj 'socialist allocation in the first round followed by market allocation in the second round'. In some cases, large private business houses would grab the licence to expand production but delay its execution to benefit from the shortages, or just keep the licence unutilized to stave off a competitor from entry into the industry. One of the original objectives of the policy to establish public sector undertakings (PSUs) was to help industrialize the economy and build infrastructure and capture the 'commanding heights' of the economic system.

Soon after independence, the sense was that the private sector was too weak to be able to handle risks, especially in capital-intensive sectors. But unlike Japan, South Korea and Taiwan, which relied on a strategy of helping the private sector grow and reduce their risks, India followed the approach of setting up public sector companies. Such thinking was not just Nehruvian socialism but strongly supported by the industrial class of the day (Chhibber 2018).[15]

But this approach failed and India's GDP growth remained low, averaging only 3.5 per cent between 1950 and 1980 in the first three decades after independence, with per capita GDP growing at only 1.3 per cent on average.[16] It was famously and wittily called the 'Hindu growth rate' suggesting—tongue-in-cheek—that Hindu fatalism was responsible for this slow growth, but as we saw later, when with better policies India grew faster, religion had nothing to do with it. India's poverty rose during this period and India fell behind many countries on social and economic indicators. Some internal liberalization was pursued in the 1980s, but it was insufficient to address the growing problems in the economy. It eventually took a balance of payments crisis in 1991 to force the political establishment to accept the need for reform.

After pursuing state-led capitalism for four decades after independence, triggered by a major economic and financial crisis, India introduced a new industrial policy in the 1990s. Given the perception that state-led capitalism had failed, there was a significant change in thinking after the 1991 liberalization. The private sector could enter many restricted areas, especially in mining, power generation, telecommunications and airlines. The state had expanded its role in certain priority areas like electricity. But subsequently, state control on the economy was reduced.

The Electricity Act, 2003, was enacted, which completely de-licensed power generation and permitted captive power plants. It also facilitated private sector participation in the transmission sector and provided open access to the grid sector. Various policy measures facilitated increased private sector participation in key infrastructure sectors such as telecommunications, roads and ports. Foreign equity participation up to 100 per cent was allowed in construction and maintenance of roads and bridges.

3. The broad strategy for state reform

What does reform of government entail? The size of India's government is not outlandishly large—but its scope is very wide and, as a result, its capabilities are declining over time. Despite the 1991 reforms, which rid us of the licence raj, the government remains involved in too many things and its new regulatory structure has reverted to a pseudo licence raj that it thought it rid itself of in the 1990s. And now judicial activism, triggered by brazen corruption (scams), creates its own uncertainty. As they say, in India, unlike in East Asia, even the corruption is unpredictable.

The size as measured by government expenditure, in fact, increased between 1980-81 and 1991-92 and has since remained in the range of 26–31 per cent of GDP—averaging around 28 per cent. But while government spend remains at around 28 per cent of GDP, overall revenues have only been in the range of 21 per cent of GDP—so that the combined deficit of state and Central governments has been around 7 per cent of GDP. As India has run a current account deficit of only around 2 per cent of GDP, this has meant that around 5 per cent of combined government deficit was financed by domestic savings. Such large financing needs for the government has led to substantial financial repression—which has affected the development of India's financial system. The Goods & Services Tax (GST) promised an increase in revenues by 2-3 per cent of GDP, but with a botched start and major design issues whose resolution is still a work in progress, that promise will not be realized for some time to come. As GST revenues fell sharply in 2020 due to the pandemic, the Central government reneged on its promise to increase state GST revenue share by 14 per cent every year and has now provided states the option to borrow on their behalf the shortfall in revenue. This has soured Centre–state relations and put the entire spirit of 'cooperative federalism' in jeopardy. This has also meant that further reform of GST—to bring in petrol, real estate and liquor into its ambit—is now unlikely.[17]

Figure 2.2: Government expenditure by Centre and states in India

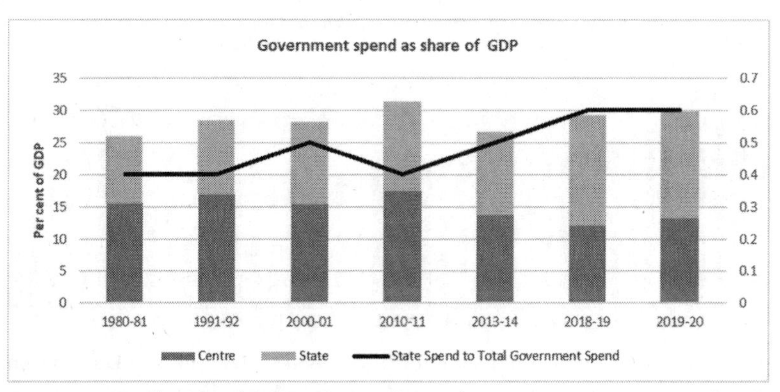

Source: *Handbook of Statistics on the Indian Economy*, Reserve Bank of India, various issues.

What has changed is the composition—more money is now spent by state governments since the acceptance of the recommendation of the 14th Finance Commission (figure 2.2).[18]

Figure 2.3: India revenue comparison with OECD and select emerging economies

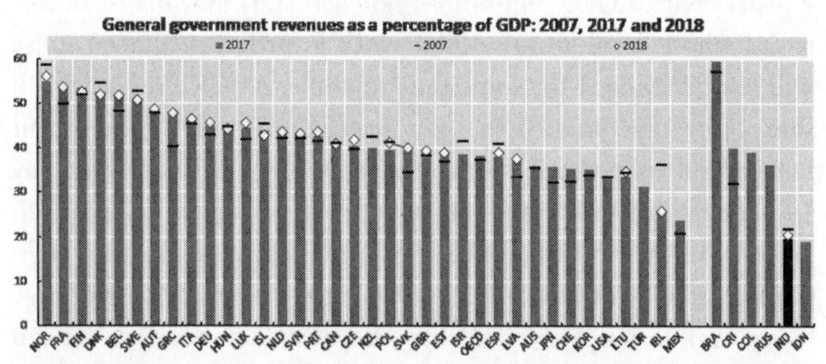

Source: *OECD National Accounts Statistics* (Database). Data from India are from the *IMF Economic Outlook* (April 2019).

Figure 2.4: India expenditure comparison with OECD and select emerging economies

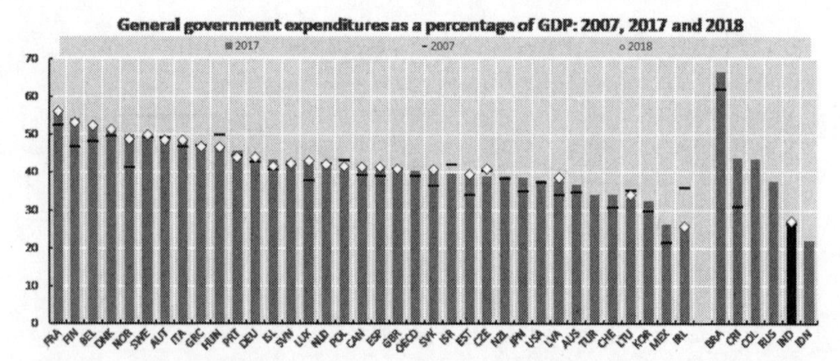

Source: *OECD National Accounts Statistics* (Database). Data from India are from the *IMF Economic Outlook* (April 2019).

Devesh Kapur (2020) makes the case, using tax revenue as a share of GDP, that the Indian state is too small. He argues that democratic countries must collect more taxes than non-democratic states. There is, however, no compelling reason why democracies need to collect higher taxes. Many socialist non-democracies who provide more government services to their citizens must also raise more taxes. But he also misses out India's huge non-tax revenues, which when added to taxes, make overall revenue numbers much larger. India also runs large fiscal deficits both at the Centre and in the states, so a better comparison would be to compare India's total government spend as a share of GDP. Here, as figures 2.3 and 2.4 show, India spends as much a share of its GDP as many countries with higher GDP levels (members of the Organisation for Economic Co-operation and Development or OECD).[19,20] So the case that India's government size is too small is not so clear-cut. It spends enough but spends it very badly so that the number of technical people—teachers, doctors, judges—are too few. We come back to this issue in Chapter 4. But what is clear is that the scope of government—the number of areas it intervenes in—is very wide and its capabilities are stretched. Its size is not too small—it just tries to do too many things.

Figure 2.5: State reform: reduce scope, improve capability, increase effectiveness

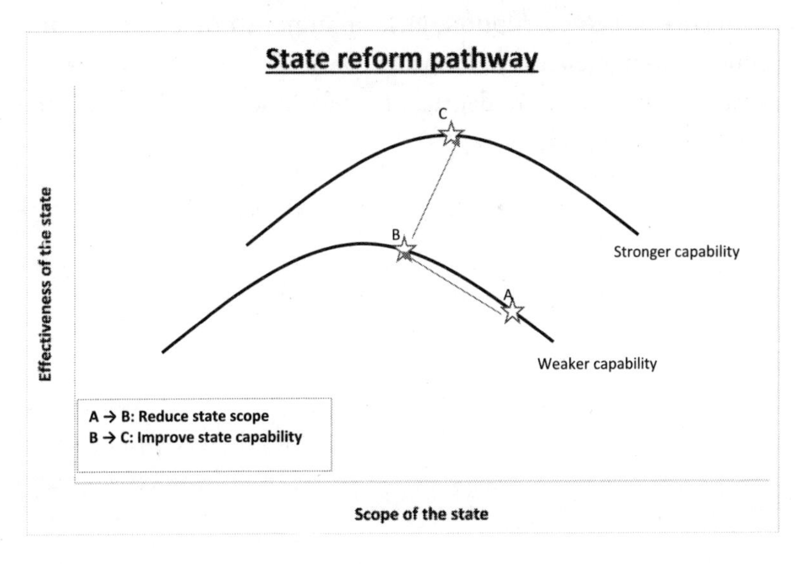

Figure 2.5 demonstrates how state effectiveness is determined by its scope of intervention and capability.[21] For any specific level of capability, greater state intervention is beneficial up to a point, but if the scope gets too interventionist for any given level of capability, the state's effectiveness declines. Too much intervention reduces effectiveness as the state tries to do too much. Effectiveness can be improved by reducing scope and, over time, increasing capability.[22] This two-part strategy for improving the effectiveness of the state was first laid out for large parts of the developing world in the *World Development Report* 1997.[23]

India was hugely interventionist until 1990. For the sake of comparison, we show that, broadly, the degree of intervention of the Indian state is more than in South Korea, and the capabilities of South Korea's state are much higher. China's state is more interventionist but also more capable. New Zealand carried out huge state reforms in the 1980s and became much less interventionist but also far more capable (figure 2.6). For India, the 1991 reforms meant that by 2020 the degree of state intervention declined to some extent, but the capability of the state had also declined—due to corruption, lack of administrative reforms and reduced competence. To improve India's state effectiveness, it must further reduce its degree of intervention and build up the capability of the state.

Figure 2.6: Direction of state capability and scope in India and selected countries

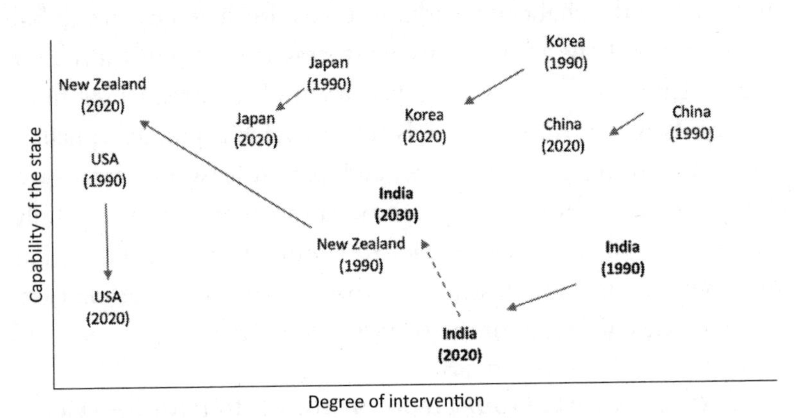

Source: Adapted from Fukuyama (2004).

India underwent a phase of liberalization after the 1991 reforms but some thirty years later, the legacy of the public sector and government control remains large at the central and state levels. Controls have shifted from licensing to regulatory bodies and a large public banking system remains, allowing the business–politician nexus enormous power, patronage and opportunity to shift downside risks to the taxpayer and derive huge profits on the upside.

China started its economic reforms under Deng Xiaoping in 1979-80, but after fifteen years carried out a major administrative reform in 1995 to prepare China's administrative system for the twenty-first century. In Malaysia, Mahathir placed as much emphasis on administrative reforms as he did on economic reforms. India started its liberalization in 1991 but it missed the bus on administrative reforms. Had India followed the Chinese pace, it should have carried out such reforms in 2005-06[24]—during the period of the UPA-I government—but coalition realities probably held it back from doing so. India certainly had another opportunity to do so again when UPA-II came to power, but it did not take up the challenge. Perhaps it was distracted by the global crisis and perhaps administrative reforms are not politically easy for a democratically elected government. The bureaucracy finds hundreds of ways to stall such reforms; a big political push is needed, and their time frame would span at least a decade—too long for the electoral cycle. But what is becoming increasingly clear, especially after its inability to handle the pandemic, is that without a major administrative reform India cannot be ready to take up the challenges of the twenty-first century.

4. Fixing welfare: Going from product- to people-based subsidies

India is becoming a welfare state before becoming a developed state—but it even does welfare badly. The compulsions of its democratic system have forced it to address the problems of poverty with subsidies rather than more long-term sustainable solutions. As a result, India now spends almost 4 per cent of GDP on subsidies (almost as much as it spends on public education and health) but also delivers them in a very ineffective manner with high leakages. Again, the contrast with China is striking. China has addressed poverty by creating jobs and providing basic services—health, education, sanitation—and not through subsidies.

Even those emerging market economies that use subsidies have shifted away from product-based subsidies (food, fuel, fertilizer and so on) to more people-based subsidies (cash transfers) to reduce costs and provide the poor more flexibility in their decision-making. India must move in this direction, reduce its subsidy bill, and release more resources for health, education, water and sanitation. Despite its significant costs, India's welfare system is neither comprehensive nor very effective: subject to huge leakages and corruption, and not well-knit into a coordinated whole.

Subsidies on the three Fs alone—food, fuel and fertilizer—cost 2.5 per cent of GDP, greater than the sum assigned to all development schemes. In the 1960s and '70s, when India had mass poverty, subsidizing products such as food or fuel made some sense; but today, when poverty has declined, product-based subsidies also benefit the non-poor and distort markets. We need to move away from product- to portable people-based subsidies, especially also as India will witness 300 million migrants over the next fifteen years, who must be able to get subsidies if they are eligible where they live rather than where they come from. Cash transfers have proven to be the best delivery option to reduce costs all over the world, through better targeting without diluting benefits.

A study by the NCAER found that in 2005, the Public Distribution System (PDS) cost Rs 3-4 to deliver Re 1 of subsidy.[25] There are two parts to this cost coming from problems at the fair price shops (FPSs)—where leakages (outright corruption) were abundant—and from widespread mistargeting errors (due to an outdated ration card system based on household surveys carried out in 1993-94). A subsequent evaluation carried out by NCAER (2016) showed some improvements, especially as the ration cards were updated and Type I (exclusion errors) were reduced.[26] Despite all its faults, the PDS became a lifesaver for the poor and migrant population. During the pandemic and now, due to the plight of the migrants after the pandemic, a One Nation One Ration Card system has been rolled-out. But this will only increase, not reduce, leakages and corruption as hapless migrants are denied rations in places where they have very limited connections and standing.

But the bigger problem and second cost lies in the operations of the Food Corporation of India (FCI) which procures, stores and moves grain from surplus to deficit states, and does all this very badly. The costs of this operation are very high. Fixing the FCI may be one solution but doing away with it altogether must also be an option.

One bold solution would be to shift not only to cash transfers on the consumer side but also on the producer side, as in Mexico and in Turkey.[27] The Pradhan Mantri Kisan Samman Nidhi (PM Kisan) scheme is a start and could be expanded if all other producer and input subsidies were done away with. This would allow the government to collapse fertilizer and all other input subsidies into a cash subsidy, allow the private movement of grain from surplus to deficit states, with the government buying small quantities needed for its strategic reserve. Public stocks would decline from the current level of 80 million tonnes to around 20 million tonnes, with huge fiscal savings. The entire food market would shift out of government hands into private hands. Several emerging economies such as Mexico and Turkey have made such a switch with savings of around 60 per cent. For those concerned about such a sudden shift, transition arrangements could be made with the shift to cash transfers occurring first in urban areas and even by keeping ration shops only for below poverty line (BPL) households for a while.

India cannot afford to rely only on western-style welfare. It runs one of the world's largest 'workfare' (cash-for-work) programmes, the MGNREGA scheme—but with mixed success, and implementation problems. Part of the problem for effective implementation of MGNREGA is that there are at least eighteen other uncoordinated schemes that deal with rural and land development. Moreover, the MGNREGA scheme itself is overly complicated as it has seven stated objectives—so it's difficult to measure success, especially as none of these seven have any clear yardstick for success. Even the basic objective of 100 days of employment is not based on any assessment of needs. Some states may need 50 days, and others may need as many as 150.

Ironically, developed states with better administration have made greater use of these schemes than the needier backward states, widening further the gap between them—the opposite of what one would expect for a scheme designed to help the genuinely needy. The assets created have not been durable and their creation is not consciously linked to any district- or block-level development plan. In 2013-14, it cost Rs 175 to deliver Rs 132 of wages, of which about Rs 90 went to beneficiaries (using a leakage rate of 30 per cent).[28] But if no sustainable assets are created, it is better to shift to a simple cash transfer to help the beneficiaries and save money.

Since 2018, MGNREGA work has been allowed on private small farms of backward communities, which has helped improve land productivity and its employment potential by enabling the shift from traditional cereals to more lucrative cash crops, vegetables and fruit. But these remain a very small part of the total scheme so far. MGNREGA work has been allowed for building toilets—but that diffused its core objectives even further and has now fortunately been stopped.

Health-related schemes also need significant review and rationalization. Of India's Millennium Development Goals for 2015, it is furthest behind in maternal and infant mortality (and neo-natal mortality). Despite so many schemes, 'out of pocket' expenses on health, at 63 per cent, are the highest in the world. But in health, cash transfers are not the best answer, as shown by the poor experience with Janani Suraksha Yojana. Better results are being achieved by the recently introduced Janani Shishu Suraksha Karyakram (JSSK), which is a cashless scheme designed to provide a combined package for the mother and child from seven months of pregnancy to one month after pregnancy. It has helped reduce the maternal mortality rate as well as the neo-natal mortality rate. The Ayushman Bharat scheme, which provides health insurance, had a start with ten million beneficiaries in its first year but it should not be an alternative to a functioning health system without which over a billion people are left at the mercy of unregulated private providers. The scheme is in poor shape due to the pandemic and will need a reboot in future years.

India clearly needs reforms to unshackle the economic system from state controls, reduce the footprint of the state so that the government's slogan of 'maximum governance; minimal government' can be realized. India has a public sector balance sheet with a large portfolio of public sector companies whose total assets exceed $500 billion (18 per cent of GDP). It must, over the next ten years, convert this balance sheet of capital in PSEs into a balance sheet of public infrastructure which can deliver services and crowd-in private investment for sustained long-term growth and poverty eradication. We take this issue up in the next chapter. But while reducing the scope of government is one phase of the reform, improving state capability to perform vital functions must also be a key part of that reform. We take up these issues in Chapter 4, after we review what India should do with its socialist legacy of PSUs, which we address in Chapter 3.

3

Bharat's Other Ratnas: Dealing with State-owned Enterprises

These are not the crown jewels [ratnas] of India's economy but bleeding ulcers.

—Arun Shourie, former minister of disinvestment.

We all know about the 'Bharat Ratna', India's highest civilian award. Many of our independence fighters have received the Bharat Ratna, and more recent awardees include the great cricketer Sachin Tendulkar and the famous singer Lata Mangeshkar. They are the venerated who's who of India.

But India also has other Ratnas—the more than 230 PSUs that were once the commanding heights of India's socialistic economy and still account for about 20 per cent of the GDP and 15 per cent of stock market capitalization through fifty-odd listed firms.[1]

Prime Minister Modi made a pledge to US investors almost two years ago, which he repeated to German investors recently, that 'the government has no business to do business'. And while the government has stated its intent to privatize many of them—so far it has had very little success.

India calls its state-owned enterprises public sector undertakings. Despite all the rhetoric of private sector development and economic reform, India still has over 230 central PSUs, of which seven are Maharatnas, seventeen are Navratnas and more than seventy are Miniratnas—the 'crown jewels' of India's socialist legacy. There are also over 1,000 PSUs in state and municipal hands. It is time to clean up this costly legacy. But how to do this and what approach to take towards them is not so straightforward, given the vast network of vested interests that are keen on their perpetuation.

1. The declining role of PSUs in the Indian economy

Since the 1991 liberalization, the role of PSUs has begun to decline, largely because the private sector has expanded rapidly. PSU share in employment in the organized labour force and its share of value added in GDP is now around 5 per cent—down from 10 per cent in 1990. But they still retain substantial assets: over 20 per cent of GDP. Their share in manufacturing and mining has declined but remains significant.

About half of the PSUs are in manufacturing and mining, and the rest are in the service sector—transport, telecommunications, financial and technical services. Service sector PSUs are just over 100, while non-service ones are around 130. There are over 1,000 state-level public sector enterprises (SLPEs) but they do not follow any classification system and are not all covered in a uniform manner across states. The combined assets of all PSUs declined from around 35 per cent of GDP to just over 20 per cent. Over the same period, the sales-to-GDP ratio declined from 20 per cent of GDP in 1990 to about 14 per cent of GDP: a much smaller decline, indicating that the sales to asset ratio (also sometimes referred to as the turnover ratio) increased from 0.5 in 1990 to around 0.8 in 2015. Value added created by PSUs as a share of GDP and the ratio of PSU employment to total organized employment in the economy has declined from around 8 per cent of GDP in 1990 to under 5 per cent of GDP in 2015. Post the 1991 liberalization, although the number of PSUs has remained more or less the same, their share in the economy measured by value added, employment and sales has declined, as the private sector has expanded faster. This is a pattern we see in several other countries with state capitalism such as in Brazil and China, where the share of state enterprises has also been declining.

There have been very significant changes in the value added from PSUs in different sectors of the economy. PSU value-added share in mining declined from 80 per cent in 1990 to less than 50 per cent by 2003-04 and is under 20 per cent today. The share of PSUs in the service sector has remained low. In the manufacturing sector, it declined from 20 per cent in 1990 to under 10 per cent in 2004-05 but has surprisingly risen again in the last three years, mainly due to the oil and petroleum PSUs, and those dealing with by-products such as chemicals and fertilizers.[2]

The PSUs can be classified into three tiers: loss-makers, profit-makers and those that fluctuate between profit and loss and could potentially be turned around either through better performance in state hands or through disinvestment. Combined, PSUs make profits, but about 30 per cent of them are serial loss-makers,[3] and the return on capital (ROC)—except for the largest PSUs—is below that of comparable private firms. If the loss-makers alone were shut down, India could increase public infrastructure investment by 10 per cent. Besides financial costs, their productivity is also low. Labour productivity in PSUs has grown at 2 per cent per annum as against 5.2 per cent for the economy.[4]

PSUs have many hidden costs, as well. In addition to government equity, some PSUs also rely on soft loans from the government. These soft loans are in addition to their borrowing from the financial sector and international agencies. The soft loans have been criticized as they remove a hard budget constraint and allow inefficiency to persist and work against the objective of greater commercialization in the functioning of PSUs. Surprisingly, such soft loans continued to rise even after the 1991 liberalization. Some of these loans were paid back but in many cases were delinquent and were written off, and some turned into equity. The government was keeping a lifeline to loss-makers through these soft loans, while at the same time trying to get them to improve, sending very conflicting signals.

The larger PSUs appear to be doing even better than private companies of similar size, based on their reported data. For example, the return on assets and return on capital in the largest seven PSUs—the Maharatnas—appear to be better than firms in the private sector and companies of similar size based on foreign direct investment (FDI), though the value of assets, especially land, needs careful scrutiny.[5] Independent audits are needed to assess their performance. But in the case of the next category of PSUs—the seventeen Navratnas—the performance of private firms of similar size is much better, except for the better performance of the Navratnas over their private sector comparators during the period of high growth from 2003-04 to around 2008-09. It is also interesting that the returns on both assets and on capital for the Navratnas went up during the period of rapid growth and has declined quite sharply since the global economic crisis.

PSUs in the service sectors, such as Air India, MTNL and BSNL, and those providing a range of other types of services both financial and non-financial, have done poorly relative to those in mining and manufacturing. This is also not surprising, given the lack of service orientation in PSUs. Not only is the performance of PSUs in the service sectors worse, but their presence could have also adversely affected the performance of private sector firms in those sectors. This is because the government introduces regulation and preferred policies to favour PSUs to get a better deal than the private competition in that sector. Arpita Mukherjee (2015) stated that in service sectors with erstwhile public monopolies, the vested interests of the government and PSUs adversely affect the performance of the entire sector.[6] This is probably a bigger issue in the airline sector than in the telecommunications sector. The presence of PSUs in the telecom sector has not had a negative effect on the industry because of a more effective regulatory environment, which has not hindered private sector companies. Telecom Regulatory Authority of India (TRAI), the telecommunications regulator, has had its share of criticism, but it has not been accused of helping PSUs against the private sector. But in aviation, the Director General of Civil Aviation (DGCA) has not worked as effectively in creating a level playing field and has favoured Air India. It has deliberately or unconsciously affected the performance of private sector airlines. But service-sector private companies have also performed poorly for a variety of other reasons.

PSUs have also underperformed on various productivity indicators used to measure firm performance. Profit before interest, taxes per employee (PBITE) and net sales per employee (NSE) have increased fivefold and value added per employee

(VAE) has increased fourfold, respectively, between 1990 and 2019. But labour productivity in PSUs—measured by VAE—increased considerably slower, at 2 per cent per annum, than average labour productivity growth of around 5.2 per cent for the economy (including low-productivity sectors such as agriculture) over the same period.

A major objective in setting up PSUs was to increase employment and this objective was pursued vigorously. Between 1970 and 1990, employment in PSUs almost doubled from 1.1 million in 1970 to almost 2 million in 1990 (around 10 per cent of the organized labour force). The objective was not only to create more jobs but also to improve the skills base of the labour force. This was to be done by a focus on skills development, training and human resource development. At the same time, PSUs were also told to give special preference to Scheduled Castes (SCs) and Scheduled Tribes (STs).

In summary, there was, and probably still exists, considerable overemployment in the PSUs. Their total employment, which had reached a peak of 2 million employees in the central PSUs, is now only 1.25 million employees for about the same number of firms. This would suggest that under the guise of job creation, overemployment of around 60 per cent existed in the PSUs. Some of this has now been corrected and the remaining workforce is given better training and skills development. But despite these efforts at improving the skills of PSU employees, the growth in labour productivity in PSUs is much below than that of the economy.

2. Efforts to reform and privatize since 1991

While privatization of PSUs was not part of the liberalization package of the 1991 reforms, efforts to try and improve their performance was. But some change was envisaged even in the way the state managed its enterprises. Greater delegation of decision-making, more commercialization for profitable PSUs and restructuring of loss-making firms through the Board of Industrial Financing and Restructuring were included. Other elements of the liberalization involved: (i) free entry to private sector firms in industries reserved exclusively for PSUs; and (ii) disinvestment of a small part of the government's shareholding (while still holding majority stocks) and listing PSUs on the stock exchanges. The most significant of industries affected by the former policy were telecommunications, petroleum (from extraction to refining and marketing), electricity generation and distribution, several basic goods industries like steel, aluminium, mining and air transportation. For the latter, ensuring that the listed PSUs follow the stock exchanges' listing requirements necessitated disclosure and governance regulations, appointment of independent directors, independent remuneration and audit committees. Another change was withholding or withdrawing budgetary support to loss-making ('sick') PSUs. Subsequently, sick PSUs were denied permission to revise wages and salaries. Loss-making PSUs were encouraged to lay off workers to seek commercial viability, failing which they were to be closed.

But between 1992 and 1998, privatization was not pursued aggressively as there was no strong pressure brought on India externally or internally to do that. The IMF did not insist on this as part of its financial conditionality and strong labour unions ensured that the political costs of privatization would be high. Strong political and vested interests, and deep-seated bureaucratic preference for PSUs where jobs could be had, made sure there was no strong internal constituency for privatization. The BIFR was created to track performance of PSUs and advise them—especially the sick ones—on investment and restructuring. Three categories of PSUs were formed and named: Maharatnas, Navratnas and Miniratnas, and performance contracts (MOUs) were signed with them to create incentives for better performance.

The NDA government under Prime Minister Vajpayee, which came to power in 1999, was the first one that followed an aggressive privatization policy but faced political and bureaucratic hurdles. A separate Ministry of Disinvestment was created in 1999,[7] and the objective of disinvestment under it was not just to raise revenue but also improve efficiency. Over thirty companies were either fully privatized or 50 per cent of their stock divested, including one of India's most successful privatization initiatives—the sale of Maruti to Suzuki was completed during this period. Privatization, which in India is euphemistically called 'strategic disinvestment', was pursued with determination but opposition was faced, especially from labour unions, who had extracted many concessions from the government. But opposition came even from within the NDA government and the bureaucracy, as control over PSUs meant jobs, patronage and the ability to make money through PSU contracts.

The UPA-I government that came to power in 2004, dependent on the communists, did not try to privatize PSUs, although a few were shut down. Prime Minister Manmohan Singh explained his constraints quite clearly: 'We are a coalition government, and that limits our options in some ways. Privatization happens to be one such area.' It instead encouraged restructuring of state-owned firms by creating the Bureau for Restructuring of Public Firms to improve productivity and reduce losses. A National Investment Fund was also created to collect disinvestment receipts, with the idea that it would be strategically deployed rather than used as part of budget receipts. Following fiscal pressures after the 2009 crisis, the criterion was gradually relaxed until the fund, for all practical purposes, became part of the Budget.

UPA-II, from 2009–14, pursued aggressive disinvestment (share sales), not privatization. Its main objective was to raise revenue for the national budget; not necessarily to improve performance, although that may have turned out to be its unintended outcome, as firms were prepared for listing in the stock market. With the arrival of the NDA government again in 2014, there was an expectation that the disinvestment pursued quite aggressively by NDA-I between 1999 and 2004 would be taken up again, and while not much has happened in the first term, so far there are signals that more effort will be made in the second term. The government has announced a list of PSUs for closure and for privatization, including Air India, but it remains to be seen how much progress will be made on this front, now further delayed by the onset of COVID-19.

3. What does the evidence on PSU performance tell us?

There are a vast number of studies on PSUs around the world. Many of them show that privatization improves labour productivity and even profitability of PSUs but not necessarily overall efficiency and productivity. A comprehensive survey of this literature (Megginson and Netter 2001) concluded that divested (fully and partially privatized) firms almost always become more profitable and more efficient. An OECD survey soon thereafter also came to the same conclusion. Subsequent surveys (Muhlenkamp 2013) have questioned these findings and shown that the previous surveys suffered from flaws.[8] It questions whether privatization leads to greater efficiency and argues that public and private sector firms perform the same when subject to competition and better regulation. Some have argued that many of the studies suffer from methodological flaws, as the gains from privatization maybe due to selection bias, as better-performing PSUs may be privatized first.

The most recent survey by UNDP's Global Centre for Public Service Excellence (GSCPE 2017) shows that privatization is likely to lead to positive results in markets with greater competition and better regulation. This is more likely in developed countries but not so in middle-income and developing economies, where the results of privatization are more mixed. Factors affecting PSU performance can be economy-wide variables: GDP growth rate, sector- or industry-specific variables including concentration of firms, size of the firm, export orientation and capital intensity, to name some of the most important ones. In addition, the share of private equity (degree of privatization) and MOUs[9] can also potentially affect a firm's performance by encouraging commercialization, reducing political interference and giving the PSU management clearer performance goals and targets, and pay and other incentives for improved performance. There is some empirical evidence globally that MOUs can improve PSU performance.[10]

There are many studies that try and discuss the performance of PSUs in the Indian context. But very few of these use rigorous techniques and are therefore largely descriptive.[11,12,13,14] When we look at the more rigorous ones, we get some interesting findings.

In a recent paper, Ritika Jain (2016) uses technical efficiency of a firm as the performance variable, instead of financial rates of return.[15] She applies a stochastic frontier analysis technique to generate technical efficiency by industry and by firm, and then examines the impact of disinvestment and the ideology of the state government in which the enterprise is located, as well as whether the state government belongs to a political party that is different from the Central government. The results indicate that disinvestment—even partial disinvestment—has a strong positive effect on the firm's performance. The political ideology of the state government as well as whether the state government and the Central government belong to different parties has a significant effect on performance. Her results are, however, dependent on the credibility of the method used to calculate technical efficiency, which is derived as a residual in the stochastic frontier analysis and is therefore dependent on how well specified the model is itself.

Gupta (2005) showed that disinvestment (even the sale of minority shares) had a positive effect on PSU financial performance, ostensibly because new owners injected greater commercial drive, which helped improve profitability.[16] Nandini Gupta (2011) focused on the evaluation of performance of the central public sector undertakings (CPSUs) based on data of 213 manufacturing and non-financial service sector firms from CMIE (Centre of Monitoring the Indian Economy) for the period 1988–2009.[17] This paper supported the fact that the sale of both partial and majority equity stakes, accompanied by the transfer of management control from government to private owners, has an economically significant positive impact on the performance of CPSUs. The paper also considered the impact of the disinvestment on the compensation of employees and employment. It shows that the improvement in profitability following privatization is not accompanied by a decline in worker compensation and employment, after controlling for observable and unobservable characteristics of the firms such as firm size, industry Herfindahl index and year dummies to control for contemporaneous macroeconomic shocks. The paper did not look at all at the role of MOUs and focused entirely on the role of disinvestment. It was also using data from the period largely before the new improved MOUs were introduced.

But this result has been challenged by recent studies, as it did not factor in the effect of MOUs. Gunasekar and Sarkar (2014) show that when PSUs with and without MOUs are considered, much of the financial performance improvement using ROA, attributed to privatization, is due to the performance effect of MOUs.[18] The positive effect of privatization disappears once the MOU performance effect is considered. So, a policy of selling a minority stake (up to 49 per cent) as a disinvestment measure is unlikely to have any positive effect on financial performance. In their first paper, Chhibber and Gupta (2017) had analysed the financial performance of India's 235 PSUs using firm-level data over the period 1990–2015 from the Public Enterprise Survey (time series panel data set).[19] The paper investigated factors that explain the financial performance—ROC and ROA of these PSUs. The results did show a positive effect of MOUs on their ROC, but not on ROA as was shown in the Gunasekar and Sarkar paper.

However, this result holds only for the non-service sector (manufacturing, mining) and not for service sector firms. In the case of service sector firms, divestment (share sales) had a positive impact on performance, making them ideal candidates for more aggressive privatization. The results also show that larger PSUs—the Maharatnas—appear to perform better on financial indicators than smaller PSUs and even better than private firms of similar size. GDP growth has, as expected, a positive effect on PSU performance and soft loans have a negative effect, as they reduce the pressure on firm performance. Export orientation and capital intensity have no clear effect on PSU performance.

In a subsequent paper (Chhibber and Gupta 2019), the focus is on explaining the factors affecting the efficiency and productivity of India's PSUs, using various measures of productivity, instead of financial indicators.[20] In this paper, VAE is used as a measure of labour productivity, and value added per capital and value added per asset to measure productive use of capital and assets.[21] The results show that MOUs—have no positive, and sometimes negative, effect on performance. The results provide very clear support for share sales (divestment) and privatization (strategic divestment) as opposed to MOUs to improve the performance of PSUs. They also indicate that the MOU system is not producing the results for which it was designed. There is also the possibility that PSUs only agree to benchmarks which are easily achievable and are gaming the MOU system. They have a cosy relationship with their sectoral ministry and can use that relationship to ensure high MOU ratings even when their productivity parameters are low or even declining.

4. Performance of PSUs after strategic disinvestment (outright privatization)

In addition to partial share sales (divestment) India also had a unique experiment with full privatization (strategic divestment) during the period of the NDA-I government from 1999 to 2004. What does the evidence on the performance of PSUs that underwent strategic disinvestment tell us? Some thirty entities were strategically disinvested during that period. Of these, several were hotels, sold largely for their land and assets. Some PSUs were sold to other PSUs, and therefore did not really pass into private hands. Twelve companies were fully privatized between 1999 and 2004 under the NDA-I government, where over 50 per cent of their shares and management control passed into private hands, ceding management control to the private sector.

The performance of these twelve PSUs—Bharat Aluminium, CMC, Hindustan Teleprinters, Hindustan Zinc, Hindustan Teleprinters Limited, ICI India, Indian Petrochemicals, Jessop and Co., Lagan Jute Mills, Maruti Udyog, Modern Food Industries, Paradeep Phosphates and Videsh Sanchar Nigam—shows considerable improvements after strategic disinvestment. The weighted ROC tripled on average from around 5 per cent in 1999–2004 to 15.1 per cent in 2010–15 and went even higher in the high-growth phase 2004–09 to average of around 25 per cent. The ROA for these firms also stayed high—higher than that of the Navratnas that remained in public hands. It also jumped up in the high-growth phase and remained over 15 per cent in the period 2010–15—of course, it was also high in the period 1999–2004.

The experience of privatization undertaken by the NDA-I government from 1999–2004 has turned out to be quite positive. The results provide very clear support for share sales (divestment) and privatization (strategic divestment) as opposed to MOUs to improve the performance of PSUs.[22]

5. Getting government out of the business of business

India needs a ten-year plan for reform of the PSUs instead of the piecemeal annual announcements of closure, privatization, divestiture followed so far. For now, it should keep the Maharatnas in the public sector but try to make them world-class companies. For the others, with few exceptions, the ten-year plan should include their sale or closure. The plan could have two phases of five years each; with Phase 1 focused on PSUs that require closure and those in mining, manufacturing and services where outright sales do not require other sectoral reforms. Phase 2 could be reserved for PSUs where other reforms are needed to provide alternatives to citizens for services currently provided by the PSUs.

The Maharatnas should, for now at least, stay in state hands, the total assets of which are around Rs 10 trillion ($133 billion), which is about one-third of the total PSU assets of about Rs 30 trillion ($500 billion). In any case, the Maharatnas—Bharat Heavy Electricals Limited (BHEL), Coal India, GAIL (formerly Gas Authority of India Ltd), Indian Oil, NTPC (formerly National Thermal Power Corporation), Oil and Natural Gas Corporation (ONGC) and Steel Authority of India Ltd (SAIL)—are collectively doing better than private companies of similar size. Their ROC and ROA have been higher than those of comparable private firms by 4 per cent and 2 per cent, respectively. However, even in this category the situation has seen a reversal of trends in the last three years: the private sector has shown a surprising improvement in ROC and ROA, while the Maharatnas are showing a continuous decline in performance. Therefore, among the Maharatnas, SAIL, BHEL and Indian Oil need serious restructuring and better leadership to make them world-class companies.

The remaining two-thirds of state assets are in the 17 Navratnas, 73 Miniratnas and 120-odd companies that are not given a ratna status. The performance of the Navratnas is consistently worse than that of comparable private companies, with ROC roughly 2 per cent lower. Many of the companies in this group could be privatized in Phase 1—especially Bharat Electronics, Mahanagar Telephone Nigam Limited (MTNL), National Mineral Development Corporation (NMDC) and Oil India.

The Miniratna companies are the ones that are ripest for strategic disinvestment in Phase 1. A plan to sell most of these companies should be developed, with those in manufacturing and the services sector high on the list for immediate sale, as these are the worst performers. There will be many arguments made against selling these companies to the private sector, but there seems to be no reason to run these as public companies except to provide employment to a small number of people and to be able to provide managerial positions to party members once any new government comes into power. A far more serious issue is that of tainted contracts and procurement, where lucrative deals are handed out to cronies.

It is often argued that PSUs should be prepared for privatization through restructuring prior to the sale. But it is not evident that such restructurings are helpful or get higher valuations. The buyer may or may not value any of these restructurings and may have very different ideas of how to improve the company. So, operational restructuring is often not advisable. On the other hand, financial restructuring may be needed for many PSUs, as they often have a web of complicated financial relationships or, like Air India, are saddled with large debt.

But even for those that do, we need a long-term plan to look for alternative ways to serve national and consumer interest. For example, it will be argued that the FCI is needed for India's food policy objectives. But if India reforms its food policy and allows private traders to play a much bigger role in the purchase, storage and sale of food (along the lines of the *Shanta Committee Report*, 2016) the FCI could be run as a small non-profit agency. Poor consumers could be provided cash transfers instead of the elaborate system of FPSs. Mexico provides a good example of how it got rid of a costly state-owned enterprise CONASUPO over a ten-year period and replaced it with a well-run cash-transfer system called PROCAMPO.

However, such huge changes in the entire food-marketing chain will take time and cannot be done overnight. But without a clear plan on where India needs to be ten years from now, it is hard to make any change at all. The same logic applies to India's numerous fertilizer PSUs. Farmers (especially small farmers) should be paid a cash subsidy to help them purchase fertilizers and other inputs. But the private sector should gradually take over the production and distribution of fertilizers and get the numerous fertilizer PSUs out of the system altogether. Again, Mexico (through its PROGRESSA programme) and later Turkey were able to make this transformation with huge savings to the budget.

At the state-level, more than half the state-level public enterprises (SLPEs) should be shut down. In fact, over 300 of the registered companies are 'non-working' and should be wound down immediately. There is no reason to keep them open, except that the state does not know what to do with employees on the payroll of these companies. But despite repeated admonitions by the Comptroller Auditor-General (CAG), these have not been closed. But even among the 'functioning PSUs', there are many loss-making companies that have outlived their usefulness and are candidates for closure. A centralized account should be created to know the full financial picture of all the remaining SLPEs, just as has been done for the PSUs. A dividend policy should be enforced so that profit-making SLPEs provide a return to the taxpayer. Privatization should be pushed for those in the mining and manufacturing sectors, and much greater commercialization for the service PSUs in water, electricity distribution and transport.

There is a case to keep some of the power and oil companies in public hands, at least in the first phase. For example, the Power Grid Corporation could remain in government hands until complete unbundling has occurred in the power sector, after which it too could go into private hands. Some of the oil companies could also, for now, remain in government control until fuel prices are liberalized and brought under the GST. There was a case earlier for defence-related PSUs on security grounds, such as Hindustan Aeronautics Limited (HAL). That case may yet exist, but with the government opening the defence sector to private investment and consciously encouraging the private sector to enter this excluded area, the case for defence sector PSUs becomes weaker. It may, in any case, help bring in foreign partners into these companies to upgrade their technology and make them more cost-conscious. But even in the security area, the case for PSUs is now much weaker and even these could be included in plans for privatization in Phase 2.

6. The process matters

How and to whom these companies are sold does matter. Russian-style or Latin American-style privatization—where most of the state assets were sold to 'oligarchs'—must be avoided.[23] Transparent processes, competitive bidding and ensuring that some of the funds are set aside for worker compensation are vital for strategic disinvestment to succeed. Strategic sales are considered the optimal way to get the best returns from privatization, but this need not be so. In democratic countries with reasonably developed capital markets, open market sales (share sales) could be designed to widen ownership and create a greater public stake for the sales. India now has many large private companies that are functioning well, with professional management and which are not family-owned. Employees could also be provided shares—employee stock option plans (ESOPs)—in companies when they come under private management so that they are not so resistant to the sale and share in the upside of post-privatization.

For companies that are already listed, the concern that such large block sales will lower their share price can be countered by call-auctions and pre-announced share sales in smaller chunks over time. Foreign institutional investors (FIIs) could be allowed to purchase shares so that there would be no need to list these companies in international stock exchanges. They could be listed in the National Stock Exchange or the Mumbai Stock Exchange—which are now experienced enough to handle such sales—but with FII access, the market for these shares would be wider. The opposition to such an approach will come from trade unions, vested interests and even consumers afraid of higher prices. But considering the long-term benefits to the economy, and better services and products to the consumer, this approach is worth exploring.

Without such a bold approach we will perhaps see some temporary improvements in some PSUs but the underlying incentives for better performance will not have changed and future politicians will have the opportunity to misuse them, again. The public–private partnership (PPP) programme needs a major overhaul along the lines of the Kelkar Committee recommendations.[24] Banks are not the best place to seek long-term finance for PPP projects and efforts must be made to develop non-bank financial sources: the bond market, insurance and pension funds going directly to finance such projects. And the banking sector itself needs a dose of privatization—which we discuss in more detail in the chapter on finance and banking.

In order to avoid the charge that the government is selling the family silver to, so to speak, pay the grocer's bill—the proceeds from the privatization and sales of assets of closed firms should not go back into the budget but instead should be put into the

National Infrastructure Investment Fund and used to pay worker compensation so that the people can visibly identify how the proceeds are being utilized. Such an approach also follows the best practices of the IMF's fiscal rules which have inexplicably been eroded in India and even the IMF has acquiesced in this relaxation of the fiscal rules for India.

It is time to make the slogan 'The Business of Government Is Not Business' a reality. Just kicking the can down the road again and again will not work. A litmus test would be the sale of Air India.

4

Strengthening the State's Capability to Deliver

Reforming an existing order is one of the most dangerous and difficult things ... Those who benefited from the old order will resist change very fiercely. By contrast, those who can benefit from the new order will be less fierce in their support, because the new order is unfamiliar, and they are not certain it will live up to its promises.

—Nicolo Machiavelli, Italian philosopher and historian

A major puzzle in India is that the government appears to do a few things well but its ability to provide basic services across the board remains very weak. India has a competent central bank—the Reserve Bank of India (RBI); it has an Election Commission (EC) that can run elections as well if not better than any other democratic country; it has a space agency, the Indian

Space Research Organisation (ISRO), that can launch satellites cheaper than anyone else. But India seems unable to properly deliver basic education or provide primary healthcare and water and sanitation. In this, India is not unique in the developing world, but some have solved this problem. Many East Asian countries like Taiwan, China, South Korea and now Vietnam were able to do this through well-monitored competent bureaucracies. Some like Bangladesh have managed, despite having a less competent bureaucracy, by allowing non-government organizations (NGOs) to deliver these services.

1. Classifying government services

Arturo Israel, a public administration expert, provides a useful way of thinking through this problem by a dual classification of service delivery: specificity (or discretion)[1] and transaction volume.[2,3,4] Figure 4.1 provides an illustration for India using Israel's classification.[5] Government functions are classified into four quadrants, based on the specificity of the tasks they perform and transactions volume. The RBI,[6] ISRO and the EC perform very specific tasks with considerable discretion—they have high specificity and low volume of transactions. At the opposite end are services that have large volume of transactions but lack specificity in the sense that it is difficult to measure performance and/or ascribe it to a specific input. Low scores in the school system could be due to poor administration, bad teaching, lack of educational supplies or even poor nutrition for the children. The same applies in even greater measure to health, where poor health outcomes could be due to a variety of factors, and the most important ones, such as water and sanitation, and mothers' education, may not even be in the health sector. The same problem also afflicts the police and the judiciary, where transaction volume is sufficiently large and specificity is also low, although perhaps not as much as in health.

The volume of transactions is lesser in higher education or tertiary education in quadrant 3 (Q3), but they also suffer from lower specificity, except for some elite institutions (figure 4.1). Railways, electricity providers, telecommunications providers are in quadrant 2 (Q2) where they have high specificity—measures of performance—but have high transactions volume. Such services are best commercialized or provided by the private sector, as far as possible. In electricity, for example, generation and distribution could be in private hands with transmission in a semi-public agency. Rail lines could be in the public sector but wagons, catering and so on could all be in private hands.

Figure 4.1: Classifying government activities by specificity and transaction volume

Specificity		
	Q1 RBI Election Commission ISRO	Q2 Telecom Financial regulation Electricity Railways
	Q3 Foreign policy Higher education Tertiary health	Q4 Judicial system Police Primary education Primary health
	Transaction Volume	

Source: Adapted from *Institutional Development: Incentives to Performance,* Israel (1987).

Agencies in quadrant 1 (Q1) perform better whereas those in quadrant 4 (Q4) are the most difficult to deliver as they lack specificity (it is hard to measure their performance and ascribe it to a factor) and have high transactions volume. So central banking, or rocketry, or running an election are very specific tasks, and when run by agencies that are given considerable discretion in their decision-making can be run very effectively. School teaching or primary healthcare are high-volume transactions with little specificity. The education and health outcomes are dependent on many things, of which the effectiveness of the teacher or the primary healthcare worker are only one part and often not the most important part. You have lack of specificity (discretion) and large volume, making accountability very difficult. Higher education has more specificity—so India can run a few institutes like the Indian Institute of Technology (IIT) and Indian Institute of Management (IIM) reasonably well—but even here a mass of higher education institutions can exist, basically providing degrees but no skills.

It also explains why governments are keen to deliver things like toilets, water, gas cylinders and bank accounts, where they can show the beneficiary immediate results, but do not show the same interest in delivering the more difficult services like health and education, which may have much better long-term development outcomes. This new welfarism helps win elections but not development.[7]

Aircraft maintenance, airports, ports, highway maintenance and commercial banking have some specificity and larger volumes of transactions than a central bank, or an election commission, but if interfered with by political masters can also deteriorate quickly. Courts have specificity but even larger transactions than these agencies and enormous opportunity for corruption as the Indian system shows. Transparency through information technology (IT) is one solution where discretion in decision-making is not needed. So, payment of taxes, electricity and water utilities, registration of property and so on, can be digitized with huge improvement in service, and post-pandemic, this shift will increase greatly.

What this means is that services like basic health and education must be localized, with some overall guidelines and regulations. Local governments do this well in some states like Kerala, but there is a risk that in some states such as Bihar and Uttar Pradesh, local elites will control the hiring of teachers and primary health workers and turn these into jobs for their friends and family and their supporters. NGOs could be another option, as in Bangladesh, and NGOs like Pratham are already highlighting the problems in India's education system. Local property taxation to fund these services will also provide greater ownership and control over the provision of these services, which lack specificity and have a high volume of transactions. Corporatization, or private provision of a range of services with appropriate regulation is another option. Telecommunications and transport are already moving in this direction. Much of India's electricity sector could also be privatized.

Reform of the state is not an easy process, especially in a democratic set-up with a five-year electoral cycle. It's a long-term project and may need decades of reform. Resistance builds up very quickly from those who will lose out and, as Machiavelli says it very accurately, the support from the beneficiaries is scattered and weak. Many countries carried out such reforms after war and conflict when state administrations were rebuilt. It is important, therefore, to start with some priorities and take on something achievable but does require strong leadership and mobilization of citizen support.

One way to prioritize state reform is to assess how citizens view the state and its various branches. A poll carried out just before the 2019 elections by the Centre for the Study of Developing Societies (CSDS), Lokniti and Azim Premji University showed that the army and courts remain the most trusted, as does the district collector, the official responsible for state administration at the district level—much higher than the chief minister of each state (province) and even the prime minister (figure 4.2).[8] The high trust in the judiciary is surprising, given the high level of judicial corruption and the huge backlog of cases, whereby justice is denied for so long. The police and government officials in general (other than the district collector) get low marks on trust, and the least trusted are political parties.

Figure 4.2: Trust in state institutions in India, 2019

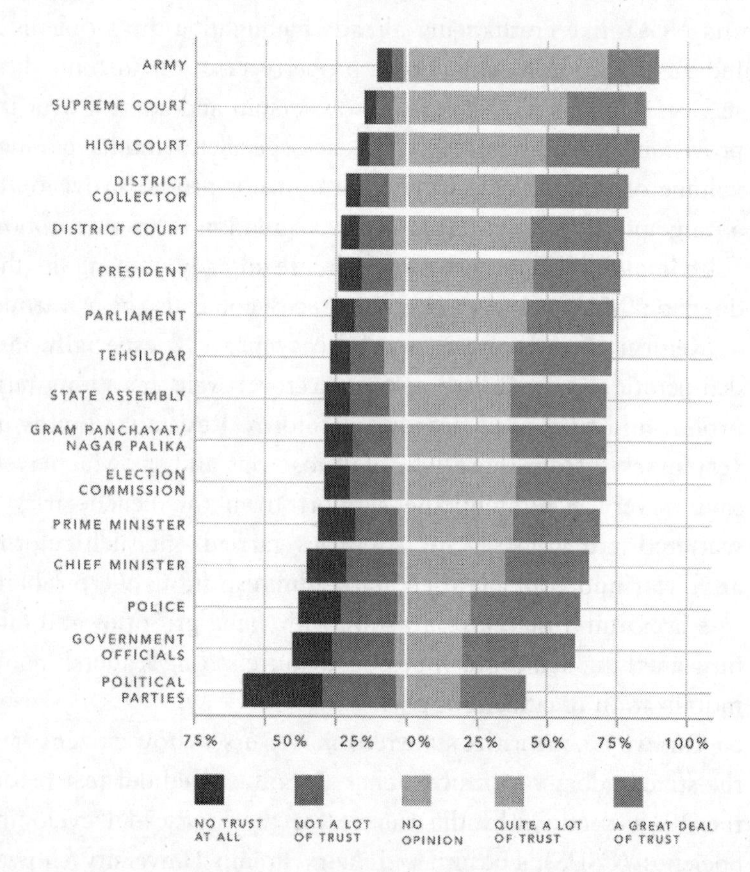

Source: *Politics and Society Between Elections*, CSDS, Lokniti and Azim Premji University (2019).

Broadly, among the three branches of government, the judiciary gets the highest marks, the legislative bodies are second and the administrative branch of government is the least trusted.[9] Based on this, an administrative reform of government would be a good place to start.[10]

India's boutique government: Small but hugely expensive

The size of the civil service is by itself not large, but its composition needs a huge restructuring—there are too many clerical and administrative staff, and too few technocratic experts, teachers and health workers. Devesh Kapur (2020) argues that the size of the state is small because it has too few judges, police officers, teachers, doctors and so on.[11] That is probably true, as the share of general government employment to total employment was around 1 per cent, the lowest in Asia in the 1990s (Schiavo-Campo, Tommaso and Mukherjee 1998), and has not changed much since then. In most Asian countries it is above 2 per cent, and in Malaysia and Sri Lanka over 3 per cent.[12] On the other hand, the small size comes with a very heavy cost. In India, the ratio of the average wage of a general government employee to per capita GDP is now around 4—amongst the highest in the world—whereas in most of Asia that ratio lies between 1 (Vietnam, China) and 2.5 (Indonesia, Sri Lanka, Philippines). Even South Korea, Thailand and Malaysia have a ratio of general government wage to per capita GDP of around 3-4. With a ratio of 7 until 1980, India was in the category of some former French-ruled African countries like Senegal, but while that ratio has declined to 4 it remains too high. In much of the Arab world and Turkey, that ratio is around 2-3. India runs a boutique government—small relative to its needs but very expensive relative to its income.

Another factor that has contributed to huge inefficiencies in the civil services is the compression ratio—the ratio of average salaries in the highest to those in the lowest bracket. India's wage compression ratio has declined considerably. This has come about by keeping salaries of the top levels low and rapidly increasing salaries at the lower end of the bureaucracy. The 7th Pay Commission defined the compression ratio as the ratio of the entry-level employee at Grade A to C at 3.12 and for the ratio of the highest paid at Grade A to Grade C at 3.74. The upper end of the civil service has seen its real wages fall well below that of the private sector, whereas at the lower end salaries (including benefits) can be more secure and are even higher than in the private sector.[13] This has meant that the pay, and as a result the quality, of the inductees at the higher-end, with discretionary decision-making authority, has declined, whereas those at the lower-end, who make up more than 90 per cent of the government labour force, end up paid a much higher wage than in the private sector. India spends too much on its government as it pays too high a salary at many lower levels of government and ends up having too few government teachers, health workers, police officers and judges.

However, that just means India's public spend is quite large, but is spent badly. It does not mean India should increase government spending but that it should reorient its spending better. Almost 50 per cent of total governmental expenditure is non-developmental, with large chunks going to administrative salaries, pensions and interest payments. India also spends too much at central and state levels and very little (3 per cent) at the local administration level. The same amount spent at the local level would allow it to hire many more teachers or nurses and compounders as local wages are much lower than those determined at state capitals or at the Centre in New Delhi.

At the apex of this bureaucracy sits a mandarin-like elite administrative service who are competent and smart but who are shuffled around like a deck of cards at a bridge game and therefore have no time to develop the in-depth expertise needed to remain abreast of global developments in those fields. They lack the technical edge required to lead India's government policy in their sectors to retain our competitive edge and they often suffer from excessive political interference in their functioning. A more professional, performance-based civil service with promotions based on regular testing rather than a time-bound lifelong sinecure is needed to maintain a meritocratic culture. There is much to learn from the civil service systems of East Asian countries such as Japan, South Korea, Singapore and Taiwan.[14] Much greater specialization is also needed at the top of the bureaucracy, instead of the generalist model India adopted from its colonial administrative system.[15]

The new bureaucratic elite are the regulatory bodies, often headed by retired senior government officials, not by technically competent experts as is the case in most other parts of the world. We need a blueprint of a modern regulatory structure, which can then be developed over the next five years in a systematic manner—more transparent, less complex and headed by professionals with domain expertise, not career bureaucrats. We need a system that will minimize regulatory capture[16] but does not choke private investment, and which allocates resources in a transparent and efficient manner. This should also allow private investment in many sectors where it is currently restricted, including natural resources and defence production, and help avoid the coordination problems that have led to a situation in which India, with the second-largest reserves in the world, now imports record levels of coal.

Figure 4.3: India's property tax is amongst the lowest in the world

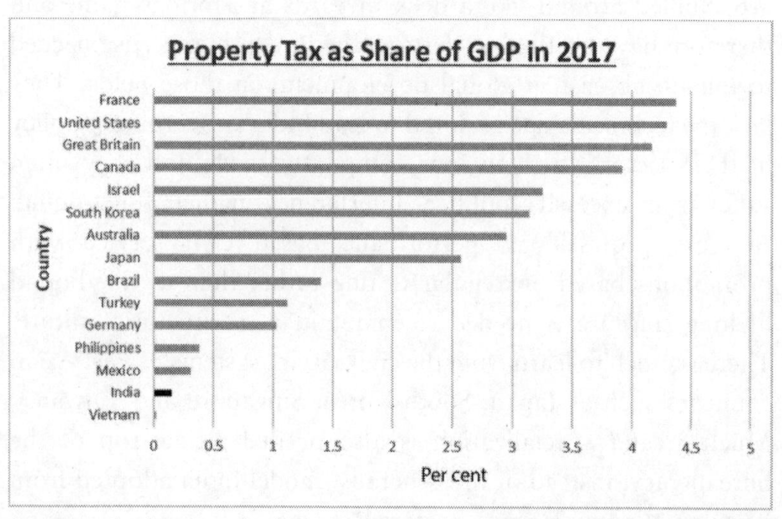

Source: Authors' calculations based on OECD and World Bank databases.

A regulatory review is needed to assess the effectiveness of regulations. One principle that must be kept in mind is that while more complex regulations can create more effective outcomes, they also require a much greater capacity to manage, implement and monitor those regulations. If that capacity does not exist, a simpler regulatory structure should be considered. A big deficiency in India is that it has complex and overlapping regulations which are hard to administer and monitor. As a result, corruption abounds and often the left hand of the government does not know what the right hand is doing. Civil society can play a big role in highlighting failures in administering regulations and should be seen by regulatory bodies as an ally not an enemy, especially in natural resource management. In the financial sector for example, RBI and the Securities and Exchange Board of India (SEBI) are considered competent but disentangling the roles and responsibilities of different regulators should also be investigated; a clean-up of the nested relationships between the RBI and the government must be a priority as well.

2. More devolution to sub-national government

A review is also needed of the roles and responsibilities of the central, state and local governments. The proliferation of national flagship schemes has blurred the role and responsibilities of the Centre and the states and diminished accountability. The idea that the Centre will design national schemes, which will then be implemented in a prescribed manner by state governments and districts with huge variability in their capacity and governance quality is itself absurd. The 14th Finance Commission shifted about 10 per cent of the divisible pool share of resources to the state level—but much remains to be done to shift more resources to the local level (figure 4.3). As Kapur (2020) has shown, India's share of local government spend and hiring is much lower than in most developed countries but also much lower than in authoritarian centrally dominant countries like China, where delegation and devolution are very substantial, making government far more effective.[17] One argument that is often made is that India does not even collect enough revenues for the needs of the Centre and the states, so there is limited scope for shifting more resources to the local level. But this argument is spurious. A rise in property taxes—which remain amongst the lowest in the world—is the most obvious way to provide more resources at the local level without eating into state and Central government revenues. It remains a surprise why this most obvious way to raise resources for municipal and civic infrastructure and help build 'smart' cities has not been utilized so far.

One big issue that India will face going forward is the changing composition of population in states. The southern states' population growth rates are much lower than those in the north. Several Northeast states and even West Bengal have lowered their fertility rates hugely. Their quite legitimate gripe is that if resources are decided largely by population, they are being penalized for faster development and better education and health services, which have pushed their population growth down. This will become an even bigger battle by 2026, when the decision will have to be made on the distribution of parliamentary seats, which currently are based on the 1971 census.

Some creative options can be considered to reduce this tension between the states with fast-growing populations versus states with slow population growth. One option is to give credit to states which have reduced population growth rates. This would encourage efforts to control the population in those states where the fertility rate remains very high. The 15th Finance Commission has given a 12.5 per cent share to demographic performance so as to reward states that have pursued faster economic and social development, and have reduced their birth rates.

A second would be to give credit to states which have seen greater in-migration. The common misperception is that intrastate migration is large, but interstate migration is quite low. But as the 2016–17 Economic Survey pointed out, interstate migration is hugely underestimated and during the decade 2001–11 could have been as high as 60 million, and by 2019, when the pandemic struck, was as high as 200 million. Creative ways to give credit to states with in-migration between 1971 and 2011 could be considered. This would also encourage states receiving migrants to provide them better services, which they are now usually denied, and discourage discrimination against migrants.

Some worry that in the mind of the Central government, devolution may have gone too far. The 15th Finance Commission was asked to examine 'the impact on the finances of the Union government of substantially enhanced devolution to the states following the recommendation of the 14th Finance Commission coupled with the continuing imperative of the national development programme—including New India 2022'. Does this suggest that the government is having second thoughts on the fiscal devolution it accepted earlier?

Other countries such as Brazil and Indonesia did claw back big-bang decentralization to some extent, but in our view, India needs even further decentralization—especially to local levels. But in India, such an approach will be counterproductive as the 2014 devolution did not lead to any change in the total amount of funds to the states, just in the way they were delivered. Whereas earlier funds were tied up in central flagship schemes, they were now to be provided in an unfettered form to the states to decide how best to spend them. In fact, India needs even greater devolution going forward and remains, in form, a highly centralized country. And, as the latest GST imbroglio shows, is quite willing to go back on promises made to the states. In the end, the 15th Finance Commission has kept the share the same. It has reduced from 42 per cent to 41 per cent because Jammu and Kashmir and Ladakh have become union territories (not states) and will be largely funded from the central pool.

A third concern is regarding the request to the commission to examine 'control or lack of it in incurring expenditure on populist measures'. Given the growing concerns over rising state deficits—especially in Bihar and Punjab—the concerns over excessive state spending are well taken. But it is again very subjective as there is no clear definition of 'populist' programmes. Who decides what is 'populist' or realistic? And what of the populist programmes in the Union Budget? Telling states how to spend their money did not work well earlier and will not work well now. In the spirit of 'cooperative federalism', state governments must be allowed to make their own choices and face the electorate on their own performance. Any restrictions added on would deliver an additional blow to 'cooperative federalism' that GST initially generated, but has been set back, perhaps irreparably, by the 2020 GST imbroglio. The 15th Finance Commission has allocated about 0.5 per cent of GDP for incentivizing states to improve the finance of their state electricity distribution companies.

3. Other considerations: Smaller states and more time zones to improve governance and productivity

One issue that has not generated enough focus is the optimal size of states in India. Some are too large to be governed well. The break-up of states, politically tortuous as it has been, has led to improved economic development. The creation of Haryana and Himachal Pradesh in the 1960s led to very rapid progress in both states. These had been neglected parts of a much larger Punjab state but took off after their creation. Similarly, Uttaranchal (now Uttarakhand) has done well after being hived off from Uttar Pradesh, as has Jharkhand after its split from Bihar and Chhattisgarh from Madhya Pradesh. The latest is the split of Telangana from Andhra Pradesh.

Obvious candidates for further splits are Uttar Pradesh with a population of 230 million, Bihar and Maharashtra with a population of over 120 million each. With a projected population of 1.5 billion and assuming an optimal state size of 30 million,

India should eventually become fifty states. By this logic, even Madhya Pradesh (even after the creation of Chhattisgarh), West Bengal, Tamil Nadu and Rajasthan are candidates for split-ups.

The current government is pushing for faster development of India's eastern states. Among other factors, one issue that has not got enough attention is the diminution of productivity in the Northeast from being forced into an India-wide time zone.[18] Maulik Jagnani (2019) has shown significant effects of sleep timings on years of schooling as well.[19] With productive hours considerably affected, especially in winter months, a natural productivity boost would come from the creation of two time zones for the country. One obvious natural longitudinal line would be with Odisha, Bihar, West Bengal and the Northeast in one time zone and the rest of the country in another natural time zone.

Dealing with the cancer of corruption

> *Just as it is impossible to know when a swimming fish is drinking water, so it is impossible to find out when a government servant is stealing money.*
>
> —Kautilya, Indian philosopher

Corruption in India is now an accepted way of life. It's a dead weight loss. A new Netflix series, *Bad Boy Billionaires*, shows how deep the rot is in India's corruption-ridden society. Whether corruption is increasing or decreasing is unclear. India ranked 94th in 2012 and 2013 rankings of the Transparency International, based on perceptions of businesses. This was the time when scams were being exposed under the UPA government. India's ranking then improved to 76th position by 2015. But

2020 rankings show a jump up to 86th position (table 4.1).[20,21] Transparency International's own Corruption Barometer for Asia, which surveys citizens not businesses, shows that in 2017, 41 per cent of respondents said corruption had increased over the previous year; by 2020, this number had increased to 47 per cent. Whether it is going up or down, what is clear is that India has the highest rate of bribery across all of Asia (table 4.2).[22] And the joke in Asia is that even 'corruption' in India is inefficient. In much of Asia if you pay a bribe your work gets done, whereas in India even that is never sure.

Table 4.1: Transparency International's 'Corruption Perception Index' for India

India	2012	2013	2014	2015	2016	2017	2018	2019	2020
TI Score	36	36	38	38	40	40	41	41	40
TI Rank	94	94	85	76	79	81	78	80	86

Source: *Corruption Perceptions Index 2020,* Transparency International (2021).

How does one address it? Corruption is a symptom of a dysfunctional interface between the government and society. But the moment also provides us an opportunity to initiate wider reforms to tackle corruption.

First, we must consider the issue of how much discretionary power the government should have and where it should be placed. As James Madison, a founding father of the American Constitution wrote in the Federalist, 'In framing a government to be administered by men over men, the great difficulty lies in this: you must first enable the government to control the governed; and in the next place oblige it to control itself.' In India, the discretionary power of the executive has, over time, become too great. Laws and rules, contradicting each other and accumulated over the years, are open to interpretation by officials.

Second, corruption can be reduced through greater competition or contestability. If the services that people need are provided in a contestable way, corruption will decline. This has been proved in the case of telecommunications. Twenty years ago, every household in India wanted a telephone and people paid bribes to get ahead in the queue for connections. With the arrival of mobiles, no one bothered about fixed-line connections, but corruption moved to a higher level—to procure 2G spectrum licences. India got it right with 3G licences, using auctions, which shows that more competition and careful design can reduce corruption. The opportunity for corruption exists wherever there are excessive controls and public monopolies. Easing access to these services will reduce corruption.

Third, greater transparency is needed wherever major financial resources are involved. 'Follow the money' is a good guide to look for places to prioritize. Procurement, licensing and other major public transactions are all areas in need of greater public scrutiny and transparency. The procurement and mining laws, where public funds and assets are involved, need major upgrading to bring them to global standards. The citizens' Right to Information Act has been a significant milestone. But its use is not easy and public officials find many ways to withhold information. E-services are an effective step forward and wherever introduced have helped citizens meet their basic services in a transparent manner.

Fourth, we need incentives against corruption. Singapore had one of the most corrupt customs services in the world. It realized that to be a trade and service centre for the region, it would have to root out corruption. It now pays its civil servants the equivalent of private sector wages. Public sector wages have risen over the years in India as well and while not equivalent to private sector levels, they are nevertheless competitive. But the public sector requires more merit-based hiring to dispense with the system of paying bribes to get stable jobs in PSUs.

Table 4.2: 'Did you have contact with a public official and pay a bribe?'

	Had contact, didn't pay a bribe	Paid a bribe	Don't know/ Refused
Japan	98%	2%	0%
Maldives	97%	2%	1%
South Korea	90%	10%	0%
Nepal	88%	12%	0%
Malaysia	87%	13%	0%
Vietnam	85%	15%	0%
Sri Lanka	84%	16%	0%
Taiwan	83%	17%	0%
Philippines	81%	19%	0%
Myanmar	80%	20%	0%
Mongolia	78%	22%	0%
Thailand	76%	24%	0%
Bangladesh	76%	24%	0%
China	72%	28%	0%
Indonesia	70%	30%	0%
Cambodia	63%	37%	0%
India	61%	39%	0%
Total	81%	19%	0%

Source: *Global Corruption Barometer: Asia 2020*, Transparency International (2021).

Fifth, election financing is a major reason cited for political corruption. The US faced the same problem around 150 years ago. Meaningful election financing reforms could be enacted in the US only in the 1970s. Two areas to start election financing reforms would be raising funds for electioneering and containing alleged vote-buying schemes. India has unfortunately moved in the opposite direction by introducing an opaque system of electoral bonds, whereby donations to political parties can be made without disclosure and without scrutiny by the EC. It is no wonder that political parties are the least trusted institution in the country.

Sixth, India needs a serious judicial reform to ease the backlog of cases. We also need more predictability in outcomes, both in the judiciary and in the administration. The judiciary remains small and arcane in its procedures—and judicial activism has amplified but is very selective and one might even say capricious, often at the cost of further delays in the cases piled up at the doors of the courts. Digitization of the court system, hiring more judges and modernizing the system by increasing systems of arbitration and commercial courts are needed to reduce delays. As the saying goes, 'justice delayed is justice denied', and India is denying justice on a gigantic scale and is then open to massive corruption in the judicial system.[23]

India signed the UN Convention Against Corruption that sets global standards on tackling corruption in 2005 and ratified it in 2011. But it still has a long way to go to meet global best practices. The passionate response to corruption in every citizen survey has sent a strong message to the government that citizens demand serious and urgent action. Such reforms aren't easy as they will be opposed by narrow interests that have much to gain from the status quo.

If Kautilya in the *Arthashastra* could lay down the methods of dealing with corruption, surely modern India, with ambitions of becoming a global power, can take on the scourge of corruption. All developed countries had to tackle corruption systematically at some point. India now has a historic opportunity to do the same.

5. Conclusion

To conclude, India does not need a smaller government or for that matter a much larger one, but a more focused, smarter and more accountable government with much clearer roles and responsibilities. A two-pronged strategy of reducing its scope[24] (not size) and improving state capability is the way forward. Countries that have grasped this nettle have escaped from the 'middle income trap'. China is on its way, but many others have floundered. That India will grasp the nettle in the coming years and revive its long-term prospects is a hope all of us must ensure. At 8-9 per cent GDP growth, India can not only eliminate poverty but become an industrial country in three decades. At 4-5 per cent growth, India is unfortunately stuck in the middle-income trap for another fifty years.

The coronavirus has exposed the inefficiencies in government more sharply. India's inability to manage the pandemic was inevitable given the weak health system, with one of the lowest public health spending as a share of GDP in the world. But other inadequacies were also exposed, including a very weak and badly run social safety net and lack of coordination between the Centre and the states, and very inadequate funding for local government which is at the front line of the fight against the pandemic. Trust in public institutions was surprisingly relatively high in India but may now have declined as more and more people lost lives and livelihoods.

This chapter and Chapters 2 and 3 together have shown a two-pronged strategy for improving the effectiveness of government, reducing its scope and improving its capability. Let it do a set of fewer things and do them well—keep the regulatory system simple and transparent and avoid doing what the private sector and civil society do better. India must also decentralize and devolve much more—but also build up greater capability in local government. If India is to reset for the twenty-first century, our future and those of our children lies in reforming the government now for rapid, sustained long-term growth and a happier society. No quick fixes will work. Only then can we say that 'Government Work Is God's Work'.

Part II

Building the Foundations: Developing Human Capital

5

New Lessons for Indian Education

The best investment for one year is to grow grains; the best investment for ten years is to grow trees; the best investment for a lifetime is to educate people.

—Guan Zhong, Chinese philosopher and politician

In 2015, a photograph from Hajipur (Bihar) went viral.[1] It showed a building where students were taking their tenth-grade board examinations. The photograph drew interest not because of the students inside that building but because of their families and friends who climbed the building walls to help the students cheat. Outrage, disbelief and even jokes followed, as the photo made international headlines. However, this episode reflected a painful reality. The education system in the country, and not just in Bihar, suffers from deep-rooted challenges. Learning outcomes, which are well below where they need to be, reflect these challenges. Indian students lag behind students from other parts of the world and, as technology and innovation increasingly shape the twenty-first century, disadvantages are piling up for young Indians.

To make matters infinitely worse, COVID-19 threatens to reverse decades of progress, limited as it may have been. Many children who have experienced a disruption in their education may fall behind or never return to school. Between May and June 2020, an Oxfam survey of five states—Bihar, Jharkhand, Chhattisgarh, Odisha and Uttar Pradesh—found that 80 per cent of parents surveyed reported that education was not delivered during the COVID-19 lockdown.[2] About 1.5 million schools closed during the first lockdown, affecting 289 million students. As children around the world dropped out of school, millions were forced to work to support their families.[3] With the largest school-age population in the world, one can imagine the hit taken by poor children in India. All this will have serious economic consequences. According to one World Bank estimate, Indians will lose $440 billion in lifetime earnings as a result.[4]

India's education sector is vast and complex, and it is difficult to focus on all its facets in a chapter in a book. We have made a conscious choice to focus our attention mostly on school education. We merely touch on tertiary or vocational education here. The reason is that so much that is deficient in Indian education can be traced to the early years of students. From their health in the early years to what they learn in their formative years has a profound impact on their later lives. We believe that if the foundations are good, Indian students will be better prepared for what life has to offer them.

The centrality of education to development

In 1990, UNDP published the first *Human Development Report* (HDR). Since then, the HDR has consistently promoted what HDR 1990 called the 'human dimension of development'.[5] That first HDR argued that there was an 'essential truth' which placed humans at the centre of development. Development affords people more options. One option may include having more income as a means to improved well-being. However, that is not the only option. People may want a longer life, personal freedoms, security, community participation, human rights, etc. The HDR helped expand the conceptual underpinnings of development.

The HDR directly challenged a misconception that human development could be promoted only at the cost of economic growth. The report argued that this was a false trade-off, which 'misstates the purpose of development and underestimates the returns on investment in health and education'. In fact, the HDR contended that private returns to education were well over 30 per cent in Africa, Latin America and Asia. At that time, developing countries as a group were spending more as a share of their national economies on their militaries compared with education and health combined. The HDR noted that there were '... eight times more soldiers than physicians in the Third World'.[6]

Similarly, from the very first *World Development Report* (WDR) in 1978, the World Bank has also been pushing education (and health) onto the centre stage of development. The first WDR makes it clear that experience suggests that poorer people 'are unlikely to share equitably in economic growth, mainly because they have less access to the productive assets needed to generate incomes—land, credit, education and jobs in the modern sector'.[7] That we are still seeking its rightful place for education in economic development discourse in the twenty-first century tells you how frustratingly slow the progress has been in this area.

Four decades later, the 2018 WDR highlights the powerful and positive impact that education has on different aspects of human welfare. It is an effective tool for raising incomes by making workers more productive. Research indicates that each additional year of schooling is associated with an 8–10 per cent increase in earnings.[8] This positive association of education with higher earnings is seen in every region of the world (figure 5.1).[9] Women benefit even more from education. Not only do incomes rise across the board, but the threat of unemployment decreases in well-functioning labour markets.

Figure 5.1: Schooling is systematically associated with higher wages

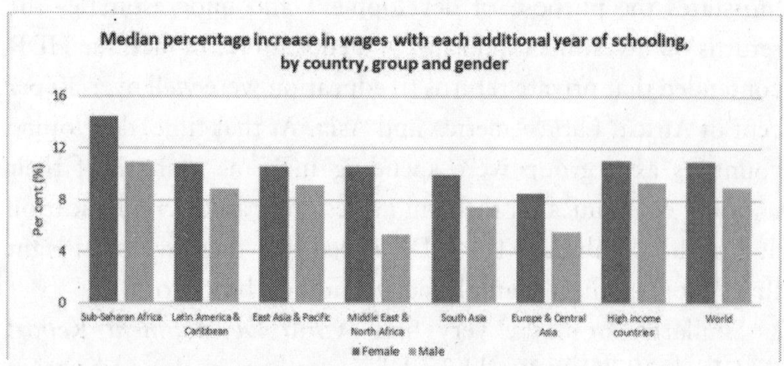

Source: *World Development Report 2018*.

In the Indian context, there is voluminous research on the critical links between education and development. For example, Jean Drèze and Amartya Sen, who have written extensively on India, cite eight reasons why basic education is critical to development: (i) there are powerful effects on quality of life (from freedom to communicate to leading an informed life); (ii) economic opportunities depend on educational experiences; (iii) voice and security are closely linked; (iv) positive general and public health outcomes; (v) education brings about changes in public perceptions of the 'range and reach' of human rights; (vi) better understanding and use of legal rights; (vii) voice of women (with other positive impacts on mortality of children, nutrition, etc.); and (viii) reductions in class and caste divisions.[10] Moreover, for many girls and women, a sound education is essential to navigating out of 'a nexus of poverty, violence, child labour, early marriage, abuse within and outside families, and lack of care and nutrition'.[11] Such benefits are intergenerational.[12] However, despite all that we know about the benefits of education, there is a bitter reality to contend with, especially in India.

A global learning crisis

In the 2018 WDR, 'Learning to Focus on Education's Promise', the World Bank begins with a simple statement: schooling is not the same as learning. This may be self-evident, but it has not always been so. For decades, developing countries have worked hard to raise enrolment ratios. Countries around the world have made much progress on that front. Literacy levels have risen globally and India too has benefited from that trend. However, along with the evolution of the global economy, learning has become central to education. It is simply not enough for children to go to school, progress through school systems and leave unprepared for the rigours of modern economies.

The 2018 WDR paints a picture of a global 'learning crisis', highlighting the steep hill many countries have to climb to improve education in a meaningful way. When third-grade students in Kenya, Tanzania and Uganda were asked if they understood the sentence 'The name of the dog is Puppy,' in English or Kiswahili, three-quarters responded in the negative.[13] In Brazil, where fifteen-year-old students have shown improvements in mathematics skills, the rate of progress is such that it will still take them seventy-five years to get to a rich country's average. Even worse, at the current rate, it will take 250 years for Brazilian students to reach the rich-world average for reading. But it isn't just that cross-country differences are so stark. Often, the differences within countries are even more so. In Uruguay, sixth-grade students from poor families are rated as 'not competent' at five times the rate of wealthy children.[14]

What we know about the deficiencies of current learning systems is matched by what we do not know. Even before COVID-19, 260 million children globally were not in school.[15] That means any global assessment of student learning does not include the impact of such a large chunk of school-age children being out of school. But it gets worse. For many developing countries, including India, there is limited data available to create an evidence base for informed policymaking.

Until 2009, India used to participate in the OECD's Programme for International Student Assessment (PISA), which measures fifteen-year-olds' ability to use their reading, mathematics and science knowledge and skills to meet real-life challenges. In the 2009 assessment, Indian students, who came from the well-performing states of Himachal Pradesh and Tamil Nadu, had reading and mathematics scores that were closer to those of students from Kyrgyzstan than the average of OECD students.[16] The Indian government decided to end its participation in PISA because it argued that the assessment did not relate to what Indian children were taught in school.[17] On the other hand, China has been part of PISA and has been topping the rankings. There is a view that Chinese students appearing in PISA do not represent the full Chinese system and that the government picks the provinces that participate and that this helps inflate its ranking. However, this is no consolation for India, given that India's 2009 participants were from the best states and India still ranked 73 out of 74 countries.

The 2018 WDR argues that the global 'learning crisis' is driven primarily by deficiencies in four key ingredients: unprepared learners, ineffective teaching, inputs that don't reach the classroom and terrible governance. If India and other developing countries want to make substantial progress in the quality of learning outcomes, these four aspects merit careful attention. In popular discourse, governments are either not spending enough on education or are not focused on quality, and that makes the education sector churn out unproductive workers. It is in this context that we read about companies in India (and elsewhere) complaining about the lack of qualified workers. However, this is an incomplete diagnosis. Governments could spend a lot more money on the education sector and still wind up with terrible learning outcomes. An anecdote will illustrate this point.

In 2013-14, one of us (Soz) visited a small village called Bandi Payeen in the upper reaches of Baramulla in northern Kashmir.[18] This village, measuring roughly 1 km by 0.5 km, had eight government schools—a high school, three middle schools and four primary schools. Not one of those eight schools had enough teachers, students, chairs, desks, or anything. On the other hand, a middle school in a village close to Baramulla town had only nine students in eight grades and almost a dozen teachers, most of whom were found chatting outside during Soz's visit to the school. These are not isolated examples. This was happening across Baramulla and perhaps across India. Government schools did not appear to be serving the interests of students even though teachers in these schools are widely perceived to be more qualified than those in private schools. Is spending more money on such an inefficient and unbalanced system going to improve learning outcomes? We find that hard to believe.

A proper diagnosis is fundamental to reformist policies and eventual improvements in learning outcomes. Let us first take the issue of unprepared learners. This is not the children's fault. They suffer from malnutrition, limited support from families or other environmental challenges. Even if they get a decent opportunity in life, poverty pushes children to the back of the classroom. It is an uphill struggle from the very beginning. With 30–40 per cent of children malnourished in India (and in other poor countries), the foundations of the learning system are teetering from the start.

Effective teachers make up the second key ingredient for effective learning. Teachers, according to the WDR, 'are the most important factor affecting learning in schools'. However, teachers often lack the skills or motivation to help their students learn. While this is a problem across countries, the challenge is particularly pronounced in developing countries such as India. The WDR reports that 'fifteen-year-old students who aspire to be teachers score below the national average on PISA in nearly all countries'.[19] Teacher education is often poor and their subject-matter expertise and teaching skills are shaky at best. A study of fourteen Sub-Saharan African countries found that the average sixth-grade teachers were no better at reading than the best-performing sixth-grade students.[20] The point here is not to excoriate teachers but to highlight a problem that bedevils learning systems in developing countries.

The third area relates to missing inputs that are critical for classroom learning. As we alluded to in the Bandi Payeen example, there really aren't many resources available to help teachers improve learning outcomes. If school budgets are overwhelmingly devoted to salaries, there is little left over for basics such as textbooks, desks or even floor matting. Computers and internet connections are a dream for most government schools in India. Yes, more resources would help bring in the kinds of inputs that can help students learn better. However, as the Baramulla examples indicate, throwing money at the problem may not help. Improved public expenditure efficiency combined with additional resources may be necessary if students are to improve their standing.

Finally, the WDR argues that poor governance systems are damaging for student learning. How schools are managed is of high importance when it comes to improving learning quality. But it isn't only school principals who may be failing. Governance systems also include oversight, transparency and accountability mechanisms that are critical to improving school performance. Of course, this means leaders of education departments who monitor the performance of school systems. But it also means the involvement of parents and community members in how schools create an environment conducive to learning.

These four ingredients matter greatly for improved learning. Certainly, these are not the only ingredients that matter. Education systems are complex, face diverse and deep-rooted challenges and are not amenable to easy solutions. For instance, the challenges of university-level learning are considerably different from those facing high schoolers. However, regardless of what level of education we are talking about, it appears inconvertible that a good beginning will yield dividends later on. James Heckman, a Nobel laureate in economics, has been a lifelong advocate of investing in early childhood development. Heckman points out that by the time students from 'disadvantaged families' enter pre-school (ages three to four), it may already be too late to secure a productive future for them. If Heckman had his way, policymakers would focus on children from birth until five years.

Such investments have high social returns, will reduce deficits, and increase economic growth.[21] That means the traditional view that seeks to link learning outcomes to what happens in schools, colleges and universities is incomplete. If we want better learners, we have to help those in need from the very early days.

Evolution of India's education sector

At independence, adult literacy in India was about 18 per cent. A country with hundreds of millions of people, most living in poverty and beset by food insecurity, focused on education for the masses. It is easy for us in the twenty-first century to talk about education quality and bemoan past mistakes. However, India's founders and their successors pushed hard to get children into schools. By subsidizing education in IITs and IIMs, a cadre of quality professionals was developed. Affirmative action helped bring marginalized communities into the education system.[22]

Education policy has evolved considerably since Independence. The Kothari Commission (1964–66) framed education as necessary for increasing productivity, developing national cohesion, modernizing the country and strengthening social and moral values.[23] Given the low literacy rates prevalent at that time, the Kothari Commission recommended free and compulsory education for children up to the age of fourteen. The Commission formulated the three-language formula (children would learn Hindi, their state language and English), stressed equality of opportunity (including gender) and prioritized science and mathematics.

Between then and now, there have been many initiatives to help improve India's education system. In 1986, the Rajiv Gandhi government implemented the National Policy on Education (NPE) to help prepare the country for the twenty-first century.

The NPE shifted focus to issues of access and quality.[24] Under the NPE, the Central government allocated development expenditure for primary education even as curriculum development remained with the states. Operation Blackboard (1987–88) sought to improve the resources available to primary schools. The National Programme for Nutritional Support to Primary Education (1995) provided a cooked meal every day for children from first to fifth grade. The Movement to Educate All (2000) aimed to achieve universal primary education by 2010.[25] The Government of India (GoI) launched the Sarva Shiksha Abhiyan (SSA) in 2001 as its flagship elementary education programme to provide universal education to children between the ages of six and fourteen years.[26]

In 2009, the Right to Education Act (RTE) was enacted to keep up the momentum for universalizing basic education. The RTE enabled every child between the ages of six and fourteen years the right to be admitted to a quality school. The RTE further mandated that schools should have separate toilets for boys and girls, drinking water, a library and access for disabled children.[27]

As a result of such policies, India has made substantial progress in spreading literacy and in improving gross enrolment (particularly at the primary school level). According to the National Sample Survey (NSS) 75th round on Household Social Consumption: Education, 77.7 per cent of Indians over the age of seven are literate (73.5 per cent in rural and 87.7 per cent in urban areas).[28] The Annual Status of Education Report (ASER), an undertaking of Pratham, an NGO, found that for ten years since 2007, enrolment of children aged six to fourteen had exceeded 95 per cent. For the first time, in 2018, children out of school dropped below 3 per cent. The proportion of girls between eleven and fourteen years of age that was out of school was 4.1 per cent in 2018. This is a vast improvement compared to 2005, when the ASER reports began to be published. Enrolment ratios had also improved for girls in the 15-16 group. Meanwhile, the percentage of children enrolled in private schools plateaued at just above 30 per cent, starting in 2014 after rising steadily since 2006.[29]

The status of Indian education

These are heart-warming improvements. However, despite this progress, the 2018 WDR highlights some disturbing findings on India. Drawing on that, 'In rural India in 2016, only half of grade five students could fluently read text at the level of the grade two curriculum, which included sentences (in the local language) such as "It was the month of rains" and "There were black clouds in the sky".'[30] Such shortfalls in learning start early and Indian children have a steep hill to climb, both in reading and mathematics (figure 5.2). As students advance through different grades, they learn little and learning gaps increase over time (figure 5.3).

Figure 5.2: Shortfalls in learning start early

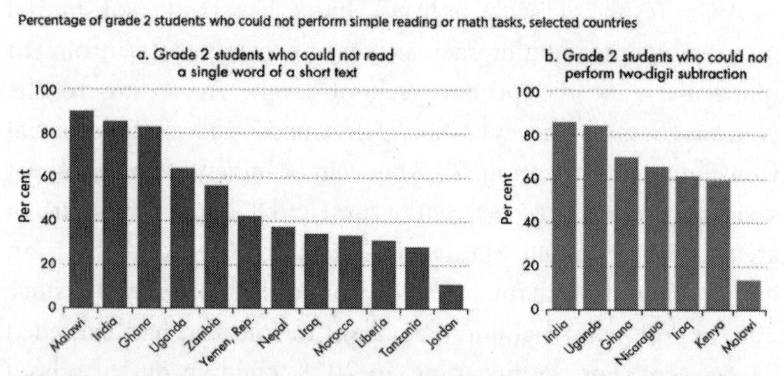

Sources: WDR 2018 team, using reading and mathematics data for Kenya and Uganda from Uwezo, Annual Assessment Reports, 2015 (http://www.uwezo.net/); reading and mathematics data for rural India from ASER Centre (2017); reading data for all other countries from U.S. Agency for International Development (USAID), Early Grade Reading Barometer, 2017, accessed May 30, 2017 (http://www.earlygradereadingbarometer.org/); and mathematics data for all other countries from USAID/RTI Early Grade Mathematics Assessment intervention reports, 2012–15 (https://shared.rti.org/sub-topic/early-grade-math-assessment-egma). Data at http://bit.do/WDR2018-Fig_O-1.

Note: These data typically pertain to selected regions in the countries and are not necessarily nationally representative. Data for India pertain to rural areas.

Source: *World Development Report: Learning to Realize Education's Promise*, World Bank (2018).

Figure 5.3: Students often learn little from year to year

Assessed grade-level performance of students relative to enrolled grade, New Delhi, India (2015)

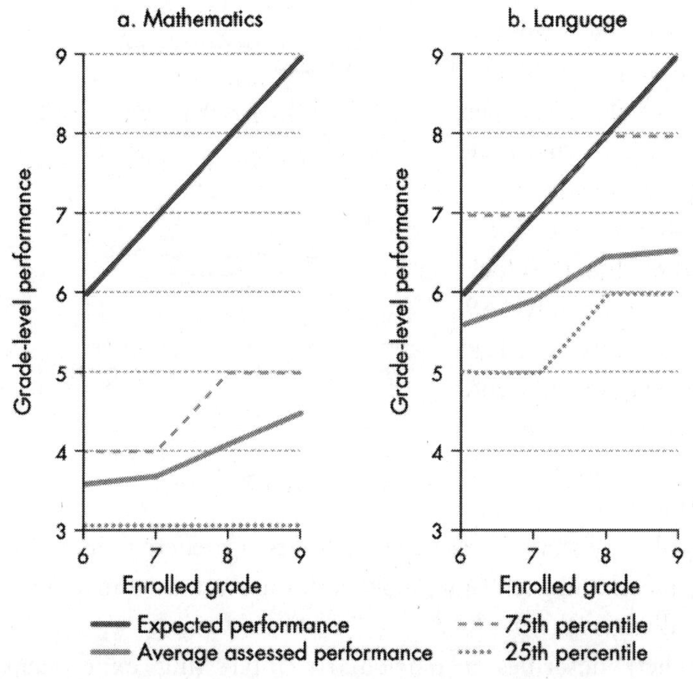

Source: WDR 2018 team, using data from Muralidharan, Singh, and Ganimian (2016). Data at http://bit.do/WDR2018-Fig_0-4.

Source: *World Development Report: Learning to Realize Education's Promise*, World Bank (2018).

There is broad consensus that quality of learning has not kept pace and that the education system has massive inequalities—spatial and social—and students have 'very low levels of practical skills'.[31] The economist Lant Pritchett describes the problem as '... a massive mismatch between their aspirations of how they will be able to use their schooling and their actual capability'.

Figure 5.4: Students are often unable to apply what they learn

Can you measure length?

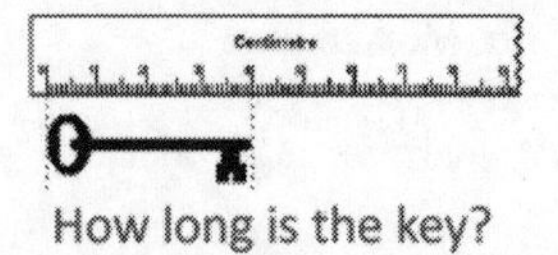

How long is the key?

86% of all youth get it right.

What is the length of this pencil?

Less than 40% could give the right answer.

Source: ASER 2017: *Beyond Basics Presentation,* ASER Centre.

Using data from ASER surveys, Pritchett has documented that youth (ages 14–18) have a distressingly low ability to solve simple problems. For example, 83 per cent could tell what time it was when the clock struck three o'clock. However, when the clock struck 4.45, only 59 per cent were correct. In another experiment, if a girl went to bed at 10.30 p.m. and woke up at 6.30 p.m., only 60 per cent could say that she slept eight hours. Pritchett points out, 'While most could tell time, most could not use time in simple, practical ways.'[32]

Pritchett describes a particularly interesting experiment developed by Educational Initiatives, a company that develops education technology products. To demonstrate the difference between rote learning and actual understanding, the company asked youth to measure an object against a ruler. The object was placed at the end of the ruler and the youth were asked to provide the length of the object. Eighty-six per cent answered correctly. However, when the object is placed anywhere else (away from the starting edge of the ruler), only 40 per cent measured correctly (see figure 5.4).[33] These are significant learning deficiencies with ramifications for productivity, employability and well-being.

An ASER Centre report indicates that 60 per cent of youth want to study beyond grade twelve. Of these, only 43 per cent can do simple division such as a three-digit number divided by a one-digit number. Less than 40 per cent can calculate a 10 per cent discount. Pritchett concludes that '... substantial numbers of Indian youth have educational aspirations—college or university level study—for which they are totally, radically, completely unprepared'.[34]

As you can imagine, as this army of youth progresses through different levels of the education system, good opportunities aren't available to most. Karthik Muralidharan, an economist who has written extensively on Indian education, compares the design of the post-Independence Indian education system to a 'filtration system' driven by 'sorting' rather than human development, and says that most structural weaknesses can be explained by this.[35] Muralidharan explains that sorting picks out the most capable students and does little to prevent everyone else from falling behind. For every IIT or All India Institute of Medical Sciences (AIIMS) graduate, there are thousands who don't make it to university, or end up getting an education that is of little value in the modern world.

Yamini Aiyar at the Centre for Policy Research (CPR) is a passionate advocate for education reforms. Aiyar suggests that several factors are responsible for poor learning outcomes.[36] First, the way education is financed is problematic. Elementary education is highly dependent on Central government financing because state governments spend disproportionately on wages and other liabilities. Schemes such as Sarva Shiksha Abhiyan (SSA, now called Samagra Shiksha) finance much of the non-wage expenditure. Unfortunately, this funding is not tailored to local contexts. Furthermore, central funding follows an annual budget cycle, which is not efficient and causes delays because it takes time for funding to get released and reach local communities. These financial elements are over and above the oft-repeated complaints of limited public funding of education in India.

If things were not complex enough in terms of financing, Pritchett and Aiyar find that public school education is far more expensive to provide than private school education. They estimate that the 'accounting cost' per student in a government school in the median state in 2011/12 was Rs 14,615 ($265) while the median child in private school cost Rs 5,961 ($108). By aggregating this cost differential across states and all government schools, Pritchett and Aiyar conclude that, over a year, this excess cost is about Rs 500 billion or 0.6 per cent of GDP. They next calculate the economic cost, which is 'what it would take public schools at their existing efficacy in producing learning, to achieve the learning results of the private sector'. The excess economic cost was Rs 2.32 trillion (2.78 per cent of GDP or about $50 billion).[37]

As alluded to earlier, before India spends more on the education system, it must utilize existing resources better. One final point on public expenditure on education is important. It varies significantly across states (see figure 5.5).[38] In eight states analysed by the CPR, state governments contributed 80–95 per cent of the total education expenditure.[39] However, while the absolute spending on each student is vastly different from state to state, as a proportion of states' budgets, spending is roughly similar—between 12 and 15 per cent.

Figure 5.5: Government expenditure on students varies sharply

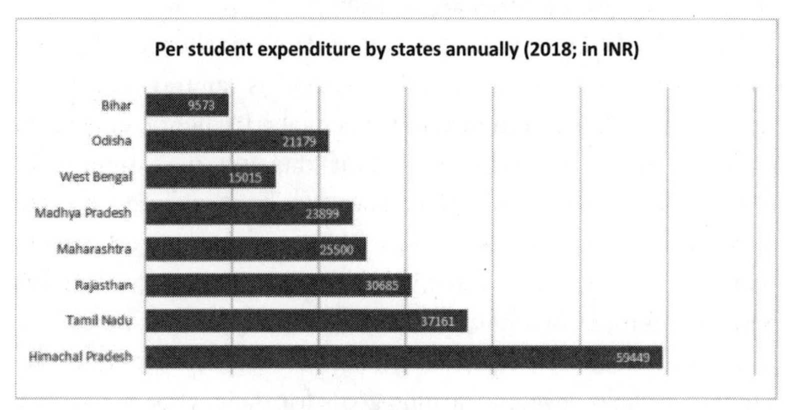

Source: Adapted from *State Education Finances: A Deep-Dive into School Education Finances in Eight States*, Centre for Policy Research (2020).

There is also a problem with how education achievement is assessed. While experts would like to create accountability systems for learning outcomes, the government's systems have focused on other things. Pritchett describes a 'dashboard' approach that enables large bureaucracies to monitor 'process compliance and inputs'. In India's case, Pritchett gives the example of the Education Management Information System (EMIS) programme called District Information System for Education (DISE), launched as part of the SSA scheme. This system was a 'report card' on schools. It included data from each district and aggregated it to the state level. In the 2016-17 reports reviewed by Pritchett, he found 977 distinct numbers reported. Pritchett notes that 'not one of those numbers is any direct measure of student learning' (and interestingly, a previously included measure of learning, pass percentages, was dropped from the 'report card').[40] These dashboards can tell us a lot about schools, their facilities and the number of students and their gender. However, they don't tell us about what these children are learning.

The education system also suffers from challenges that are common in the public sector. The system is far too centralized to be governed and administered effectively. In theory, education policy in India has held districts as the unit of planning. In practice, district-level planning does not happen because there isn't enough functional or financial autonomy to plan and execute policies and programmes that would be more relevant to schools and communities in a particular district. It is not clear that those in charge of education departments at the district-level have the capacity to help develop learning goals for their schools and they certainly do not have the authority and autonomy to do so. More importantly, much of the action happens at the level of schools and local communities. As things stand right now, it is difficult to imagine local-level functional autonomy to put together learning goals that communities could help conceptualize, plan, implement and monitor.[41]

Sadly for Indian schoolchildren, their teachers can often be the problem. Sometimes it can be teachers who are either not sufficiently qualified or not well-trained to help students learn. For instance, in 2003, the Government of Bihar started a massive recruitment drive. In a mad dash to close the gap, recruitment rules were relaxed (teachers only had to provide degrees and not write any competitive examinations). A decade later, a scandal broke out when it was revealed that at least 20,000 of the new recruits (3,62,000 had been hired) had forged their degrees.[42] But even if the degrees are genuine, teacher training is abysmal. The thousands of teacher training institutes are 'low-grade degree shops' that really do not teach potential teachers how to manage classrooms or how to inculcate learning habits in students.[43]

Even when these poorly trained teachers are recruited, they don't always show up for work. UNESCO's *Global Education Monitoring Report* 2017 found that 24 per cent of teachers in rural India were absent during unannounced visits in 2010 (1,300 villages).[44,45] While there have been improvements in 'input-based measures of school quality' such as the availability of toilets and electricity, midday meals, payment of salaries on time, etc., reductions in teacher absence rates have not kept pace.[46] A BBC story on a teacher who remained absent for twenty-three years of her twenty-four-year career may have been amusing to many but it is no laughing matter to children who need all the help they can get.[47] Teacher absenteeism is not really about poor pay. Government schoolteachers often make ten times the local median salary.[48]

While the focus of this chapter is on school education, India's tertiary education sector also requires substantial reforms. India has 993 universities and 39,931 colleges—the largest number of higher education institutions in the world.[49] Over 65 per cent of these are private, and more than half are in rural India.[50] The laissez-faireism of the 1990s helped the sector rapidly expand with the entry of private players. However, significant challenges—lack of world-class research institutions, unemployability of graduates and a stagnation in the number of PhDs—remain unaddressed. India's near-total absence in global rankings of universities is telling. One reason for this is that there has been no clear long-term policy on the development of higher education. 'Having no policy on higher education has itself been the policy,' writes Jandhyala Tilak.[51] Higher education faces the same issues as schools do—faculty shortages, low funds, inequalities of access and the unhelpful separation of teaching and research in universities.[52]

The National Education Policy 2020 and the way forward

More than three decades after the formulation of the 1986 education policy, India has a new National Education Policy (NEP). This policy has been in the making for several years. The NEP lays out a broad and inclusive vision for Indian education. It sets an ambitious goal to '... have an education system by 2040 that is second to none, with equitable access to the highest-quality education for all learners regardless of social or economic background'.[53]

The NEP directly addresses what it believes will help India achieve this aim. It argues that previous education policies '... focused largely on issues of access and equity'. Furthermore, it acknowledges the role of the Right of Children to Free and Compulsory Education Act (RTE), 2009, in establishing the legal underpinnings for achieving universal elementary education in India. The NEP takes this forward by its focus on improving learning outcomes, given the consensus on how much they lag. The NEP also stresses the manner in which Indian education should reform and evolve. The NEP states:

> [The] purpose of the education system is to develop good human beings capable of rational thought and action, possessing compassion and empathy, courage and resilience, scientific temper and creative imagination, with sound ethical moorings and values. It aims at producing engaged, productive and contributing citizens for building an equitable, inclusive and plural society as envisaged by our Constitution.

The NEP also tries to address some of the issues in India's tertiary education systems as well. For example, it aims to raise the

General Enrolment Ratio (GER) from 26.3 per cent to 50 per cent by 2035; establish a National Research Foundation, and single and multi-discipline universities of education and research; create an umbrella Higher Education Commission of India (HECI) to replace other regulatory bodies, etc.

There are many other details about the NEP that are worth reviewing. We should acknowledge that the NEP's focus on strengthening learning outcomes, promoting inclusion and equity and nurturing socially responsible students is welcome. But for some observers, elements of the policy's vision may be overly nationalistic or moralistic. It may even be difficult to implement such elements and it is unclear how these would contribute to the development of a productive labour force. Even so, the focus should be mainly on how the NEP is implemented to achieve goals related to quality, equity and inclusion. In a country with deep institutional incapacity, implementation challenges can derail the most well-intentioned policy reforms.

In this context, the NEP appears to minimize the criticality of governance and management of the sector. Just the school system includes over 1.5 million schools, about 8.7 million teachers and 260 million students spread across hundreds of districts and thousands of villages. The governance challenges that affect the current system will not go away just because there is a new policy in place. The institutional foundations of the reform effort must be central to this exercise. Otherwise, it will fail.[54]

Karthik Muralidharan and Abhijeet Singh highlight the NEP's implementation challenge by cautioning policymakers about gaps between the 'high quality of policy design' and 'low quality implementation'. To underscore this challenge, they point to a large-scale randomized control trial in Madhya Pradesh where they 'found no notable effects on school functioning or student achievement of an ambitious reform that aimed to improve school management, largely through the type of school development plans that are recommended in the NEP'.[55] An associated problem is that of reporting on outcomes. Independent assessments found that the reported learning outcomes were inflated. To overcome this challenge, Muralidharan and Singh suggest greater investment in independent ongoing measurement of learning outcomes that are based on representative samples.[56]

The NEP does well to recognize the necessity of strong foundations and including children as young as three years old in the overall framework. There is a need to extend this further by focusing on child nutrition from birth onwards. Let us not forget that if we truly want to strengthen foundations, we need to ensure that expecting mothers are healthy and babies between zero and three years have the kind of nutrition that helps them prepare for joining the NEP framework at age three. This may not seem like an 'education sector' issue but it fundamentally is.

An immediate concern for policymakers is to make sure that children who have dropped out of school or have found their learning disrupted due to COVID-19 do not fall behind in perpetuity. This was already a problem before the pandemic. As students progressed from one grade to another, their learning deficiencies stuck. Both for addressing pandemic impacts and also more generally to reduce learning gaps, conducting remedial learning could be helpful. This could be accomplished through Pratham's 'Teaching at the Right Level' (TaRL) approach, which 'has shown that tailoring instruction to children's learning levels can produce massive learning gains'.[57] Moreover, India must prepare for any future large-scale disruptions to learning and have a plan in place for the delivery of education in crises.

This is where technology can help. But it is not a panacea. EdTech (education technology) has not yet demonstrated its ability to transform poorly performing education systems.[58]

However, COVID-19's impact on educational institutions, students and their communities has been profound. On the one hand, the digital divide may have become more extensive and deeper as poorer, unconnected children fall behind further; on the other, it is also true that thousands of start-ups and billions of dollars of funding for EdTech are creating intriguing possibilities in India. It is too early to say if EdTech will help all learners and teachers to do better. However, it is quite likely that EdTech could be a valuable complement to traditional teaching methods and also act as a backstop should an emergency force the closure of schools again. The threat of a growing digital divide is just as real as the promise of EdTech. To mitigate the former and leverage the latter, government policies and programmes must integrate technology with different aspects of the education system—learning, teaching, assessing, monitoring and financing. For a big and poor country like India, technology holds much promise. Nowhere may this be truer than for the education sector.

There is no getting away from the flawed and inadequate funding of public education. As Aiyar points out, the Central government's one-size-fits-all style of financing leaves little room to address local learning needs in a specific location. Why not put states in charge of determining what central assistance should be used for?[59] The idea here is for the Central government to provide 'block grants' to states with autonomy to states in how those funds are used. Aiyar proposes two types of untied grants. The first would be for infrastructure needs under the RTE and the second would be to support plans articulated by states. Finally, the funding would be based on multi-year plans as opposed to annual cycles, which does not allow for proper programme implementation. A deeper reform would push the financing to districts and blocks (a smaller administrative unit) with the ultimate goal of schools being empowered to articulate their plans and needs. This is obviously not easy, given how limited institutional capacity is in the education sector. However, for truly transformational changes, this capacity must improve dramatically. It is a difficult ask but there will be no far-reaching reforms without this.

There is an urgent need to change the way teachers and administrators are assessed. Administrative responsibilities may distract teachers from their main job, which is to teach students. It can also be distracting in another key way. Aiyar notes that '... the career ladder for teachers—as they move to becoming headmasters, cluster- and block-level officers, and finally district education officers—is primarily focused on administration rather than supporting teaching/learning'. In this context, the NEP seeks to reduce administrative work and strengthen teacher training. Should that happen, it would be a welcome break from the current system.

We end here with teachers. No education system will reform without a well-trained and professional community of teachers. We have discussed at length the shambolic teacher training and certification system in India. That is where basic reforms are of critical importance. We may ask for teacher accountability, but we must first hold those people accountable who train and certify teachers. In Finland, whose students consistently perform exceptionally on PISA, there is no emphasis on teacher accountability. Why? Because in addition to having a master's degree, Finnish teachers must go through the 'most rigorous and selective professional schools in the entire country'.[60] Only 10 per cent of applicants get into the five-year master's programme to become elementary school teachers.[61] This may seem like a novel concept, but if teachers are qualified and trained exceptionally well, they will become the lynchpin for transforming Indian education.

6

A Healthier India

It is health that is the real wealth and not pieces of gold and silver.

—Mahatma Gandhi, leader of India's freedom movement

On 21 June 2020, *The New York Times* published a story on Neelam Kumari Gautam, a thirty-year-old pregnant woman.[1] Neelam went into labour and her pain was unbearable. Her husband, Bijendra Singh, put her in the back of an autorickshaw and over a fifteen-hour span sought to admit her at eight hospitals in Delhi. No one would admit her. COVID-19 was spiking in India. Despite government orders to hospitals to provide emergency care, Neelam and many others were denied care. Neelam died, as did her unborn child. Her husband now cares for their little son, who is a victim of a health system that broke down completely, especially when the second wave of the pandemic hit in March 2021. That Neelam, a middle-class woman living in India's biggest metropolitan area, suffered such a cruel fate may seem eye-opening to observers outside India. But Indians can relate to this story because they live it every day, especially in rural India.

If the health system so grievously fails middle-class families, imagine the situation in poor, rural areas. In the Narwaw area of Baramulla in north Kashmir, one of us (Salman Anees Soz) chanced upon a medical sub-centre during a visit to a village. Sub-centres are usually single-room operations that are the 'most peripheral and first point of contact between the primary healthcare system and the community in the rural areas'.[2] Located on top of a ramshackle shop, the centre could only be accessed by a flight of rickety stairs. On a bright, sunny afternoon, I climbed the stairs to see for myself the miracle of basic healthcare in India's villages. A closed door and a rusty lock greeted me at the top of the staircase. A conversation with the shopkeeper revealed that the sub-centre was often closed because its health worker lived in Baramulla town and she found her commute to be tedious. That health worker is among those lucky people to have a government job but found it cumbersome to travel 5–10 km for work. That there was no accountability was clear because the health worker had made absenteeism a habit.

Besides, it is unclear how well-trained that health worker really was. People usually prefer going to private clinics or to tertiary hospitals even for basic care. You only have to visit AIIMS in New Delhi, India's premier tertiary care hospital, to see how burdened parts of the health system are. While some of India's health indicators have improved, there are major gaps in the provision of healthcare in India. For a country that aspires to global leadership, the health system is languishing and will prove to be a significant drag on the country's economic prospects. Amartya Sen has been a leading proponent of placing health (and education) at the centre of India's development debate. Sen once famously remarked, 'India is the only country trying to become a global economic power with an uneducated and unhealthy labour force.'[3]

Unfortunately, policymakers and influential commentators in India don't always take Sen's advice. When discussing economic reforms, the focus is more on privatizing public sector entities, attracting foreign investment and building hard infrastructure. Education and health do not get the same national attention. Perhaps this is because these are in the domain of state governments as opposed to the Central government. Another reason could be that those in charge may not fully understand the connections between health, education and economic development. Whatever the reason, this attitude must change. The COVID-19 pandemic is a wake-up call for Indian policymakers to re-examine their priorities. To develop a prosperous society and to do it sustainably, a good health system is a prerequisite, not a by-product.

Invest in health to grow the economy

Good health is foundational to sustainable economic growth and investing in good public health can create intergenerational benefits. There is evidence that 'a well-educated, healthy and well-nourished workforce pays bigger dividends to the economy than simply building new roads and bridges'.[4] In 2018, the IMF 'identified poor public health as the twelfth-most important hurdle for ease of doing business, ahead of crime, tax regulations and policy instability'.[5] A study of the growth trajectory of ten industrialized countries over 100–125 years found that 'about one-third of economic growth in advanced economies in the past century could be attributed to improvements in the health of global populations'.[6] Improvements in health reduced constraints on human productivity and the pace of long-term growth improved by 30–40 per cent.

Researchers at the McKinsey Global Institute (MGI) confirm the finding that poor health outcomes are a chronic drag on economies.[7] MGI released its findings as part of a report published in July 2020, just as the pandemic was gaining strength. The report analyses the impact of 'proven interventions' on the health of individuals. These interventions take the form of public sanitation, medicine, surgeries and other interventions recommended by global and national health institutions. MGI analysed data for 200 countries. Some of the report's observations are well known. For example, the report suggests that 'over the past century, improved hygiene, better nutrition, antibiotics, vaccines and new technologies have contributed to tremendous progress in global health' (figure 6.1). The report also discusses 'dramatic improvements in survival rates for people with certain types of cancer, heart disease and stroke in many countries'. These improvements have led to better quality of life and a rapid expansion of the labour force and its productivity.

With labour force improvements came prosperity and as countries became wealthier, they invested more in 'better food and safe environments', creating a virtuous cycle of 'improved health and higher incomes'.[8] The really interesting part relates to the finding that 'the cost of ill health was more than $12 trillion in 2017, about 15 per cent of global real GDP'. This is a highly significant finding, especially for countries like India. Even with low female labour force participation rates (LFPRs),

India has a huge reservoir of labour. MGI predicts that labour force growth will slow down from an annual rate of 1.8 per cent over the last fifty years to just 0.3 per cent in the next fifty years. That means labour productivity will be hugely important in the twenty-first century. But we know that without better health outcomes, there is little chance of creating the kind of productive labour force that India needs to achieve a good standard of living for its citizens.

Figure 6.1: As health improved in the twentieth century, life expectancy more than doubled and the global labour force expanded

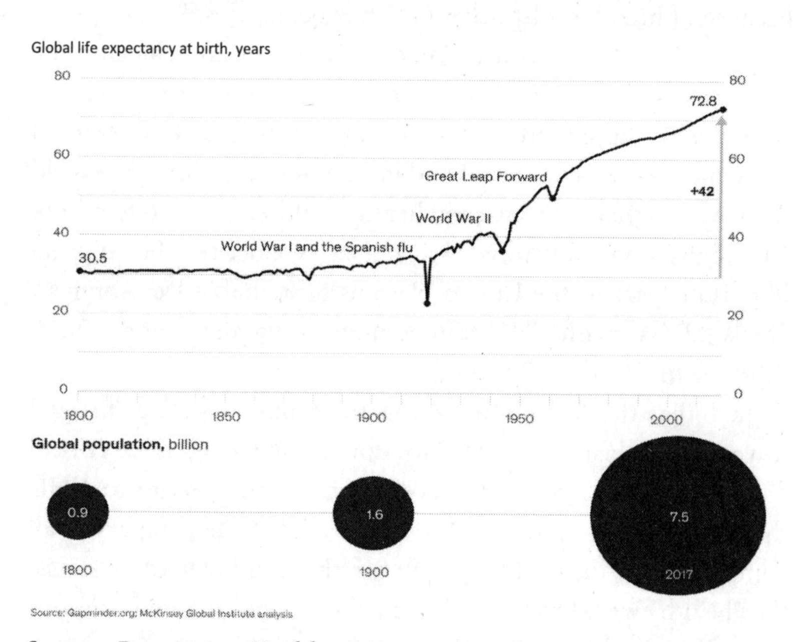

Source: *Prioritizing Health: A Prescription for Prosperity*, McKinsey Global Institute (2020).

The universal health coverage (UHC) goal

When we talk about health policy, it is useful to see how the world is addressing this issue. The overarching goal is the achievement of universal health coverage (UHC). From the perspective of WHO, UHC means 'that all people have access to the health services they need, when and where they need them, without financial hardship'. This includes 'the full range of essential health services, from health promotion to prevention, treatment, rehabilitation and palliative care'.[9] Of course, WHO notes that about half the people in the world do not receive the health services they need, and that 100 million people are pushed into poverty each year because of high out-of-pocket health expenditures.[10]

According to the World Bank, UHC is key to achieving the institution's twin goals of ending extreme poverty and increasing equity and shared prosperity. Calling health a 'foundational investment in human capital and in economic growth', the World Bank argues that without good health, children can't go to school and adults are unable to work.[11] It is no wonder that health is an important part of the United Nations Sustainable Development Goals (SDGs), with UHC gaining momentum ahead of the 2030 deadline for meeting SDG targets.

In India, the focus often is on the limited funding directed towards the health sector. No doubt, financing is a critical part of the UHC goal. However, there is much more to UHC than financing. According to WHO, UHC 'encompasses all components of the health system: health service delivery systems, the health workforce, health facilities and communications networks, health technologies, information systems, quality assurance mechanisms, and governance and legislation'.[12]

India's progress on UHC is poor. Using data from the Global Burden of Diseases, Injuries, and Risk Factors Study (GBD)

2019, researchers assessed UHC effective coverage for 204 countries and territories from 1990 to 2019.[13] India's UHC effective coverage index stood at 47 in 2019. In comparison, Brazil was at 65, Russia at 69, China at 70 and South Africa at 60. More advanced nations like Germany (86), Japan (96) and the US (80) were further along. India scored particularly badly on antenatal care, treatment of certain cancers and diseases like asthma. The main takeaway was that India remains far from the frontier. But there was an added concern. It turns out that the rate of annualized change in the index was the highest in South Asia, which India dominates, during 1990–2010. This pace slowed considerably during 2010–19. To understand why, we must examine the key challenges facing India's health system.

What ails India's health system?

Less than half of India's population has access to effective healthcare (figure 6.2).[14] Access to and the quality of healthcare available very much depends on where one lives and who they are. There is a big disparity between health outcomes in urban centres and rural India. There is an urban bias in healthcare. Health disparities have a gender element as well. Women find it harder to access healthcare. One Harvard study found that of the outpatient visitors to AIIMS, only 37 per cent of women got access to healthcare. In comparison, 67 per cent of men were able to access care. Caste also plays a part in healthcare access. A study in Karnataka found that caste dictated not only the quality of health infrastructure but the length of consultation time, the behaviour of healthcare workers, etc.[15] Some two million Indians need life-saving surgeries each year and only 5 per cent of them can get them.[16]

Figure 6.2: Less than 50 per cent of Indians have access to effective healthcare

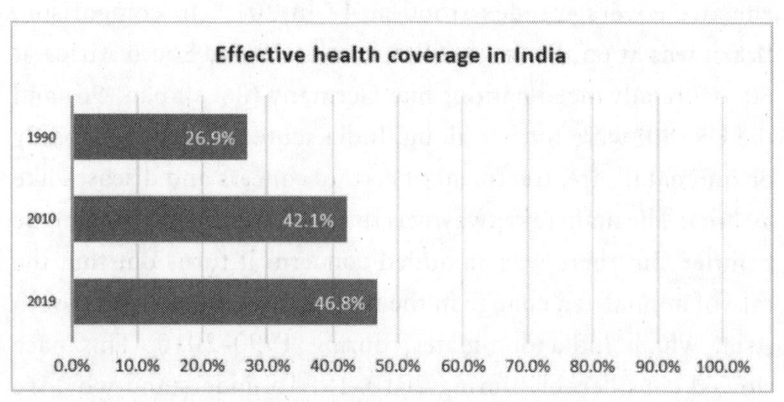

Source: Institute for Health Metrics and Evaluation.

The other problem facing India's health system is that its infrastructure is deficient, overcrowded and undermanned. The capacity to take on patients remains well below internationally recommended levels. The number of beds available is grossly inadequate. The fact that 'it remains common in government hospitals to have up to five sick newborn babies sharing a cot' illustrates this.[17] India has about 0.5 hospital beds for every 1,000 citizens. China has almost nine times that number while countries like Japan and South Korea have far more than that.[18] Shortage of health infrastructure guarantees overcrowded health facilities for a country as populous as India. The general disrepair of the country's infrastructure exacerbates these problems—poor infrastructure hinders the transfer of patients, medicine and human resources between rural and urban areas.[19]

Of course, national averages hide geographical disparities. Health outcomes can vary dramatically depending on where one lives in India. India's most populous state, Uttar Pradesh, spends less on healthcare (per capita) than every other state in the country.[20] While seventeen states have a surplus of infrastructure (including Kerala, Arunachal Pradesh, Gujarat, Karnataka, Tamil Nadu), India's most populous states register huge deficits in the required number of health centres. This is based on government estimates of the number of buildings required to service the population in these areas.[21]

Healthcare systems are also quite diverse. For instance, Kerala and Tamil Nadu, among India's best-performing states on health, have very different approaches to the provision of primary healthcare. While the development of the healthcare sector has been driven by the private sector since the mid-1980s in Kerala, the public sector has been an equally important part of the expansion of Tamil Nadu's healthcare services (with a significant increase in public spending over the 1980s and 1990s).[22,23] Kerala has nearly two times more private hospitals than public hospitals. In Tamil Nadu, the shares are almost equal.[24] Having said that, it is important to note that local governments in Kerala have played an important role in the expansion of primary healthcare—its success is based on a devolution of power to local bodies in 1996 which brought primary health centres (PHCs) and sub-centres under the jurisdiction of villages.[25]

To complete this grim picture, there is a severe shortage of qualified health workers. A 2019 report found that India is facing a shortage of two million nurses and 6,00,000 doctors.[26] According to WHO, India has less than nine medical doctors for every 10,000 people.[27] Unsurprisingly, better-off countries have a much higher ratio. China has more than double and the US has triple that ratio (figure 6.3).[28] The pressure on healthcare workers is such that they sometimes become victims of attacks by irate care-seekers. AIIMS added a taekwondo course for its doctors in 2017 to help them defend themselves 'should they be attacked while on duty at the overcrowded, undermanned hospital'.[29]

Figure 6.3: China has double the number of medical doctors per 10,000 people

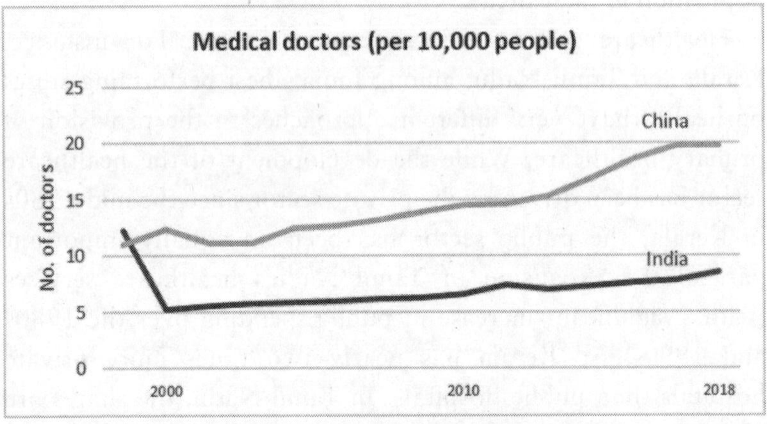

Source: *The Global Health Observatory*, World Health Organization.

The financial costs associated with healthcare impose an extreme burden on the most vulnerable in India. While the cost of healthcare at government-run facilities is nominal or free, most Indians are forced to turn to private health providers. Only 46 per cent of rural Indians and 35 per cent of urban Indians go to government hospitals.[30] Even at government hospitals, however, citizens shoulder the costs of drugs, diagnostic services and basic medical supplies.[31] A common sight in most hospitals in India is of patients accompanied by multiple family members. Family members run errands to ensure doctors and nurses can do their jobs. Even in the best government hospitals, patients are referred to private diagnostic centres for tests that should ordinarily be performed in the hospitals.

It should come as no surprise that, on an average, a rural household spends Rs 16,676 ($228) and urban households spend Rs 26,475 ($362) on medical bills every year.[32] An incredible 63 per cent of health spending in India is out-of-pocket (OOP) (figure 6.4).[33] While OOP used to be fairly high in China as well, it has come down over time to about 28 per cent of total health expenditures.[34] Additionally, 'lack of preventive care and little chronic disease management, meanwhile, leads to sicker patients, resulting in more expensive care and adding pressure to the financial side of the equation'.[35] At independence, only 8 per cent of healthcare was private; today over 70 per cent of India's healthcare spending is private.[36,37]

Figure 6.4: Health expenditure in India

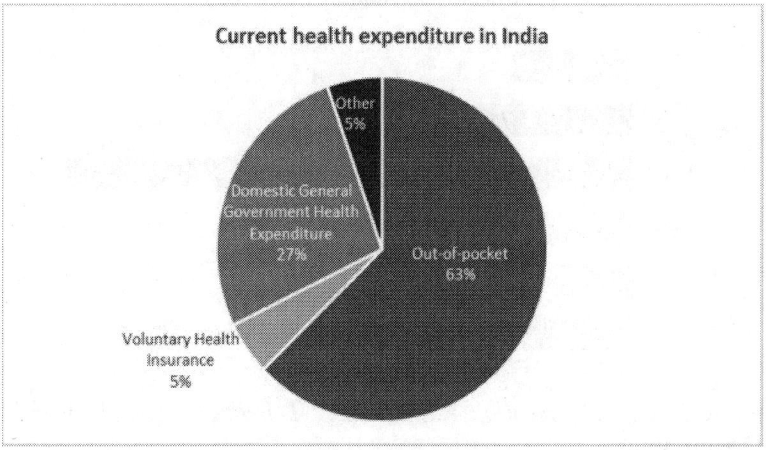

Source: *Global Health Expenditure Database*, World Health Organization.

To say that India's healthcare sector is underfunded would be an understatement. According to World Bank and WHO estimates, India spends 3.54 per cent of its GDP on healthcare (figure 6.5).[38,39] This includes both public and private expenditure, most of which is OOP. Public sector spending (state and central) is a little more than 1 per cent of GDP (figure 6.6).[40] This figure has remained stagnant for the past fifteen years.[41] Successive governments have made commitments to ramp up public health expenditure. The current government is targeting 2.5 per cent by 2025.[42,43] A WHO estimate from 2018 indicates that the Indian government spends less than $20 per person per year on health, about 7 per cent that of China.

Figure 6.5: Total health expenditure in India and select countries

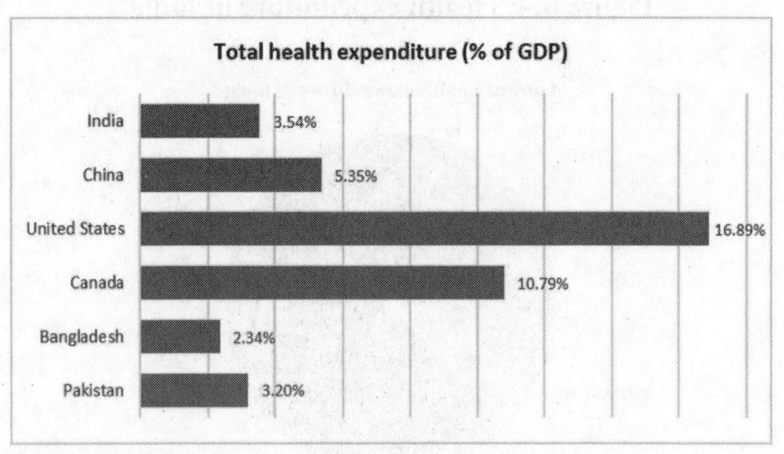

Source: *Global Health Expenditure Database*, World Health Organization.

Figure 6.6: Total public health expenditure in India and select countries

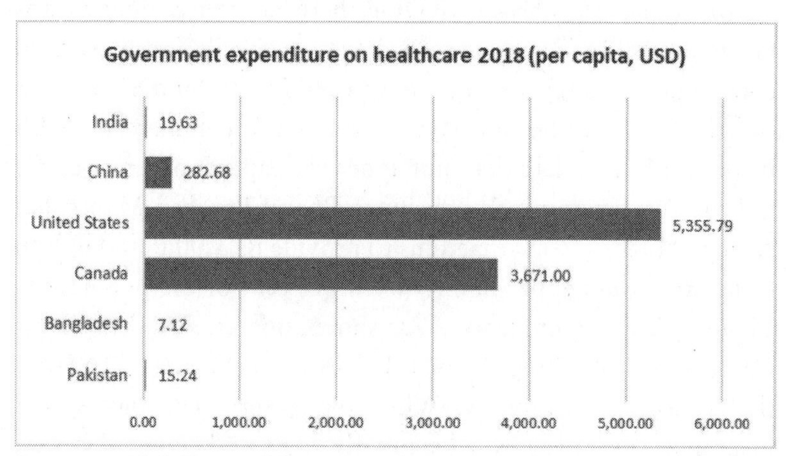

Source: *Global Health Expenditure Database*, World Health Organization.

Even the low public expenditure on health is not spent efficiently and that shows up in health outcomes. Tarun Khanna, Nachiket Mor and Sandhya Venkateswaran found that India's healthcare system underperforms its peers. They note that 'in 2019, it [India] had a Disability Adjusted Life Years Rate (DALY Rate) (i.e., the number of healthy life years lost on account of death and disability per 1,00,000 population) of 33,643. This is well above that of Vietnam (26,783), Colombia (24,212), and Thailand (29,338).'[44] Worse, some South Asian countries like Bangladesh, with lower PPP adjusted per capita incomes had better health outcomes. Among other factors, they point to waste in the already low government spending on health. They cite the examples of Kerala and Telangana and other urban areas where 'government hospitals carry out large numbers of excess C-Sections, well above the WHO recommended rate of 10 percent, but have not shown concomitant declines in maternal and perinatal mortality rates.'[45,46]

To alleviate the pressure of OOP, there has been a shift towards health insurance. However, according to the NSS's 75th household consumption survey, 86 per cent of rural Indians and 81 per cent of urban Indians did not have any public or commercial health insurance.[47] This data does not appear to capture progress under the current government's Ayushman Bharat Pradhan Mantri Jan Arogya Yojana (2018) that aims to provide Rs 5,00,000 ($6,900) in health coverage per family to 40 per cent of the population. There are two components of Ayushman Bharat: Health Wellness Centres and Pradhan Mantri Jan Arogya Yojana (PM-JAY), the insurance component. While the government claims that insurance coverage has substantially improved under PM-JAY, verifiable data is difficult to come by.

Even when health and other insurance coverage is available, it is underutilized. Manish Sabharwal and Rajiv Mehrishi found that the Employees State Insurance Scheme (ESIS), which covers almost 130 million people is sitting on cash reserves of Rs 800 billion ($10.78 billion). They note that the 'Employees' State Insurance Corporation's (ESIC) unspent reserves are larger than the Central government's healthcare budgetary allocation'. With pay-outs low, the annual profits of ESIS persist at Rs 100 billion ($1.35 billion).[48] Reforms to address these shortcomings are very important and urgent.

Beyond the health sector's considerable problems, there are two areas that require special attention—malnutrition and sanitation. India continues to face a serious child malnutrition problem that impacts health outcomes as well as labour productivity at a mass scale. Even before the onset of the pandemic, there was evidence that child undernutrition may be on the rise.[49] A look at the first round of state-level data from the National Family Health Survey

(NFHS)-5 is worrying. The percentage of underweight and stunted children in West Bengal and Maharashtra has increased.[50,51] In West Bengal, children under five years who are anaemic has increased from 54.2 per cent to 69 per cent; in Maharashtra, from 53.8 per cent to 68.9 per cent; and in Bihar from 63.5 to 69.4 per cent.[52] Stunting and wasting have also increased (data on only twenty-two states has been released so far—data for states like Uttar Pradesh is yet to be released).

Sanitation and access to clean water and food are also important for a healthy population. Twenty-one per cent of communicable diseases in the country are linked to poor sanitation and unsafe water.[53] Service delivery of water, sanitation and solid waste management in urban India remains weak. For instance, government data indicates that urban consumers receive only 70 litres of water per capita per day against the recommended 135–150 litres.[54] Low expenditures only partially explain poor service delivery. Other factors such as better leadership, community involvement and establishing PPPs could be more helpful.[55] According to Water Aid,[56] out of India's population of about 1.3 billion, 163 million people don't have clean water; 732 million (over half the population) people don't have a decent toilet; and over 60,000 children under the age of five years die each year from diarrhoea caused by dirty water and poor toilets.

In this context, the government's Swachh Bharat initiative has been a highly visible effort to eliminate open defecation and improve solid waste management. Prime Minister Modi has lent his considerable political clout to this initiative, and it has met with some success. A World Bank evaluation in 2020 noted that the coverage of 'safely managed' toilets among households without toilets increased by 6.8–10.4 percentage points compared with a control group. Open defecation reduced by 7.3–7.8 percentage points. The evaluation also highlighted the 'significant positive impacts on hygiene awareness among adults and children' but also noted that 'the interventions of school campaigns and intensive follow-up were of limited additional impact'.[57] While the government declared rural India open-defecation free in 2019, these claims have since been questioned. The pandemic has worsened the situation with open defecation seeing a fourfold increase, a substantial decrease in the use of sanitary toilets in rural areas, and 6,00,000 toilets facing an acute water shortage and another 1,20,000 with no water supply at all.[58] As long as sanitation challenges remain, as with malnutrition, good health outcomes will be harder to come by.

What India can do to achieve UHC

South Korea's success as an Asian economic tiger is frequently highlighted as what might have been for India. South Korea is one of those rare countries to break out from the ranks of middle-income countries to become a high-income, advanced economy. However, less highlighted is the manner in which South Korea achieved the progress that it has. The fact is that improvements in the health sector have helped South Korea develop remarkably well. But this does not happen automatically. It requires a lot of effort and investment and that is how South Korea managed to achieve universal healthcare in a generation.[59] South Korea spent only 2.3 per cent of its GDP on healthcare in 1970. By 1997, they had ramped up this figure to 6 per cent of GDP.[60]

In 1977, South Korea introduced mandatory social health insurance and achieved universal coverage by 1989.[61] Since 2000, South Korea has had a single-payer national health insurance system—a system that is generally considered to be effective. On a range of health indicators, the country is among the best in the world. Its UHC effective coverage index stood at 89 in 2019, even better than that of advanced nations like Germany and the United Kingdom (UK). South Korea has received plaudits for effectively dealing with the COVID-19 pandemic. Of countries with a population of more than fifty million, South Korea has among the lowest per capita caseload and deaths.[62] What many people may not appreciate is that South Korea's population density (527/km^2) is higher than India's (464/km^2). Undoubtedly, South Korea's economy has made great strides but without an effective healthcare system, it would not be where it is today.

That brings us back to India. What can India do to improve its health system? How can India achieve UHC? Before we get to specific ideas for India's health system, a few caveats apply. First, the meaning of UHC in the US should not necessarily apply in India. After all, a wealthy country can deploy many more resources. Besides, the health challenges in one country may differ from those in another country. Second, and this is certainly the case in India, access to health financing will not necessarily guarantee access to healthcare. Think caste, income levels, geography. There is a temptation to think that egalitarian principles require the same level of sophistication in care in rich and poor countries alike. Such thinking will not lead to increased access to care. The goal for poorer countries must be to maximize coverage with a basic service package to ensure a healthy population.[63] Finally, when thinking of improving health outcomes, we must adopt a broader framework that includes improvements in public service delivery in areas such as clean water, sanitation and solid waste management. With these caveats out of the way, we recommend the following improvements in the health sector.

Strengthen coordination, collaboration and knowledge exchange at different levels of government. India's federal structure empowers states to deliver health services. The Central government has an important coordination and policy planning role and also implements national health initiatives. However, this federal structure appears to be more centralized with limited opportunities for local stakeholders to have a say in broad policy formulation. A decentralized health system will likely be more effective to universalize healthcare in India. For this to happen, the Centre and states should have an institutionalized coordination mechanism and this should be replicated at the level of states, districts and blocks. Feedback loops along this entire chain can have many desirable impacts, including the implementation of good practices and improved disease surveillance.

Strengthen community engagement. In India, the focus of healthcare is on physicians and hospitals. But community-based healthcare could become a foundational pillar for India's health system. More than half of the 218 essential, cost-effective interventions identified by the Disease Control Priorities Network are delivered through PHCs and local approaches.[64] In the Chinese city of Xiamen, growing incidence of chronic diseases led to the creation of a new model of primary healthcare. They call it Joint Management by Three Professionals. A specialist develops a treatment plan, a general physician implements it and a community worker provides health education.[65] Community healthcare can also impact health literacy, which leads to improvements in care, such as higher rates of vaccinations. Kerala provides an example of successful decentralization of healthcare and the increased role for community-based care.[66] Such systems have a natural link to improved sanitation and hygiene outcomes, which are critical for overall health improvements.

To improve child nutrition, also focus on maternal nutrition. In 2004, the Copenhagen Consensus, a think tank, assembled a panel of scientists and economists, including four Nobel laureates. It asked the panel what cause they would support if they had $75 billion to invest. A similar exercise was held in 2008 and

2012. The winning intervention in each of the three years was the same: 'Interventions to Reduce Chronic Undernutrition in Preschoolers'.[67] A 2012 research paper on malnutrition revealed that for every $1 spent on addressing malnutrition led to benefits of $30. In India's case, a $1 investment in reducing stunting resulted in benefits in the range of $45 to $139. This is as close to a 'no-brainer' as you can get in economics. Yet, the latest NFHS data shows that in several parts of India, children born between 2014 and 2019 are more malnourished than the previous generation.[68] Part of the reason relates to mothers' nutritional health and to low birth weight (LBW). If mothers' nutritional status is poor, then LBW is a likely outcome. LBW is, in turn, the biggest determinant of child malnutrition.[69] Therefore, to reduce child malnutrition, mothers' nutrition should receive much more attention than it has so far.

Ramp up expenditure on healthcare. The government currently spends less than $20 per person per year on healthcare. According to current growth trends mapped by the GBD Study, spending is projected to only increase to $93 by 2050.[70] In the first budget after the pandemic struck, the government announced a steep hike in health expenditure. However, part of this hike was related to the procurement of COVID-19 vaccines, which, incidentally, the government failed to procure in a timely manner. Another part had to do with improvements in water and sanitation. While clean water and sanitation are important for good health, such spending is usually not listed under health. It may seem like an increase in health spending but could hide continued underspending in a critical area. More importantly, increased public health expenditure should be part of a broader strategy that can help determine where the additional funds would go. India cannot afford to be in a situation of unproductive government spending. Expenditures must be linked to outcomes and concrete objectives. One way to do this would be to create a multi-year plan to increase health spending to the middle-income country average with health outcome goals that are in line with the averages of middle-income countries.

Improve quality through personnel training and certification. A joint World Bank (International Bank for Reconstruction and Development, IBRD), OECD and WHO report found that the increase in institutional deliveries from 14 per cent to 80 per cent had failed to make a dent in maternal and child mortality in India 'due to the poor quality of care provided at health facilities'.[71] While health infrastructure requires attention, India's strategy should give primacy to well-trained personnel, development of basic health packages and ensuring accountability standards across public and private healthcare systems. There is an acute shortage of healthcare workers in India and the situation is likely to worsen. To improve health outcomes, training and certifying this workforce is exceedingly important. This can happen through a proper plan that has national and local elements, and with coordination between agencies at all levels of government and a collaborative effort with the private sector.

Meet patients where they are.[72] Both physically and through telemedicine, India should maximize the opportunity to provide basic healthcare close to where people live. There is now an opportunity for India to combine community healthcare with digital health to deliver preventive care without people having to crowd district-level and tertiary-care hospitals, which can focus on delivering services that they are meant for. Digital tech has shown promise to plug the gap between the demand and supply of mental health professionals in places with low investments.[73] Technology could help India transform its health sector in ways that were previously unimaginable. There is no one way to make this happen. But imagine the following scenario: a villager goes to a sub-centre. A health worker takes down the basic history and inputs it into a tablet. The data is stored and sets up an appointment with a general physician who views the patient's medical history and then discusses the case with the patient via telemedicine. The follow-up is left to the health worker or, if need be, the patient is referred to the next-level health facility. Electronic medical records are generated and stored. Of course, this will require enabling legal and institutional reforms, including data protection and security.

India can build on existing strengths to realize the health sector's economic opportunities. India's pharmaceutical industry is one of the world's biggest. India's capabilities in producing generic drugs are world-renowned. Affordable and high-quality generics have yielded positive health outcomes for millions around the world, including in developed countries. For example, 25 per cent of all medicines consumed in the UK are produced in India while African countries now can fight AIDS better thanks, in part, to Indian drugs. However, to truly become the world's pharmacy, an achievable ambition, India must continue to move up the value chain, encourage a sharp focus on quality, promote policies that diversify sources of raw materials, reduce the dependence on drug price controls and encourage collaboration between Indian and international pharma industry participants.[74]

COVID-19 is hastening the adoption of technology around the world. Countries that were going slow on telemedicine adoption or on the health sector's digital transformation are suddenly finding huge interest in this area. McKinsey and Company notes that global digital-health revenues will rise from $350 billion in 2019 to $600 billion in 2024. This includes telemedicine, online pharmacies, wearable devices, etc.[75] China is among those nations that are exploring the role of digital care across the healthcare value chain. India must not fall behind in this area. A far better health system is possible and it can be done within a few decades. In healthcare, COVID-19 presents a distinct opportunity for India to leap ahead and dramatically alter people's well-being and the economy's overall health.

7

Women in the Workforce

If you want something said, ask a man; if you want something done, ask a woman.

—Margaret Thatcher, former prime minister of the United Kingdom

Gunjan Bansal went to an elite high school, topped her class and dreamt of becoming an architect. But Gunjan always knew that she would be married into a family as conservative as her own, and that working outside the home would not be permitted. For Gunjan, a good education was about finding a better matrimonial match, not finding a good job. And when the time came, things unfolded exactly as she had imagined. She is married and does not work. Family norms are just one among many deterrents facing women looking to build careers.[1]

Stories like Gunjan's are emblematic of the hurdles to women's economic empowerment in India. This is despite progress in a number of important areas. Indian women now are more educated, healthier, marry later, have fewer children and live longer. Yet, they find it more difficult to become part of India's economic growth story. It is not as if policymakers have not paid attention to this problem. Right since Independence, there has been a lot of focus on improving the status of women. And this has succeeded to an extent. However, complex and deep-rooted social norms as well as governance and policy deficiencies constrain progress. As Finance Minister Nirmala Sitharaman observed during her maiden Budget speech in 2019, 'It is not possible for a bird to fly with one wing. Similarly, it is not possible for the country to succeed without women's participation.'[2]

This chapter first lays out the importance of gender equality to economic development in broad terms. We then review India's progress in women's empowerment as well as the challenges that policymakers must confront. After that we place India's progress in the global context. In the next section, we present ideas for closing the gender gap, based on international experience. Finally, we present a set of recommendations that we believe are implementable and necessary for women to take their rightful place in India's economy.

Why gender equality matters for the economy

In 1970, Danish economist Ester Boserup explored gender inequality and the role of women in development in her seminal book, *Woman's Role in Economic Development*.[3] Boserup proposed an interesting theory—global differences in gender norms and levels of inequality could be explained by whether a society had traditionally engaged in plough agriculture or not. Based on research on Asia, Africa and Latin America, Boserup planted the seed of a greater focus on gender issues in development. Many have built on Boserup's work, seeking a more complete understanding of the drivers of lower levels of female economic participation, political representation and entrepreneurship.[4]

Closing the economic gender gap is not just about women. It is about men too. For instance, men in societies with higher levels of gender inequality reported poorer health outcomes. United Nations Population Fund (UNFPA) researchers have found that men who are more involved in family affairs, including as caregivers, '... live longer, have less physical and mental health problems, are less likely to consume alcohol and drugs, are more productive at work, have fewer accidents, are more likely to be satisfied with their lives and are more emotionally connected to their partners and children'.[5]

World Bank economists Ana Revenga and Sudhir Shetty pointed out that experience in the decades preceding the publication of the 2012 WDR on Gender Equality and Development indicated that 'gender disparities remain even as countries develop'. They argued that gender equality improves development outcomes in three main ways. First, with women comprising over 40 per cent of the total global labour force, the more their skills and talents are utilized, the greater the boost to growth and development. Second, as women become more empowered and have greater control over household resources, the more beneficial household decisions tend to be for children. Finally, they noted that as women's participation in social, political and economic roles improves, this leads to 'greater provision of public goods, such as water and sanitation'.[6]

Improving gender parity has particular relevance to India. Achieving gender equality could annually add $770 billion to

India's GDP by 2025, according to a report by McKinsey and Company.[7] This opportunity predominantly hinges on women participating in the labour force in greater numbers. Seventy per cent of this opportunity lies in increasing women's participation by just ten percentage points. In a different estimate, the IMF claimed that India's GDP would be 27 per cent higher if women participated in numbers equal to men.[8] The factors that impact women's economic participation are reflections of norms, agency and voice, opportunities, skill levels and education, mobility and policies.[9,10] For instance, there is a broad positive relationship between female labour force participation (FLFP) and female political representation.[11,12] Both of these are influenced by mobility, the ability to network, wide perceptions about women's roles, comfort with women occupying public office, etc.

The limited economic footprint of Indian women

It is undeniable that gender inequality remains entrenched in India. While women face considerable social inequities, in this chapter we focus on inequality of economic opportunities. A key measure of economic inequality is women's participation in the labour market.[13] The International Labour Organization (ILO) defines the LFPR as a measure of the proportion of a country's working-age population that engages actively in the labour market, either by working or looking for work. ILO estimates that the global average LFPR was 66.3 per cent in 2020, down from 70.2 per cent in 1990. While the male LFPR was 80 per cent in 2020, female LFPR was only 52 per cent.

That difference may seem shocking, but it is nothing compared to what we see in India. Using the same ILO data, India's male LFPR was 80 per cent in 2020, down from 87 per cent in 1990.

However, female LFPR was a dishearteningly low 22 per cent in 2020, down from 32 per cent in 1990 (figure 7.1). That is a 48-percentage-point differential with male LFPR. Only a few countries, including Yemen, Iraq and Syria, have lower rates of women's economic participation.[14]

On the surface, all this is puzzling. Since Independence, Indian women have made substantial gains. In 1951, a woman was likely to marry at age fifteen and have six children in her lifetime. The average woman today marries at twenty-two and has two children.[15] Women now live longer than men, girls and boys are enrolled in schools at similar rates, and the percentage of institutional births was 79 per cent in 2015-16. Ten years earlier, the rate was half that.[16] However, these gains have not translated into higher levels of economic engagement for Indian women. India's most educated and productive women have not joined the workforce.[17,18] Instead of increasing their labour force participation, Indian women are exiting the job market.

Figure 7.1: India's female labour force participation rate has been declining

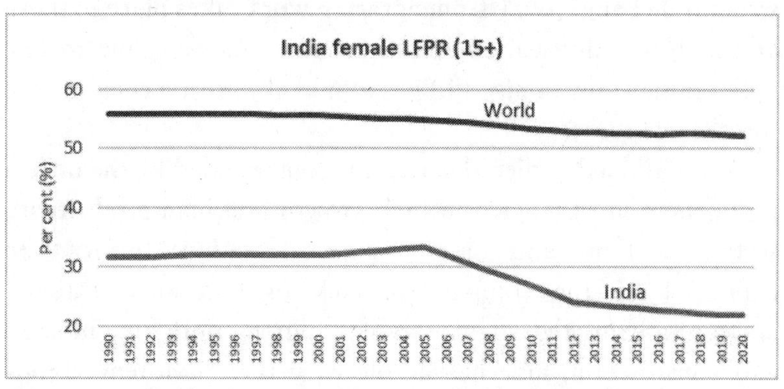

Source: *World Development Indicators*, World Bank.

Some might point to cheerier reasons for this decline—more females staying in school and seeking higher education, etc. However, there isn't conclusive evidence supporting such a claim.[19,20] Additionally, NSS data shows that women with secondary education have the lowest LFPR. In fact, studies have shown that there is a U-shaped relationship between educational attainment and FLFP. Rather, as the ILO's Ruchika Chaudhary and Sher Verick find, lack of representation and opportunity in high growth and high productivity sectors, social attitudes and issues related to personal safety are to blame.[21]

Traditionally, a large part of India's female workforce is composed of rural women engaged in agrarian work. Here lies the root of the decline. A fall in employment among married women in rural India almost exclusively accounts for the overall decline in FLFP.[22] Researchers at the Institute of Labor Economics (IZA) found that declining FLFP is concentrated among twenty-five to sixty-five-year-old married women in rural India. Among urban women, FLFP has been stagnant.[23] The fact that 75 per cent of rural working women continue to be employed in agriculture has other implications.[24] As structural change away from agrarian work takes place in these areas, this traditional economic avenue will continue to dry up.[25] India's declining FLFP is unlikely to reverse in the foreseeable future.

As mentioned earlier, this trend is compounded by the under-representation of women in high growth and high-productivity sectors, and in 'emerging occupations'.[26] While this can be explained by the comparative lack of vocational training among women, the stigma around 'dirtier work' in industry and construction, also has a role to play.[27,28] Moreover, jobs in new sectors also tend to be further away from home.[29] This conflicts with women's traditional household and caregiving responsibilities.

Female labour participation dramatically varies from state to state (table 7.1).[30] At the lowest end of the spectrum, we have Bihar with an abysmal 4.3 per cent female LFPR. And on the other end, Himachal Pradesh, with 59.2 per cent of urban and rural women above the age of fifteen participating in its labour force.[31] While Himachal Pradesh performs better than the global average, Bihar's female LFPR has halved in just one decade.[32]

It is an unenviable situation that India finds itself in. First, women participate in the economy at rates that are among the lowest in the world. Then, as women's status improves along a number of dimensions, they start exiting the job market. Worse still is the situation in states such as Bihar whose FLFP is worse than in the world's worst-performing countries.

Table 7.1: Female LFPR of India's six most-populous states (home to over 50 per cent of the country's population)

	Rural and Urban	Rural	Urban
Uttar Pradesh	13.6%	14.8%	9.7%
Maharashtra	31.6%	38.5%	22.1%
Bihar	4.3%	4.0%	6.5%
West Bengal	22.2%	20.9%	24.8%
Madhya Pradesh	27.9%	31.8%	17.4%
Tamil Nadu	37.0%	28.9%	43.9%

Source: Adapted from *Periodic Labour Force Survey 2018-19*, Ministry of Statistics and Programme Implementation (2020).

What explains lower female participation in the Indian economy?

There are a variety of factors—social, economic and governance—that have led to a low and declining female LFPR in India. Opportunities in agriculture, the predominant traditional source of employment for rural women, have been shrinking.[33,34] This means that on the demand side, the number and nature of jobs for women have changed.[35]

The loss of economic opportunities for women in agriculture has not been offset by increasing economic avenues in other sectors. In fact, women are under-represented in high-growth and high-productivity sectors, and 'emerging occupations'.[36] Less than 19 per cent of new job opportunities in the ten fastest-growing sectors have been taken up by women.[37] Demand for technical skills has accompanied these new opportunities. Consequently, women who, as a group, have far lower levels of vocational training and tertiary education have lost out.[38] This partially explains why gains in primary and secondary education have not translated into an increase in women's employment.

However, economic reasons alone do not explain the decline in female LFPR. Gender norms seem to be the biggest and most pervasive barrier to women seeking paid economic opportunities. An Indian woman's mobility, participation in the labour force and the judgement of which economic opportunities are appropriate, remain household decisions.[39] And within their households, women often do not have much decision-making power.

Some researchers argue that as households become more affluent, the pre-existing stigma around women working becomes 'affordable' as the trade-off of losing some material comfort lessens.[40] For instance, the stigma around 'dirtier work' in factories and construction, and working alongside strangers, has discouraged women from seeking employment in sectors other than agriculture.[41]

A woman's role as a caregiver is nearly always the priority. According to a survey, nearly 48 per cent of Indian women quit work midway due to family commitments.[42] Like in many parts of the world, domestic responsibilities and work remain gendered in India. Eighty-four per cent of respondents in a Pew survey held the belief that when jobs are scarce, men have a greater right to job opportunities. And well-intentioned laws don't always help. As Swati Narayan notes, 'Workplace crèches, though legally mandatory in all offices with more than 50 employees and MNREGA worksites, are rare. Anganwadis, too, have yet to be expanded into crèches.'[43]

Mobility is critical to the pursuit of paid employment. It is not a stretch to suggest that the exacting cost of safety and the fear of harassment discourages women from working. A study found that women in Delhi don't take up better education opportunities due to the risk of street harassment.[44] In fact, women are willing to spend an additional Rs 17,500 ($250) each year and twenty-seven extra minutes daily in commute time on safer routes. Men are only willing to spend an extra Rs 9,950 ($140) and twenty-one minutes.[45] Moreover, news reports of local violence have a strong effect on reducing the willingness of urban Muslim and lower-caste women to work.[46]

Public spending on women-specific schemes has largely stagnated. When India introduced gender budgeting in 2006, 4.8 per cent of the budget was allocated to women-specific schemes. This rose to a high of 5.9 per cent in 2011-12 but has declined and stagnated since. In the 2020-21 Budget, this figure was only 4.7 per cent. Of this, only 0.94 per cent of the government's total spending has been allocated to schemes that specifically target and spend on women.[47] Moreover, many agricultural and social programmes and female-focused programmes were relegated to an 'aspirational, but not practical' list in the economic survey.[48]

Even for women seeking employment (those part of the labour force), there is a woeful lack of opportunities. For instance, in Kerala, a state generally lauded for its progress on human development indicators, 57.8 per cent of rural women and 53.1 per cent of urban women (ages fifteen to twenty-nine) were unemployed in 2019. To put this into perspective, there is a difference of 30 points between men's and women's employment. The COVID-19 pandemic appears to have made the situation worse for women. Rural women saw the steepest decline in employment and the slowest recovery as of August 2020.[49] A survey conducted by Azim Premji University found that 71 per cent of casual workers who are women lost their jobs after the March 2020 lockdown.[50] Only 59 per cent of men lost their jobs.

Beyond labour force participation, there are other indicators of gender economic inequality. According to the 2017 Global Findex, 77 per cent of Indian women had a bank account. This was a major improvement over 2014, when only 26 per cent of women had bank accounts. However, as Women's World Banking points out, 48 per cent of the accounts were inactive in 2017. That means there were about 278 million women with either no accounts or inactive accounts. Very few women access broader financial services. Of the women who have bank accounts, only 16.7 per cent save formally compared to 10 per cent in 2014.[51]

The situation for women is even worse in terms of access to credit. Access to bank loans or dependence on informal channels of credit remained largely unchanged between 2014 and 2017. Only 5 per cent borrowed from a bank in 2017. The share of women borrowing to either operate a business or expand it halved to only 3 per cent between 2014 and 2017.[52] Rubbing salt into these wounds is a finding in a 2015 report of the RBI that women heads of household pay a higher interest rate compared to males.

Another key aspect of economic empowerment is property ownership, especially land. On a number of measures, stronger property rights and inheritance rights lead to improved social outcomes. In such situations, women earn and save more money, are far less likely to suffer domestic violence, more money is devoted to education and children are healthier.[53] Yet, despite laws such as the Hindu Succession Act of 1956 and subsequent legal precedents that mandate equal inheritance rights for men and women, the gender disparity in land ownership in India persists. A 2013 survey by Landesa, an advocacy group, and UN Women, found that one in four women in Andhra Pradesh, Bihar and Madhya Pradesh were unaware that they had a right to inherit their family land. Only one in eight women inherited their family's agricultural land. Women were reluctant to press for their rights, worrying about offending family members.[54] In rural India, just 14.2 per cent of all landowners were female in 2014, a slight increase from 12.3 per cent in 2009.[55]

Indian women in the global context

In nearly every country, women participate in the workforce at lower rates than men do.[56] However, this gap varies across countries and geographic regions. Overall, there has been a global decline in FLFP. This has gone down from 56 per cent in 1990 to 52 per cent in 2020 (modelled ILO estimate). A drop in women working in their early childbearing years may explain this downward trend. In 1995, economist Claudia Goldin discovered that FLFP was a U-shaped function.[57] This means that as there is economic development, FLFP first falls before it picks up. This can explain why countries with some high GDP/capita and low GDP/capita have similarly high levels of female economic participation. While the U-shaped function on an average persists across countries, it does not neatly explain FLFP differences between countries at similar levels of development. Jayachandran finds that gender norms explain this variation. This is particularly relevant for India where there haven't been positive returns to education.[58]

While there is a lack of equal economic opportunities for women, India performs particularly poorly. World Economic Forum (WEF) ranked India 149 out of 153 countries in its 2020 Economic Participation and Opportunity index.[59] Only Pakistan, Yemen, Syria and Iraq perform worse. As in India, sociocultural norms prevailing at multiple levels—caste, community, religion and region—have broadly discouraged women from taking up paid employment across South Asian countries.[60] Overall, FLFP is fairly low across South Asia, except for Nepal, which has one of the highest female participation rates in the world (over 80 per cent).[61] However, only India's FLFP demonstrates a downward trend (figure 7.2).[62]

Figure 7.2: Female LFPR in South Asia

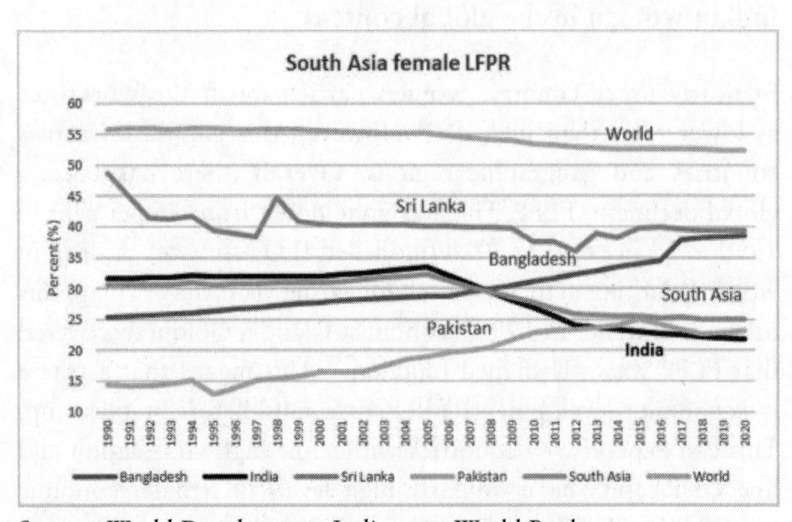

Source: *World Development Indicators,* World Bank.

In Bangladesh, FLFP has grown alongside the explosive growth of its garment export industry. Today, garments account for 75 per cent of Bangladesh's export earnings and 80 per cent of the sector's employees are women.[63] FLFP in Pakistan has generally been increasing. Between 1992 and 2014, its FLFP doubled.[64] In an interesting contrast to the trend in India, Pakistani urban women with post-secondary education are three times more likely to seek employment than women with primary education only. However, like in India, a growing link between marriage and lower levels of participation seems to be emerging.[65]

How other countries promote women's economic participation

The preceding discussion shows that gender inequality is not a uniquely Indian problem. However, India's progress on economic empowerment is mixed and there are signs of deterioration. How other countries approach gender inequality has lessons for India. There is little space here to provide details of what is happening globally. But a few case studies illustrate the many ways India can make progress on gender equality, especially in economic terms.

Publicly funded support for women during their childbearing years has been instrumental in keeping women in the workforce. Japanese public policy has increasingly become more supportive of female economic participation. This includes recent reforms under former PM Shinzō Abe's 'Womenomics' agenda. For many decades, female employment in Japan has followed an M-shaped pattern—high levels of participation right after higher education, followed by a drop during marriage and childbearing years, and a return to the labour force after.

However, this pattern has become less pronounced with time. Researchers at the Brookings Institution find that with every new generation of Japanese women, the break from this pattern increases.[66] According to ILO estimates (World Development Indicators or WDI), in 1990 Japanese FLFP (15+) was 50.13 per cent. In 2020, this figure is 52.7 per cent. It appears that Japanese public policy, as opposed to greater education attainment, has facilitated and supported greater FLFP. In addition to generous maternity and paternity leave, there has been a dramatic expansion of the government's provision of day-care facilities under the 'Womenomics' agenda. Other reforms include lower tax rates for married women; better-compensated family leave; enhanced child-care availability; and targets for women's representation in business leadership.[67]

Like Japan, Norway has had generous publicly funded comprehensive parental provisions and subsidized day-care for children for many decades. In 1970, only 13,000 Norwegian children were enrolled in day-care centres. By 2012, the number was about 2,80,000 with 90 per cent of children between the ages of one and five enrolled in government day-care centres.[68] Norway has also given fathers the right to child-care leave since 1977.[69] In 1990, Norwegian FLFP (15+) was 55 per cent. In 2020, this figure was 60.2 per cent.

Many countries, including India, have tried to increase FLFP through paid family leave. Of course, India's maternity benefits are limited to the formal sector, which is extremely small. But even so, researchers find that a large percentage of women do not return to work after maternity leave. To deal with this issue, Uruguay tried a novel experiment. To enable a more flexible return to work after maternity, the government paid a subsidy that helped formal sector beneficiaries get full pay even after working for only half the time. Luciana Etcheverry found that 'mothers are more likely to be employed following the implementation of the parental care subsidy in the short and medium-term.'[70] Etcheverry finds that one to three years after the birth of a child, there is an 'increase in the likelihood of employment for mothers'. Furthermore, 'mothers of young children employed in the formal-private sector have a significant increase in income and job experience compared to mother of young children employed in other sectors'.

These examples from Japan, Norway and Uruguay show that policies can have an impact on gender inequality. However, these policies must be tailored to India's context. What may work in Japan is not necessarily going to work in India. For example, the increase in paid maternity leave from twelve to twenty-six weeks in India applies to only 1 per cent of women.[71] And in a country that still has poor enforcement of anti-discrimination laws, there is every chance that the law will end up hurting women.[72] Invasive questions about matrimony and childbearing can be a routine part of the recruitment process in India.[73]

What India can do to feminize the economy

There are no quick-fix solutions to reducing gender inequality. Despite Mr Abe's efforts on behalf of Japanese women, *The New York Times* reported that women hold less than 12 per cent of corporate management jobs. This is below Mr Abe's target of 30 per cent. Even though female LFPR has increased, more than half work part-time or in contract jobs that offer no career advancement. These workers have suffered disproportionately during the COVID-19 pandemic, losing income and working hours.[74] The goal should be to continue pushing for reforms in gender norms and in sustained improvements in the enabling environment for women's economic empowerment. In that context, the following recommendations are relevant for India:

Keep pushing girls' education: Despite the positive association between the education of girls, and lower poverty and improved living standards, girls continue to be excluded from India's education system. This has clear implications for labour force participation later on in life. Swati Narayanan notes that, 'While education is now more inclusive, with three-fourths of women literate, only 37 per cent complete Class 10.'[75] A renewed focus on girls' and young women's education is a key step in creating equal opportunities in the labour force.

Sensitize schoolchildren. There is evidence that norm-changing interventions are more effective for children. Particularly, in the case of young boys who are more likely to hold inequitable ideas about gender than girls do.[76] An opportunity to change attitudes might be in the curriculum itself: school textbooks appear to be riddled with gender stereotypes.[77] Narendra Nath Kalia noted in the *Economic and Political Weekly*, 'Almost 20 years ago, India's official educators promised to deliver a curriculum that would recognize and nurture the fundamental equality between men and women.' Kalia wrote that in 1986! A recent UNESCO report shows that women continue to be under-represented in school texts and are shown mostly in traditional roles.[78] This requires an urgent, time-limited and methodical review of school textbooks by an independent commission of educators and gender specialists.

Acknowledge the female farmer. In a 2018 report, Oxfam India highlighted the role of women in Indian agriculture. The sector employs 80 per cent of all economically active women in India; they comprise 33 per cent of the agriculture labour force and 48 per cent of the self-employed farmers. As the 2018 Economic Survey noted, rural-urban migration by men is leading to greater feminization of agriculture. Despite this, only 13 per cent of rural women own land.[79] Agriculture policy will have to adapt to this demographic shift in rural India. When we think of farmers, we typically think of men. Public policy should be rebalanced in the direction of female farmers.

Strengthen financial inclusion. To improve women's access to finance, the government could create more awareness of financial services available to women and actively promote the benefits of financial services for women. Improved regulation, financial literacy and technology can support these efforts.

Create awareness of women's property rights. While there are laws and policies that are designed to improve women's property rights, often women are simply not aware of their existence. A sustained campaign to create such awareness with complementary support through community dialogue with participation of women's groups and government representatives could help create change over time.

Monitor impact of maternity benefits law. There is a strong link between the provision of maternity leave and women's LFPR (ILO recommends fourteen weeks). However, Alice Newton at the World Bank finds that there is only a positive correlation for up to 140 days (20 weeks) of leave.[80] Beyond this, women may appear to be unattractive hires for employers and lose out on skills/experience. Does India's twenty-six-week maternity benefit help or hinder women's participation? There is a question about who should bear the burden of financing this benefit. Currently, it is just employers in India. Meanwhile, governments in Canada, Australia and UK share this burden.[81] Is something like that feasible in India?[82] Time will tell.

Prioritize safer commutes. There is evidence that simple interventions such as rapid bus transit systems, streetlights and women-only spaces can help.[83] Some of this is already happening. However, much more needs to happen and in a systematic way.

Feminize the police. In 2019, women made up only 9 per cent of India's police force.[84] This is far below the global average of 35 per cent.[85] More women in police means not just more job opportunities but also greater sensitivity towards female complainants in cases of abuse and sexual violence.

Collect more gender-disaggregated data. India has severe limitations in socio-economic data. Without data, evidence-based policymaking is impossible. To the extent that policymakers wish to promote evidence-based policymaking, the entire system of data collection and reporting requires an overhaul. As part of that overhaul, collection of gender-disaggregated socio-economic data across all sectors will be a great contribution for women's empowerment in India.

Focus on women's political empowerment. Around the world, women's empowerment, participation and political representation have been observed to grow in tandem.[86] Low levels of female LFPR contribute to 'female under-representation in democratic politics', but as gender norms change, barriers to women in the political and economic spaces are simultaneously lowered.[87] Empirical evidence shows that 'women's political representation is positively associated with many health outcomes, including life expectancy' for everyone, especially children.[88] While steady strides have been made in improving representation, India falls far behind the 25.5 per cent global average for women in Parliament.[89] It is also a fact that low political candidacy for women is another formidable challenge and, as Geetika Dang notes, 'In almost all political systems, no matter what electoral regime, it is the political parties, not the voters that constitute the real gatekeeper to elected offices.'[90] India's political parties must step up for India's women. For India's sake.

8

Protecting the Vulnerable

Power has only one duty—to secure the social welfare of the People.

—Benjamin Disraeli, former prime minister of the United Kingdom

The 'worst constituency in India' is how the *Mint* newspaper characterized the Singhbhum Lok Sabha constituency in Jharkhand during the 2019 parliamentary election.[1] Singhbhum's profile piece begins by describing a scene in a hospital waiting room. A mother is holding what the reporter describes as a 'featherless pale-skinned newborn bird'. Of course, it is not a bird. It is the woman's two-month-old daughter, Rohivari. The little girl appears frail, struggles for breath and seems totally unprepared for the burdens of the poverty that is all but guaranteed for children born into such circumstances. However, special as Rohivari must be to her family, she is not unique. Over 60 per cent of Singhbhum's children are underweight—the worst in the country. But just like Rohivari, Singhbhum is also not unique. Child malnutrition is prevalent in wide swathes of India. The Singhbhum story is a grim reminder of the pervasive vulnerability and destitution that dominate the everyday lives of millions of Indian families.

It is not difficult to imagine how economic shocks can make things worse for malnourished children. However, malnourishment is only one factor that creates vulnerabilities. Loss of a job, a chronic health condition, an accident, or even retirement can move people into poverty and destitution. As India locked down in March 2020 to slow the spread of COVID-19, Scroll.in, an online news portal, reported on the impact on children around the country. One such case was that of ten-year-old Asha Yadav, whose daily meal at home was a 'fistful of rice with sugar or salt'.[2] On 'better days', Asha's mother would give her a little dal or some potatoes. Hailing from Gonda district in Uttar Pradesh, one of the poorest in the country, Asha is one of almost 100 million children whose meals were affected by the lockdown.[3] Normally, children would get meals at school. With schools shut down, the usual meal of rice, vegetables, milk and fruit under the government's Mid Day Meal Scheme (MDMS) was no longer available.

The MDMS is a key part of India's social protection system that provides food and non-food safety nets for poor and vulnerable Indians. Asha's story tells us how vital a safety net like the MDMS is for millions of school-going children. Unfortunately, this story also exposes weaknesses in the social protection architecture that led to Asha not having her nutritious meals when she most needed it, when her family was likely dealing with a shock to personal finances because of the pandemic.

In this chapter, we discuss the importance of safety nets and present an overview of India's social protection system, its evolution, coverage and deficiencies. To contextualize India's safety nets, we will review global experiences and understand how much progress India has made and what some of the key areas of progress are. We will also present a summary of debates around the further evolution of India's social protection system before concluding with recommendations for a post-COVID-19 social protection architecture.

Why safety nets matter

Social safety nets are not a new idea, even for India. In international development discourse, the idea of safety nets took more coherent shape in the 1980s and 1990s as part of a debate on humanitarian and development assistance.[4] The World Bank's WDR on poverty (1990) argued that a strategy for achieving rapid and politically sustainable improvements in the quality of life for poor people 'must be complemented by well-targeted transfers, to help those not able to benefit from these policies, and by safety nets, to protect those who are exposed to shocks'.[5]

Since then, SSNs have become an integral part of poverty-reduction strategies. If policy or other shocks threaten to push people into extreme poverty and deprivation, SSNs come to the rescue. Over time, the role of SSNs has expanded to address issues of hunger and nutrition.[6]

While there is no single definition of social protection or an exhaustive list of interventions, the work of international institutions is a useful guide. The United Nations Children's Fund

(UNICEF) defines social protection as 'the range of policies and programmes needed to reduce the lifelong consequences of poverty and exclusion'. The World Bank notes that social protection and labour interventions 'help individuals and societies manage risk and volatility, and protect them from poverty and destitution'.[7]

These interventions are categorized into three buckets: (i) SSN/ social assistance programmes; (ii) social insurance programmes; (iii) labour market programmes. SSNs are 'non-contributory' interventions, which help individuals and households cope with chronic poverty, destitution and vulnerability. Examples include unconditional and conditional cash transfers, non-contributory social pensions, food and in-kind transfers, school feeding programmes, public works and fee waivers. Social insurance programmes are 'contributory' interventions with an aim to 'help individuals manage sudden changes in income because of old age, sickness, disability or natural disaster'.[8] Individuals pay insurance premiums to be eligible for coverage or contribute a percentage of their earnings to a mandatory insurance scheme. Labour market programmes can be contributory or non-contributory programmes and are designed to help protect individuals against loss of income from unemployment or help them acquire skills and connect to labour markets (active labour market policies). Unemployment insurance and early retirement incentives are examples of passive labour market policies, whereas training, employment intermediation services and wage subsidies are examples of active policies.[9] These three categories are represented in India's social protection systems to varying degrees, as we shall see shortly.

SSNs can have profound development impacts. As a supplement to household income, safety nets enable more spending on health and education, which can lead to a more productive labour force in the future. Food assistance can ensure a smoother consumption pattern in countries where livelihoods may have seasonal patterns. Finally, interventions targeted at women and children can have impacts on how households consume food. Imagine children receiving a nutritious meal at school, freeing up food for other family members. Safety nets that target women can also help improve their health or their status within households. If safety nets target rural areas, there is a strong potential to improve economic growth through impacts on labour productivity and purchasing power.[10]

Contrary to the belief that safety nets/welfare schemes are wasteful,[11] such programmes can have a multiplier effect on the GDP. Recent evidence shows that an additional dollar spent on social protection leads to an accumulated increase of $3 in South Korea, $1.7 in Japan and $1.5 in Mongolia (within three years of the investment).[12] Social protection (like maternity programmes) can also increase FLFP, which can lead to major GDP gains.[13]

How India fares on safety nets

India has made massive strides in reducing extreme poverty. Between 2006 and 2016, India lifted 271 million people out of poverty.[14] However, World Bank researchers note that while a majority of Indians are no longer poor, nearly half remain vulnerable. Malnutrition remains stubborn and India remains home to the largest population of food-insecure people.[15] Jean Drèze and Anmol Somanchi make a similar point noting that 'Significant progress occurred (for the first time) between the third and fourth rounds of the National Family Health Survey (NFHS), i.e. between 2005-6 and 2015-16. However, partial findings of the fifth round, released a few months ago, suggest no further progress between 2015-16 and 2019-20—just before the COVID-19 crisis.'[16] Many Indians live dangerously close to the poverty line and are constantly at risk of slipping under. The COVID-19 pandemic has made this vulnerability even more apparent. Estimates of Indians at risk of sliding back into poverty range between 12 million and 260 million.[17] A study by Azim Premji University reported that an astounding 230 million Indians—enough to make the world's fifth-largest nation—dropped below the $5/day threshold.[18]

Given the magnitude of poverty and vulnerability in India, policymakers have focused on three aspects of social welfare. The first strand is the pursuit of stronger growth, which theoretically enables job creation and income security. The second strand is the provision of public goods such as education, health, water, etc., as a way of strengthening the country's socio-economic foundations. The third strand is about protecting the most vulnerable sections of society by weaving a variety of safety nets.[19] Since the 1980s, India has succeeded in moving to a higher growth trajectory. This growth has not always been inclusive and most certainly has not created the kinds of employment opportunities that, for example, China has been able to create. Even so, India's growth has yielded many positives, including more fiscal space for the state to focus on public goods and safety nets. Unfortunately, it is here that things have gone less well. Provision of public goods remains poor. Safety nets are, essentially, compensation for other failures and weaknesses.[20]

India has a long tradition of implementing safety net programmes. The PDS, which is the world's largest social protection scheme,[21] was introduced in the 1940s as a by-product of British India's war effort.[22] Since then, India's social protection programmes have expanded substantially. There is also a marked trend towards a rights-based approach to social welfare.[23] MGNREGA, National Food Security Act (NFSA), RTE, etc., are all part of a shift to help poor and vulnerable populations have access to 'justiciable claims'.

Before the Modi government took office in 2014, five programmes accounted for the bulk of India's social protection expenditure. These include (i) PDS; (ii) Integrated Child Development Scheme (ICDS); (iii) MDMS; (iv) MGNREGA; and (v) pensions for widows/elderly.[24] Seventy per cent of the country's social protection budget was spent on programmes such as the PDS and MGNREGA (figure 8.1).[25]

Since then, additional significant programmes have been introduced. The PM Kisan scheme was introduced in 2019. Its objective was to provided minimum income support of Rs 6,000 ($80) per annum for 120 million eligible farmers.[26] The price tag for PM Kisan was initially set at Rs 75 billion ($10 billion) per annum. For 2019-20, the scheme was revised to benefit nearly 20 million additional farmers. The scheme covered a total of 145 million beneficiaries, by allocating Rs 872.18 billion ($11.7 billion) from the Central Government.[27] The revised budget was Rs 543.70 billion ($7.3 billion) in 2019-20.

The government also introduced Ayushman Bharat, a health initiative that combined health insurance with wellness centres. This was not a totally new scheme because it subsumed an existing insurance programme. The revised budgetary allocation for PM-JAY in 2019-20 was Rs 32 billion ($429 million). Of course, as some have pointed out, this funding is inadequate to serve the intended beneficiaries and may instead fragment the already weak health system.[28] Other than these programmes, India also has 400 benefit transfer programmes at the central level and about 2,500 programmes at the state level.[29]

Data from India's Ministry of Finance reveals that public spending on social security and welfare schemes has been rising since the 1990s. In 2018, the government spent 4.64 per cent of its total expenditure on social welfare (figure 8.2).[30] This is approximately 1.7 per cent of the real GDP (Central Statistics Office) for that year.[31] While the range of programmes India offers is wide, India chronically underspends on safety nets compared to most countries, even other low-to-middle-income countries (LMICs).[32] According to the World Bank, only 1.5 per cent of India's GDP is spent on social protection, much of it on PDS.[33]

Figure 8.1: India's budget allocation for various social protection programmes

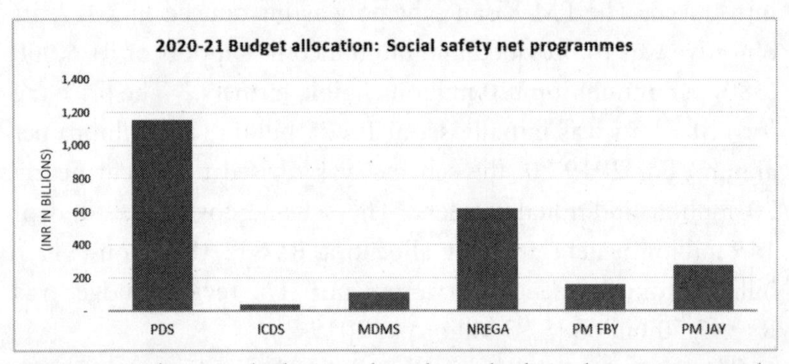

Sources: Authors' calculations based on budget documents; 'Eight Charts Show the Modi Govt's Spending Patterns on Flagship Welfare Schemes', The Wire (2020).

Besides inadequate spending, there are other aspects that merit attention. The first has to do with coverage of various schemes and ease of access for potential beneficiaries of schemes. Overall, the rural coverage of safety nets is more extensive. While the coverage of in-kind programmes (PDS, MDMS) is fairly balanced (94.7 per cent rural; 92.1 per cent urban), employment schemes (MGNREGA) only target beneficiaries in rural India, as do most other programmes.[34] This lopsided coverage needs to be addressed, as India is likely to be more urban than rural by 2050.[35]

Figure 8.2: Public expenditure on social security and welfare in India

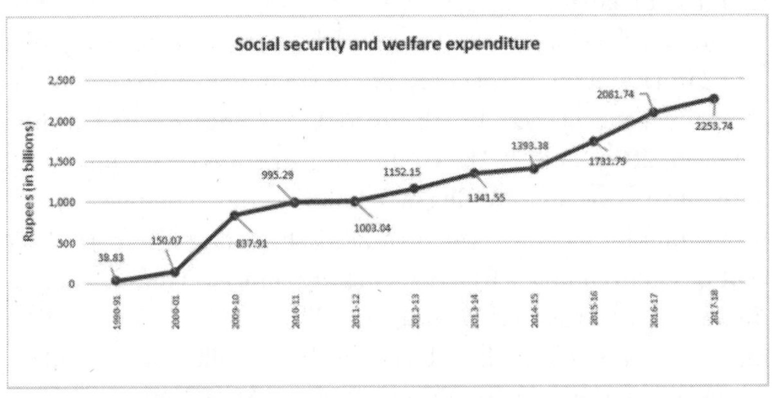

Source: *Indian Public Finance Statistics 2017-18,* Ministry of Finance.

Furthermore, the experience of poverty, inequality and, by extension, vulnerability can vary across (and within) states. Moreover, there are differences in efficiency—implementation and leakages and take-up.[36] The reasons for this are fairly intuitive. Varying demographic and economic profiles, as well as resources and state capacities, are to blame. The demand for SSNs also varies. India's poorest states—Chhattisgarh, Madhya Pradesh, Uttar Pradesh, Odisha, Jharkhand, Rajasthan and Bihar—are home to 45 per cent of India's population and 62 per cent of its poor.[37]

The experience with COVID-19 has also made clear that existing safety nets are not strong enough to withstand serious shocks. For example, between May and June 2020, 35 per cent of students surveyed by Oxfam had not received rations under MDMS. Similarly, despite an additional infusion of Rs 4 billion ($54 million) this year, MGNREGA was close to exhausting 70 per cent of its funds just six months into FY2021.[38,39] Of course, MGNREGA already has a chronic year-on-year (YoY) cycle of wage arrears.[40] The plight of migrants has not led to any significant changes.

Other developments compound these problems. The mandatory linking of benefits to Aadhaar has led to exclusion of many beneficiaries. Of the forty-two hunger-related deaths between 2017 and 2018, twenty-five are linked to failure to authenticate or link Aadhaar.[41] Politics, too, complicates the provision of safety nets. Madhya Pradesh, a state where 42.8 per cent of children under five years old are underweight, decided to do away with eggs in their Anganwadis (childcare centres). This may suit a particular political ideology but is unhelpful to children who need all the nutrition they can get.[42,43] Moreover, nearly 100 million people cannot access PDS because the Central government uses the 2011 census rather than more recent projections.[44]

As India's economy grapples with the pandemic and its aftermath, other threats loom on the horizon. Limited employment opportunities for a growing youth demographic, employment-limiting technological innovations and impacts of worsening climate change could overwhelm India's safety nets. All this is happening in the context of a weakening of traditional, family-based safety nets due to migration, urbanization, etc.[45] Finally, given that safety nets are tangible, they are prone to becoming political tools. This phenomenon has influenced the design of programmes to favour short-run consumption, smoothing over the problem of addressing the root causes of poverty and vulnerability.

The global safety nets landscape

Safety nets have been a part of the global discourse on poverty reduction for a long time. In 1990, following a decade of renewed conversations about poverty reduction, two important things happened—economist Martin Ravallion came up with the $1-a-day poverty line[46] and the World Bank's WDR on Poverty defined a 'New Poverty Agenda'.[47] The first created a simple yet enduring visual of extreme poverty. The other defined pathways to end this extreme poverty—and while doing so, stressed upon the need for safety nets as an integral companion to development policies.[48]

As an aside, there is an interesting backstory to how Martin Ravallion came up with the now-famous $1-a-day poverty benchmark. In the late 1980s, a group of World Bank economists observed that many developing countries had poverty lines at an income of about $370 a year. This was a basic amount that many countries thought was necessary for life's essentials. Sitting at dinner with his wife one day, Ravallion had an 'epiphany'. He divided the $370 figure by 365 days of the year and the '$1-a-day' concept was born! Of course, the benchmark is more complicated than that, but it is a powerful illustration of how the global poor people live.[49]

Since then, SSNs have grown in importance, and 'implementing appropriate national social protection systems' by 2030 is an SDG target (SDG 1.3).[50,51] However, despite lofty goals, the global picture is troubling. Only 45 per cent of the world's population is covered by at least one social protection measure, according to estimates from the ILO's *World Social Protection Report* 2017–19.[52] Additionally, only 29 per cent have access to 'comprehensive' social security (figure 8.3).

Unfortunately, India performs much worse than these global averages. If we exclude nutritional benefits offered under PDS, only 19 per cent of Indians are covered by at least one social protection related to unemployment, maternity, severe disabilities, old age pension, children and benefits for vulnerable groups.[53]

While looking at global averages, gaps in certain parts of India's SSNs become apparent. This includes disability coverage (only 5.4 per cent of Indians are covered), unemployment benefits (India ranks eighth from the bottom) and maternity protection.[54]

Figure 8.3: Global public expenditure on social protection (% of GDP)

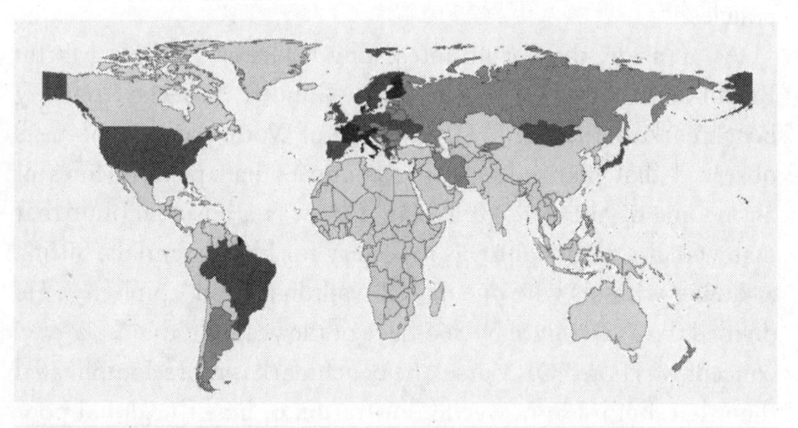

Source: *World Social Protection Database*, International Labour Organization.

Ideas for India

Social protection works! There are many examples from India and around the world that demonstrate this. However, instead of copying any one model, there is likely a need for multiple models in India, given the country's socio-economic diversity. It wouldn't be a stretch to argue that models may have to differ from state to state and even within states; there are plenty of differences that may require even more localized solutions. With that said, it is always a good idea to explore what is happening in other parts of the country or the world. After all, MGNREGA grew out of an employment guarantee scheme adopted by Maharashtra to combat the severe drought between 1970 and 1973.[55] In a similar vein, PM Kisan is modelled after Telangana state's Rythu Bandhu scheme, which provides cash payments of Rs. 8,000 ($105) per acre to almost six million farmers.[56] Piloting innovations in districts or states and then mainstreaming them has worked and should be encouraged. However, it is also a good idea to keep an eye on innovations taking place elsewhere in the world.

Survivor's pension in Sweden. European countries are far ahead on the spectrum of social protection systems. While India is justifiably focused on issues such as food security, a country such as Sweden has very different concerns. For example, when someone dies, their survivor (a child, or a spouse or partner) may be eligible to receive a 'survivor's pension'. The way the process works is as follows: when a person dies, the Swedish Tax Agency informs the Swedish Pensions Agency. The latter agency assesses whether there are survivors who are entitled to some form of survivor's pension. The pensions agency informs the survivors about the benefits. In some cases, the agency may ask the survivors for additional information. That's the extent of the process.[57] Imagine a time when you are not excluded from a benefit simply because you have a biometric mismatch but rather, you receive your benefit without having to ask for it.

South Korea's safety net problem during COVID-19. It is well known that South Korea did a good job of containing the COVID-19 pandemic in 2020, though the situation worsened in 2021. As of the writing of this book, South Korea's cases per million ranked the country 157th out of 222 countries and territories tracked by Worldometer.[58] South Korea's death rate ranking was 164. However, what is less well known, and what might be of interest to India, is that the safety net system buckled under the pressure of COVID-19.

After the Asian financial crisis in 1997, South Korea expanded its SSN. The coverage of the Employment Insurance Scheme (EIS) was expanded and a universal public assistance programme was introduced. These changes helped South Korea weather the 2008-09 GFC. However, during COVID-19, this system proved inadequate. Due to the lockdown, economic activity slowed, especially in the small business sector. The self-employed, who account for 25 per cent of the total workforce, had no access to EIS. To support the small business sector and the self-employed, South Korea adopted a short-term Emergency Relief Allowance (ERA), for the entire population in April 2020. This measure in the universal basic income (UBI) style came in for criticism as a populist and inefficient safety net. Instead, the government is now considering universal unemployment insurance, modelled after systems in countries like Germany and Denmark.[59] Why may this be relevant to India? Close to 90 per cent of India's workers are in the informal economy with few, if any, protections.[60] From 'workfare' job guarantee programmes to unemployment insurance schemes, there is a lot to explore for India.

What India must do

India has improved safety nets over the last few decades. These safety nets have played a big role in poverty reduction and in building the country's human capital. During crises, these safety nets have worked, although not always as well as they should. COVID-19 overwhelmed India's safety nets, just as the pandemic overwhelmed safety nets around the world. As COVID-19 threatens to unravel years, perhaps decades, of progress, what should India's social protection architecture look like going forward?

There is an emerging school of thought that recommends a form of basic income as a way to guarantee a minimum income, smooth consumption during shocks, drive demand and reduce poverty and vulnerability. However, a pure UBI programme would be expensive to implement. Surbhi Bhatia and Vishnu Padmanabhan calculate that this would amount to at least 10 per cent of the GDP (at the current poverty line levels and Rs 1,215 or $16 per month).[61] Karthik Muralidharan and Maitreesh Ghatak suggest a leaner 'Inclusive Growth Dividend'.[62] This scheme will put Rs 120 ($1.60) in the pockets of every Indian every month and cost 1 per cent of the GDP. They claim that, unlike UBI, this would be just one part of a person's income stream and will help mitigate extreme poverty; and make a part of future income predictable. Reetika Khera proposes a more gradual rollout as another approach. She suggests providing UBI first for vulnerable groups, such as pregnant women, disabled people, widows and the elderly, would make the programme more affordable.

However, we believe that there are two fundamental problems with this debate. First, there is the standard difficulty of developing sound delivery systems and administrative capacity for a UBI-style programme. But there is a bigger, more critical consideration. There appears to be a search for a panacea, a silver bullet to secure the lives of India's marginalized communities. Safety nets must be part of a broader framework, which does not neglect the other elements of inclusive growth and provision of public goods. Within that broad framework, safety nets should have their own framework, their own architecture. Many elements are already in place for this architecture. To this end, we propose five recommendations.

Build a social protection system. India has hundreds of schemes at the central and state government levels. This is problematic for multiple reasons. Coordinating these schemes is a challenge. You need a sprawling bureaucracy to implement these schemes and help avoid the usual problems of corruption and duplication. This is a serious issue in a country with limited institutional capacity, especially at local levels. As Junaid Ahmed, the World Bank's country director in India notes, China and Indonesia implement only about 10 national social assistance programmes. India has almost 400. While India doesn't have to copy other countries, modern safety nets are part of systematic approaches rather than piecemeal efforts.[63]

Strengthen delivery systems. Institutional delivery mechanisms, especially at local levels, need strengthening. MGNREGA helps explain continued challenges of delivering social programmes in India. Despite MGNREGA's many successes, delayed payments still dog the programme. Wage arrears are common and lead to diminished interest from potential beneficiaries. A key cause of payment delays is technology. It appears that in 2019-20, almost Rs 16 billion ($214 million) of wage payments 'were rejected' owing to faulty account details. Economist Jean Drèze notes that these rejected payments 'are accompanied by a bewildering collection of error codes that are often difficult to understand, even for professional bankers'.[64] Drèze found that it took government agencies two years to figure out the meaning of 'inactive Aadhaar' as an error code associated with MGNREGA payments. This astounding factoid is not only about the folly of an over-reliance on technology but, more importantly, about the complementary institutional capacity that remains a hurdle to the effective delivery of these critical programmes.

Different states need different strategies. Different states have different priorities and needs, and must be allowed to spend their centrally issued funds for social protection programmes differently.[65] The World Bank's July 2020 India Development Update suggests a system in which funding is a blend of two components—a basic central allocation that can be topped off with 'block grants' customizable to states. This could allow states flexibility to determine their own needs and implementation capacity, and establish better-suited programmes.

More safety nets for urban India. COVID-19 exposed a glaring hole in India's safety nets when millions of urban workers started streaming to their homes in rural areas. Within three weeks of the imposition of the lockdown, the unemployment rate tripled in urban India. Most urban workers are informal, have no written job contracts or any access to benefits. There is no MGNREGA for them to flock to in urban India. The government's relief package bypassed most urban workers. In fact, by the time the government acted, millions had already reached their homes, possibly carrying the virus with them. This is sufficient reason to think in terms of universalizing job guarantees. MGNREGA's self-targeting mechanism works well and should work well in urban areas.[66] This is not only about COVID-19. India is likely to be more urban than rural by 2050.[67] Urban workers will require a more secure safety net.[68] A universal job guarantee can be an important element of India's social protection framework.

Don't forget old people. India's socio-economic discourse focuses disproportionately on young people and their challenges. Owing to rising life expectancy, the share of elderly will rise over time. By 2050, a fifth of the population will be above the age of sixty. As of now, only 12 per cent of this population group has access to a formal pension system.[69] Most Indians have no retirement savings. While there are some 'contributory' pension schemes such as the Atal Pension Yojana (APY) and the National Pension Scheme (NPS), the World Bank estimates that only a small proportion of people benefit from them. Of the almost 400 million workers in the unorganized sector, only about 4 per cent benefit from these schemes. Economists Jean Drèze and Reetika Khera have pointed out that social pensions, modest as they are, appear to be valued highly by beneficiaries and leakages are limited. They argue in favour of moving towards universalization of pension benefits. The associated costs appear to be modest.[70] Using technology to implement this expansion could mitigate some of the added costs. The Mercer Global Pensions Index scores the adequacy of India's pension benefit levels at 38.7. This is far below China's 53.4 and Brazil's 72.5. India needs to scale up pension benefits and coverage at mission-mode pace. The lives and dignity of an entire generation of India's elderly are at stake.[71]

Ultimately, a comprehensive human capital framework offers the best protection against shocks and vulnerabilities. The ability of people to survive shocks on their own must be enhanced by improving their productivity, opportunities and incomes ('promotional instruments'). Additionally, there should be 'preventive instruments'—social insurance pprogrammes—and 'protective instruments'—tax-financed redistribution after a shock.[72] The foundations are important. Safety nets are only one part of the bigger puzzle. By undersupplying public goods, the Indian state continues to limit the capacity of its citizens and underutilize an avenue to reduce risk.[73] Even most aspirational examples of welfare states, such as the Scandinavian countries, have first made investments in public goods like education, healthcare systems and security.[74] India cannot and must not avoid that path.

Part III

Freeing Markets and Unleashing Competitiveness

9

Labour: India's Demographic Dividend or Disaster?

India's labour laws are anti-worker.

—Atal Bihari Vajpayee, former prime minister of India

India entered its so-called demographic dividend around 2005—expected to last until 2055. It is a period when a country has a surge of working-age population of fifteen- to sixty-four-year-olds, which supports the elderly and the young. India has already utilized almost a third of the period of its demographic dividend[1]—it saw a period of explosive growth from 2003–12—but has not been able to sustain that growth. And given the nature of its growth, India has created less employment for every unit of its GDP growth—the elasticity of employment-to-GDP has been declining.

Japan, Hong Kong and Singapore entered such a phase of demographic dividend in the 1960s and grew very rapidly to become developed countries. China entered its demographic dividend coinciding with economic reforms in the 1980s and has seen very rapid and sustained growth for over three decades. Brazil entered such a phase in the 1960s as well, but while it had a sharp growth spurt for a decade from 1966–75, that spurt was not sustained. The Arab world entered their demographic dividend phase in the 1990s but without growth, and employment frustration among the population—especially the educated youth—led to the Arab Spring a decade ago. Their dividend became a demographic disaster.

Whether a country realizes its demographic dividend depends on how capital, labour and land come together to generate income and employment. The division of income depends enormously on initial attributes as well as on technological change and how that change is generated, spread and determined by market forces, by government policies and regulations, and in the end by specific interests and competition. But before we go further, it may be useful to look at an economic construct of the dualistic structure of developing economies and what structural transformation means for them.

1. Economic dualism and structural transformation

In 1954, Arthur Lewis, an economist from St Lucia, published *Economic Development with Unlimited Supplies of Labour* and introduced what came to be called a dual sector model or the 'Lewis model'. [2] Lewis argued that the central process of development consists of moving a large mass of underemployed workers, with low productivity (in Lewis's terms, workers whose marginal product is 'negligible, zero or even negative'), out of a 'subsistence' sector, where living standards are necessarily low, into a modern 'capitalist' sector, where output per worker can be higher because it is 'fructified by capital'.[3] In 1979, he was awarded the Nobel Prize in economics for this work, which led to the creation of a new field in economics called economic development.

Lewis did not consider dualism as rural-urban, or even agriculture vs non-agriculture. You could have a segment of agriculture that used capital and was modernized. At the same time, you could have parts of the urban sector where a mass of people provides services in what is loosely called the informal sector. Dualism could be described as modern vs traditional (via technology) or formal vs informal (via the labour market). His model has been criticized from many angles. If there is an unlimited supply of labour, then wages should stagnate, but they often do not. If wages are stagnant due to their unlimited supply, then wage shares should decline over time—but they do not. Why does capital not spread across the economy rather than stay in a modern enclave sector? Investment in human capital (through education and skilling), as distinct from physical capital, can be another option for the use of capital and drive development.[4]

Lewis did not discuss duality between agriculture and non-agriculture as others did. Fei and Ranis interjected a third phase in the Lewis transformation: when the demand for food would rise and there would be a need to invest part of the surplus in increasing food supply. This is turn would require modern farming techniques to generate an increase in food supply.

While all these criticisms remain valid, nevertheless, the underlying appeal of the Lewis model in describing the process of transformation of a traditional economy or the lack of it remains very valid. Other complications could be added; for example, restrictions on the use of capital, land or, for that matter, labour could accentuate the dualism. Arbitrary and capricious restrictions in labour market flexibility can accentuate dualism as even the modern sector prefers under these circumstances to hire more casual labour and adjust their production systems accordingly. Firms prefer to remain in the informal sector rather than grow larger and face all the tax and regulatory requirements spread across myriad labour laws and face the depredations of India's labour-inspector raj. Land-use restrictions affect decisions on location, employment and size in ways that are often unpredictable.

2. India's dualistic labour market and employment challenges

In this section, we will analyse these laws in detail and the recently introduced changes to those laws. But before we go there, an assessment of the magnitude of the employment challenge India faces must be made.

India's working age population will increase by at least twelve million per year until 2030—roughly adding a Belgium every year. India's LFPR is around 0.5—reasonably high for men at about 0.8 but shockingly low 0.20 (and declining) for women. The reasons why it is so low are still a puzzle, with explanations ranging from the need to perform unpaid housework[5] to lack of appropriate jobs to safety issues, discrimination, inadequate training for women and overall patriarchy. But even with this low LFPR, it means people cannot find suitable employment, as India generates about 5 million jobs every year and the demand is for 6 million. As a result, an additional million people every year must find some means to survive by becoming self-employed—hawking and selling their labour on the streets.

India would need to create at least 8.5-9 million jobs every year until 2030 to reach a Lewis turning point—6 million to meet the employment needs of everyone entering the working force and looking for a job; 1.5-2 million more if the LFPR of women rises to 0.5, making the average LFPR 0.65; and another 1 million to gradually absorb the sink of underemployed people eking out a precarious living on the streets. At present, according to the World Bank's report on jobs in South Asia,[6] India creates 0.75 million jobs for every 1 per cent growth. This means India would need to grow at 12 per cent per annum to create adequate work to realize its demographic dividend—a tall order for an economy which had slowed down to 4-5 per cent pre-COVID-19. Even reaching 8-9 per cent GDP growth (the rate India grew in 2003–08) would be a huge achievement. Therefore, India must generate more employment from its growth, at least 1 million jobs for every per cent of GDP growth—more inclusive growth.

It is in this context that one can view India's economic transformation and how it has differed from other countries, especially in the Asia region. During its high-growth phase from 1980–2008, total factor productivity (TFP)[7] grew at 2.6 per cent annually, with the service sector providing half of it, according to the World Bank (2012).[8] The manufacturing sector showed TFP growth of only 0.3 per cent—much lower than even in Pakistan. By contrast, China shows enormous growth in manufacturing TFP, which grew 1.4 per cent during its initial growth phase after China's economic reforms from 1978–93, and then rose to 3.1 per cent from 1993–2004. While TFP growth in agriculture and services was lower in China than in India, China was able to generate a huge number of jobs in manufacturing—and pull people out of agriculture, raise standards of living and reduce poverty.[9] Export-led manufacturing, whereby China became the factory of the world, created the jobs which millions of low-skilled workers could move to and improve their standard of living, send remittances back to their rural families and build a better life.

By contrast, India saw a boom in the service sector where high-skilled jobs were created, but it meant that a large mass of low-skilled labour was left languishing in rural areas or drifted to urban centres and looked for ways to make a living selling things on the street or taking up jobs in construction at wages which kept many of them below the poverty line. India became the back-office IT centre for the world, but its benefits were not spread to masses of low-skilled labour. This dualism between a few skilled workers getting jobs in fast-growing IT and service sectors, and masses of unskilled labour underemployed or self-employed but poor, is largely because India missed the bus on manufacturing whereas China successfully got on. Today, Vietnam is following this model and, in some sectors like textiles and apparel, Bangladesh is too. On the other hand, India is headed in the opposite direction—a recent survey by the Centre for Economic Data and Analysis (CEDA) of Ashoka University and the Centre for Monitoring Indian Economy (CMIE) shows that in the period 2016-17 to 2019-20, manufacturing employment in India fell from 51 million to 40 million.[10] It also states that agriculture has been the fallback option. The agriculture sector employed 145.6 million people in 2016-17. This increased by 4 per cent to reach 151.8 million in 2020-21. While it constituted 36 per cent of all employment in 2016-17, the figure rose to 40 per cent in 2020-21, underlining the sector's importance for the Indian economy. Employment in agriculture has been on the rise over the last two years with YoY growth rates of 1.7 per cent in 2019-20 and 4.1 per cent in 2020-21. These trends are also confirmed by the CMIE household survey which shows the share of agriculture in total employment has gone up from 35.3 per cent in 2017-18 to 36.1 per cent in 2018-19 and then to 38 per cent in 2019-20 and on to 39.4 per cent in 2020-21.[11]

To get around the rigidities in hiring and firing that constrain the ability to adjust to production demands, businesses have increasingly used contract labour. The share of contract workers in factories among total workers increased from 26 per cent in 2004-05 to 36 per cent in 2017-18, while the share of directly hired workers fell from 74 per cent to 64 per cent over the same period. India has the largest share (about a third) of a category called 'casual wage workers' or in colloquial use 'daily workers' in South Asia. India's share of casual workers is even higher than in Pakistan (17 per cent), Nepal (10 per cent), Bangladesh (22 per cent), Afghanistan (14 per cent), or Bhutan (4 per cent). Sri Lanka and Maldives have none.[12] *The Periodic Labour Force Survey Report (2018-19)* indicates that 70 per cent of regular wage/salaried employees in the non-agricultural sector did not have a written contract, 54 per cent were not eligible for paid leave and 52 per cent did not have any social security benefits.[13]

Figure 9.1: Vulnerable employment and the Human Development Index

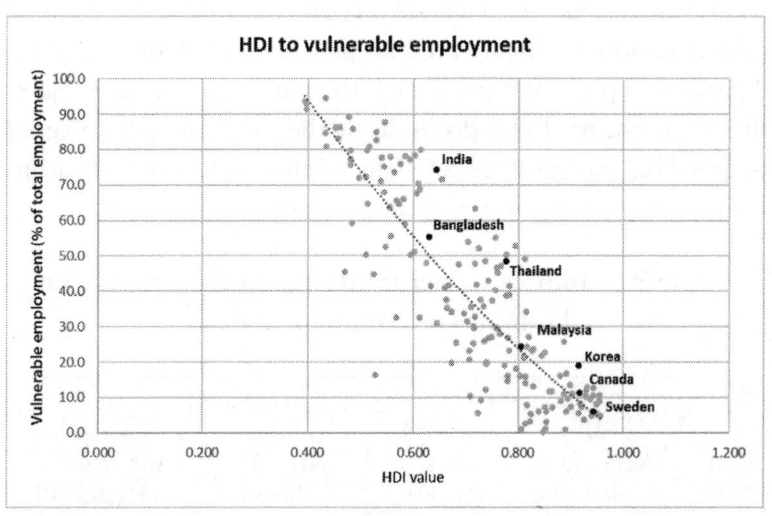

Source: *HDI Indicators* 2020, UNDP.

Instead of trying to adhere to these laws, firms prefer to hire casual labour for whom these laws and regulations need not be applicable. As a result, the mass of India's workforce has very little social protection. UNDP's *Human Development Report* provides data on the share of vulnerable employment in total employment—it is, as one would expect, highly correlated with Human Development Index (HDI). But India sticks out as a huge outlier. With its level of HDI, based on cross-country comparisons (figure 9.1) India's share of vulnerable employment should be at most 50 per cent but it is above 75 per cent, much higher than even in Bangladesh. India's labour protection and safety nets are amongst the weakest in the world. This was exposed vividly during the sudden lockdown, when millions of migrant casual workers had to trudge back to rural areas under horrific conditions in the largest mass migration seen since the Partition of India. Chhibber (2020), using the share of vulnerable employment, created a Vulnerability-Adjusted HDI. The exercise calculates how far India's HDI drops with a shock of 1 per cent, 2 per cent, 5 per cent (table 9.1). If the shock is of intensity higher than 1 per cent, India drops from the medium-HDI category to low-HDI category, as its Vulnerability-Adjusted HDI drops below 0.55, the cut-off for medium human development.

Table 9.1: India's vulnerability to shocks: Impact on Human Development Index

HDI 2019	Inequality-Adjusted HDI	Vulnerability-Adjusted HDI (1% shock)	Vulnerability-Adjusted HDI (2% shock)	Vulnerability-Adjusted HDI (5% shock)
0.647	0.477	0.5703	0.4936	0.2635

Source: Chhibber (2021).

Ahsan and Pages (2008) find that registered sector employment and output gets reduced by laws that increase employment protection or the cost of labour disputes substantially. The share of value added that goes to labour does not increase by such laws and so they do not benefit labour. Labour-intensive industries, such as textiles, are the hardest hit by amendments that increase employment protection while capital-intensive industries are the most affected by laws that increase the cost of labour dispute resolution. These adverse effects are not alleviated by the widespread and increasing use of contract labour.

Until the mid-1990s, India's protectionist trade regime hurt labour. Hasan, Mitra and Ramaswamy (2003) find a positive impact of trade liberalization on labour-demand elasticities in the Indian manufacturing sector. These elasticities turn out to be negatively related to protection levels that vary across industries and over time. Furthermore, they find that these elasticities are not only higher for Indian states with more flexible labour regulations, but they are also impacted to a larger degree by trade reforms. Aghion, Burgess, Redding and Zilibotti (2008), following delicensing, showed that industries located in states with pro-employer labour market institutions grew more quickly than those in pro-worker environments.

Li, Megistae and Xu (2011) believe that labour flexibility is a key factor that explains China's advantage with respect to India in productivity growth in manufacturing.[14] It also explains the much smaller size of Indian firms (median size 18 employees vs 134 for China) and the link between firm size and city complexity that underpins China's advantage and higher productivity. It has been argued that labour rigidity (arising from the fear of having to take prior permission for retrenchment/closure even if businesses are not viable, i.e., lack of an easy exit option), and high administrative burden (since the multiplicity of labour laws has resulted in multiple inspections, returns and registers), explain why firm sizes have remained small in India. This has constrained growth of firms. Amongst registered factories, the Annual Survey of Industries (2017-18) indicates that 47 per cent factories employ less than twenty workers and provide only 5 per cent of total employment and 4 per cent of total output.

Hasan and Jandoc (2010) find little difference in the size distribution of firms between states believed to have flexible labour regulations versus those with inflexible labour regulations. However, on restricting attention to labour-intensive industries, they find a greater prevalence of larger-sized firms in states with flexible labour regulations. But the idea of a missing middle category—the lack of firms of the size that employs 100–1,000 workers—is not borne out by the data. Kishore (2015) shows that in 1980-81 only 31.5 per cent of factory workers were employed in this middle category of firms but by 2011-12 that share had grown to 45.6 per cent. But this growth did not come from small firms growing larger; instead, it came from large firms becoming smaller. Employment in firms larger than 1000 workers fell from 44.7 per cent in 1980-81 to 28.5 per cent in 2011-12. Outsourcing by larger firms may explain some of this, but labour laws were not responsible for this decline. But what is clear is that average factory size has declined, not grown, in India, and may explain why India has struggled to compete in manufacturing. India does not have a missing middle-size factory problem, it has a small-size factory problem.

The 6th Economic Census (2013-14) reported that there were fifty-nine million establishments in India employing 131 million people (of which 72 per cent were self-employed and 28 per cent hired at least one worker. According to the Periodic Labour Force Survey for 2018-19, 79 per cent of the workers were in establishments with less than ten workers. More than 70 per cent of manufacturing employment is in firms with less than ten workers. Labour laws explain to a large extent why firms remain small—because most labour laws in India apply to firms employing more than ten workers.

3. The new labour codes

In 2020, India tried to clean up twenty-nine labour laws into four labour codes, on (i) wages; (ii) industrial relations; (iii) social security; (iv) occupational safety, health and working conditions.

The labour codes on wages and industrial relations apply to all establishments, with limited exceptions. The codes on social security and occupational safety increases the thresholds for factories from ten to twenty (with power) and twenty to forty (without power). According to PRS Legislative Research, a report of the ILO (2020) shows that collective dismissals need to be authorized by public authorities only in twenty-two countries (including India, Pakistan and Thailand).[15] Of these, seven countries (including India, Sri Lanka and Colombia) do not require consultation with workers' representatives. On the other hand, notification to both workers' representatives and competent authorities are required in most countries, but no prior permission is needed.

The Industrial Relations Code 2020 increases the threshold to 300 workers,[16] after which prior permission will be required but retains the notice and compensation requirements specified under the Industrial Disputes Act, 1947. While the increase is welcome, the question that arises is, why have any requirement at all and instead why not insist on prior notification to workers, especially as the data does indicate that the previous requirement of 100 workers did not affect firm size.

To promote the growth of smaller establishments, some states had amended their labour laws to increase the threshold of their application. For instance, Rajasthan increased the threshold of applicability of the Factories Act, 1948, from ten workers to twenty (if power is used), and from twenty workers to forty (if power is not used) and the law on the threshold of hiring and firing without government permission from 100 to 300 workers in 2014. The Economic Survey (2018-19) noted that increased thresholds for certain labour laws in Rajasthan resulted in an increase in growth of total output in the state and total output per factory.[17] But attribution of this growth to labour flexibility has been questioned by Maira and Mehta (2020).[18]

According to Manish Sabherwal, a well-known expert on labour issues, India suffers from labour-inspector raj and at the same time many labour codes and laws are not enforced, and corruption abounds. He says, 'India's labour laws are a mess. It is practically impossible to comply with 100 per cent of them without violating 10 per cent of them.'[19] The new codes try to make things more transparent by enabling provisions for web-based inspections in some cases and third-party certification and create some provisions for common registers and returns. However, details have been left to delegated legislation. Further, in certain cases, such as the Code on Social Security, compliance reporting on different aspects (such as provident fund and insurance) may continue to be required to be made to different authorities. The codes also increase the quantum of fines and imprisonment in several cases and allow for the compounding of offences in certain cases. The Industrial Relations Code removes the requirement for reference to the government and publication of award in the gazette and replaces industrial courts/tribunals with two-member labour tribunals (with one judicial and one administrative member). Whether this will reduce the labour-inspector raj remains to be seen.

The Code on Occupational Safety and Health increases the threshold for contract labour provisions from twenty to fifty workers. Further, it shifts from the contractor to the principal employer, the primary responsibility of providing welfare facilities.[20] The Industrial Relations Code makes provisions for recognition of a negotiation option for unions with 51 per cent membership.[21] But the code weakens collective bargaining rights by requiring a two-week notice for strikes. But the implementation of the new codes has been delayed due to the pandemic.

4. Skilling and employability

According to Shukla et al. (2019), the proportion of formally skilled workers in India is extremely low, at 4.69 per cent of total workforce, compared to 24 per cent in China, 52 per cent in the US, 68 per cent in the UK, 75 per cent in Germany, 80 per cent in Japan and 96 per cent in South Korea.[22] This situation can be attributed to three factors—poor education and learning, weak incentives to train workers (largely casual workers) and the limited number of jobs that require deep training. According to the latest *India Skill Report* (2019), only 45.6 per cent of the youth graduating from educational institutions are employable.

Using the International Standard Classification of Occupations (ISCO-08), Shukla et al. find that a little above half (56 per cent) of the labour market is dominated by people who are classified at Level 2 skills—those who can operate machinery and electronic equipment, while 30 per cent constitute skill Level 1 type—simple and routine manual and physical tasks. Nearly 11 per cent of the population can be classified at skill Level 3, who can record work, simple calculations and have good communication skills in specialized fields, while the smallest share is that of skill Level 4, who have decision-making capability and creativity. Slightly more than over half of skill Level 1 individuals are in the fifteen to thirty-five years age group, whereas this group constitutes about 40 per cent of other skill-level types.

On the flip side, the *India Skills Report* 2019 shows that 63 per cent of employers across all sectors felt that only 'some job seekers' or 'no job seekers' meet the required skills.[23] The job providers want people with acquired skills and experience. Newcomers to the job market do not have such skills. Eighty-four per cent of students surveyed cited interest in exploring internship opportunities; however, only 37 per cent of employers offer internships to freshers. This mismatch must be addressed.

One state that has done well is Andhra Pradesh. To enhance employability, the Andhra Pradesh government's key mandates are training in domain-specific industry-recognized courses, 'modular market' demand courses and soft skills training. This is well in line with the findings of the *Skills Report* that the top ten Indian states with the highest employability registered not only high domain expertise but also high non-technical skills. Furthermore, when the survey asked employers to cite three highly desirable soft skills apart from technical knowledge, employers ranked communication skills in the first spot, followed by adaptability and learning agility to meet the challenges brought about by disruptive technologies and changing job environments.

Concluding thoughts

Whether these new codes will help reshape India's employment intensity, improve wages and working conditions remains to be seen. The evidence so far is mixed. The Economic Survey of

2018-19 says that states like Rajasthan are already seeing the benefits of relaxation in labour market flexibility introduced in 2014.[24] Others dispute these claims. It is probably too soon to make conclusive judgement.

The pandemic has, in any case, forced the government to shelve these laws. What will emerge after the pandemic is unclear. Several states like Madhya Pradesh and Haryana are moving in a perverse direction by trying to bring in laws to reserve jobs for people from the state. The best that can be done is to allow even further experimentation by states but under the rubric of a broad national legislation, not allowing detrimental laws like those being considered in Madhya Pradesh and Haryana, which will set off a race to Balkanize India's labour market. The new laws allow that kind of flexibility with permission.

But what is clear is that India must find much greater employment for a large mass of semi-skilled workforce the way China and many East Asian countries did, and now Vietnam and Bangladesh are showing that it can be done. Vietnam has seen the sharpest recovery from the pandemic on the back of exports of low-technology products. India must realize that the high-tech service sector alone will not solve its employment challenge.

India must also reshape the incentives for a more skilled work force that will then attract higher levels of investment, which in turn will demand labour at various skill levels and create the incentives to acquire those skills. It's about turning the current dismal state of employment and working conditions into one where the demand for skilled and semi-skilled labour matches its supply and provides adequate wages and employability to India's surging demographic bulge.

10

Land, Infrastructure and Urban Transformation

Buy land, they're not making it anymore.

—Mark Twain, American writer

In the previous chapter we focused on labour. But how labour combines with other factors of production determines productivity and competitiveness. This is determined not just by labour laws but also by a host of policies that regulate the use of land, the development of infrastructure and how urbanization and city development help bring out the structural transformation that Arthur Lewis talked about.[1]

A major reason why India remains uncompetitive is that it has mismanaged its most important and scarce underlying factor of production—land. This has affected the use of capital and the development of infrastructure that is needed for any modern economy to grow and prosper. India is urbanizing rapidly but in an unplanned manner. It has begun to address the issue of red tape through efforts to improve its rankings on the World Bank's ease of doing business, which has improved to 63 from 142 in 2014. But the costs of doing business remain high because land is expensive, inflexible labour laws have prohibited a well-functioning labour market and logistics costs remain high. This is despite some recent efforts to invest more in infrastructure and move up the rankings on the Logistics Performance Index (LPI), which measures the time it takes to move products. India has made it way up to the 44th place, but remains below China, Malaysia and Thailand and somewhat better than Indonesia and even Vietnam. But as we will show in the chapter, the costs of using this infrastructure remain very high due to India's pricing policies for fuel, electricity and freight tariffs.

Land misallocation and land acquisition

Ejaz Ghani argues that distortions in land markets are much bigger than those in labour markets.[2] He attributes a huge decrease in output per worker in the manufacturing sector to factor misallocation. Most of this decline originates from the misallocation of land and buildings. He goes on to argue that land misallocation has implications for capital allocation through financial markets. Because land is the best form of collateral due to its immobility (i.e., the debtor can't run off with land), land misallocation leads to massive capital misallocation. While borrowers can often pledge 80 per cent of the land value against loans, for most other forms of fixed investment, the loan-to-collateral value ratio is substantially lower.

Misallocation in labour market inputs had no adverse impact on the allocative efficiency of financial loans. The capital misallocation has worsened over time as large manufacturing firms have moved out from cities and into rural areas in search of more land. As a result, financial misallocation is far greater in the organized manufacturing sector than in the unorganized. Land appears to be a minor concern in services. Ghani et al. (2018) compare the role of factor market distortions in services with the manufacturing sector.[3] As most services tend to be less land-intensive compared to manufacturing, they argue that land distortions have not constrained productivity growth in services. This is one factor that explains India's success in services relative to manufacturing.

While India's Logistics Performance Index is improving, India still has some catching up to do in infrastructure and returns to infrastructure spend remain very high. In a simulation exercise, Chhibber and Kalloor (2017) show that if public infrastructure investment increases by 5 per cent of GDP, India's GDP growth rate will increase by 1 per cent.[4] Supporting this finding in a different way is a Standard and Poor report which shows that for every 1 per cent of GDP spent on infrastructure, the multiplier effect on India's GDP is two.[5] This report also argues that (i) infrastructure development is critical for improving India's manufacturing competitiveness and achieving higher growth; (ii) timely execution of projects within budgeted costs will be the key challenge, even if funding is available for economically viable projects; (iii) power generation and transmission are improving, but transportation infrastructure capacity constraints continue to limit corporate performance and investments; and (iv) successful infrastructure development can provide a boost to many sectors, including steel, cement, auto, real estate and others.

Land acquisition also emerges as the major factor that owners of projects cite as the factor responsible for delays in infrastructure projects, according to Nallithiga et al. (2017).[6] The top five important causes of construction delays in transportation infrastructure projects are land acquisition, environmental impact of the project, financial closure, change in orders by the client, poor site management and supervision by contractor.[7] The story is consistently the same in study after study. These delays are primary responsible for rising non-performing assets (NPAs) for loans given by the banking system to infrastructure projects discussed in the chapter on banking and finance.

In 2013, India passed a new land acquisition act—Right to Fair Compensation and Transparency in Land Acquisition, Rehabilitation and Resettlement Act, 2013 (LARR)—with bipartisan support to provide adequate compensation to landowners and define clearly for which purposes land could be acquired. These were defined as: for strategic purposes relating to naval, military, air force and armed forces of the Union, including central paramilitary forces, or any work vital to national security or defence of India, or relating to state police, or for the safety of the people; or for infrastructure projects; or for building housing to resettle people affected by disasters and for poor families. The Act defines the landowner as including a person who is granted forest rights under the Scheduled Tribes and Other Traditional Forest Dwellers (Recognition of Forest Rights) Act, 2006.

The Act included compensation not only for the land acquired but also landowner compensation for replacement housing and livelihood compensation for those working the land. These costs were set at very high levels making land acquisition very costly. It also introduced the clause that the law shall apply even when private companies buy land from willing sellers, without any involvement of the government.

For a typical rural household that owns an average of one acre of land, the Act will replace the loss of annual average per capita income of Rs 3,700 ($50) for the rural household, with:

- four times the market value of the land, and
- an upfront payment of Rs 45,000 ($600) for subsistence, transportation and resettlement allowances, and
- an additional entitlement of a job to a family member, or a payment of Rs 5,00,000 ($6,700) up front, or a monthly annuity totalling Rs 24,000 ($320) per year for twenty years with adjustment for inflation—the option from these three choices shall be the legal right of the affected landowner family, not the land acquirer, and
- a house with no less than 50 square metres in plinth area, and
- additional benefits may apply if the land is resold without development, used for urbanization, or if the landowner belongs to SC/ST or other protected groups per rules of the Government of India.

Many have argued that with this law, land acquisition for industry has become prohibitively costly. Before this law came into effect, land zoning laws were used to exploit poor farmers. Their agricultural land would be acquired at cheap prices and rezoned as industrial land when its market price would rise hugely. Politicians and corrupt officials in cahoots with industry made huge profits. They would often acquire far more land than was needed for industrial production and convert it into staff housing which would later be sold commercially. The landowners would be paid limited compensation, face displacement and were often left poorer. This issue came to a head when Tata Motors wanted to acquire 1,000 hectares of land to build a Nano car plant at Singur in West Bengal. When the Mamata Banerjee government denied them that option, they moved the plant to Gujarat where then Chief Minister Narendra Modi offered them the land for a song.

When the NDA government came to power, it introduced a new law in 2015 to water down some of the provisions of the 2013 Act—which it had earlier voted for. But land is such an emotive issue that even with a considerable parliamentary majority, it has not been able to get this law passed. Instead, it has removed the mandatory features of the law and thereby made it possible for individual states to modify the law. According to Lopez and Chari (2021),[8] 11 states have amended land reform laws to allow industries and non-farmers to buy large parcels of agricultural land and put them to non-agricultural uses, and thereby by-pass the LARR. These 11 states are Andhra Pradesh, Gujarat, Haryana, Karnataka, Madhya Pradesh, Maharashtra, Punjab, Rajasthan, Tamil Nadu, Uttarakhand and West Bengal.

One option is to lease land instead of selling it. Farmers have an emotional attachment to their land, as it has often been in their family for generations. Leasing allows them to keep the title and get compensation for its use, including jobs for their youth and housing in the new real estate developments. This option, the brainchild of Chandrababu Naidu, was proposed for the new capital city for Andhra Pradesh, Amravati, on the banks of the Krishna River after it had to give up Hyderabad to Telangana. He had helped build Hyderabad—also called Cyberabad—into India's foremost IT city. Facing opposition by farmers to the forced acquisition of fertile agricultural land, he proposed a land-lease model. Unfortunately, the project ran into huge opposition and was subsequently abandoned by the new government of Y.S. Jagan Mohan Reddy that came into power in 2019.

But while this project may have been abandoned for other reasons as well, the land-lease model does hold promise if it can be made to work with the government leasing the land and on-leasing it for industrial and real estate development. Further experimentation may be needed to see its potential.

Transport and power infrastructure: Improving but remain costly

The need for India to catch-up on infrastructure, which started with the first NDA government starting the Golden Quadrilateral Highway (GQ) project is well recognized. In that vein, on 15 August 2021, in his Independence Day speech, the prime minister announced that India would spend Rs 100 trillion ($1.33 trillion) through the Pradhan Mantri Gati Shakti National Plan to bring new employment opportunities for youth. Gati Shakti, goals are to reduce travel time and increase productivity of industries by helping India's local manufacturers to be globally competitive. But infrastructure, finance and other key reforms must go hand in hand.

In a country with poor infrastructure, normally Say's Law operates. Build a road, and commerce and business will follow. Das et al. (2019)[9] used the construction of India's Golden Quadrangle (GQ) central highway network, together with comprehensive loan data drawn from the RBI, to investigate the interaction between infrastructure development and financial sector depth. They identify a disproportionate increase in loan count and average loan size in districts along the GQ Highway network. Importantly, however, results are concentrated in districts with stronger initial financial development, suggesting that while financing does respond to large infrastructure investments and help spur real economic outcomes, initial financial sector development might play an important role in determining where real activity will grow.

Power generation and distribution is improving but distribution remains a big problem in India with state distribution companies (DISCOMs) in deep financial distress. The Institute of Energy Economics and Financial Analysis ascribes the problem to absence of competition, unsustainable cross-subsidies, economically inefficient tariff-setting processes, expensive thermal power purchase agreements (PPAs) and a lack of modern technology and infrastructure development which add to DISCOMs' losses.[10] But even as power availability improves, based on IEA reports, India's electricity prices are very reasonably low for consumers and provided free for the agricultural sector (figure 10.1), but remain amongst the highest in the world for producers (figure 10.2).[11] Electricity prices for consumers average $0.86/kWh or $86/MWh as against $117/MWh for industry.

This cross-subsidization is also a feature of rail tariffs in India, where passenger traffic is subsidized by high rail tariffs on commercial traffic. The National Transport Development Policy Committee (NTDPC) (2014) had noted that in several countries, passenger fares are either higher or almost equal to freight rates. However, in India, the ratio of passenger fare to freight rate is about 0.3. The Economic Survey of 2017-18 said the share of Indian Railways in freight movement has been declining primarily due to a non-competitive tariff structure.[12] According to the same survey, a set of measures are prioritizing investments in important areas, namely dedicated freight corridors, high-speed rail, high-capacity rolling stock, last-mile rail linkages, port connectivity and attracting private and foreign direct investment, but these will take time to show results.

Figure 10.1: India has low electricity prices for consumers

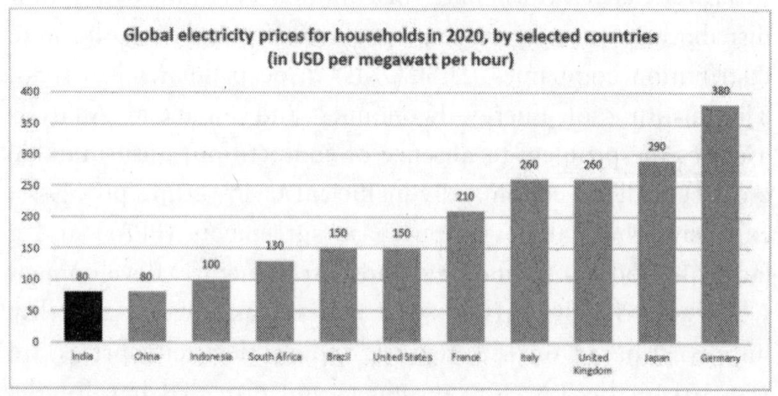

Source: *World Energy Prices*, IEA (2019).

Figure 10.2: But India has very high electricity prices for producers

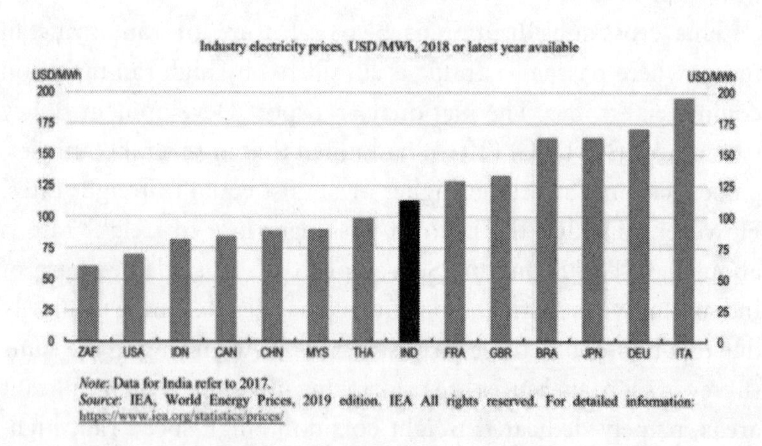

Source: *World Energy Prices*, IEA (2019).

Programmes like the Ujwal DISCOM Assurance Yojana (UDAY) were designed specifically to provide much-needed reforms, but while there was some initial success, the problems of DISCOMs have resurged—especially during the COVID-19 pandemic when electricity demand fell sharply, but guaranteed contracts with power generators had to be honoured. The 15th Finance Commission has provided incentive allocations to states to improve the functioning and finances of their DISCOMs. In its report, the 15th Finance Commission has allowed an additional borrowing limit of 0.05 per cent of gross state domestic product (GSDP) per cent for a state, for reduction in aggregate technical and commercial losses as per targets and another 0.05 per cent borrowing space for reduction in the energy cost-revenue gap. Also, the introduction of direct benefit transfers (DBTs) to all farmers in a state, in lieu of free electricity given to them, will entail an additional borrowing limit of 0.15 per cent. The government is also considering measures to reduce cross-subsidization of electricity between consumers and producers.

Figure 10.3: India's petrol prices are higher than other emerging economies

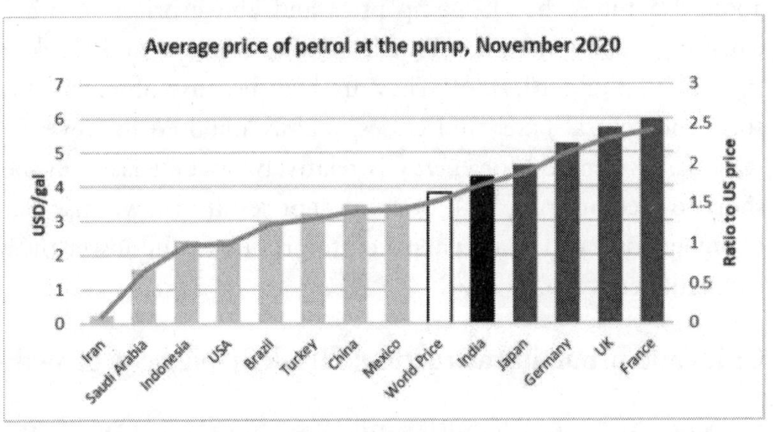

Source: 'Gasoline Prices', GlobalPetrolPrices.com (November 2020).

Figure 10.4: India's diesel prices are higher than other emerging economies

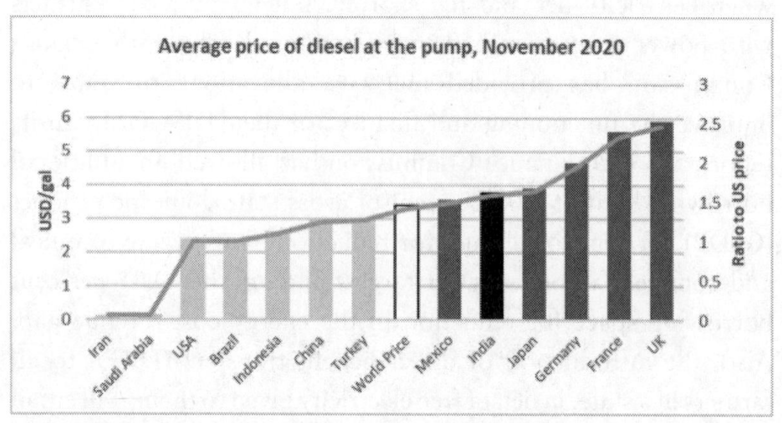

Source: 'Diesel Prices', GlobalPetrolPrices.com (November 2020).

Very high petrol and diesel prices also add to the cost of doing business in India and work against the development of the manufacturing sector, where energy needs are the highest. India's petrol and diesel prices are higher than average world prices, about 1.5 times the US pump price and above prices in other emerging economies like Brazil, China, Mexico and Turkey (figures 10.3 and 10.4).[13,14] They are high because of exorbitant state and central taxes and cesses, mainly imposed for revenue reasons. As demand for energy is relatively price-inelastic in the short to medium run, high prices do not result in lower use but in higher costs which are passed on to producers and lower their competitiveness.

Cities and urban infrastructure: Higgledy-piggledy growth

In combination with demography, urbanization will determine whether India prospers or not. Cities can be engines of growth, innovation and better living, but if not well planned, cities can breed greater inequality, insufferable air quality, huge waste of travel time and poor liveability. India's major cities, which are likely to generate GDP larger than many developing countries today, have developed in an unplanned manner and therefore score very poorly on liveability.

Urbanization also offers substantial opportunities to reduce poverty, in part because it is more cost-effective to meet many basic needs in cities than in rural areas. Providing electricity to the 200 million urban residents who currently lack access would require only $1.37 billion per year till 2045. Generating this electricity from low-carbon options (consistent with avoiding a 2°C temperature rise) would cost only 1 per cent more. This demonstrates that relatively small amounts of resources need to be mobilized to deliver basic services and infrastructure to the urban poor—an essential precursor to inclusive and sustained economic growth.[15] In many countries, migration to cities, even to the periphery in slums, has led to improvements in health and life expectancy as access to healthcare, water and electricity even in very rudimentary ways has improved livelihoods. But they remain cesspools of poverty and huge inequality, and more planned development and smarter cities could massively increase the benefits of urbanization for lives and livelihoods.

Oxford Economics' Global Cities Report estimates that seventeen of the twenty fastest-growing cities in the world between 2019 and 2035 will be in India.[16] By 2030, MGI projects that Mumbai will generate a GDP of $200 billion, Delhi $150 billion, Ahmedabad $95 billion, Hyderabad $82 billion, Bengaluru $70 billion—these are sizes of many developing countries today. But to make these cities more liveable and productive will be a major challenge. In 2019, New Delhi and Mumbai ranked a low 118th and 119th, respectively, on the Economist Intelligence Unit's Global Liveability Index 2019 that covered 140 cities.

Table 10.1: City centre floor area ratio (FAR) values in different cities

City	Floor area ratio (FAR)
Sao Paulo, Brazil	1.00
Mumbai, India	1.33
Chennai, India	1.50
Delhi, India	1.20–3.50
Amsterdam, The Netherlands	1.90
Venice, Italy	2.40
Paris, France	3.00
Shanghai, China	8.00
Vancouver, Canada	9.00
San Francisco, United States	9.00
Chicago, United States	12.00
Hong Kong, China	12.00
Los Angeles, United States	13.00
New York, United States	15.00
Denver, United States	17.00
Tokyo, Japan	20.00
Singapore	12.00–25.00

Source: *Urbanization beyond Municipal Boundaries: Nurturing Metropolitan Economies and Connecting Peri-Urban Areas in India*, World Bank (2013).[17]

On a visit to Singapore in 1973, Mrs Indira Gandhi was asked whether she was impressed by what she had seen, to which she reportedly responded, 'It's a city. We can build twenty of these anytime.' The reporter shot back, 'Madam, why don't you? It might transform the country.' But nothing changed as the votes were largely in the rural areas. India's cities grew in an unplanned manner until 2005, when a central flagship programme, the Jawaharlal Nehru National Urban Renewal Mission (JNNURM) was introduced to help guide and finance urban development. Since 2014, there has been an even greater focus on urban development; and JNNURM was renamed AMRUT (Atal Mission for Rejuvenation and Urban Transformation). This has been complemented by other programmes like the Smart Cities Programme, Swachh Bharat Mission and a revamped Pradhan Mantri Awas Yojana—Housing for All (PMAY-HFA), which was largely a rural programme earlier. But all these schemes, just like JNNURM, still reflect a very top-down approach to development. A Sagarmala scheme to build twenty cities (port-led development) along India's coastline has been on the anvil for some time now, but progress is slow.

India's third tier of government—the panchayats and urban local bodies (ULBs)—remain very weak, both in their capacity and in their finances. According to Kapoor and Sinha (2020), the Constitution allows eighteen functions to be devolved to ULBs, but this must be granted by states, who are reluctant to do so.[18] More than that, they can take away revenue-generating jurisdictions from municipal authorities by declaring them industrial townships. Municipal finance issues, which we discussed in Chapter 4, need urgent attention, particularly the issue of property taxation and user charges. India's actual urbanization is much larger than shown by census data, as many peri-urban areas are still run by panchayats so that they can remain classified as rural for tax purposes. But such structures do not allow for better professional management and they remain deprived of many services and facilities that an urban designation would provide them.

India's urban development is also very top-heavy. Based on the 2011 census, Class-I cities—those with populations of 1,00,000 and above—had only 26 per cent of the total national population in 1901 and 44.6 per cent in 1951, but now have 70.2 per cent of the population. Forty-two per cent of the urban population now lives in fifty-three cities with a population size above one million. The Indian urban system—in terms of distribution of population in different size-class of cities—has clearly become more unequal. The small and medium cities' share in total urban population has consistently declined over the years. Megacities have become congested, clogged and polluted, and also show significant social polarization. There is a gridlock situation for the cities, inhibiting their potential for becoming effective economic and social change sites. The top-heavy character of India's urban system also adversely impacts the balanced regional development of the country.[19]

Land-use regulations and transport infrastructure also have a major impact on whether cities are efficient and reduce disparities. Harari (2016) shows that the shape and spread of Indian cities are hugely impacted by factors such as floor area ratios (FARs) that discourage compactness, very odd for a country with high population density.[20] In India, over time, FARs have been reduced ostensibly to avoid congestion in the city centre and India now has the lowest FARs in the world (table 10.1), resulting in huge city sprawl and very un-Smart cities. The development and location of public transport—metros, bus lanes, etc.—also have a huge impact on mobility and spatial development. Some cities such as New York and Sao Paulo have used changes in FARs as an incentive for urban rejuvenation.

Mumbai municipality has also tried them but has done so in an unplanned manner, largely to raise revenue, resulting in further problems.[21] Besides FARs, examples of regulations that are impacting the effectiveness of urban development are the Urban Land Ceiling Act, which has been claimed to hinder intra-urban land consolidation; rent control provisions, which prevent redevelopment and renovation of older buildings; regulations hindering the conversion of land from one use to another; and, more generally, complex regulations and restrictions in central cities, as opposed to relative freedom outside the administrative boundaries of cities.[22] Many other aspects of efficiency are also affected by spatial development, such as delivery of services like water, electricity and sewage.

Akbar et al. (2018) find that there are huge variations in mobility speed across Indian cities. Megacities like Kolkata, Bengaluru, Hyderabad, Mumbai, Delhi and Chennai have very slow mobility—less than 15 miles (24 km) per hour—but so do much smaller cities like Varanasi, Patna, Gaya, Darbhanga and Ranchi.[23] This they attribute to the fact that uncongested mobility is a key factor determining speed in Indian cities—so speed is slow most of the time, not only at rush hour. In India, traffic moves slowly as there is very poor infrastructure and all forms of transportation coexist on the same road—from cycles, two-wheelers, cars, trucks, buses to push-carts/pull-carts, and stray dogs and cattle as well. Chandigarh, which has the best roads and fastest mobility has average speeds slower than Chicago, the slowest city in the US. There are no obviously good solutions other than building better public transport—metro, sky trains, bus lanes, etc.

Allow more local experimentation and strengthen state–Centre cooperation

What this and the previous chapter on labour have shown is that reforms of factor markets, the so-called second-generation reforms, especially labour and land, will not be easy, unlike the 1991 liberalization, which was mainly in product markets, where the reforms were relatively more straightforward and were mainly in areas under the jurisdiction of the Centre. India is now entering reforms that have concurrent jurisdiction. The states must also come on board and, in many cases, reforms must be applied and enacted to suit local conditions, where city mayors and councils must be engaged with. This does not mean that no national standards must be legislated. We don't want a race to the bottom, by competing states diluting land and labour laws to attract investments. But it may be better to enact broader laws which protect the interests of the exploited—however, enabling details may be left to state-level laws and regulations.

Similarly, in urban development and urban governance, reform is urgently needed. The urban land regulations and city zonal laws are counterproductive to India's future urban development. India's FAR must be increased to avoid urban sprawl and inefficient urbanization. The land laws, in general, now make land prohibitively expensive to acquire. Land-leasing may be a better way forward, where the land remains in the original owner's hands. India will have to allow more experimentation, which is best done by the states.

Chapter 4 also discussed the need for more empowered city governance—elected mayors—and with greater authority to raise local revenues through property taxes and user fees. India clearly needs to pay much greater attention to urban development. India will urbanize but if it wants to grow at 7-8 per cent, how its cities grow, how they deliver the benefits of agglomeration, how they take care of new entrants and whether they become centres of innovation or cesspools of social conflict, crime, bad air quality, sanitation and clogged traffic, will be determined by how aggressively and smartly India meets these challenges.

11

India's Financial Sector: A Whodunnit

If you owe the bank $100 that's your problem. If you owe the bank $100 million, that's the bank's problem.

—J. Paul Getty, American-British industrialist

India's financial system is in trouble, and unless it's fixed there is not a hope in hell it will become an economic powerhouse in the twenty-first century. It's like a patient with serious cardiac disease. At a minimum, it needs something akin to multiple bypass surgery but even simple angioplasty, to fully clean the clogged arteries, has not been performed.

The banking system, which is the heart of the financial system, has been weakened over the years. The cardiologists (regulatory bodies) overseeing this patient have been arguing for many years that India's financial system is fine because it has not suffered a cardiac arrest (a banking crisis). Individual banks have gone under, but they have typically been dealt with by merging them with another bank—the most recent, at the time of writing this, being the Laxmi Vilas Bank—merged with a subsidiary of DBS Bank in November 2020.

Multiple committees have been set up to improve the financial and banking systems, but their recommendations have been ignored or at best taken on piecemeal. Some minor reforms are undertaken—especially after another failure like the collapse of Infrastructure Leasing & Finance Services (IL&FS) Ltd or the exposure of a financial scam such as the Vijay Mallya or Nirav Modi scandals, but then inertia sets in. While the financial system has not suffered a fatal cardiac arrest—there has been no run on the banks—smaller heart attacks have occurred and been patched up. Rising NPAs are a sure sign of the growing disease. The NPAs have been there for some time, growing rapidly during India's credit boom of the 2003–08 high-growth period but then exploding after the 2009 financial crisis when India opened the credit spigots to help the economy recover.[1] Efforts to resolve them began after the passage of the Insolvency and Bankruptcy Code (IBC). But the decline was very slow and even that stalled after several court rulings weakened the process by stopping the takeover of the companies which were in default.

The government announced a large package termed Aatmanirbhar Bharat Abhiyan (Self Reliant India Mission) in 2020. Much of it provided relief through financial forbearance (including a hold on the IBC) and lowered interest rates. But subsequently, the budget for FY21-22, acknowledged substantial contingent liabilities—especially relating to the FCI and by doing so increased the fiscal support. A second package was announced in June 2021 to help companies deal with the economic impact of the second COVID-19 surge. The bulk of this is once again done through credit guarantees—especially directed this time to health- and tourism-related sectors. Whether the first round and subsequent financial forbearance will lead to larger NPAs remains to be seen.[2]

If you look deeper, India has been underserved by its financial system more fundamentally than just the issue of bad loans. India has the least efficient and the least inclusive financial system in the world as well. The intermediation cost—the difference between the average deposit rate and the average lending rate—of India's financial system, is over 500 basis points. The credit-to-GDP ratio, another indicator of a healthy financial system, has grown—but very slowly to reach 50 per cent in 2019 (figure 11.1)—much lower than the fast-growing economies of East Asia, where that ratio is well over 100 per cent.[3] India has opened new accounts for tens of millions under the Jan Dhan scheme but, on most usage indicators, India's financial system remains the least inclusive.

There is collective and accumulated responsibility for the mess the financial sector is in—from scam artists, populist and corrupt politicians, crony capitalists, supplicant bankers and unclear regulations, to a web of relationships between the Ministry of Finance and the RBI. It's an Agatha Christie whodunnit like the *Murder on the Orient Express*, where the famous detective Hercule Poirot discovers that everyone is to blame for the murder.[4]

Let us try and disentangle this web to understand the collectiveness of the crime—the victim is, of course, the taxpayer and the Indian economy.

Efficiency of India's financial system

The job of any financial system is to take deposits and efficiently transfer them to borrowers who can use these financial savings to generate economic activity, which creates jobs and improves people's livelihoods. Credit flow is like blood circulation in a human body, pumped by the heart to different parts of the body to sustain life and activity. How effectively it does that depends on the strength of the heart and clear pathways (arteries) to different parts of the body.

The banking system provides that same function for the economy. How efficiently does it do that? There are reams of reports on the Indian financial system and much technical jargon to analyse it, but some basic facts and figures, with some international comparisons, will tell us in simple and understandable terms how India's financial system performs. One basic measure for a financial system's effectiveness is the cost of banking intermediation, measured by the difference between the average lending rate and the average borrowing rate. On average globally, that difference is about 200–300 basis points, whereas in India it is over 500 basis points (table 11.1).

Table 11.1: Bank lending–deposit spread for select countries

Country	2014	2015	2016	2017
Argentina	4.3	3.7	7.0	9.7
Venezuela	2.5	4.5	5.7	6.3
Kenya	8.1	6.9	7.9	6.0
India	6.5	6.0	5.4	5.1
Singapore	5.2	5.2	5.2	5.1
Myanmar	5.0	5.0	5.0	5.0
Hong Kong SAR, China	5.0	5.0	5.0	5.0
Russia	5.1	6.5	5.6	4.7
Mexico	2.7	2.8	3.4	4.6
Indonesia	3.9	4.3	4.7	4.6
Bangladesh	3.1	3.5	4.2	3.9
Philippines	4.3	4.0	4.0	3.7

Country	2014	2015	2016	2017
Pakistan	4.5	4.2	3.9	3.7
Australia	3.0	3.3	3.3	3.2
South Africa	3.3	3.3	3.3	3.1
Thailand	3.2	3.3	3.2	3.1
Israel	3.1	3.0	2.9	3.0
China	2.9	2.9	2.9	2.9
Vietnam	3.2	2.3	2.2	2.6
Canada	2.5	2.7	2.6	2.6
Sri Lanka	0.3	1.0	3.4	2.6
South Korea	1.7	1.7	1.8	1.8
Malaysia	1.5	1.5	1.5	1.7
Japan	0.8	0.7	0.7	0.7

Source: Global Financial Development Database (October 2019).

Very few countries have an intermediation ratio higher than 500 basis points. Argentina, Kenya, Russia and Venezuela are in that group. Thailand, Indonesia, Bangladesh and Pakistan have intermediation costs in the range of 300–400 basis points—lower than India. China, Sri Lanka and Vietnam are in the range of 200–300 basis points, and Japan, Korea and Malaysia are the most efficient with intermediation costs under 200 basis points. Surprisingly, Singapore and Hong Kong have intermediation costs of 500 basis points. Nevertheless, within Asia, India has the most inefficient financial system and these costs are passed on to borrowers, reducing India's competitiveness.

This picture of India's banking sector does not show out so clearly when standard measures of productivity are employed. As Sengupta and Vardhan (2020) show, operating costs as a percentage of total income and average total assets—standard measures of the cost of intermediation—fell dramatically between 1991 and 2010 but have since started to show some increase.

They show through various measures such as comparison of loan borrowing rates and deposit rates with risk-free government yield and real employee compensation that the benefits of productivity improvements have not gone to borrowers, or depositors, or bank employees but has gone to shareholders—who have been forced to use it for provisioning of bad loans. But since 2015, due to stricter provisioning requirements, the size of NPAs has become so huge—especially for state banks that the government has been forced to inject large sums into PSBs.[5]

Figure 11.1: Credit-to-GDP growth: India and selected comparators

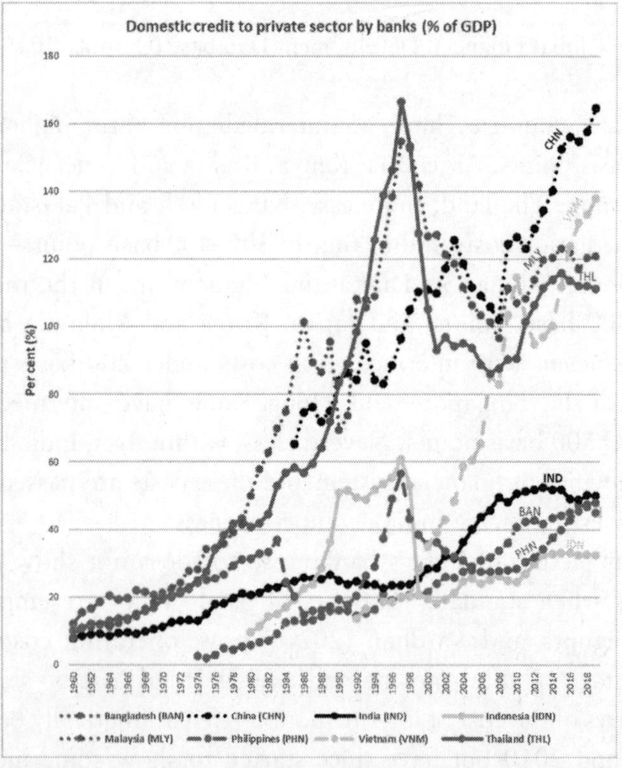

Source: *World Development Indicators*, World Bank (October 2020).

One would expect high NPAs if the banking system provides a lot of credit to the private sector. But despite all the pressures for directed lending and a huge unmet demand for credit, the amount of credit India's banking system provides to the private sector is relatively small. In 2019, the ratio of credit to the private sector by the banking system to GDP was only 50 per cent—similar to Bangladesh and to weaker economies in East Asia such as Indonesia and the Philippines, and much smaller than the rapidly growing economies of China, Malaysia, Thailand and Vietnam, where that ratio is well over 100 per cent of GDP and in the case of China, over 150 per cent of its huge GDP (figure 11.1). Not only is banking intermediation costly in India, but there is also, as a result, much less of it.

Why is India's banking system so inefficient?

There are at least four factors that explain why India's banking system is so inefficient.

- High NPAs
- Statutory liquidity requirements
- Directed lending requirements
- Inefficiencies in public sector banks (PSBs) and costs of financial inclusion directives

Rise in high non-performing assets

The issue of NPAs is not a new one. In the past, it was kept hidden. India nationalized a large part of its banking system in 1969. Since then, public sector banks (PSBs) have dominated Indian banking. Subsequently, private and foreign banks were allowed in—especially after India liberalized its economy in

1991 and grew so rapidly that by 2018-19, almost 40 per cent of gross advances were from private banks. In 2008, just before the global financial crisis, private banks had more NPAs than PSBs. Revealed NPAs in PSBs were surprisingly small. But once more stringent criteria were applied, especially after 2015, the hidden NPAs in PSBs were exposed (tables 11.2 and 11.3).

Part of the reason for large NPAs was directed lending. PSBs were required to lend 40 per cent of their total loans to the farm sector and to MSMEs. If farm debt got too high and farmer agitations began, mass loan waivers were introduced.[6] Pressure would also build up just before a major election to write down MSME loans. But a bigger part of the NPAs comes from connected or crony lending, which went to politically well-connected corporates. And when they were unable to pay, instead of their loans being declared NPAs, corporate debts were restructured, especially for well-connected crony capitalists. It was known as 'phone call' banking where a phone call from the finance ministry to the manager of the state bank called for a restructuring of loans to a major corporate, presumably with some payback to the party in power.

Once a PSB was in serious difficulties, it was either merged with a bigger PSB or fresh capital at taxpayers' expense was injected to reach capital adequacy requirements. Private banks did not suffer from these pressures. Things got worse after the global financial crisis: as India used fiscal and monetary stimuli to revive the economy, PSBs were instructed to lend heavily. These loans also formed a substantial part of the subsequent NPA problem. Raghuram Rajan, then governor of the RBI, called it 'riskless capitalism'[7] and Arvind Subramanian, the chief economic advisor, called it 'stigmatized capitalism'.[8] The NPAs contributed considerably to the high intermediation spread as banks were required to provision against these NPAs and these provisioning needs kept rising.

Table 11.2: NPAs in all commercial banks—public and private

Year (End March)	Gross NPAs as % of total assets	Gross NPAs as % of gross advances	Net NPAs as % of total assets	Net NPAs as % of net advances
Mar 2021		7.5		2.7
Sep 2020		9.3		3.7
Mar 2020		8.5		3.0
2018-19	5.6	9.1	2.1	3.66
2017-18	6.8	11.22	3.4	5.96
2016-17	5.6	9.34	3.1	5.34
2015-16	4.7	7.49	2.7	4.43
2014-15	2.7	4.27	2.5	2.38
2013-14	2.4	3.84	2.3	2.12
2012-13	2.0	3.25	2.0	1.68
2011-12	1.7	3.08	0.8	1.28
2010-11	1.4	2.45	0.6	0.98

Source: *RBI Financial Stability Reports.*

Table 11.3: NPAs in public sector banks

Year (End March)	Gross NPAs as % of total assets	Gross NPAs as % of gross advances	Net NPAs as % of total assets	Net NPAs as % of net advances
Mar 2021		9.5		4.8
Mar 2020		10.8		5.1
2018-19	7.3	11.6	2.8	4.81
2017-18	8.9	14.59	4.5	7.97

Year (End March)	Gross NPAs as % of total assets	Gross NPAs as % of gross advances	Net NPAs as % of total assets	Net NPAs as % of net advances
2016-17	7.0	11.68	3.9	6.89
2015-16	5.9	9.28	3.5	5.72
2014-15	3.2	4.95	1.8	2.92
2013-14	2.9	4.37	1.6	2.57
2012-13	2.4	3.62	1.3	2.01
2011-12	2.0	3.32	1.0	1.52
2010-11	1.4	2.44	0.7	1.09

Source: *RBI Financial Stability Reports.*

In 2015, the RBI persuaded the government to allow it to get tough with recalcitrant corporates. There was a moment, a fleeting one though, at the end of 2015, when we thought the system was seriously going to address the NPA problem. An IBC legislation was introduced in Parliament. At that stage, gross NPAs (GNPAs) were some Rs 4 trillion and net NPAs (NNPAs) were around Rs 2 trillion—provisioning was around Rs 2 trillion (tables 11.2 and 11.3). A strict regime of classification and provisioning was introduced, made even stricter in early 2018. The balance of power shifted from the borrowers to the bankers. India's 'riskless capitalism' now became risky. Corporate bosses could not borrow with impunity and faced the threat of losing their companies.

Harsh Vardhan (2021) argues that this pressure led to deleveraging by large corporations whose debt-equity ratio fell from over 0.25 in 2014 to under 0.20 by 2018.[9] Banks also became more risk-averse, and their risk-weighted assets dropped from over 70 per cent in 2014–17 to 65 per cent by 2019 and even further in 2020 and 2021. They shifted their lending to consumer lending and through non-banking financial companies

(NBFCs) at least until 2018 when the IL&FS crisis halted NBFC lending. The share of industry in bank credit fell from 43 per cent in 2011 to 31.4 per cent by 2020. Consumer loans rose from 18.7 per cent to 27.6 per cent.

The first round of resolution was started, especially in the steel sector, where valuations increased, and recovery rates were high. But the process was slow. The IBC was a good reform, but it was useful only for dealing with one-off bankruptcies. It was too slow to deal with systemic problems where large parts of the corporate sector and the banking system were in distress. For that, an asset resolution trust company was needed. But such an approach would require that the government put up the money to take these assets off the books of the banking system and park them in an asset resolution agency.*[10] Instead, the government doubled down to make the IBC process stronger. Stricter ordinances were brought in to strengthen the IBC process and a clever piece of financial engineering was used to recapitalize the state banks, without the cost showing on the fiscal balances of the government.[11] According to a World Bank assessment in 2018, before IBC, the time taken to resolve stressed loans was 4.3 years and the recovery rate was 26 per cent for financial creditors. Two years into IBC, this improved to 48 per cent recovery, which takes about 1–1.5 years through the IBC (79 resolution cases).

But as GNPAs rose above Rs 10 trillion (above 6 per cent of GDP and over 11 per cent over advances) and pressure began to build up in the system, also exacerbated by demonetization and global oversupply in some sectors such as steel, and overcapacity in some like the power sector, the cry for latitude went up again.

---

* In September 2021, the Cabinet approved the establishment of the National Asset Reconstruction Company Limited (NARCL) with a Rs 30,600 crore guarantee. https://www.thehindu.com/business/Economy/government-sets-up-bad-bank-to-clear-the-npa-mess/article36495756.ece

Corporate bosses (promoters) realized, for the first time, that they could lose their entire company or companies. Several went to court and, while initially, the court upheld IBC, subsequent rulings raised doubts on some interpretations of the act. For example, the Supreme Court ruled that the National Company Law Tribunal (NCLT) has jurisdiction to adjudicate disputes related solely to the insolvency of a corporate debtor and not beyond that. It also held up taking power companies into the resolution process. That fleeting moment when it looked like India might get serious about banking reform was lost.

With COVID-19, as the lockdown sent the economy off the cliff, the IBC has been shelved for at least one year and may never be the same again. And a much bigger stock of NPAs will emerge post-COVID-19. The *RBI Financial Stability Report* for 2020 estimates:

> Macro stress tests for credit risk indicate that the GNPA ratio of all SCBs may increase from 8.5 per cent in March 2020 to 12.5 per cent by March 2021 under the baseline scenario. If the macroeconomic environment worsens further, the ratio may escalate to 14.7 per cent under very severe stress.

But surprisingly, despite the pandemic, the GNPA ratio for all commercial banks declined from 8.5 in March 2020 to 7.5 in March 2021. It did rise for private commercial banks from 4.8 in March 2020 to 5.1 in March 2021 and also rose for foreign banks as one would expect during a pandemic. But for public sector banks it has fallen very drastically from 10.8 in March 2020 to 9.5 by March 2021. Some argue that the state banks, should be applauded for having made efforts to resolve bad loans through the IBC process more aggressively and through provisioning.

There is some evidence that some borrowers are taking on new loans with the government guarantees provided post-COVID-19 to pay back even back NPAs. Whichever of these is the right explanation needs to be assessed carefully. The RBI's ability to regulate and monitor state banks was compromised earlier and it would be a pity if we could end up back to the bad old days of Indian banking. The RBI's 2021 Financial Stability Report still shows that under extreme stress GNPAs for the system as a whole could rise to 11.8 in the future, down from its scenario projection of 14.8 per cent in the 2020 report. The share of large borrowers in the aggregate loan portfolio of State Banks stood at 52.7 per cent in March 2021, but they accounted for a share of 77.9 per cent of the total GNPAs—so they account for a larger part of the problem—not smaller borrowers.

Sane and Feibelbaum (2021) argue that the IBC process should be fixed to allow more restructurings—even by existing promoters if they bring in new capital.[12] They believe that the IBC process is much too fixated on resolution and liquidation rather than on restructuring. It had become a very mechanical process, with very little judicious and discretionary judgements on future viability of firms. As they say, 'bank employees—both public and private—are considered public servants under the Prevention of Corruption Act (POCA). As a result, they face perceived legal risks in the judgments they make about restructuring loans. In such a position, it is easier to mechanistically choose among bids rather than engage in complex negotiations with borrowers.'

The IBC no doubt needs improvement, but it's a useful mechanism for dealing with individual cases—not systemic problems which will require much more drastic and quicker methods—such as an asset resolution agency, to quickly clean up the large block of NPAs. Delay will be very costly for the post-pandemic recovery.

Statutory liquidity requirements (financial repression)

Fiscal dominance is the other reason why India's banking system is so inefficient. Financial repression—a method by which the government forces the financial system to finance its deficit—has a peculiarly Indian term called the statutory liquidity ratio (SLR). The SLR is the amount of its assets the banks are required to hold in liquid assets. Very conveniently, the government's security bonds were declared to be liquid assets, so a bank could meet SLR requirements by buying them.[13] The SLR rate[14] was around 20 per cent in 1949 but reached a peak of 38.25 per cent in 1992 and since then has been declining but remains at 18 per cent. Very few countries in the world have SLR requirements, and even in Bangladesh and Pakistan, which still maintain SLR requirements, they are lower than in India.

There is also a complex and nested relationship between the RBI and the government, which weakens the former's ability to supervise the banking system and carry out monetary policy. The RBI stopped buying government bonds in 1997 so that the automatic monetization of the deficit was curtailed. But the RBI remained the debt manager for the government, whereas in most countries, debt is managed by the finance ministry or by an independent debt office. The problem with having the RBI as the debt manager is that it sets up a conflict of interest for the RBI. Its primary mandate is to control inflation, for which it may need to keep interest rates high, but as debt manager it wants to keep interest rates low to sell government bonds.

These conflicts then create incentives for the RBI to force the banking system to hold government bonds—especially after it stopped buying government bonds. For this, the SLR is a useful tool and explains why SLR has remained so high for so long. Another cost of all this financial repression is that the development of the corporate bond market has been held back.[15] And it may also help explain why the government is reluctant to further privatize the banking system.

Directed lending

All commercial banks are required to lend 40 per cent to agriculture, exports and MSMEs. This directed lending ostensibly to priority sectors puts additional burden on the banking system. In 2015, not satisfied with these directives, a Micro Units Development and Refinance Agency Bank (or MUDRA Bank) was established to ensure more funding to microenterprises. Much of the initial advances were simply old loans which were reclassified as MUDRA loans. With the downturn due to COVID-19, almost all of it will have to be written down as a loss to the taxpayer. But the amounts are small compared to the large NPAs of the corporate borrowers. They nevertheless add considerable costs to the banking system. Until 2012, bank lending to NBFCs, which was on-lent to priority sectors, was counted as meeting part of that bank's priority-sector lending requirement. But that was stopped and added to the burden for banks to now compete with NBFCs for borrowers in priority sectors.

One reason for directed lending is to improve inclusion. But as NPAs in priority sectors have gone up, it is not clear that this is the best way to improve financial inclusion. In most countries, specialized banks or development finance institutions are created to cater to priority sectors. In no country do you find all commercial banks having to direct a part of their lending to priority sectors—at least not as high as 40 per cent of all lending. It would be better to designate one or two banks for this kind of priority lending and back them with fiscal support for subsidized lending and leave the remaining banks to do 'proper and fit' commercial banking. And NBFCs can play a much better role in reaching these priority sectors as they are closer to the ground and have much better information of the risks involved in such lending, and much lower transaction costs due to less burdensome regulations.

Inefficiencies in public sector banks and costs of financial inclusion directives

One of the most momentous decisions of India's move towards a socialistic economy was the nationalization of the banking system. A major reason why India nationalized its banking system in two phases in 1969 and 1980 was to direct lending to priority areas—agriculture, MSMEs and exports.[16] Other factors were that many banks were owned by corporate promoters who were usurping much of their lending towards their own companies. But this problem could have been resolved by forcing them to put limits on self-lending or by forcing corporate businesses to sell their banks to non-business owners, as is the case in the USA and UK. Instead, Prime Minister Indira Gandhi wanted to send a loud political signal of her government's socialistic orientation through bank nationalization.[17] Nationalization put over 90 per cent of India's banking system into state hands.

State banks have dominated Indian banking since 1969, when the first wave of nationalization was enacted, followed by a second round in 1980. By 1992, there were twenty-one state banks that controlled more than 90 per cent of Indian banking (in terms of deposits and loans). There is still considerable debate in India on whether nationalization was a good thing. Since the liberalization of the economy in 1991, private banks have been licensed and grown rapidly so that state banks now control 70 per cent of the banking system.

Until recently, when the BJP-led government announced its intention to sell two state banks, no major political party in India has ever been for the privatization of state banks. Private banks were licensed for the first time again after liberalization and several of them, such as HDFC (India's largest private bank), ICICI and IDFC, emerged from state-owned development finance institutions into banks. India today has twenty-two private sector banks. They grew rapidly, especially during India's high-growth period from 2000–12. State banks' shares in the market have gradually declined so that by 2019 they now have around a 40 per cent share of the Indian banking sector (about 63 per cent of deposits and 57 per cent of loans). These shares would have fallen further but all government deposits and those of state-owned entities must be kept in state banks. No state bank has been privatized but over time there has been de facto privatization of the Indian banking sector. Several sectors, such as airlines, telecommunications and retail banking, have been dominated by private banks.

Rising NPAs—especially in state banks—have resulted in reduced stock market valuations of state banks. One single private bank, HDFC, had a valuation larger than all state banks combined in 2019. There has been a growing clamour for reform and even privatization of state banks. Over the years, innumerable committees have been set up to reform the banking system but their implementation has been limited and spotty. The most comprehensive of these was the Narasimham Committee II report of 1998 which led to a wide set of recommendations on the role of the RBI, reform of the banking system and the role of state banks. Reforming state banks has been the most difficult aspect of these recommendations. Recently, the focus has been on mergers and consolidation. A Bank Business Bureau (BBB)[18] was set up to improve the selection of bank managers and monitor the progress of state banks—but its powers are limited and often overruled by the banking department of the finance ministry.

Facing mounting losses, India has been forced to recapitalize its state banks. A partial recapitalization was carried out in 2018 with a clever piece of financial engineering. Banks issued bonds, which were purchased by the government and used to recapitalize the banks themselves. This meant that the fiscal liability of the government was only the interest payment on these bonds—no market player was involved in this transaction. But in return, the state banks were asked to carry out some internal reforms, such as better credit controls and risk management to improve their efficiency. The government then announced a mega-merger of state banks and in 2020 reduced their number from twenty-one to twelve—but whether this merger will improve the efficiency of the banking system remains to be seen.

The Oriental Bank of Commerce and United Bank were merged with the Punjab National Bank (PNB) to create the country's largest state-run bank after State Bank of India (SBI). Similarly, Syndicate Bank was amalgamated with Canara Bank, and Andhra Bank and Corporation Bank merged into Union Bank. Also, Allahabad Bank was amalgamated with Indian Bank. But such mergers are not a serious reform, as merging weak banks with stronger banks often ends up weakening the entire banking system. There was an expectation that much of the money would go to stronger banks and the weakest ones would be shut down. Instead, a larger share went into the weaker banks.

Another source of transactional costs is the Jan Dhan scheme, by which state banks were forced to open accounts for the unbanked. Only 53 per cent of people aged fifteen and over had a bank account in 2014. Under the Jan Dhan scheme, this shot up to 80 per cent by 2017. These accounts, however, were not very active until recently. According to the World Bank's *Global Financial Inclusion Report* 2017,[19] 48 per cent of these had not made a deposit or withdrawal—amongst the highest percentages in the world; only 8 per cent had borrowed from a financial institution; and only 20 per cent had saved at a financial institution. These numbers have increased a bit after the government deposited small sums of money into the Jan Dhan accounts but even so their usage is low—partly because these are one-time transfers and some of them may be precautionary savings. Kale, Nageswaran and Bhandari (2021)[20] estimate that the share of bank account holders not using their accounts in the previous 3 months is down to 30 per cent—and these are prominently women, who are poor and under the age of thirty-five. They suggest improvements in the incentives and functioning of Banking Correspondents (individuals engaged by banks to serve the unbanked) to target greater usage among this group.

The RBI has started preparing a new Financial Inclusion Index (FI-Index). The index will be a single value between 0 and 100, where 0 represents complete financial exclusion and 100 shows full financial inclusion. And, it will have three broad parameters with weights—access (35 per cent), usage (45 per cent) and quality (20 per cent). The full details of this index are not yet available but a press release from the RBI states that the FI-Index for the period ended March 2021 was 53.9 as against 43.4 for the period ended March 2017, suggesting some improvement.[21]

Despite all these efforts by the government, financial inclusion remains low. Forcing state banks to open accounts for the unbanked increases their costs but does not genuinely increase financial usage. For many of these people, a postal bank would probably be a better solution, as access would be much easier. Mobile banking is another mechanism that has worked well in some developing countries. Forcing banks to open accounts is not the way forward. Neither is having all state banks pursue directed lending. The government is better off having one or two banks focus on specific sectors or establish development finance institutions for these purposes—not mess it up with state commercial banks.

Non-bank financial companies (NBFCs)

The NBFCs play an important role in the financial system as they often know the smaller borrowers better.[22] If you think of the banking system as the main blood vessels, i.e., they bring the blood into the heart and carry it out, the NBFCs are the smaller vessels and capillaries. They typically do not take deposits, but they can raise funds in the market, and they also borrow from banks to on-lend in the market. They are also much better at reaching the last-mile customer often not reached by banks, due to asymmetric information and the costs of reaching creditors with weaker financial assets. About half of their funding comes from banks, about one-quarter from mutual funds, another 20 per cent from insurance companies and the rest from deposits. NBFC lending accelerated in the decade 2004–14 when India grew at a rapid rate, but really took off at a tearing rate in 2015–18, when the banking sector lending ground to a halt as NPAs were revealed. In 2008, when total formal credit was Rs 30 trillion, the share of NBFCs was 12 per cent and by 2018, with total formal credit rising to Rs 118 trillion, the NBFC share had risen to 18 per cent. They were also a major supplier of retail credit to the MSME sector and played a key role in housing finance.

Table 11.4: Non-performing loans in NBFCs

Year	GNPA Ratio	NNPA Ratio
Mar-2015	4.1	2.5
Mar-2016	4.5	2.5
Mar-2017	6.1	4.4
Mar-2018	5.8	3.8
Mar-2019	6.1	3.3
Mar-2020	6.8	3.4
Mar-2021[32]	6.4	2.7

Source: *RBI Financial Stability Report*, 2021.

But that tearing growth came to a grinding halt with the collapse of IL&FS, a large NBFC mired in debt to the infrastructure sector, when it suffered a minor cardiac arrest—India's Lehman moment. It also exposed the weakness in the regulation of the NBFC sector by RBI, which, as supervisor, had allowed this very rapid growth, creating the conditions for NPA problems in the NBFCs. Their GNPAs, while rising, have remained lower than banks at around 6.8 per cent in March 2020 but, as with state banks, have surprisingly now fallen to 6.4 per cent in March 2021. Once again, this could be due to new government guaranteed loans being used to pay back old NPAs. The RBI has now required a 20 per cent liquidity credit requirement for NBFCs above Rs. 50 billion and enhanced supervision. But an asset quality review will be needed to decide which NBFCs should be allowed to continue.

This shadow banking is an important part of any growing financial system and provides an important source of funding to parts of the economy that banks do not service efficiently but clearly needs more attention and better supervision.

The role of the regulator

There are five regulatory bodies in the financial system in India. The dominant ones are RBI and SEBI for capital markets. There is also a regulator for insurance—Insurance Regulatory and Development Authority of India (IRDAI), one for pensions—Pensions Fund Regulatory and Development Authority (PFRDA), and another for commodity markets—Forward Markets Commission (FMC).

Of these, the relationship between the RBI and the government has been the most complicated and debated. There is a web of nested relationships between North Block (Ministry of Finance) and Mint Street (RBI), which has created huge conflicts of interest and needs to be untangled for a modern financial regulatory system. It has often been described as a traditional marriage between a husband (Ministry of Finance) and wife (RBI), and the government is the mother-in-law; where disputes are settled within the home, not in public; and there is no question of divorce. But recently the disputes have spilled out in the open and become more like a modern marriage and divorce as well.[23]

With the appointment of outside experts as RBI governors, there was increasing hope that gradually the RBI would be made more independent[24] but that hope has been belied and the RBI governorship has gone back to the bureaucracy. The establishment of a monetary policy committee (MPC) and inflation targeting was another signal of greater independence. But by keeping interest rates too high the MPC lost credibility with the business community, while it became the darling of the financial investors. India's economy, with a heavy weight of food and fuel inflation, driven by supply shocks, is in any case not suitable for inflation targeting and may have ended up doing more harm than good.

The relationship between the regulator RBI and the owner of state banks, i.e., the government, is complex. The RBI is the regulator of the banking system and approves the appointment of bank CEOs to ensure they are 'fit and proper'. It has often turned down CEOs for private banks—but for PSBs, those appointments are made by the Ministry of Finance. In general, the supervisory power of the RBI over state banks is diluted. RBI staff sit on the boards of PSBs, and RBI is thereby complicit in all their decisions, which it is supposed to supervise and regulate. RBI is the debt manager for the government, which complicates its monetary policy role.

Most other regulators are too weak or too compliant with the government. When the Life Insurance Corporation (LIC) was forced to take over the bankrupt IDBI bank, the regulator IRDAI did not even raise an objection. The FMC should, in any case, be merged with SEBI to avoid overlapping regulatory authority.

The way forward

Who is to blame for the mess? India now has the least efficient financial system in the world, and it is also amongst the least inclusive. India has, so far, avoided a financial collapse—but has come close to it. The large share of PSBs has meant that depositors have not been concerned that their banks will collapse. Despite very low deposit insurance,[25] there is no run-on weak banks as the public expects the government to cover the losses. Perhaps a collapse would have forced quicker reforms, as was the case in the Asian financial crisis or the Turkish crisis for those countries affected. But in India, despite rising NPAs, the problems have been largely swept under the rug.

As in the *Murder on the Orient Express*, everyone involved is to blame for the situation India finds its financial system in.

Some, such as former Deputy Governor of the RBI Viral Acharya, blame everything on the government—that fiscal dominance is the cause of all problems.[26] Others, such as former Chief Economic Advisor Arvind Subramanian, blame crony-capitalism—that India's 'stigmatized' capitalism is the cause of all problems. Yet, others blame populist politicians, who led to nationalization, and subsequent directed lending and forced financial inclusion initiatives such as Jan Dhan accounts, for the woes of the financial sector. A weak and compromised regulatory system—some might even call it regulatory capture—is also a contributor. Just because India escaped the Asian financial crisis and to a large extent the GFC, top regulators crowed that India's financial system was safe and sound. All these actors are collectively responsible for where things stand today.

Underlying governance is also a mismatch between assets and liabilities. India is trying to use banking deposits (typically short-term) to finance infrastructure projects or other industrial projects with longer gestation times. There is a mismatch. India must rely much more on bond issues for this type of financing. But as Vardhan (2021) points out over 85 per cent of bond issues are AA, whereas the average commercial borrower is rated BBB. He suggests a well-run, independent credit-enhancement institution to handle this problem. But how to run such an institution transparently and professionally will itself be a challenge in India.

The decision to allow corporates to own banks, as proposed by a recent RBI committee, is not the right way forward. Imagine Vijay Mallya, wilful defaulter, owning an entire bank. India will move from a corruption-ridden state banking sector to one in which the keys to the banking sector will be handed back to corporate houses to take deposits and do with them as they wish. India will then become a typical crony-capitalist country if it is not one already. We have seen this story before, during the run-up to the Great Depression in the 1920s—made famous in the movie *The Great Gatsby*—and in subsequent crises in many parts of the world including the Latin American debt crisis of the 1980s, the Asian financial crisis in 1997 and the Turkish banking crisis of 2001. It's a movie that ended badly. The decision to allow some large well-run NBFCs to be allowed full bank licences may be acceptable—if they are not owned by corporates. Instead of handing over the keys of the banking system to the corporate sector,[27] it would be better to focus on genuine and much-needed reforms.

The seven key elements of reform needed are:

1. **Reprivatization of the banking system:** After consolidation, India now has 12 PSBs—these could be reduced to at best four PSBs to ensure regional coverage and the remaining privatized. Two are slated for privatization and we will have to see how that process unfolds.
2. **Remove directed lending from commercial banks:** Establish or designate one or two banks to perform priority sector lending. For MSMEs, a MUDRA Bank to provide non-collateralized lending has already been set up and NBFCs are a major source of credit for MSMEs; their growth should be encouraged. Jan Dhan accounts could be transferred to the newly established Indian Post Payments Bank, a more suitable entity for such accounts than a scheduled commercial bank.
3. **Swift clean-up of the existing NPAs:** NPA resolution, now slated to rise to around 15 per cent of advances, should be swift. The IBC process was not designed for system-wide problems. An asset resolution agency will be needed to remove the NPAs from the banks for separate resolution.*[28]

* In September 2021 the government established the National Asset Reconstruction Company Limited (NARCL).

In any case, no privatization of PSBs will be possible without removing their NPAs. Promoters whose NPAs are transferred must lose their equity.

4. **RBI should be given full supervisory powers over all PSBs,** and they should not sit on the boards of these banks.
5. **The RBI should not be the debt manager for the government:** This function should be with a treasury department in the Ministry of Finance and removed from the RBI.
6. **SLR requirements should be eliminated** to encourage fiscal discipline. SLR requirements are a rarity and have been eliminated in most modern emerging economies. Such a move will also encourage the development of a corporate bond market.
7. **An asset quality review of the NBFCs** should be performed, weaker ones closed, and stronger ones encouraged, particularly for priority sectors such as housing, exports and MSMEs—especially as banks are released from directed lending requirements.

This will no doubt not be an easy reform. But without such sweeping reforms India will plod along and be stuck for a long time in the low-middle income category of countries.

Part IV

Re-engineering the Economy

12

Agriculture: A New Menu Needed

If agriculture fails, all else will fail.

—M.S. Swaminathan, Indian agricultural scientist

One of the late R.K. Laxman's best cartoons from the mid-1960s portrays a smiling food minister looking out of a window at a heavy monsoon downpour saying, 'This year we can tell the Americans to go to hell.' Fifty years ago, a good monsoon meant that that year, India was not dependent on food aid and would not have to go hat in hand to the Americans for food under the PL-480 programme. US President Lyndon Johnson held back PL-480 food shipments off the Bombay harbour until India toned down its criticism of US's Vietnam policy, and thus triggered India's desire to achieve food self-sufficiency. India responded to this by not only unleashing a green revolution and the PDS, but also setting up an elaborate system of grain procurement and buffer stocks at the FCI.

What a different world we are in today. Our agriculture is not as vulnerable to the monsoon, and we have mountains of grain—we maintain costly buffer stocks of more than twice our needs. But while India's food situation and the world have changed, our food and broader agricultural policy is stuck in a fifty-year-old mindset. And ultimately, the problems in the farm sector are tied to developments in the non-farm sector.

Back in the day, we set up the FCI to procure grain from farmers at prices set by the Commission for Agricultural Costs and Prices to encourage production, subsidized agricultural inputs such as fertilizer, pesticide, water and electricity, and provided cheap food to consumers through FPSs. This helped India get rid of its dependence on food aid, made it self-sufficient in grain production and brought about the Green Revolution. But today, our needs are different, and the world has moved on.

What India needs to do is to move a large share of its population out of dependence on farming. Today, India derives only 15 per cent of its GDP from agriculture but almost 40 per cent of its population remains dependent on farming—as against about 10 per cent in China and less than 1 per cent in the US. Nearly 61 per cent of the farmers surveyed said they would prefer to leave farming if they found employment in the city, according to a 2018 Centre for the Study of Developing Societies (CSDS) report. Over 45 years to 2016, according to the agricultural census, the average size of the Indian farm has shrunk by more than half—from 2.28 hectares to 1.08 hectares. Plus, of 146 million farms, nearly 100 million are marginal, or smaller than 1 hectare in size. At the state level, according to Rangarajan and Dev (2021) the average size of farm holdings in 2015-16 ranged from 3.62 hectares in Punjab, 2.73 in Rajasthan and 2.22 in Haryana to

0.75 in Tamil Nadu, 0.73 in Uttar Pradesh, 0.39 in Bihar and 0.18 in Kerala.[1]

Of the roughly 40 per cent population dependent on farming, more than 50 per cent do not even own land but work as labourers as they have nowhere else to go for work. A CSDS Lokniti study (2018) revealed that only 26 per cent of farmers would prefer to remain in farming.[2] More farmers prefer direct income support transferred to their bank accounts than even input subsidies—and only 8 per cent of the farmers feel their problems come from low prices. Almost 50 per cent feel their problems are linked to low productivity, lack of irrigation and poor institutional arrangements in agriculture. The Lewis model we discussed in Chapter 9, which predicts that rural wages will stagnate until surplus labour has been absorbed into non-farm occupations, has not materialized. This has forced the creation of a slew of inefficient subsidy programmes to help farmers and employment guarantee schemes which take up more funds than productivity-enhancing investments on irrigation, roads, electricity and R&D.

The government had promised a doubling of farmers' incomes by 2022. That was a stretch target and unlikely to be achieved in any case—even before the pandemic. What ails Indian farmers today is not just the need to move people out of the farm sector but also the need for a leap in productivity, a better crop mix to move to more in-demand products with more lucrative prices, much-improved farm-to-plate marketing chains, protection against climate change and new mechanisms for reducing risk and uncertainty.

Some key analytical constructs to understand agriculture

Much has been written about Indian agriculture and it can get into huge complexities. But to better understand the forest from the trees, so to speak, a few analytical constructs may be instructive to understand better the complexities of farm policy and its intended and often unintended consequences.

Figure 12.1 on agricultural supply response provides a simple construct to explain why farm pricing is very important and complex. If you want more supply along a supply curve S1 you need to raise farm prices. But if farm prices are raised too high, farm products become unaffordable. This brings in the critical role non-price factors play in balancing adequate returns to farmers with providing produce at affordable prices to consumers. In period 1 we have demand and supply balanced at price P1. But as the population expands and incomes rise, the demand for food shifts to D2. If supply does not increase, prices will rise to P2—this is the increase in prices farmers will need to increase supply. But at P2, food prices will rise to unaffordable levels. One option is to import more food. But that will require foreign exchange. The other option is to find ways to improve productivity—by which the supply shifts from S1 to S2 so that prices can go back to P1, and demand and supply have both increased. More farm products are being demanded and now produced at an affordable price.[3]

Supply shifts are caused by investments—these could be on-farm investments that improve productivity such as soil improvement, terracing, irrigation, or much broader collective investments—large irrigation projects, better seed varieties. The on-farm ones can be incentivized by higher prices but could also be due to better land titling, provision of cheaper credit and pricing of water and electricity. The much larger shifts typically come from public investments in irrigation, research and extension, rural electrification and connectivity. Rural roads play a role as well as they open new markets and IT connectivity increases information and knowledge of new farm practices, better information of markets, weather conditions and access to credit and inputs.

Figure 12.1: Agricultural supply response: Price and non-price factors

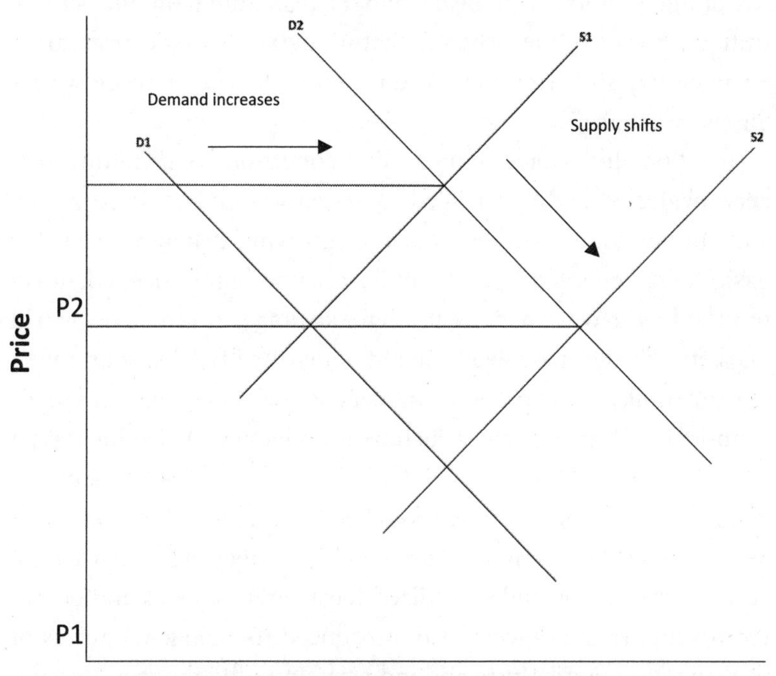

The bigger the supply shifts caused by investment and expenditure in irrigation, roads, electrification and new seed varieties, the more agricultural produce can be provided at affordable prices. If demand keeps increasing, then supply shifts are needed to keep farm prices affordable. This applies to any farm product but does not mean it must apply to every farm product. A country could have surpluses in some items and deficits in others, so trade can play a key role. India can export extra grains and import lentils or potatoes. But for key commodities that are needed, countries like to be self-sufficient in normal years and use some buffer stocks if the rainfall fails or a crop disease knocks out a part of the produce.

Forward markets also typically develop—these use private stocks to ensure farm products are provided at predetermined prices. Cropping patterns can also change, depending on the supply shifters. For example, when irrigation expands in a certain area, farmers may shift from less water-intensive crops to more water-intensive crops.

In 1965, India faced famine-like conditions. Agriculture had been neglected as India placed all its efforts on industrialization and supply could not keep up with growing demand—even for basic food items like cereals. India became highly dependent on food aid as it was short of foreign exchange to buy it on world markets. The US provided food aid under the PL-480 programme, but this rankled Indian policymakers as the US demanded India's support in return on issues such as the Vietnam War. This forced India to foster the Green Revolution, ironically, with heavy support from the US through the Rockefeller Foundation. India invested heavily as well in supply shifters, such as irrigation, high-yielding and rust-free seeds and subsidized fertilizer, pesticides and credit. Farm support prices were also introduced to change the terms of trade between agriculture and industry. Initially, the focus was on wheat, but subsequently, new high-yield rice varieties were also introduced.[4] Since irrigation was key to its success, the spread was uneven, with huge benefits to Punjab, Haryana and western Uttar Pradesh, where irrigation was well-developed.

Hayami and Ruttan (1971) attribute the slow diffusion of high-yielding seed varieties which would spur productivity shifts to the lack of suitable adaptations to local conditions.[5] When local research institutes were able to provide the necessary adaptation, diffusion accelerated. If irrigation is available, farms are of a certain size and innovations generate individual cash returns, then they are likely to get adopted quickly. Agarwal (1983) shows that diffusion of innovations in rural areas is more complex, and the type of innovation, and the social and economic characteristics that they are introduced into, determine the pace of adoption.[6]

Farm products are also sometimes subject to a cobweb cycle, where prices fluctuate sharply from one year to the next. Sugar cane, onions, potatoes, pulses, oilseeds as well as meat and poultry products are most susceptible to such cycles as their storage costs are high and trade is restricted. For an Indian diet, onions are very important and rising onion prices have been known to bring down governments, if they happen just before an election. A sudden drop in supply, say due to bad weather, can then increase prices, which then causes a sharp increase in production in the next crop cycle the following year, leading to a sharp price drop and the cycle goes on. These volatile farm price cycles discourage the production of those items and investment in their productivity. The 2019-20 Economic Survey shows how the cobweb model explains huge fluctuations in pulse prices between 2018 and 2019. Tomatoes, onions and potatoes (TOP) also go through periodic price fluctuations that would be explained by a cobweb model. According to an SBI Ecowrap report for 2017, tomato prices rise every 2.4 years, onions every 2 years, potatoes every 2.8 years, and they fall in subsequent years: a typical cobweb cycle.

Some price-stabilizing mechanisms are then needed. Forward markets play a stabilizing role, but even so farm prices are subject to greater volatility than non-farm prices. Trade can be a stabilizing force, so removing trade restrictions, which are common in agriculture, is another option; but arranging sudden imports of the volume India needs is not easy. In 2019, India had to arrange onion imports from Iran, but it took several months for supplies to arrive and abate the rise in prices.

One mechanism India developed to stabilize prices of cereals and some essential commodities for the farmer was the Bureau of Agricultural Costs and Prices whose main function is to establish minimum support prices (MSPs), and for the consumer the Essential Commodities Act, which includes cereals, potato, onion, pulses, oils and oilseeds, which are subject to trade and price regulations. In the past, MSP was set below the market price, but gradually—and partly under political pressure—a cost-plus concept developed by the Swaminathan Report came into being, with MSP set at 50 per cent over the cost of production. As a result, India's MSP now bears no relation to market prices or international prices. Between 2010-11 and 2013-14, international food prices were high, and MSP was below them, but since 2014-15, MSP for wheat is around 1.5 times international prices, and for barley and jowar, twice as high as international prices. Only for rice do we see some parity between the MSP and the international price, largely because international rice prices have not fallen as sharply as they have for wheat (figure 12.2).[7]

A third issue for farm products is the high costs of marketing. Farm products are perishable, not consistent in quality and shape, and provide a price premium for freshness. As a result, the supply chain from farm to plate can be costly. Mitra et al. (2018), using data from potato cultivation in West Bengal, show that regulations on packaging and processing, and marketing, can also add to these costs—so the plate-to-plough price differentials can be huge and cartels can develop that drive up the differential between consumer and producer prices.[8] RBI surveys in 2019 show that the share of farm price to retail price is about one-third in perishables like potatoes, onions and green chillies, to 75 per cent in non-perishables like soya beans, groundnuts and red chillies.[9] For rice it is about 50 per cent and for lentils, around 60 per cent. This does not factor in on-farm losses and transport losses to the mandis, which can be as high as 30 per cent.

Among the top three government policies that help farmers are, in that order, government procurement, readily available market information and denotification of crops from the Essential Commodities Act. Among the measures that might help realize better prices and make the right cropping decisions were more reliable weather information, better storage facilities, government advisory on crops and better market information (app-based). Econometric analysis carried out with the survey data showed that teledensity, all-weather roads and the number of markets per cropped area had a major effect in reducing retailer and trader margins. The online National Agriculture Market (eNAM) has been shown to help integrate onion markets in Maharashtra.[10]

Another way to reduce the bargaining power of buyers against farmers is to mobilize them into cooperatives. One instance where that worked well in India is the milk revolution that was pioneered by Dr Verghese Kurien—initially in Gujarat but one that has now spread to many parts of the country and made India the largest milk producer in the world. According to Hitesh Bhatt (2019) who now directs the Institute of Rural Management Anand (IRMA), founded by Dr Kurien, India largely depended on milk imports in the 1950. Operation Flood, begun in 1970, helped the country's milk production soar, providing livelihoods to millions of farmers through the cooperative model.[11]

The success of Operation Flood helped to make the associated brands into household names: Amul (Gujarat Cooperative Milk Marketing Federation), Verka (Punjab State Cooperative Milk Producers Federation Limited), Milma (Kerala Cooperative Milk Marketing Federation) and Nandini (Karnataka Milk Federation). According to the *Agriculture Skill Council of India* report, around 8.4 million small and marginal dairy farmers depend directly and indirectly on the dairy sector for their livelihood. From these, 71 per cent are women. Moreover, of the total workforce engaged in dairy activities, 92 per cent are from rural areas. Further, around 69 per cent of dairy workers belong to socially and economically disadvantaged communities.

Figure 12.2: India MSP and international prices for cereals 2020

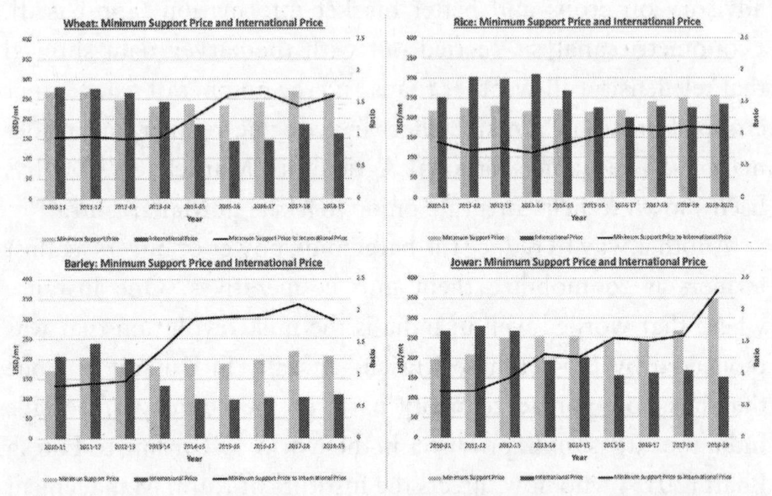

Source: *Agricultural Statistics at a Glance 2019*, Ministry of Agriculture and Farmer's Welfare, Government of India (2020).

State-sponsored cooperative farming has been tried in other agricultural commodities but in a half-hearted manner and often opposed by larger farmers. Singh (2017) explains how Charan Singh—who later became Prime Minister of India—opposed Jawahar Lal Nehru's ideas of joint and cooperative farming.[12] He felt copying Soviet-style cooperative farming could not work in India, where farmers were wedded to their soil. But as the White Revolution in milk shows, joint approaches, where farmers produce on their land but cooperate in marketing and supply chains, can also be made to work. There is now mounting evidence that well-designed joint farmer-producer organizations (FPOs) can be made to work.

If farm size is very small, and irrigation and other investments require a certain size, then group farming provides a better alternative to individual farms, especially for commercial farming, such as for fruits and vegetables (Agarwal 2020).[13] Rangarajan and Dev (2021) also argue that FPOs are the way forward.[14] They cite the work of Verma et al. (2020) for which farmers were surveyed in Maharashtra and Bihar (see table 12.1), where organically grown FPOs show huge increases in income and productivity.[15] Even promoted FPOs do much better than non-FPOs. India has only 10,000 FPOs but needs at least 1,00,000, and they should be encouraged and helped through credit, market knowledge and other inputs.

Table 12.1: Farmer-producer organizations

Benefits of joining FPOs: Maharashtra and Bihar						
	Changes in gross income (% respondents)			Changes in productivity (% respondents)		
	Increase	Decrease	No change	Increase	Decrease	No change
Promoted FPOs (PFPOs)	64	9	27	56	5	38
Organically evolved FPOs (OFPOs)	98	0	2	97	0	3
Non-FPO	32	34	34	29	40	32

Note: Sample: PFPOs = 303; OFPOs = 99; Non-member = 171.

Source: *Are Farmer Producer Organizations a Boon to Farmers? The Evidence from Bihar, India*, Verma et al. (2020).

Despite the Bali victory

That desire to not allow any outside power to interfere with its food security played itself out in the WTO discussions in Bali in 2014, where India rightly opposed a push by the US and others to limit the size of its food subsidy. The WTO system does not allow support for specific products but does not object to income support. India objected to these restrictions on its support through price supports. But having won that battle, India must now try and modernize its food security system for its own sake, rather than under pressure from the WTO.

India's food subsidy bill has risen considerably in the last few years because of open-ended grain purchases at high MSPs, large and costly stockholdings and a food distribution system riddled with inefficiencies and leakages. The government now buys a major share of the marketed grain: 50 per cent in the case of wheat and 40 per cent in the case of rice. It is now holding almost 80 million tonnes (Mt) of grain, more than twice the strategic buffer stock needed. The new National Food Security Act (NFSA) will expand the scope and coverage of the PDS. To understand the likely impact of the new act on the food subsidy bill and to deliver on its promise, it is important to understand the shortcomings of the existing PDS and its impact on the grain market and on the users of the system.

A 2018 study by the OECD and the Indian Council for Research on International Economic Relations (ICRIER) calculated a Producer Support Estimate (PSE), which measures the combined effect on farm income of all the subsidies provided through inputs and purchase prices but offsets them against all the controls on trade and prices that end up costing the farmer in lower income. They concluded that:

> On the one hand, restrictions stemming from agri-marketing regulations, together with export restrictions targeting several commodities, exert downward pressure on prices, with Indian farmers receiving prices lower than those prevailing in international markets across most commodities over the last two decades. On the other hand, there are programmes that provide huge subsidies for farm inputs, such as fertilizers, electricity, and irrigation water. These domestic and trade policies have combined to reduce Indian farm revenue by an estimated 5.7 per cent in the past three years—amounting to an 'implicit taxation' of about Rs 1.7 trillion per year. At the same time, funding for public services—such as physical infrastructure, inspection, research & development, and education and skills—that are essential to enable the long-term productivity and sustainability of the sector, has not kept pace.[16]

The study's conclusions are based on data until 2016 and, as we have shown in figure 12.2, MSPs have continued to rise whereas international prices have not increased as much and as a result, the farm PSE, if extended further, would not be as negative. Nevertheless, the important point is that this complex web of interventions has benefits to some parts of the farm sector but have huge negative effects on others. Larger farmers gain hugely as they get the bulk of the input subsidies and price support. There are also huge regional and state-wise disparities in the current system which need to be assessed and analysed.

Any reform of India's food policy must start at the consumer end. As far back as the early 1980s, Krishna and Chhibber (1983) showed that even then India's wheat procurement and distribution policy was badly flawed.[17] With memories of the bad years of the 1960s when US President Johnson held India to ransom over food aid, India was now holding too much in precautionary stocks at a high cost. In 2005, a careful evaluation of the PDS by National Council of Applied Economic Research (NCAER) concluded that, considering all the inefficiencies of the PDS, the Indian government spends Rs 3.65 to transfer Re 1 of real benefits to the poor. About 57 per cent of subsidized grains do not reach the target group, and a little over 36 per cent is siphoned off the supply chain. Implementation of the PDS is plagued by large errors of exclusion and inclusion and ghost cards. The PDS is a less efficient mode of income transfer. The economic costs of grains are higher than the market prices in most states. Only 23 per cent of sample FPSs are viable. The rest survive on leakages and diversions of subsidized grains.

After the Bali meeting, India had three options: continue with the current system but try to reduce leakages through e-monitoring, undertake comprehensive reforms by shifting entirely to DBTs and shrink the FCI into a tiny buffer-stockholding agency, or effect partial reforms by introducing DBTs in major urban areas and allowing private traders to purchase and supply grain to the FCI for the remaining requirements. A committee led by former minister Shanta Kumar in 2015 opted for partial reform but has gone further by suggesting revisions to the NFSA.[18] It makes five sensible and practical suggestions.

First, get the FCI out of the business of procurement in grain-surplus states like Punjab, Haryana, Madhya Pradesh, Chhattisgarh, Andhra Pradesh and Odisha, and shift its focus to eastern Uttar Pradesh, Bihar, Assam and West Bengal. The FCI can purchase grain above its NFSA needs from surplus states, but the actual purchasing should be handled by the states themselves.

Second, the report pushes for a national warehousing system under a PPP model to reduce wasteful storage and transport costs. Farmers can deposit their produce at these warehouses and receive up to 80 per cent of the MSP value of this produce from banks—and then sell it later at market prices. This will be a major improvement as it would reduce storage costs and wastage.

Third, the panel suggests that state bonuses, which are given on top of the centrally announced MSPs, be the responsibility of the states, and levies which states use to finance these bonuses be made uniform at 3 per cent. This would help avoid the costs of huge bonuses paid by the states and financed by the levies they charge the FCI to procure from their farmers.

Fourth, the panel moots shifting to cash payments for inputs like fertilizers, and rationalizing the price of urea so that the price distortion of nitrogen–phosphate–potassium (NPK) mix, caused by urea pricing, is reversed. Smuggling to neighbouring countries and other distortions caused by urea pricing would also be removed. Huge productive investments in the fertilizer sector are needed but have been held back by the absurd pricing system, which has made India even more dependent on fertilizer imports.

Fifth, the panel suggests amending the NFSA and reducing the subsidized population to 40 per cent instead of the current 67 per cent. It also suggests BPL consumers get more subsidized grain—7 kg instead of the current 5 kg—but that the issue price be linked to MSPs, except for the very poor. Further, in cities that have a population of more than one million, FPSs should be replaced by DBTs.

If implemented, these recommendations would provide more food for the poorest population, reduce FCI costs, bring private trade back into the system and give poor urban consumers greater choice in their food basket. It will hurt labour unions that are gaming the FCI system and states that use bonuses as a political handout, which they get the Centre to pay for through levies. This would hugely reduce the massive leakages and corruption in the food chain. If India can implement these reforms in the coming years, it would also avoid unnecessary battles at the WTO. But for now, these reforms have not been adopted.

Most countries that graduated from low-income to middle-income status shifted from 'product-based' subsidies to 'people-based' ones. This makes eminent sense. In a low-income country, when more than 50 per cent of the population is poor, cash transfers are infeasible and subsidies on products that form the bulk of the expenditure of the poor make sense. But as countries like India move to middle-income status, and the extremely poor population drops to about 20 per cent, DBTs are a preferred method of targeting. Mexico, where the cash transfer programmes originated, also had two separate schemes for consumers and farmers. PROGRESA, a conditional cash transfer (CCT) scheme, paid poor families but on the condition that their children attend school and are inoculated. PROCAMPO was designed to help small farmers and as a rural anti-poverty programme. Given the independently evaluated success of these schemes in helping reduce poverty, similar schemes were adopted in many Latin American countries, and have now spread to Turkey, Iran, West Asia as well as Africa.

In Asia, both Philippines and Indonesia have used cash transfer programmes. Mexico is now considering merging the two schemes to avoid double-dipping. It has long ago reformed and abolished CONASUPO, the equivalent of our FCI. Direct income support to farmers has also been found to improve land titling, increase farm investment and allow small farmers to adopt new crops and techniques more easily. Moving to 'people-based' subsidies translates to better targeting, as well as being less costly, with smaller leakages and corruption. They do not distort markets or encourage the wasteful use of scarce soil and water. New technology, wider financial access and Aadhaar help the process.

So, why all the farm protests?

In September 2020, India suddenly, passed three farm acts:

1. The Farmers' Produce Trade and Commerce (Promotion and Facilitation) Act, 2020
   - expands the scope of trade areas of farmers' produce from select areas to 'any place of production, collection, aggregation';
   - allows electronic trading and e-commerce of scheduled farmers' produce;
   - prohibits state governments from levying any market fee, cess or levy on farmers, traders and electronic trading platforms for the trade of farmers' produce conducted in an 'outside trade area'.

2. Farmers (Empowerment and Protection) Agreement on Price Assurance and Farm Services Act, 2020
   - provides a legal framework for farmers to enter pre-arranged contracts with buyers, including mention of pricing, and defines a dispute resolution mechanism, which requires farmers must go into arbitration and give up their right to go to court.

3. Essential Commodities (Amendment) Act, 2020
   - removes foodstuff such as cereals, pulses, potatoes, onions, edible oilseeds and oils from the list of essential commodities, removing stockholding limits on agricultural items produced by horticulture techniques except under 'extraordinary circumstances', and requires that imposition of any stock limit on agricultural produce only occur if there is a steep price rise.

One major worry of farmers in Punjab, Haryana and western Uttar Pradesh, where the wheat–rice–sugar combo prevails, is that the eventual intent is to abolish government markets where they get assured prices. The bigger worry of farmers—especially larger farmers with surpluses—is that the lucrative MSP system and FCI procurement will be reduced. Although MSP is not mentioned, the removal of cereals, pulses, potato, onions, edible oilseeds and oils from the Essential Commodities Act sends a signal that the MSP system may eventually be weakened or even removed entirely. A second big concern of the farmers is that a dispute resolution mechanism has been established under the farm laws that removes their right to go to court and this is done at the behest of corporate interests. The third worry, more from the perspective of state governments, is that the farm laws prescribe to states without adequate consultation with them on a subject which is under the 'concurrent' list in India's Constitution.

Figure 12.3: Trends in production of major crops in India (1950-51 to 2018-19)

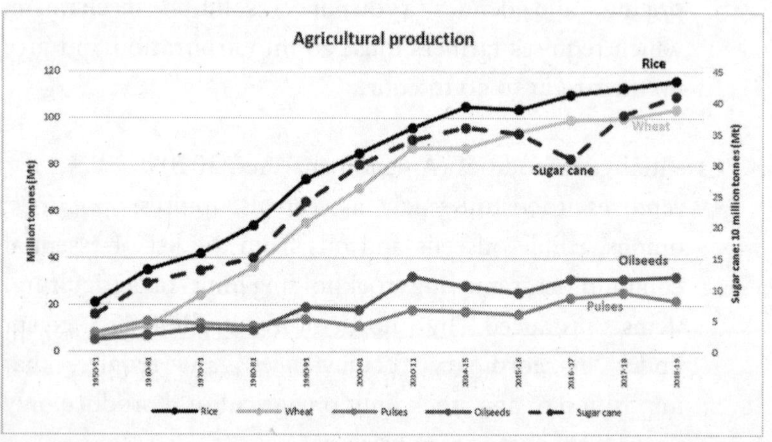

Source: *Agricultural Statistics at a Glance 2019*, Ministry of Agriculture and Farmer's Welfare, Government of India (2019).

Even though the farm bills do not mention MSP, this has become the main bone of contention, as they anticipate that the findings of the *Shanta Committee Report* will be brought in eventually. The most vocal opposition has come from Punjab and Haryana, where FCI procurement is highest and the mandi system is most prevalent. The Government of India has not only been forced to declare that it does not intend to change the MSP system, but it has also raised MSP for rabi crops—wheat to Rs 1,975 per quintal; barley to Rs 1,600; gram to Rs 5,100; mustard and rapeseed to Rs 4,650; lentils to Rs 5,100; and sunflower to Rs 5,327. Of these, the big-ticket item is wheat, the MSP of which has been increased from $250 to $260 a tonne, well above the international price of $175 in August 2020 (figure 12.2). At these prices, India cannot afford to even export the surplus grain procured as it would entail a huge loss. FCI stocks of wheat and rice are at their all-time highs. They peaked in June for wheat and in April for rice. In 2016, FCI stocks in the central pool in those months were 32.64 Mt for wheat and 22.16 Mt for rice. By 2018, they had risen to 43.57 Mt for wheat and 24.87 Mt for rice.

By 2020, despite COVID-19, FCI stocks ballooned to 55.83 Mt for wheat and 32.24 Mt for rice. This helps explain why the focus of the agitations is not just the change in the farm laws but is also to preserve this inefficient procurement system that is hugely lucrative to a few states. It ensures that India keeps producing larger and larger quantities of wheat, rice and sugar cane (figure 12.3), even in water-scarce areas like Punjab and Haryana, using up large quantities of scarce groundwater, encouraged by free electricity to pump water and assured procurement. Mihir Shah and P.S. Vijayshankar (2020),[19] point out that agriculture consumes about 90 per cent of India's water supply, and of this, 80 per cent is consumed by just three water-guzzling crops: rice, wheat and sugar cane. India's food demand patterns have changed—moving away from basic cereals to vegetables, fruit and lentils—and more land needs to be freed up for these. But this will not happen if the government keeps buying all the cereal surpluses at above 'world' prices and providing huge support to sugar cane farmers, especially in western Uttar Pradesh. India does need farm reforms—but these rushed-through farm laws will not do it.

Historical practices, notably the Green Revolution, prioritized the single objective to maximize production over other nutritional and environmental dimensions. Davis et al. (2021)[20] quantitatively assess outcomes of alternative production decisions across multiple objectives using India's rice-dominated monsoon cereal production as an example. They find that increasing the area under coarse cereals (i.e., millets, sorghum) improves nutritional supply (on average, +1 per cent to +5 per cent protein and +5 per cent to +49 per cent iron), increases climate resilience (1 per cent to 13 per cent fewer calories lost during an extreme dry year), and reduces greenhouse gases or GHGs (–2 per cent to –13 per cent) and demand for irrigation water (–3 per cent to –21 per cent) and energy (–2 per cent to –12 per cent) while maintaining calorie production and cropped area. But this shift is unlikely as returns to coarse cereals are lower than those for rice—unless farmers are disincentivized from producing rice.

Conclusion: A second green revolution

The 1991 reforms left out the farm sector. Agriculture remained shackled by a maze of controls and subsidies. Unlike South Korea, China, Thailand and, lately, Vietnam and Bangladesh, India was unable to move people out of farming to better-paid jobs in manufacturing. As a result, the share of agriculture in output has fallen to 15 per cent of GDP. But almost 40 per cent of the workforce still toils away in activities related to farming.[21] The average farm size in India is about 1 hectare, and 86 per cent of farms are less than 2 hectares, with limited surplus to sell. But even those that do, get squeezed by a controlled marketing system where traders often form cartels to squeeze farmers and ensure price information is not transparent. High mandi licence fees, an important source of revenue to state governments, also restrict the entry of new traders and keeps competition low.

India has been a global laggard in shifting to cash transfer programmes—DBTs—both on the consumer and producer side. It has introduced DBT for a few items like kerosene and gas, but has kept an inefficient, costly and corruption-ridden food subsidy system in place. On the production side, there is an equally wasteful input subsidy system for farmers—credit, and fertilizer, pesticide and electricity subsidies—that hurts agricultural productivity, benefits mostly larger farmers and accelerates soil degradation. To supply the wasteful food subsidy system, India has also interfered with farm prices through MSPs, and import and export controls, thereby hurting rather than helping farmers. It is now procuring and storing huge quantities of unused grain when the country should be shifting its cropping pattern towards lentils, vegetables, fruit and proteins. India is now spending close to 3 per cent of GDP on various subsidy schemes.

Some Indian states have pioneered farm-support schemes. Telangana's Rythu Bandhu scheme supports farmers to grow two crops a year, with a direct income payment of Rs 4,000 per acre for each crop—making a total payment of Rs 8,000 per acre for the year. But there is no independent evaluation of the scheme so far. Odisha is launching Krushak Assistance for Livelihood and Income Augmentation (KALIA) and provides support to small and marginal farmers as well as landless labour. PM Kisan targets some 120 million small and marginal farmers who have less than 2 hectares (about 5 acres) of landholding with a payment of Rs 6,000 a year as minimum income support—costing about 0.4 per cent of GDP. One criticism of PM Kisan is that it leaves out the landless. But instead of making the farmer scheme more complicated, it is best to strengthen the MGNREGA to help landless labour.

Expand PM Kisan and MGNREGA and reduce input subsidies such as free electricity and wasteful fertilizer subsidies that disproportionately benefit the larger farms. The shift to PM Kisan which is a broader production-based subsidy, could also be used to reduce MSPs for specific commodities. This shift could be designed to be budget neutral. It would enhance productivity, as farmers would be able to take greater risks in their crop-mix and would increase rural demand and thereby help recovery.

It would put more income in the hands of farmers and landless labour, boost rural demand and give farmers greater choice in cropping patterns. It would also ensure that less paddy and sugar cane are grown, especially in parts of the country where water is scarce. Groundwater depletion would be curtailed and land productivity would increase.

What India needs is a second green revolution. One of India's most respected agricultural experts, S.S. Johl, has been arguing for this for the last thirty years. His two seminal reports (Johl 1986; Johl 2002) laid out the case for such a revolution, but have largely been ignored.[22,23] He argued against the Swaminathan Committee formula of fixing MSP at 50 per cent above the cost of production.[24] Instead, he argued to encourage farmers, especially in Punjab and Haryana, to shift their crop production away from wheat and rice to fruits, vegetables, pulses and oilseeds, for which demand has been growing. Shifting Punjab and Haryana from the paddy–wheat cycle will also allow other states to increase their production of these items and increase incomes.

He argues that free electricity is destroying the water table; farmers should instead have the income support to pay for the electricity. Heavy fertilizer and pesticide use, combined with a lowered water table, have created a deadly cancer crisis in Punjab. Also, burning stubble to get in an early rice crop has contributed to massive air pollution in the northern Yamuna–Ganga plain and affected most major cities in northern India, including the capital New Delhi. India's heavy reliance on underground water—mainly through free electricity—has been in sharp contrast to China's strategy of water use in agriculture as brought out in Lele (2020).[25] Average farm size in China is even smaller than in India but have much higher levels of productivity.

One way to do this is to set up a system of incentives towards these crops and away from wheat and rice, whose production could be allowed to decline. Instead of increasing MSPs under pressure, the Government of India could increase payments under PM Kisan and an expanded MGNREGA. It should also improve the farm price information systems through mobile telephony and vital infrastructure for the food supply chain.

But ultimately, the bulk of India's population dependent on farming, who make up about 40 per cent of the population, are caught in a low-productivity trap in agriculture. Fifty-five per cent of these do not even own land and work as labourers. A few have benefited hugely from free electricity, no income tax, cheap fertilizer and assured MSPs in government mandis, but India's farming is in trouble. While the COVID-19 pandemic did not have a huge impact on agriculture, it needed a reset even before the pandemic struck. And the farm protests—the biggest in India's history—in response to laws hurriedly passed through Parliament during the pandemic, have exposed the vulnerability and fragility of India's farmers. Their solutions lie in a second green revolution on the farm and, for a vast majority, more employment in the non-farm sector.

13

Making in the Age of Machines

You cannot wait until a house burns down to buy fire insurance on it. We cannot wait until there are massive dislocations in our society to prepare for the Fourth Industrial Revolution.

—Robert J. Shiller, American economist

It could be a scene from a sci-fi thriller. A virus outbreak has separated people from each other. The fear of contracting the virus is keeping healthy members of a family from seeing their loved ones who are admitted in a hospital. Patients are too sick to operate phones and tablets. The fear of infection is such that even doctors and nurses minimize interaction with patients. A robot enters this desperate scene. Capable of speech and facial recognition and a tablet attached to its mid-section, the robot greets the patient and shares a pleasant surprise. On the tablet screen are comforting images of the patient's family members who are speaking words of love and encouragement.

This scene is not from a Steven Spielberg movie but from India.[1] A Bengaluru-based start-up, Invento Robotics, is the creator of Mitra, a 5-foot-tall robot who entertained Ivanka Trump during her visit to India in 2017. In fact, Prime Minister Modi launched Mitra during that visit. Mitra was not the only robot that came in handy during the pandemic. Robots helped perform elective surgeries, disinfect streets and clean buildings, among other activities.[2,3] Robots are part of a fast-emerging industrial revolution that is changing the global manufacturing landscape. So, is Mitra's story a foretelling of India's rise as a global manufacturing power? After missing the boat on labour-intensive manufacturing that propelled China and other East Asian countries to prosperity, will India do things differently at the advent of the Fourth Industrial Revolution? Will India be the twenty-first century's China?

The short answer is, 'The odds are against it.' However, it is not impossible, and we are still early into the twenty-first century. At the very least, India can do far better than it has. Of course, there is no birthright to good economic performance. At the height of the trade war between China and the US, there was a perception that China's loss would be India's gain. In 2019, India's commerce minister told Parliament: 'India can gain a lot from the manufacturing sector which moves out of China. We are focused on certain sectors that are looking to move out of China.' Such sentiments have also been voiced by independent observers. However, according to a recent report, 'China's share of global exports is actually rising, and is now even exceeding the level before the Sino–US trade war broke out in 2018.'[4] Moreover, of the companies that have been planning to shift their production outside China, India is not the destination of choice. Vietnam, Bangladesh and even African countries are vying for business. It is a competitive environment out there and those who prepare for it are likelier to succeed.

How China became a powerhouse

Manufacturing has long been viewed as a key driver of growth in developing countries. The pro-development characteristics of manufacturing stem from its unique ability (vis-à-vis other sectors) to absorb many unskilled workers, create capital inflows, cause spillover effects, etc. Export-oriented manufacturing has been instrumental in the economic growth of eastern and Southeast Asian countries. Globalization facilitated and accelerated China's growth as an industrial juggernaut. Along with globalization, unbundling of global supply/value chains played a hugely important role in this transformation. China was able to shift hundreds of millions of low-skilled workers from agriculture to manufacturing. India's transition was different, with the decline in the share of agriculture in the economic output being matched largely by an increase in the share of services. Manufacturing stagnated despite attempts by various governments to increase its share in the economy.

Figure 13.1: Comparing India and China

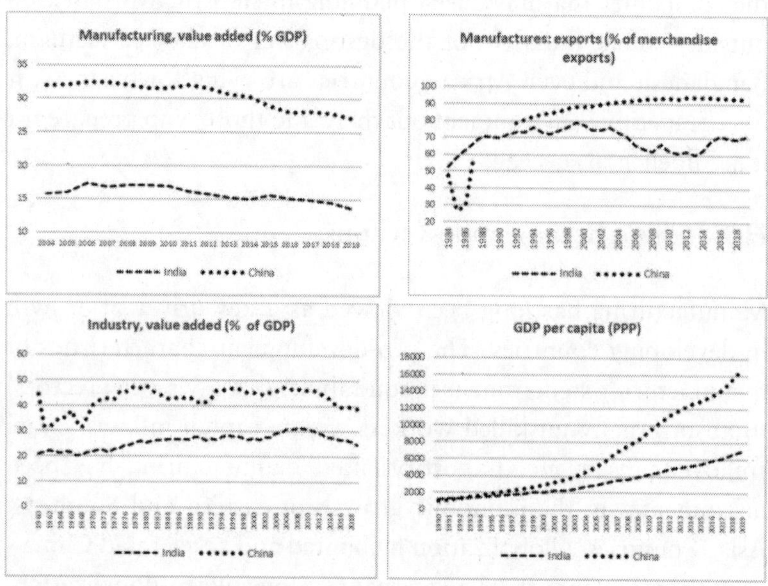

Source: *World Development Indicators*, World Bank.

After Mao's disastrous Great Leap Forward, China was an unlikely venue for one of the greatest transformations in human history. After all, China was a poor, agrarian country ruled by an authoritarian regime that had just presided over tens of millions of famine deaths.[5] In 1978, China's per capita income was lower than even India's meagre per capita income. China's population of about one billion people was 40 per cent more than that of India's. Mao had left a calamitous economic legacy. Low-quality industrial production and low-productivity agriculture were a hallmark of the economy. Tens of millions of people did not have enough to eat. Constant harassment of intellectuals left a legacy of antiquated science and technology. The educational system was in a shambles. Chinese society was 'embittered, exhausted and alienated'.[6] What unfolded next was an economic transformation that created jobs, reduced poverty, improved living standards and retooled China as a global economic power within just a few decades.

There are plenty of accounts of China's progress that benefit from hindsight. But what we found interesting is to go back to the time of China's transition to see what observers were saying then. Alexander Eckstein, an expert on China at the University of Michigan, predicted in his 1977 book *China's Economic Revolution*, that China would grow at 6 per cent per year for the rest of the twentieth century.[7] Eckstein died a year before the publication of his book. At that time, China was still recovering from Mao's cultural revolution and the Great Leap Forward. Eckstein felt that if China could avoid such mistakes, sustained 6 per cent per annum growth was possible. However, the changes that took place after Mao's (and Eckstein's) death appear to have taken China's development to an even higher trajectory than Eckstein had imagined.

One interesting account of the big changes taking place around the time Deng Xiaoping took the helm, comes via a 1984 essay by Donald Zagoria in *Foreign Affairs* magazine.[8] It abandoned Soviet-style centralized planning in favour of Chinese-style decentralization with a mix of socialist and market economics. Agricultural de-collectivization became a reality. Some private trade and commerce became legal. Light industries received an upgrade and the initial stages of a 'consumer revolution' were evident. The post-1978 period also saw a greater emphasis on education, especially in science and technology. Tens of thousands of students were sent to study abroad. There were many internal reforms, including in institutions of government as well as in the Chinese Communist Party, which saw a sort of professionalization at the time. Beyond internal reforms, there was an opening up to the outside world. The Chinese call it an 'open door' policy, a sharp departure from Mao's model of 'self-sufficiency'.

A more recent account of China's rapid rise comes from Yi Wen at the Federal Reserve Bank of St. Louis. Writing in 2016, three decades after Zagoria, Yi Wen argues that China had found the 'secret recipe' for an industrial revolution. This recipe, Yi argues, was not democracy or institutional development per se but a much humbler and gradualist approach to economic development that other industrial powers had also broadly followed. China's path was a sequence of steps that included ensuring political stability, bottom-up reforms such as those in agriculture rather than the financial sector, setting up small industries in rural areas, public and private ownership structures instead of wholesale privatization, enormous public infrastructure spending and progress along the industrial ladder, from light to heavy, and from labour- to capital-intensive. Over time, China has progressed from 'manufacturing to financial capitalism' and from 'a high-saving state to a consumeristic welfare state'.[9]

Yi notes that China was the world's leader in manufacturing in 2016. It produced nearly 50 per cent of the world's major industrial goods, including crude steel (800 per cent of the US level and 50 per cent of global supply); cement (60 per cent of the world's production); coal (50 per cent of the world's production); vehicles (more than 25 per cent of global supply); and industrial patent applications (about 150 per cent of the US level). China was also the world's largest producer of ships, high-speed trains, robots, tunnels, bridges, highways, chemical fibres, machine tools, computers, mobile phones, etc.[10] This success was not without hiccups. In fact, as Yi noted, China had tried (and failed) to industrialize several times before its ultimately successful bid in 1978. Even after 1978, there were many failures around the overall positive trajectory of China's manufacturing-led growth. Of course, the timing of China's opening coincided to some extent with the opening up of global trade. In fact, the changes in China helped lead to the kind of globalization that unfolded over the last few decades. China was a huge beneficiary of these changes, but it was also a catalyst for the transformation of the global economy.

Understanding China's rise is not simply about deriving lessons for India's future trajectory. After all, what worked for China fifty years back is unlikely to apply exactly to India today. However, glancing through history is of interest not merely for understanding what might have been but also to keep an eye out for opportunities when we least expect them. We should also not discount India's own efforts to improve its standing. India's economy today is twenty times bigger than it was in 1978 when China's transition began. That is no mean feat. However, it is only in relation to China and a few other countries that India's good progress pales in comparison. China's economy today is almost a hundred times bigger than it was in 1978. At this moment, it may seem inconceivable to us that India can catch up to China or become a manufacturing giant. However, remember China's situation of abject poverty and limited prospects in 1978. Things can change and usually do. But change is not automatic. India must put itself in a position to benefit from changes taking place in the world.

India's manufacturing story

With countries like China growing rapidly on the back of labour-intensive manufacturing, Indian policymakers have long felt the need to improve the share of manufacturing in the economy. The Manmohan Singh government enacted the National

Manufacturing Policy (NMP) in 2011. The NMP set a target of creating 100 million jobs in a decade and boosting the share of manufacturing to 25 per cent of GDP.[11] The Modi government not only reaffirmed such targets but promoted a sense of urgency in meeting them through the 'Make in India' initiative. By 2022, the government aimed to boost manufacturing's share in the economy to 25 per cent and add 100 million new jobs to the existing 50 million in this sector.[12] This target was later revised to 2025. This focus on manufacturing is part of mainstream thinking in India.

As part of a strategy to develop India as a manufacturing powerhouse, 'Make in India' pitched the country as an investment destination. The government took steps to help India improve its standing in the World Bank's ease of doing business rankings. FDI became 'First Develop India' and industrialists were urged to not leave India because of pressure from government agencies. The government expressed its intention to preserve investor capital, promote ease of doing business, implement easy and effective governance, develop a skilled labour force and invest in modern infrastructure. The goal was to make India the best investment destination in Asia.

It is undeniable that the 'Make in India' campaign attracted a lot of attention, both in India and abroad. However, it hasn't moved the needle much on manufacturing in India. Manufacturing value added as a per cent of GDP was only 13.6 in 2019, the third-lowest share since 1960. In fact, this share has never exceeded 18 per cent between 1960 and 2019. The COVID-19 pandemic may distort the shares of industry (and manufacturing), agriculture and services in total output in 2020. However, there is no reason to believe that the share of manufacturing in total output will rise in line with government targets. To understand why, we need to review both global trends as well as India-specific factors.

Figure 13.2: India faces premature deindustrialization

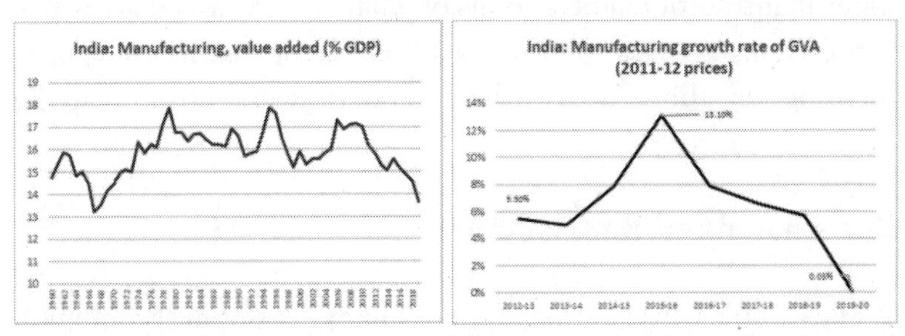

Sources: *World Development Indicators,* World Bank; National Statistical Office, Government of India.

India confronts what Dani Rodrik called 'premature deindustrialization' (figure 13.2). The phenomenon of deindustrialization is familiar to more advanced economies, where employment share of manufacturing has been on the decline for decades.[13] With the exception of some countries in Asia, low- and middle-income countries around the world have experienced 'falling manufacturing shares in both employment and real value added, especially since the 1980s'.[14] While industrialization peaked in western European countries at income levels of around $14,000 (in 1990 dollars), 'India and many sub-Saharan African countries appear to have reached their peak manufacturing employment shares at income levels of $700'.[15] This is not good news for poor countries, because industrialization is a key path to rapid growth and allows absorption of excess rural workers in urban factories where they may find more productive employment.[16]

Rodrik's findings found resonance in a 2017 World Bank report, which suggests that new technologies are reshaping the manufacturing landscape and that the old model that utilized low-wage labour may no longer be available to developing countries such as India.[17] This report argues that technologies such as 'advanced robotics, industrial automation and 3D printing are changing the landscape of global manufacturing'. The report also notes that traditional definitions of what constitutes an attractive manufacturing location are also changing with companies focusing on those areas where modern technologies can be better leveraged.[18]

But what about Bangladesh?

While Rodrik's observations apply to many developing economies, there are exceptions like Bangladesh and Vietnam. Manufacturing value added as a share of GDP is at an all-time high of 19 per cent in Bangladesh. In Vietnam, this share has gone from less than 13 per cent in 2010 to almost 16.5 per cent in 2019. Why do these countries not fit Rodrik's deindustrialization storyline? More importantly, what should India's strategy for the future be, given the jockeying for leadership of the Fourth Industrial Revolution?

Let's deal first with India's failure to boost manufacturing through initiatives such as 'Make in India'. Raghuram Rajan, the former governor of RBI, was an early critic of the initiative. Rajan argued that an incentive-driven, export-led growth or an import-substitution model was not appropriate for the times. He felt that global economic conditions were not very conducive to accommodating another 'export-led China'. Rajan also cautioned against 'picking a particular sector such as manufacturing for encouragement simply because it has worked well for China'. From his perspective, India is developing differently and at a different time than China and that 'we should be agnostic about what will work'.

Others were sceptical as well. *The Economist* magazine noted that while the government correctly argued for a skilled workforce, there was no vision for improving the underlying education sector. Similarly, while the need for improving infrastructure was clear and accepted in policy circles, there were no details about where the money would come from. Some argued that 'Make in India' was too ambitious. The growth rates needed to achieve the government's manufacturing targets would be in the 12–14 per cent range. Historically, India had not grown at that clip. The capabilities required for such growth appear to some observers to be beyond the implementation capacity of the government. Investment as a share of GDP has declined over the last several years with private investment doing worse than government investment. The Index of Industrial Production (IIP) tells its own sorry tale. From April 2012 to October 2020, there was only one month in which the IIP grew by double digits. Also, by targeting too many sectors, the initiative lost focus and neglected to focus on India's comparative advantages.[19]

Let's now turn to Bangladesh. In 2013, a Dhaka factory collapse killed over 1,100 workers, mostly women. The Rana Plaza disaster shook Bangladesh, its garment industry and their clients worldwide. A global campaign in support of workers and their safety ensued. Since then, wages have improved, as has safety. Bangladesh is now second only to China in garment exports. Its 4,500 garment export factories employ nearly 4.5 million workers.[20] Before that disaster, Bangladesh was already amid a transformation that helped the country snag low-value-added manufacturing business from China. It now exports $34 billion worth of apparel annually. The manufacturing sector has helped Bangladesh grow at a healthy rate in recent years. Its per capita income tripled in the decade since 2009, overtaking Pakistan and within striking distance of India. Extreme poverty ($1.25/day) was more than halved from 19 per cent to 9 per cent. Exports soared by 15–17 per cent and despite COVID-19, the country grew by 3.8 per cent in 2020, among the best in Asia.

There is no one factor behind Bangladesh's success. While GDP growth has increased fast, population growth has been much slower than in Pakistan and India. That means its per capita income growth is more rapid. Economist Kaushik Basu attributes this success to factors such as women's empowerment as well as the government's efforts towards grassroots economic inclusion. A focus on social indicators has helped improve children's health and education, and raised the average life expectancy to seventy-two years, higher than in India and Pakistan. Basu also notes the role of the garment industry in Bangladesh's success.

An ingredient in this success has been more flexible labour laws that have allowed firms to grow bigger in size than in India. The ability to contract labour and expand the workforce has enabled garment firms to become bigger and employ many more workers, most of them being women.[21] This has boosted female labour participation in ways not seen in India (figure 13.3). According to ILO estimates, the female LFPR in Bangladesh is 50 per cent higher than in India. What appears to have helped Bangladesh is a combination of globalization, rising wages in China and strong consumer demand for apparel. It also appears that Bangladesh's commitment to the apparel industry as the lynchpin of its manufacturing strategy succeeded because it played to the country's advantages.

Figure 13.3: Bangladesh outperforms India on manufacturing and female LFPR

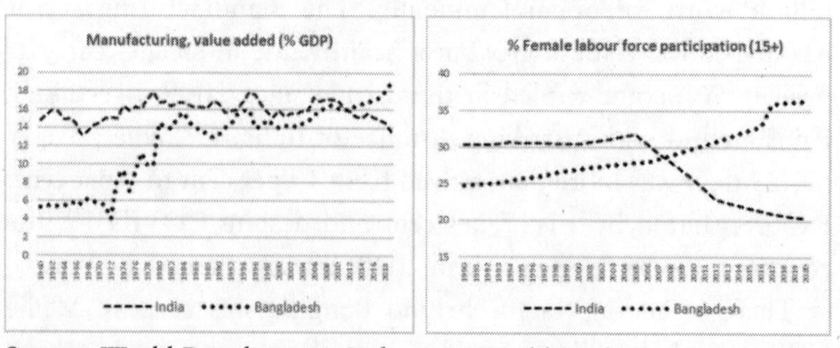

Source: *World Development Indicators*, World Bank.

Having said that, Bangladesh is discovering that it needs to keep up with the times to stave off competition from other countries, such as Vietnam and Ethiopia. Continued reliance on low-value-added manufacturing will not be a sustainable strategy. Furthermore, a regulatory environment that stifles businesses will hinder investments. Bangladesh cannot afford to sit on its garment industry laurels. It has to adapt to changing times and it appears to be doing so with a strategy focused on expanding special economic zones that leverage the country's population density and works within the constraints imposed by scarce land resources.[22]

What India must do

India must assess its situation carefully. New technologies are likely to revolutionize production. At the same time, there is a chance that the world will become more unequal as advanced countries corner a larger share of production. For India to make meaningful progress, especially as it relates to creating opportunities for young people, technology and innovation will be the key. We must remember that India needs to create at least 90 million non-farm jobs by 2030.[23] A burgeoning youth population that is turfed out of decent job opportunities by rapidly evolving technologies is going to be hugely problematic. But innovation, and the adoption of modern technologies, could also help India benefit from the vast opportunities that technological disruption has to offer.

For India to compete for a bigger share of the Fourth Industrial Revolution, there is a need to develop a long-term strategy. There is plenty of knowledge already about what the world might look like in the next thirty to fifty years. Global trends indicate a clear movement towards automation and machine learning, greater use of robotics and 3D printing and much greater reliance on data analytics and networking. For now, India is not prepared to benefit from a future defined by these trends. However, this should not condemn India to the status of an also-ran in the modern manufacturing race. After all, India has shown the capacity to compete with the best in the world in some key sectors. For example, in the last fifteen years, India has emerged as one of the biggest auto manufacturers in the world. In 2019, India produced 4.5 million vehicles, taking the fifth spot behind Germany in the global league tables.[24] This rise is despite poor infrastructure, limited connections to global value chains (GVCs) and a stifling regulatory environment. Imagine how much better India can do if the enabling environment is world class.

It is also important to keep an eye on the competition and understand what might be making others successful. China is now the world's biggest automobile manufacturer, producing 25.7 million vehicles in 2019. This shows how much further India must go in terms of competing in this sector. The other interesting aspect is that of the types of vehicles being made. Climate change is already leading to the production of more electric vehicles (EVs). In 2019, 2.1 million EVs were produced worldwide. EV sales accounted for 2.6 per cent of the total. The stock of EVs went up by 40 per cent in 2019 relative to 2018. We know what the trend is and so do other countries. Already, China, Europe and the US are dominating the EV market. China is not only producing EVs but is also deploying them. Between 2015 and 2019, China registered 4,97,000 electric buses. India has registered electric buses in the hundreds.[25] China is in a win-win situation. Of course, China is not alone. Many countries are pursuing their Fourth Industrial Revolution dreams.

The auto industry example is simply a way of suggesting that India may be in danger of ceding modern manufacturing space to others even before the competition has started. A concerted effort with a bold vision for the future and an actionable plan and an enabling environment are required if India wants to be among the best in the world. The other cautionary tale is that India should not take for granted that rising wages in China will necessarily force low-value-added manufacturing to shift to other countries. China has been using automation/robotization to address declining wage competitiveness.[26] While it may make sense for poorer countries to specialize in industries that can employ vast numbers of low-skilled and low-wage workers, more advanced economies could blunt that advantage by using robots as complements to more skilled labour.[27]

It is unlikely that India can reverse decades of stagnation in the manufacturing sector by following one specific path. More likely, a lot of things must happen simultaneously. Policymakers must focus on raising India's labour and capital productivity. India currently falls well behind global levels of productivity and competitiveness. Focusing on specific sectors may help.[28] Some economists argue that India should improve its competitiveness in its traditional areas of strength such as textiles, apparel and leather. Interestingly, they also point to the opportunity of 'servicification' of manufacturing. This basically means that manufacturing is not just about production but also about services that accompany manufactured products. Conceptual design, product strategy, sales and marketing and after-sales service is what servicification is about. India's services sector is already fairly large. It wouldn't be a big leap to adapt its service culture to the servicification model.

Another key opportunity is to think about investments that can target multiple long-term goals simultaneously. To illustrate this idea, let us think of mobility and climate change. India currently has a much smaller domestic market for vehicles than China does. As the economy grows, people will buy more vehicles and more vehicles on the roads will have implications for greenhouse gas (GHG) emissions, pollution and health. Investing in cleaner vehicles, building up the enabling infrastructure, developing new supply and service chains and getting people to move more efficiently can help reduce some of the adverse impacts of climate change. Reducing the country's infrastructure deficit can also be done in a way that maximizes the use of modern technologies. Clean energy investments will help reduce power shortages while keeping emissions low and improve the ability of businesses to compete with their international peers. These types of win-win solutions need to be built into the financial calculus of future investments.

Beyond hard investments, India must revamp its R&D capabilities. For now, India is just not spending enough on R&D to be competitive in a future that will be defined overwhelmingly by science and technology. After hitting a peak of 0.86 per cent of GDP, India's R&D expenditure has consistently declined to about 0.65 per cent of GDP in 2018. China spends 2.2 and the US 2.8 per cent of GDP (figure 13.4).[29] India's situation is also reflected in the number of patent applications filed by leading powers like the US and China. Quite simply, India is not in their league right now. The gap between India and other powers has been increasing and differences accumulate over time. If things do not change, there is simply no way for India to be able to compete. Without a greater commitment to R&D, including by the private sector, Indian manufacturing will remain a marginal player.

Figure 13.4: Patent applications and R&D expenditure—India, China and the US

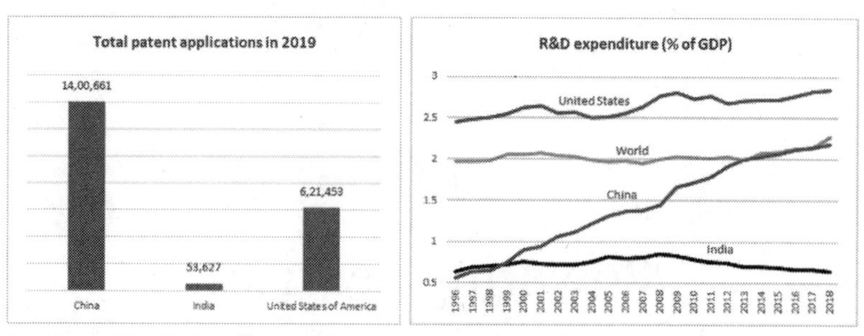

Sources: World Intellectual Property Organization; *World Development Indicators*, World Bank.

Finally, we go back to a constant theme—investment in human capital. For any country to do well in modern manufacturing, the labour force will have to move up the value chain. That means a much greater focus on education, especially early childhood education. It also means improved child health and nutrition and nurturing through the early years. We have discussed these topics in other chapters in this book. However, we keep talking about human capital because this topic does not receive the attention it deserves. If India wants to be a manufacturing power, it has to help children grow up healthy and get an education that prepares them for an uncertain future. Without that investment, there can be no transformation and the Fourth Industrial Revolution will pass India by and the gap with the world's economic powers will grow. Who wants that?

14
Powering Services

Nothing wilts faster than laurels that have been rested upon.

—Percy Bysshe Shelley, English poet

With an abundance of engineers and entrepreneurs, Bengaluru exemplifies twenty-first-century India's rising aspirations and economic growth. It is here that home-grown heavyweight firms like Wipro and Infosys made their fortunes selling IT and business services to clients around the world and, more recently, new-age unicorn start-ups (billion-dollar start-ups) like Ola and Flipkart have set up shop and thrived. The success of Bengaluru's IT services is synonymous with the rapid growth of India's services sector, particularly after liberalization unleashed parts of the Indian economy in the 1990s.

Today, India's services sector is the biggest contributor to India's GDP—more than the manufacturing and agriculture sectors combined. It accounts for two-thirds of FDI inflows into

India and 38 per cent of exports.[1] While agriculture and industry, especially manufacturing, garner disproportionate policy support and public attention, it is services that have powered India's growth in the last three decades. Whereas countries like China grew in a 'conventional' manner, leveraging labour-intensive manufacturing, India took an unconventional path, riding a services revolution to growth and poverty reduction.

India's premature deindustrialization has caused much grief to policymakers. Many efforts to boost India's industrial sector have come and gone but with little success. Meanwhile, the services sector has grown considerably, absorbed labour shed by agriculture and manufacturing, and bought time for policymakers to rethink India's growth model. One reason for India's relative success in services is a smaller productivity gap compared with other countries relative to gaps in agriculture and manufacturing. Some point to historical reasons for this lower productivity gap in services, going back to colonial times when a focus on higher education as opposed to primary education developed a small core of highly educated workers who worked primarily in service sectors.[2] That is no longer a sustainable path for India.

Policymakers must not take the contributions of the services sector to India's economic growth for granted. Slow growth and multiple challenges confront the sector. Competition is growing, the global trade environment is uncertain and technology is roiling the labour market. Even in India's vaunted IT sector, a third of its jobs could become irrelevant in the next few years.[3] Beyond these threats, India's services-led growth has failed to solve problems critical to inclusive economic development—the need for creating new jobs at a scale comparable to what manufacturing did for China. There is much for Indian policymakers to immediately contend with and reform, if India is to continue to rely on services as a primary engine of growth. For India to achieve its aspirations of becoming an economic powerhouse, policies must help maintain and expand the competitiveness and inclusiveness of India's services.

To see how India's distinctive services-led growth can flourish, it is necessary to unpack this sprawling sector and zero in on its successes and shortcomings. With that understanding, there will be opportunities to recommend reforms to maximize this sector's impact on India's twenty-first-century aspirations.

Services as a powerful engine of growth

The services sector is vast, heterogeneous and complex. The characteristics of economic agents, products produced, applicable policies and value added are incredibly varied. The Indian government identifies IT-business process outsourcing (BPO), aviation, telecom, tourism, shipping and ports as key subsectors in its Economic Survey 2020-21. Beyond these, construction, hospitality (restaurants and hotels), storage, wholesale and retail trade, communication and broadcasting, financial services, education and healthcare are also a part of the service economy. For all practical purposes, any economic activity that does not produce a tangible good and is not agricultural, is a part of the services sector.

Economists and policymakers have spent decades debating the formula for economic growth. The most repeated mantra is that export-oriented manufacturing is central and essential to growth—a silver bullet for poverty, joblessness and structural transformation in the style of China, South Korea, Taiwan and others.[4] Not just in economic and development circles, but in living rooms, people discuss the well-executed manufacturing-led East Asian growth story as a blueprint for India and other countries.

It may come as a surprise to many that services account for two-thirds of the global economic output, two-thirds of FDI, two-thirds of jobs in developing countries and four-fifths of jobs in the advanced economies.[5] Services are also the biggest growth sector for global trade. Since 2008, goods trade increased at an annual rate of 3 per cent while trade in services grew at over 5 per cent. No wonder then that the share of services in global trade has grown from 9 per cent in 1970 to 20 per cent today and could grow to 30 per cent by 2030.[6] While many predict a slowdown in global trade in the aftermath of the COVID-19 pandemic, it is entirely possible that the share of services in overall trade will continue to grow. This has huge implications for countries like India where the service sectors are dominant.

India's services-led growth has defied linear growth theories. Instead of the predicted shift from agriculture to industry to services, India transformed structurally from a predominantly agrarian to a predominantly service-oriented economy. While higher growth in the economic productivity of services vis-à-vis the productivity of manufacturing is the general norm in developed economies, this has been rare in emerging markets.[7] Service-led growth like India's has also been observed in Africa's fast-growing economies—the Lions of Africa—Ethiopia, Ghana, Kenya, Mozambique, Nigeria, Uganda and South Africa. This has led to some economists theorizing that service-led growth is a characteristic of 'latecomers to development' who have found a 'new boat' for rapid development.[8]

Figure 14.1: A comparison of the value added to India's GDP by services, industry and agriculture (1960–2019)

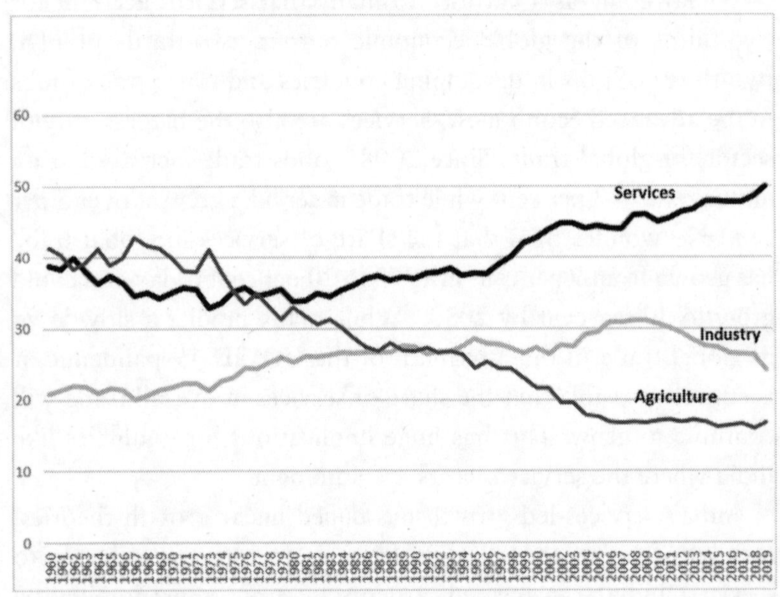

Source: *World Development Indicators*, World Bank.

The growth rate of India's services sector had started to pick up in the 1980s but accelerated in the 1990s (figure 14.1), overtaking industry's YoY growth rate to become the fastest-growing sector of the Indian economy.[9] Services, as a whole, became a net earner of foreign exchange by 1998.[10] There were also massive gains in the productivity of many subsectors. For example, in 1990, a shipping container's average turnaround time at a major Indian port was eight days. By 2005, port efficiency had doubled, and a shipping container would spend only three-and-a-half days at any major port.[11] Similarly, after the Indian government opened up the telecom sector to private players in 1994, telephones quickly lost their status as a notoriously hard-to-get luxury.[12,13]

There is broad consensus that liberalization was the main catalyst for the growth of the services sector. It opened the gates for foreign investment flows and allowed private players to capitalize on domestic demand from India's large and growing population.[14] The timing was perfect—the implementation of critical changes lined up with the rapid global IT and telecommunications revolution that was underway. This meant that many services were also becoming tradeable—a pro-growth characteristic that had previously been regarded as being limited to manufacturing. It is this ability to export and import services that has been pivotal in allowing service-led growth to become a viable pathway for economic development.[15]

Indian services also had other competitive advantages. For instance—returning to our example of IT services—well-trained, English-speaking but relatively low-cost engineers made India an attractive destination for foreign firms to set up local subsidiaries or shop for services. In the early 1990s, Indian software and computer engineers in Bengaluru reportedly earned between Rs 10,000–15,000 a month ($400–600), less than the minimum wage in the US.[16] These advantages have worked very well. In 2019-20, IT and business process management (IT-BPM) services earned $174.53 billion in revenue, of which 84 per cent ($146.6 billion) were from exports.[17]

The growth story of India's service sector is not limited to tradable services and external demand. Domestic demand, which benefited from the rapid income growth over the last three decades, has also sustained the growth of services. And it is not just in the good times that services aided India's overall growth. Some argue that India owes much of its resilience during the Global Financial Crisis to domestic demand for services. Despite the adverse impact of the crisis on services exports, the service sector still registered growth. Home-grown demand fuelled 77.6 per cent of the service sector's growth in 2008-09.[18]

The benefits of the growth of the services sector have not just been confined to the sector itself. Productivity in Indian manufacturing has benefited greatly from improved finance, transport and telecommunications. An estimated one standard deviation increase in service liberalization increased productivity of domestic firms by 11.7 per cent and foreign enterprises by 13.2 per cent.[19] Beyond firm-level benefits, individuals have gained enormously from better telecommunications services, connectivity, construction, etc.

High value but 'jobless growth': The employment problem of services

Undoubtedly, services contributed to India's rapid economic growth over the past few decades. However, this growth is not unblemished. While the overall growth of services has been fairly rapid, its subsectors offer a more mixed picture. For Indian success stories such as IT and telecom, there are sectors like transport and construction that have had more modest growth trajectories.[20] Knowledge-intensive subsectors have led a good deal of the income growth charge. As a result, a thin stratum of Indian society has accrued most of the benefits from the country's service-led growth. The share of people employed by the service sector is far less than its contribution to the GDP. According to ILO estimates, only 32.8 per cent of India's workforce was employed in the service sector (figure 14.2) and contributed to 47.75 per cent of the GDP (figure 14.1) in 2016.[21,22] Data on employment varies from source to source because it is challenging to accurately estimate the true size of the service sector and its contribution to India's GDP. The informality of a sizeable portion of the labour force, especially that engaged in services, contributes to this problem.

India's service-led growth is often described as 'jobless growth'.[23] The subsectors that have grown either tend to have a lower potential for employment generation or have witnessed declining employment elasticity (the percentage change in the number of people employed for an additional percentage point of productivity).[24]

Figure 14.2: Share of total Indian workforce in services, industry, agriculture (1991–2016)

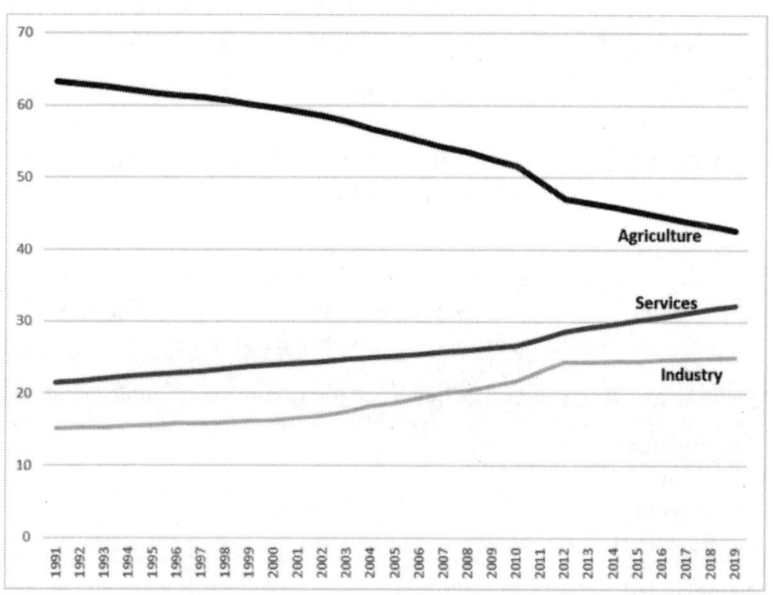

Sources: *World Development Indicators,* World Bank.

This is a serious problem. India needs to create tens of millions of non-agrarian jobs by 2030.[25] Between 1991 and 2016, the share of people employed in agriculture, which remains the largest employer, fell by 20 percentage points (figure 14.2), but it has risen in recent years.[26] Here, a comparison with China is illuminating. In the thirty-five years between 1978 and 2014,

China's agricultural employment dropped by 40 percentage points from 70 per cent in 1978 to just 30 per cent in 2014.[27] The labour released by China's agricultural sector was absorbed by both the industrial and services sectors. In fact, in 2014, for the first time since liberalization, China's agricultural sector contributed less to employment than the industrial sector.[28] In the meantime, the services sector, which has been growing rapidly, is now the biggest contributor to both output and employment in China. In India, the labour released from agriculture was also absorbed by the industrial and services sectors but not at China's scale (see table 14.1). But it should be noted that the share of labour in agriculture has risen in India in recent years.

Table 14.1: Breakdown of economic activity by sector (China and India—2019)

	Agriculture, forestry and fishing		Industry (including construction)		Services	
	China	India	China	India	China	India
Employment by sector (% of total employment)	25.3	42.6	27.4	25.1	47.3	32.3
Value added (% of GDP)	7.1	16.7	38.6	24.2	54.3	49.3

Note: For India, the value added (% of GDP) does not add up to 100 as per data source.

Source: *World Development Indicators*, World Bank.

The difficulty is that organized services by themselves are unlikely to produce the volume of jobs India needs. Many important services need skills and specializations and are unable to absorb unskilled labour.[29] In this sense, services are currently not the sponge that manufacturing has been in other countries. To solve this part of the growth puzzle—creating new jobs—the part of the economy that demands attention is the unorganized or informal one.

This may seem surprising, given the routine declarations and plans to tidy up or 'formalize the informal'. However, while flawed, India's vast informal sector has been home to 92 per cent of jobs created post-liberalization.[30] The growth of jobs in India's informal economy is in part due to a trickle-down effect from the demand for other services created by the income growth of a few organized service sectors.[31] This means that within the services' umbrella, the data on the number of people employed is somewhat under-reported because a large proportion of them work in the informal economy.[32] Services like construction, which are big employment generators driven by domestic demand, are largely informal. In January 2021 alone, construction and real estate absorbed 8.23 million workers in rural India.[33] These informal jobs also mimic the pro-development characteristics of low-skilled manufacturing.

A need to normalize the informal sector

More than 90 per cent of all Indian workers participate in the informal economy.[34] While agricultural jobs make up the largest share of informal work, 39.2 per cent of workers outside of agriculture are informal workers.[35] Far from being shadowy, among the ranks of informal workers are some of the economy's most visible participants—street vendors, domestic workers, transport workers, etc. Moreover, a third of informal workers in India are women.[36] This high level of informality is not a uniquely

Indian phenomenon—globally, more people rely on informal jobs than on formal employment. Some 61 per cent of the world's workforce earns their living in the informal economy.[37]

The term 'informal economy' was coined by British anthropologist Keith Hart in 1971 while studying migrant workers in Ghana. Since then, conventional economic wisdom has largely advocated its formalization based on concerns about illicit 'black market' activities, poor working conditions and losses in tax collections. However, many economists have come to acknowledge that the informal sector is an important source of employment and is here to stay.

However, policy measures in India have usually vilified and done little to support the informal economy. Initiatives like the 2016 demonetization and the hastily announced lockdown in March 2020 have been devastating for both wage-employed and self-employed informal workers and small businesses. The futility of efforts to somehow jolt the informal sector into formalizing has been proven time after time. While it is true that the better part of informal sector jobs is low-quality, low-productivity and low-wage, India is going to need to keep every job that it can. In this context, it is time to rethink the informal economy.

Policymakers must not abandon the intent or efforts to ensure that Indians do not find themselves marooned in low-productivity jobs in the informal sector. Creating ample opportunities in the formal economy is necessary. However, there is plenty that policymakers can simultaneously do to nurture the informal economy and its jobs, including trying to improve its productivity by creating awareness of good business practices and prevailing market conditions among enterprises.[38] Reducing the threat of extortion or 'hafta' (protection money) shake downs that India's micro-entrepreneurs or people running informal businesses are habitually subjected to by local law enforcement would also help.

In recent years, there has also been an increase in quasi-informal jobs or the so-called gig economy. Around the world (including in developed countries) and in India, technology-based platforms outsourcing the final provision of its services to 'flexi-workers' have driven this phenomenon. Think Uber or Ola for taxi services, Swiggy or Zomato for food deliveries, Urban Company for wellness and beauty services, etc. Gig workers working at such platforms increased from 8.5 million in 2016 to 15 million in 2018.[39]

While it is likely that the platform-based gig economy will continue to grow and create millions of jobs, it comes with problems that policymakers must contend with. For starters, the government needs to make a comprehensive set of rules and regulations to protect these workers. At present, there are no specific employment or labour laws that regulate gig work.[40] Existing labour laws are outdated and rife with loopholes that large platforms can exploit to avoid compliance.[41] These issues have been hotly debated in places like Europe and the US for some time now. In India, Uber and Ola drivers have locked horns with these companies over inadequate compensation and having to give up far too large a share of their earnings.

Keeping up with servicification, competition and looming changes

The value added by services and, therefore, the importance of services in the global economy continue to grow. In most major global economies, the service sectors create over 60 per cent of economic value.[42] According to the World Bank, as many aspects of production and value chains 'deglobalize', 'services will define the ability of countries and their firms to compete on the international market'.[43] Maintaining India's head start in services will be extremely important for the future.

We have already touched upon some reasons for this increasing importance of services. One is the ever-increasing ease of exporting and importing services and the emergence of services as an alternative path for economic development. Moreover, the growth of productivity of industry is on the decline. What we have not yet touched upon is the ubiquity of services, even in manufactured goods. This phenomenon is called 'servicification' of manufacturing, which means that 'the boundaries between the manufacturing and services sectors in the broader production process are becoming increasingly blurred'.[44] Products are now 'a complex bundle of goods and services, both embodied and embedded'.[45] A simple example of this is smartphones. A smartphone is not merely a physical good. While the hardware provides the bones, much of its usefulness comes from the software and apps it runs—services that are constantly created, updated and tweaked.

In 1992, Stan Shih, founder of the Taiwanese IT company Acer, observed that value-addition in IT manufacturing followed a U-shaped pattern or a 'smile'. The beginning and end of a product's production cycle—first, R&D, and at the end, marketing—command a significantly higher value than the actual manufacturing and assembly in the middle (figure 14.3).[46] This 'smile curve' is a simple visualization of the servicification of manufacturing. For instance, for one Apple iPhone 7 which was designed in California and assembled by Foxconn in China, China accounted for only $8.46 of the value. This is a very small fraction of the estimated $240 it cost to manufacture those iPhones and the retail price that started at $650.[47] In more recent models, China's value added has grown. Other popular consumer goods too can serve as easy examples. Think garments, shoes, medications, etc.

Figure 14.3: Stan Shih's smile curve

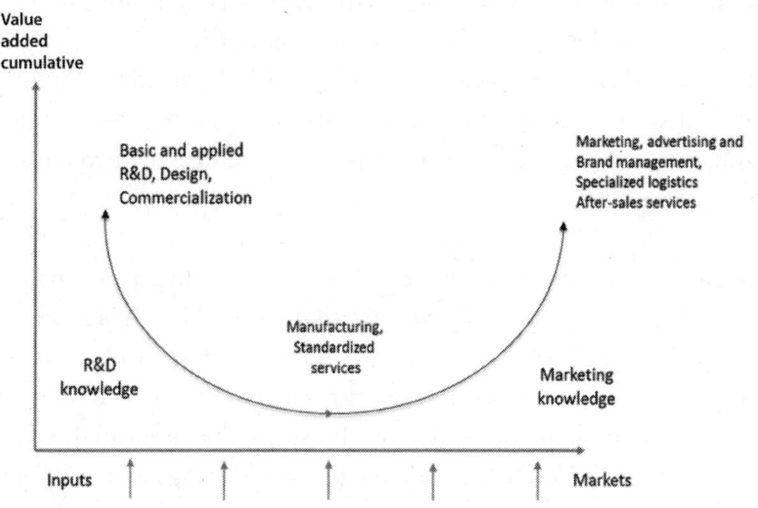

Source: *Location, Control and Innovation in Knowledge-Intensive Industries*, Mudambi (2008).

The idea of the smile curve is simple—one wants to be at the extreme ends of the production cycle as much as possible. For Acer, this meant changing its business strategy away from manufacturing components for others into more R&D and marketing its own brand-name computers. Similar wisdom can be applied to the larger economy fostering an environment where firms can engage in higher productivity services. A pivot like this is not easy and depends on the ability of firms to provide competitive high-skilled services. In this sense, we keep coming back to the need for India to make significant investments in human capital. This responsibility extends beyond just making sure that newer workers or people entering the economy have relevant skills but that the existing workforce has ample opportunity to reskill themselves. We are in an 'ever-accelerating race between skills and technology'.[48] Failure to keep up will have devastating consequences that go beyond the subsectors that demand these skills. We must remember that automation, artificial intelligence (AI) and other disruptive features of the Fourth Industrial Revolution could impact the relatively higher-skilled knowledge-intensive subsectors of the economy—the same subsectors that have been major drivers of domestic demand for other services.[49]

In India's IT sector, many workers are in peril of losing their livelihoods as most or all of the tasks they engage in get automated. In 2017, a McKinsey report warned that 2,00,000 IT professionals could lose their jobs per year over the next three years, making half of the IT sector's current workforce 'irrelevant'.[50] While this number is difficult to verify, the IT sector has seen major lay-offs and the COVID-19 pandemic has made things worse.[51] That the Indian IT sector is primarily engaged in back-end and non-innovative work is not a new finding. These red flags of future obscurity were visible right from the early days of the tech boom. A *New York Times* article from 1993 reported that while 'India has a lot of talented engineers, they aren't always doing the most advanced work' and that a 'good deal of the work done here is rated as routine, even mediocre programming'.[52]

Another thing that we have mentioned several times in this book is the need for India to invest in R&D. The success, efficiency and increased productivity of many services subsectors are entirely dependent on this. This will also give India a much-needed competitive edge. While India is cast as a major exporter of services, it is only globally competitive in computer and IT services. Unfortunately, India could soon lose this competitive advantage as well. Countries like China have increased their focus on capitalizing on the global services trade. In recent years, Beijing has been relaxing hurdles to market access by scrapping ownership requirements for foreign investment and opening up service subsectors such as science and technology, financial services and digital economy and trade.[53,54] The Chinese leader, Xi Jinping, often talks about China becoming 'cyber great power' and 'frames the information revolution as an opportunity to make up for China's relative disadvantage in previous industrial revolutions.'[55]

The Indian government has expressed concern that the country's service exports are facing increased competition from China, Brazil, Russia, Philippines, Israel and Ukraine.[56] Additionally, while services like tourism, hospitality and aviation are generally viewed as somewhat insulated from external competition, the COVID-19 pandemic has hit these sectors hard and it is unclear how long it will take them to rebound and what form their recovery will eventually take.[57,58]

Policies to create the world's service centre

Nothing mushrooms in a vacuum and good public policy is vital for the services sector. For instance, if we return to our Bengaluru example, pre-existing public sector science and technology infrastructure and tradition served as a launch-pad and an incubator for the IT and outsourcing boom that was to come.[59,60]

Most literature on Indian services notes that no integrated policy governs the sector. Unlike manufacturing and agriculture, the service sector is rarely a part of public discourse and policy debates. Instead, 'multiple, uncoordinated governing bodies adversely affect the growth of the sector' and hinder inclusive growth. For instance, in higher education some thirteen regulatory bodies work with little coordination with each other.[61] Given the heterogeneity of the services sector, it makes sense that one comprehensive policy would be difficult to draft and implement. However, consolidation and greater coordination between agencies, especially those that operate in the same space, would at least not hurt these sectors and may possibly help sector participants.

For the vast informal economy, policies should focus on improving the overall situation of the workforce. That does not only mean higher minimum wages or skilling and training programmes. The focus should be on well-being and that is a multifaceted objective. For an informal worker who must shell out money for a child's education or a sick family member's treatment, improvements mean better public services to begin with. With basic needs like health and education taken care of, workers can more productively pursue their trade and possibly be confident in taking on new opportunities. Government interventions focusing on formalization are misguided because basic support from policymakers is simply not forthcoming. If the public sector delivers on its social commitments, the informal economy will be a lot more normal and much healthier than it is right now.

For the more formal parts of the service economy, encouraging domestic private and foreign investment is very important. Despite efforts to make FDI inflows easier, India's FDI policies remain restrictive. According to the OECD's Foreign Direct Investment Regulatory Restrictiveness Index, India is more restrictive than most major economies. Only China, Russia and Indonesia have more restrictions on FDI.[62]

The service sector contracted by 16 per cent in the first six months following the COVID-19 lockdown and there was a sharp decline in demand. Overall, the government estimates that the sector contracted by over 8.8 per cent in 2020-21. It had grown by 5.5 per cent over the previous year. Providing adequate assistance to sectors that have been ravaged such as trade, tourism and hospitality—sectors that employ a significant amount of people—must remain a policy priority. Tourism and e-commerce are the low-hanging fruits where a concerted push by India could over the medium term have huge employment multiplier linkages and benefits.

Services have remained a reliable source of growth with relatively high labour productivity. Indian policymakers must pull out all the stops to make sure that it remains so. Subsectors that exhibit productivity-enhancing characteristics need a lot of knowledge-based inputs. Eventually, the key ingredients that are integral to the success of India's services are the same as what most parts of the economy desperately need—better education and better skills, more R&D, better infrastructure and suitable regulatory policies, including for the informal economy. India missed the export-led, labour-intensive manufacturing growth that fuelled China's rise. As China and other emerging nations develop their own services economies, India cannot afford to rest on past laurels.

15

Strategic Trade Policy

The world is the great gymnasium where we come to make ourselves strong.

—Swami Vivekananda, Indian philosopher

To understand Swami Vivekananda's wisdom in a modern context, an analogy with our cricket history over the last fifty years may be helpful. In the 1960s and 1970s, India produced some excellent cricketers—the Nawab of Pataudi, Ajit Wadekar, Farokh Engineer, Bishan Singh Bedi, E.A.S. Prasanna and S. Venkataraghavan come to mind. But India was only able to win on Indian dirt-track wickets. As soon as it went abroad, India lost badly as it was unable to handle the conditions outside India. Indian industry, closeted behind tariffs, had the same fate—it could sell in India but was uncompetitive outside.

A younger breed of cricketers emerged in the 1980s—they went outside and played English county cricket and built the famous team led by Kapil Dev, with players like Sunil Gavaskar, Gundappa Viswanath, Mohinder Amarnath, Dilip Vengsarkar and Ravi Shastri, that won the World Cup in 1983 and sparked a major shift in Indian cricket. Indian industry also witnessed some internal liberalization within the country under a more youthful, tech-oriented Prime Minister Rajiv Gandhi, which lifted India's growth rate.

Then followed a renaissance in Indian cricket with the arrival of Sachin Tendulkar, Saurav Ganguly, Anil Kumble and Rahul Dravid, who were ready to take on the world. India emerged as world-beaters after 2000, when it won many times outside India. Eventually, a swashbuckling side under M.S. Dhoni, with Tendulkar, Yuvraj Singh, Virender Sehwag, Virat Kohli and Zaheer Khan won another World Cup in 2011.

To match India's cricket performance, its economy took off with its fastest growth ever, averaging 8-9 per cent between 2003 and 2012. Trade with the world exploded, with India's export-to-GDP ratio reaching 25 per cent of GDP. India became competitive abroad for the first time in a range of products, including auto, pharma and IT.

Had Indian cricket withdrawn after winning the 2011 World Cup, we would not have seen the glorious wins abroad of teams led by Kohli and Ajinkya Rahane, with Rohit Sharma, Jasprit Bumrah, Ravichandran Ashwin, Ravindra Jadeja and other glorious men in the cricket blue. And India wins now not just in the men's game but also in the women's game. India used to have the occasional woman cricketer like the renowned Diana Edulji, but now produces a string of world-beaters in women's cricket, such as Mithali Raj, Harmanpreet Kaur, Smriti Mandhana, Deepti Sharma, Poonam Yadav and Jhulan Goswami. This success was built on nurturing and grooming talent from an early age, getting the best coaches from across the world and exposing the teams to global competition.

Today, Indian cricket is at its zenith and can beat any side anywhere in the world, in any format of the game. It has even beaten England at Lord's on India's Independence Day in 2021. But India's economy, unfortunately, appears to be moving inwards through its Aatmanirbhar Bharat Abhiyan and risks becoming less competitive if it is not careful. Restricting imports against dumping or to correct inverted duty structure is acceptable and using domestic reforms and to support our industry is acceptable, but where to draw the line is often not easy. And corporate interests will push India back behind tariff walls where they can sell shoddy products at inflated prices to hapless consumers. India needs to draw lessons from cricket to design a more strategic trade policy.

Export-led development remains India's best hope despite an increasingly hostile global environment. India is now the world's sixth-largest economy but remains a small player in global trade. It must integrate more globally to make the next leap forward to becoming the world's third-largest economy. Shrinking back to protectionism is not the answer at our stage of development.

India's 1991 trade liberalization was hugely beneficial—but has run its course

A balance of payments crisis forced India to liberalize its economy in the early 1990s. As a result, the role of the private sector expanded hugely. With a benign global environment between 2000 and 2013, non-oil exports grew by 18 per cent per annum and the GDP growth exceeded 8 per cent per annum—its fastest growth ever. But the benefits of this phase, which were enormous for about two decades, have run their course. India now needs a new strategic trade and industrial policy and a modernized agricultural trade policy to move India to the next phase of development.

Figure 15.1: India's share in global markets

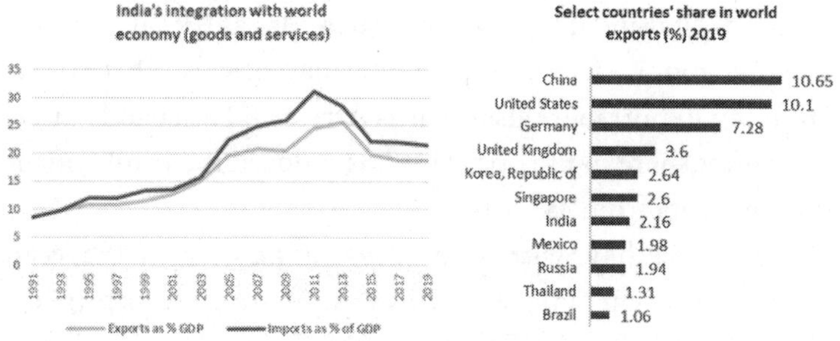

Source: *World Bank Indicators*, World Bank.

As a result of the 1991 liberalization, India's trade ratio of goods and services (to GDP) has risen enormously to around 40 per cent today (from 17 per cent in 1991). India's presence in global trade has also enhanced, with Indian share in global merchandise exports accounting for 2.1 per cent today as against 0.6 per cent in the early 1990s and share in imports rising to 2.3 per cent from 0.6 per cent. India's global exports share is much lower when compared with other export-oriented emerging economies such as China (11 per cent), South Korea (2.7 per cent) and Singapore (2.6 per cent) (figure 15.1). Exports also played a key role in their quest to become manufacturing nations. Merchandise exports account for 19 per cent of GDP in China, 35 per cent in South Korea and 15 per cent in Bangladesh, as against 11 per cent for India. According to the Economic Survey 2019-20, if India could increase its export share to 3.5 per cent by 2025 and 6 per cent by 2030, it would add almost 40 million jobs by 2025 and over 80 million jobs by 2030.[1]

India has also seen a significant shift in this period in the composition of exports. Service exports rose from 30 per cent to 40 per cent in the period 2003–08 but have plateaued at that level. Within manufacturing exports, India has lost share in textiles, leather, gems and jewellery, but has gained ground in more capital-intensive sectors such as auto, auto parts, engineering goods, electronics and pharmaceuticals. There is also a shift in our export markets towards Africa and Asia and a much lower market share in Europe. This has reduced the employment-creating benefits from exports.

India's exports have witnessed a devastating slump in the recent years with some sign of recovery this year. Share of exports (goods and services) in India's GDP that accounted for almost 25 per cent during 2011–13 was affected by the global economic slowdown and fell sharply to 19 per cent by 2017. What explains this sharp slowdown? In a recent paper, Chinoy and Jain of JP Morgan Chase attribute at least half of the slowdown to the global slowdown and the sharp appreciation of the exchange rate of around 20 per cent in the period 2014–17.[2] The remainder is explained by temporary disruptions attributable to demonetization and GST implementation. With the real exchange depreciating and the effects of the temporary shocks dissipating, exports are seeing some recovery.

According to the Federation of Indian Chambers of Commerce & Industry (FICCI), an analysis of the top twenty import markets of the world reveals that India is amongst the top five exporters only in one market, i.e., the United Arab Emirates (UAE) and amongst the top ten exporters in three more markets, namely the US, Hong Kong and Turkey.[3] In terms of market share of exports too, India has more than 5 per cent of market share only in the UAE (6.9 per cent share in 2016). It has a 2-3 per cent market share in four markets—Turkey, the US, Hong Kong and Singapore—and around 1 per cent share in six markets—the UK, South Korea, Italy, Mexico, Belgium and Spain. In all other top twenty markets, India has less than 1 per cent market share. Clearly, there is potential to increase India's share of exports in all these top twenty markets.

A mapping of the top twenty import markets (that account for almost 72 per cent of the world's total imports) according to India's exports share in these markets and the importance of these markets as India's major export destinations (matrix below—table 15.1), shows that India is well positioned in the import markets of the UAE, the US, Hong Kong and Singapore, as these are amongst India's top ten export destinations.[4] It can now use this to build a bigger export share in these markets.

Table 15.1: World's top 20 markets—their share in India's exports and India's share in these markets

Share of India's exports ↓ / India's share in these markets →	0–2%	2–5%	Above 5%
Above 5%		United States Hong Kong	UAE
3–5%	China United Kingdom		
0–3%	Germany, Japan, France, The Netherlands Canada, South Korea, Italy, Mexico, Belgium, Spain, Taiwan	Turkey Singapore	

Source: *Envisioning India 2030*, FICCI (2018).

Some improvement can be made in the US and UK markets, which are India's top export destinations, but we have not been able to garner a significant market share in these countries. The post-Brexit UK may be more conducive to trade arrangements with countries like India. Germany is another top export destination for India, but India has a mere 0.8 per cent share in Germany's overall imports. Clearly, there is room to enhance exports in this market and more broadly in the European Union (EU) as a whole—where the chances of a new trade agreement should be vigorously pursued. Of the almost $2 trillion EU imports, India supplies only a little over $40 billion. Hopefully, the agreement to move towards a free trade agreement (FTA) with the EU, if reached, will open this huge market for Indian producers.

Likewise, there is a lot of catching up to do in all the other top twenty import markets, as these neither figure in India's top ten export destinations nor does India have a reasonable market share in these countries. India's exports can also increase in parts of the world that we have neglected. For example, India provides less than 0.1 per cent worth of goods out of Latin America's total imports of almost $1 trillion. India also provides less than 0.2 per cent worth of goods out of EU's total imports of $2 trillion.

Instead of exporting more to lucrative and deeper developed country markets, in recent years India's exports have shifted, ironically, more to skilled-labour and capital-intensive products and from developed to developing country markets, especially in Africa and Asia.

India has largely missed out on the trade in networked products (NPs), where it exports only $25 billion (0.5 per cent of global trade in NPs)—both in assembled export products ($15 billion) and in parts and components (P&C) ($10 billion). Against this, China's share is 20 per cent, South Korea's is 5 per cent, Singapore's is 3.5 per cent, Malaysia's is 2 per cent, Thailand's is 2 per cent and even Vietnam's 1 per cent is double India's share. Our dismal showing in entering GVCs is due to poor logistics, unpredictable power supply and comparatively greater labour disputes. If India is to enter GVCs and regional value chains (GVCs and RVCs), it cannot at the same time become more protectionist.

Past success required a helping hand

While India's shares in global markets rose after the 1991 trade liberalization, India remains a small player in trade. India did succeed in selected products—but not by just liberalizing trade but by pursuing deliberate industry-specific strategic policies, from which there are lessons. Many blithely attribute India's rising trade shares only to trade liberalization. There is no doubt it played a key role but India's success in specific products did depend on a helping hand from the government—a light one, not a heavy-handed one.

For example, India has had some success in assembled automobile exports, but this was not accidental. It came through a strategic ten-year plan, Automotive Mission Plan or 'AMP 2006-2016', which targeted $150 billion production by 2016 and to make India a preferred destination for automobile assembly in selected segments. The National Automotive Testing and R&D Infrastructure Project (NATRiP) then added R&D to provide global excellence behind this plan. The Faster Adoption and Manufacture of Electric Vehicles (FAME) scheme, adopted in 2015, hopes to make India an electric vehicle hub in the future.

Like in automobiles, India could become a preferred destination for assembly of electronics, telecom hardware, electrical machinery, computers and office machines if it made a similar strategic plan to increase its exports from $15 billion to $150–$200 billion by 2025, especially as China looks to move out from many of these. It will need much better logistics, skilled mid-level management, predictable power supply and R&D. At present, India does not figure as a destination under consideration and appears to be losing out to Vietnam, Mexico and Bangladesh.

India is becoming somewhat of a hub for aeronautics and automobiles parts through a conscious effort to attract FDI—not foreign portfolio investment (FPI)—but with an offset policy, which requires that 30 per cent is domestically sourced. India could be a P&C supplier for a range of industries and could increase its exports from $10 billion to over $100 billion in developed markets and enter GVCs with a strategic plan.

India's pharmaceutical industry also did not grow by accident but because India enacted a patent policy in 1970 that did not comply with what came to be enshrined in the Agreement on Trade-Related Aspects of Intellectual Property Rights (TRIPS) of 1995. This allowed the pharmaceutical industry to grow stronger so that by 2005 when a TRIPS-compliant act was introduced, its internal R&D capacity could allow it to remain competitive in global markets.

India is a major supplier of IT services for design, architecture, accounting and logistics, but uses very little of these in domestic industry or for its manufactured exports. India could bring its edge in services to a range of industries in electronics and electrical machinery, defence equipment and green technology. There are some who say India should focus on services as against manufacturing, and on MSMEs rather than large firms.

These are false choices. India's edge in services should be used to give it an edge in manufacturing as well—especially in NPs. Arnold et al. (2016)[5] find that banking, telecommunications, insurance and transport reforms all had significant positive effects on the productivity of manufacturing firms.

India needs faster growth in firms of all sizes and a cascading system of contracts between large, medium and small firms with synergy across them. India badly needs more middle-sized firms employing 100–500 workers—the missing middle, for which labour reforms are needed. Some states have now made the labour market more flexible up to 300 workers, but it is also critical to safeguard labour standards and focus on skills development to build up the required labour force for the twenty-first-century world.

The potential of the Production-Linked Incentive (PLI) scheme

What our past success in some areas has shown us is that a laissez-faire approach may not be enough. A light-touch industrial policy will be needed. But ensuring that a light touch does not turn into the dead-hand of bureaucracy is not easy.

As a part of the Aatmanirbhar Bharat Abhiyan, the announcement of extension of the Production-Linked Incentive (PLI) scheme to ten more sectors with an additional outlay of about Rs 1.46 trillion over the next five years is a step in the right direction,[6] if it can be implemented smartly without becoming yet another bureaucratic trap for industry. This scheme had been introduced for mobile and pharmaceuticals manufacturing earlier this year. Now, the ten sectors to be covered under the PLI scheme are pharmaceuticals, automobiles and auto components, telecom and networking products, advanced chemistry cell battery, textile, food products, solar modules, white goods and specialty steel. The scheme envisages fresh investments leading to higher production would get cash incentives at the rate of 4–6 per cent of incremental sales.

India liberalized its economy in 1991 and reduced its applied trade-weighted real tariffs from 56.4 per cent in 1990 to 7.33 per cent in 2015 and to 4.88 per cent in 2018—well below India's WTO threshold levels, through several waves of tariff reduction. But since then, as India's trade deficit widened and imports—especially from China and Association of Southeast Asian Nations (ASEAN)—surged, several rounds of tariff increases were announced and the trade-weighted tariff for 2019 jumped to 10.3 per cent—still below WTO thresholds. Topalova and Khandelwal (2011) find competitive forces, increased firm-level productivity, both from lower tariffs from final goods as well as better inputs, due to lower input tariffs, with the latter having a larger impact.[7] The effect was strongest in import-competing industries and industries not subject to excessive domestic regulation.

One argument given for these import tariff increases is that India liberalized too rapidly, hurting industrial development, and its trade deficit—especially with China—widened. The trade deficit with China reached a peak of $63 billion in 2017-18, has since declined to $53.56 billion in 2018-19 and $48.66 billion in 2019-20, after considerable efforts to reduce it through tariffs and non-tariff barriers linked to dumping. Now that the Regional Comprehensive Economic Partnership (RCEP) negotiations are over, a review of the FTA with ASEAN, with whom we also have a rising deficit, should also be expedited.

But using import protection to manage trade deficits is a double-edged sword. As India liberalized after 1991, it saw not only high GDP growth but also an explosive increase in exports. India's non-oil exports reached around $250 billion in FY2011-12 but have since plateaued out, showing some revival in 2018-19 to around $280 billion.

But in several key Indian exports, such as engineering goods and mining, import tariffs increase the costs of production and hurt their growth. Moreover, Goldberg et al. (2010)[8] find that lower input tariffs account on average for 31 per cent of the new products introduced by domestic firms, which implies potentially large dynamic gains from trade. This expansion in firms' product scope is driven to a large extent by international trade increasing access of firms to new input varieties rather than by simply making existing imported inputs cheaper.

Also, in many products that the PLI scheme targets, upgrading technology and imported inputs will be key to their success. A 5 per cent depreciation in the real effective exchange rate would have achieved the same level of import protection across the board and encouraged exports as well. So, other than corrections for an inverted duty structure, let us not think import tariffs and other trade barriers are the right solution for 'Make in India'.

Export subsidies would subject India to WTO sanctions. In contrast, the new PLI scheme, along with a ten-year plan in each of the selected sectors for support, is the right way forward. But what is true is that India's earlier success in pharma, automobile assembly and parts did not come without selective industrial policy.

Prime Minister Modi claims the PLI scheme will boost India's manufacturing output by over $500 billion in five years.[9] This, of course, remains to be seen, as it will depend on how well it is implemented. The key to the PLI scheme's success will be transparent and smooth implementation—the heavy hand of the bureaucracy will kill it. A more streamlined system with automatic approvals done together with relevant industry bodies can make it a success. It is the first concrete positive measure to 'Make in India' and ensure the industry a level playing field.

The new PLI scheme could become a game changer along with other reforms and better logistics. It signals the recognition that laissez-faire will not work in a fiercely competitive global market where everyone else, especially China, aggressively uses industrial policy. India must get more aggressive with China to try and prise open its markets. If China wants unfettered access to India's market, it must allow the same for Indian producers. Such a strategic approach—with an end game of boosting trade instead of straightforward import protection—is the right way forward.

Behind-the-border and other supporting measures

China used its international commitments for entry to the WTO to drive home internal reforms. This was a good way to use its WTO entry. But China also cheated on its commitments to the WTO by not adhering to the true spirit of all them. For example, it cleverly used subsidized state-owned firms, and dumping and predatory pricing to grab market share when it could, and, when challenged, making small changes in product line-ups to avoid penalties. But China did drive internal reforms through external agreements. Vietnam has now been following this playbook for almost two decades with spectacular results. India has not been able to follow this strategy with the same success. Instead, it has lost out by signing FTAs without thinking through the back-of-the-border measures that will be needed to retain competitiveness.

India has started losing out even on its traditional labour-intensive exports—apparel, leather and footwear—which have fallen to around $30 billion from $40 billion a decade ago. India's competitors have taken away our markets through policies which gave them better access to logistics, credit and land, lower taxes and more competitive exchange rates.

Strategic trade policy does not mean just opening up our markets. It means using access to our markets to pry open others as well. Reviewing and renegotiating the India–ASEAN FTA is perhaps needed if the premise of the original agreement—that freer trade in services would follow free trade in goods—has not come true. Anti-dumping may require temporary tariffs or, better yet, the threat to impose tariffs, all within a WTO framework, which India must try and preserve.

To reach $1 trillion, exports must grow by 18 per cent per annum up to 2030—the same growth rate as in the golden period 2000–13. Some say that in today's difficult global markets, the era of export-led growth is over. But with abysmally low export shares, the upside for an export-led growth strategy for India is huge even if global trade grows more slowly. India has gone up the rankings on the World Bank's EDBI but has lost rank in the World Economic Forum (WEF) Competitiveness Index, which is a broader index and incorporates the EDBI data within it.

India could also consider several other measures to boost competitiveness and reduce the costs of doing business, such as:

- Establish a new development finance institution[10] or revive IDBI—where 51 per cent stake was sold to LIC—by bringing in dynamic leadership, selling government shares to private entities, and giving it the mandate to provide longer-term finance to industry.
- Remove labour flexibility restrictions for firms even further (it has done up to 300 workers in several states), to encourage the growth of firms in the 100–1,000 worker range and reduce restrictions on them to enhance competitiveness—but do it as part of a broader labour standards package.
- Reduce energy costs to industry by removing cross-subsidization to consumers and to agriculture.

- Establish dedicated Export Processing Zones (EPZs) and encourage port-led development, with special incentives to FDI for export-based labour-intensive sectors. Bring external expertise, where needed, to help run these EPZs.
- Work with RBI to gradually reduce over-appreciation of the rupee by 15–20 per cent over the next 5 years.
- Shift Corporate Social Responsibility (CSR) funding entirely to R&D and encourage R&D in private industry through tax incentives. The resulting job creation is more important than current approaches to CSR.
- Rationalize rail tariff and expedite commissioning of DFCs.
- Create a seamless and efficient road transport experience—introduce a 'One Nation, One Permit, One Tax' system.
- Establish a National Council of Logistics and Trade Facilitation outside the line ministries reporting to the prime minister. Private sector and trade stakeholders should be represented.
- Fully facilitated trust-based clearance processes through a modern risk-management system and a fully automated paperless trade environment with minimum face-to-face interactions—physical inspection of goods to be an exception.
- Target reaching cargo dwell time levels comparable to the successful Southeast Asian countries.
- Encourage growth of river transport to open landlocked areas for commerce and tourism—especially along the Ganges and its tributaries.

Concluding thought

Just as our cricket team has become a world-beater in men's and women's sections, so too can India become a world-beater in industry and trade. India will be short-sighted if it focuses on protecting its $2.7 trillion market (about the size of California's) when a global market of over $80 trillion should be our gymnasium. The world's second-largest economy, China ($13 trillion), the third-largest, Japan ($5 trillion) and the fourth-largest, Germany ($4.5 trillion) do not regard their much larger markets as large enough and are the world's most aggressive exporters. Why then should India, with a much smaller market, want to protect its growing but still small market and cut itself off from the bigger prize?

Exports have also emerged as a silver lining as India tries to recover from the pandemic, with the goal of reaching $400 billion target for FY21-22 achievable. India must aggressively support its exporters and help explore new markets and in new products. But just a few fiscal incentives will not be enough if we are to compete and join major GVCs and trade groupings like RCEP, or sign free trade deals with the EU and the US. The government and the private sector must work closely together to take on the world and build some substance into the slogan 'Make in India'. An autarchic approach to 'Make in India' will surely fail us.

PART V

Preparing for the Future

16

Changing the Climate for the Better

We are the first generation to feel the effect of climate change and the last generation who can do something about it.
—Barack Obama, former president of the United States

A group of students from the US and India travelled to Himachal Pradesh in 2018 to interview lifelong residents in different villages about their experience with climate change.[1] In Chansari village in Kullu district, a farmer told the students, 'The temperatures have risen.' He talked about the changing pattern of agriculture in his part of the world. During his childhood, his community grew kidney beans, barley, corn, wheat, potatoes. Now, they produced apples and pears. He talked about how at lower altitudes, near the Beas River, there were big apple orchards that people would pick in earlier times. Now, apple orchards have moved up to higher altitudes. Another member of the community talked about the abundance of snow when he was younger. The surrounding mountain peaks would be packed with snow until June and July. Now, pointing at the beautiful peaks around him, even though they had major snowfall that season, it didn't stay on the ground too long. It is because it is too hot, he told the students.

These and other such stories are part of a broader global debate on climate change, its trajectory, potential impacts and paths to mitigation and adaptation. Ominously, climate change threatens India more than most nations.[2] To understand India's place in the climate change debate, we need to look at the evolving global context, as well as issues specific to India. Our aim is to ultimately link India's global climate change commitments to its own capacities, ambitions and development trajectory, as well as highlight ideas to convert this enormous challenge into a tantalizing opportunity.

COVID-19 is a catastrophic shock. But it could pale in comparison to what lies ahead. As Bill Gates, the billionaire founder of Microsoft, wrote, 'As awful as this pandemic is, climate change could be worse.'[3] Gates explained in a blog that global GHGs, which contribute to climate change, will see a reduction of 8 per cent in 2020 compared to 2019. In real terms, 47 billion tons of carbon would be released into the atmosphere in 2020 instead of 51 billion tons. This reduction has enthused many who see it as a sign that GHG emissions can continue to go down. However, Gates cautions that such reductions are not possible every year. After all, this reduction has come at a cost of over 4.5 million deaths (as of August 2021), millions of lost jobs and entire productive sectors grinding to a halt. In fact, the 8 per cent reduction in emissions shows just how brutally tough it is going to be to secure meaningful reductions in GHG emissions. As Gates points out, 'To understand the kind of damage that climate change will inflict, look at COVID-19 and spread the pain out over a much longer period.' On the current emissions path, the world would see economic damage at the scale of COVID-19 every ten years.

The science behind climate change is complicated. There are various GHG scenarios and they each have very different implications. However, this much is certain: climate change will disproportionately impact poor countries and poor people, both in terms of mortality rates and economic damage. The IPCC or Intergovernmental Panel on Climate Change's latest report warns that the world has put off curbing its fossil fuel emissions for so long that a hotter future is now inevitable, under every scenario. Over the next two decades, the global surface temperature is now locked in to rise by 1.5°C. However, the report offers some hope—'aggressive emission cuts beginning now could reduce warming after 2050' and allow humanity to dodge the worst.[4]

A study by Climate Impact Lab shows that 'by 2099 under a scenario of continued high emissions growth, climate change increases death rates in low-income countries by 106.7 deaths per 100,000. Meanwhile, high-income countries are projected to see death rates decrease by 25.2 deaths per 100,000 ...'.[5] For reference, the COVID-19 crisis has raised global death rates by 14 per 1,00,000.

Many studies have shown that India will be among the worst impacted by climate change. It is a cruel irony that India will suffer disproportionately even though its contribution to the climate change crisis is relatively limited. More on that later. But let's see how all this started, what India can expect and what it must do. The pandemic could be a blessing in disguise. It could help India prepare for what is to come. It is a wake-up call.

A short detour to the history and science of climate change

In the nineteenth century, scientists had started debating the idea that burning fossil fuels could raise the earth's temperature.[6] The 'greenhouse effect' was one of several theories put forward at the time. Not many thought it was a plausible theory. In the 1930s, scientists observed that the US and the North Atlantic had warmed compared to the previous fifty years. Most believed this was part of a natural cycle. However, Guy Callendar, a British amateur scientist, started collecting data on gases, sunlight at different latitudes, use of fossil fuels, etc. That led him to conclude that humans were dumping carbon dioxide into the atmosphere and raising global temperature.[7] At the time, Callendar's was a lone voice. No one really bought it until later in the 1950s when scientists began working to confirm his theory.

It took a while for the idea of global warming to be taken seriously by policymakers. Not that policymakers were not being made aware of this emerging problem. A 1965 report to President Lyndon Johnson highlighted that burning fossil fuels could be 'deleterious from the point of view of human beings'.[8] Other US government reports in 1979 talked about climate change leading to the disintegration of the West Antarctic ice sheet, an increase of 16 feet in global sea levels: an impact that humans would feel.[9]

Millions of Americans woke up to the reality of climate change in the summer of 1988 when they learnt, 'Yellowstone National Park burst into flames; the Mississippi River ran so low that almost four thousand barges got backed up at Memphis; and, for the first time in its history, Harvard University shut down owing to heat.'[10] That year, James Hansen, then the head of NASA's Goddard Institute for Space Studies, informed a US Senate committee that 'the greenhouse effect has been detected and is changing our climate now'.

Hansen's testimony was captured by a three-column headline in *The New York Times*: 'GLOBAL WARMING HAS BEGUN, EXPERT TELLS SENATE'. Powerful as that headline was, it went unheeded as have a lot of other warnings since then. In the three decades since Hansen's testimony, 200 billion metric tons of carbon dioxide have entered the earth's atmosphere. That is about the same amount as had entered the atmosphere from the beginning of the Industrial Revolution until that point.[11] Yes, it is that bad.

It isn't that nothing at all has happened since Hansen spoke. Climate science has improved, there is much greater awareness of the threat and there is a ton of literature on mitigation and adaptation options. The threat is now on the radar screen of most politicians, even if some remain in denial. However, the question for India, as for other countries, is twofold: how bad is it going to get and what can India (and others) do? To answer the first question, researchers have been putting out a variety of scenarios that chart the possible pathways for climate change. The IPCC released the first global scenarios to provide estimates for GHGs in 1992.[12] Since then, the IPCC has regularly revised these estimates.

Table 16.1: Projected change in global mean surface air temperature and global mean sea level rise for the mid- and late twenty-first century relative to the reference period of 1986–2005

		2046–65		2081–2100	
	Scenario	Mean	*Likely* range[c]	Mean	*Likely* range[c]
Global Mean Surface Temperature Change (°C)[a]	RCP2.6	1.0	0.4 to 1.6	1.0	0.3 to 1.7
	RCP4.5	1.4	0.9 to 2.0	1.8	1.1 to 2.6
	RCP6.0	1.3	0.8 to 1.8	2.2	1.4 to 3.1
	RCP8.5	2.0	1.4 to 2.6	3.7	2.6 to 4.8
	Scenario	Mean	*Likely* range[d]	Mean	*Likely* range[d]
Global Mean Sea Level Rise (m)[b]	RCP2.6	0.24	0.17 to 0.32	0.40	0.26 to 0.55
	RCP4.5	0.26	0.19 to 0.33	0.47	0.32 to 0.63
	RCP6.0	0.25	0.18 to 0.32	0.48	0.33 to 0.63
	RCP8.5	0.30	0.22 to 0.38	0.63	0.45 to 0.82

Source: Climate Change 2013—The Physical Science Basis—Summary. Intergovernmental Panel for Climate Change.

A decade back, IPCC researchers put out four 'representative concentration pathways' or RCPs for climate modellers to use to help understand where things would stand at the end of the twenty-first century. Mind you, these are technically not the standard scenarios that IPCC usually puts out. But these four RCPs (RCP 2.6, RCP 4.5, RCP 6.0, RCP 8.5) are what we all use these days to understand what climate change can mean for us (table 16.1). For our purposes, let us just say that RCP 2.6 is the mildest (best-case scenario) and RCP 8.5 is the worst-case scenario. The other two are intermediate warming scenarios. The RCP 8.5 is also called the 'business as usual' scenario. Under RCP 8.5, the world continues spewing carbon dioxide into the atmosphere with a 500 per cent increase in the use of coal and warming of up to 6°C by 2100 (likely range being 2.6–4.8°C). This scenario poses an existential threat to life. Fortunately for all of us, this scenario now appears highly unlikely. As you may have noticed, rapid changes in technology and commitments from various governments, including India, will likely ensure that we do not meet the fate that RCP 8.5 has in store for us.

That said, climate change has cast its shadow already. We are witnessing rising seas, devastating droughts, scorching and seemingly unending wildfires, killer heatwave and more frequent and powerful cyclones and massive floods: they are now a regular part of our lives. During our time at the World Bank and the UNDP, there have been countless natural disasters that victims described as having never witnessed before in their lives. The 2014 Kashmir floods, which one of the authors lived through, ended up being the costliest natural disaster that year. Hundred-year floods (statistically speaking, a flood of a magnitude that has a one in hundred chance of occurring each year) have become almost routine. The rise in the frequency and destructive power of meteorological disasters has prompted much hand-wringing in policy and scientific circles. Many believe that a 2°C warming of global temperatures could be devastating. Some in the climate activist community warn that at 2°C warming, 'It's expected that more than 150 million additional people would die from the effects of pollution, storms that used to arrive once every century would hit every single year, and that lands that are today home to 1.5 billion people would become literally uninhabitable, at least by the standards of human history.'[13]

Not everyone believes that the impacts will be that terrible. Certainly, according to some experts, economic cost-benefit analysis does not justify adherence to the 2°C target. Nobel laureate William Nordhaus has argued that 'the international target for climate change with a limit of 2°C appears to be infeasible with reasonably accessible technologies even with very ambitious abatement strategies.[14] Nordhaus suggests that a target of 2.5°C 'is technically feasible but would require extreme and virtually universal global policy measures in the near future'.[15]

Others, including Joseph Stiglitz, a Nobel laureate himself, disagree that 1.5–2°C warming targets will impose enormous costs. A World Bank-supported commission co-chaired by Stiglitz and Nicholas Stern concluded that climate goals were achievable at a 'moderate price' and within the absorptive capacity of the global economic system.[16] Stiglitz finds that Nordhaus and other proponents of a higher than 2°C target are underestimating the damage caused by climate change. In line with the scientific consensus, both sides in this debate agree that climate change is a reality. They differ on the economic costs it is imposing and how far we need to go to mitigate those costs.

This threshold of 2°C warming is linked to the Paris Agreement. In 2015, 196 parties negotiated the agreement whose 'main goal is to limit global warming to well below 2, preferably to 1.5 degrees Celsius, compared to pre-industrial levels'.[17] India is among the 189 countries that have ratified the Paris Agreement. As part of the agreement, countries have committed to submit their climate action plans, known as nationally determined contributions (NDCs), for reducing emissions to achieve the global target of below-2°C warming.

While there are some reasons for optimism, the reality is not that good. In 2016, atmospheric concentrations of carbon dioxide passed 400 parts per million (ppm). This was the first such occurrence in several million years.[18] In 2017, a year after the Paris Agreement was ratified, not even one industrial nation was on track to fulfil its Paris commitments. Of all the signatories, only seven countries were 'in range' of their Paris targets. India was one of them.[19] In 2018, GHG concentrations reached record levels for carbon dioxide, methane and nitrous oxide.[20] In 2019, global surface temperatures were the second warmest since records began in the nineteenth century.[21]

What about 2020, the year in which we started writing this book? It was the warmest on record and GHG concentrations (driven by fossil fuels, land use and agriculture) may have set a new record.[22] In early 2020, NASA reported that Greenland and Antarctica were melting six times faster than in the 1990s.[23] The World Meteorological Organization (WMO) noted that the summer of 2020 was the warmest recorded for the northern hemisphere.[24] Flood waters in Bangladesh covered almost a third of the country at one point in 2020.[25] The California wildfires torched over 2 million acres, the size of ten New York cities.[26] In September 2020, a heatwave shattered records in western Europe. In November, Hurricane Eta cost Honduras an estimated 20 per cent of its GDP. These are warning signs. India must prepare for an uncertain, even difficult future.

Hope for the best, prepare for the worst

But is India really going to be badly affected by climate change? If yes, what types of impacts can India expect and how can those impacts be mitigated? If mitigation is not an option, can we adapt to those impacts? How will that affect the economy and life as we know it? What can or should India do? The remainder of this chapter is devoted to these questions.

At a minimum, India must prepare for 2°C warming. However, it is prudent to not take a minimalist approach to the biggest issue of the twenty-first century. There is sufficient evidence to indicate that India will be badly affected by climate change. India's actions to ward off the impacts of climate change won't just be about good global citizenship. It will be about protecting India's interests, its development gains and, above all, ensuring a viable future for generations to come.

In 2015, a series of intense heatwaves swept across India. Over a two-week period, temperatures soared in major cities. Almost 2,400 people died. This was the fifth deadliest heatwave ever recorded globally.[27] The year 2016 was the warmest on record for

India. In 2017, a study based on fifty years of data compiled by the Indian Meteorological Department (IMD) showed that India was 'two and a half times more likely to experience a deadly heatwave than a half century ago'.[28] The study found that there was a 25 per cent increase in the number of heatwave days across India and that areas in the south and west were the worst affected. In 2018 (the sixth-warmest year on record), it was reported that in the fifteen years preceding 2018, India recorded eleven of its fifteen warmest years.[29] A 2019 study warned that coastal cities like Mumbai, Chennai and Kolkata could be submerged by 2050.[30] In June 2020, a report by the Indian Ministry of Earth Sciences confirmed that average temperatures had risen by 0.7°C during 1901–2018 and that this rise was primarily due to global warming caused by GHG emissions.

Some of these grim findings relate to worse than the best-case warming scenarios. However, to put things in perspective, 2°C warming could mean that in comparison to 2015, there could be '32 times as many extreme heatwaves in India, and each would last five times as long, exposing 93 times more people'.[31]

In 2018, the World Bank issued a report that highlighted the potential impact of climate change on India by 2050. The report argued that changing monsoon patterns and rising temperatures could cost India 2.8 per cent of GDP and 'depress the living standards of nearly half the country's population by 2050'.[32] The report argues that even if the Paris Agreement commitments come through, temperature rise in India would be between 1°C and 2°C by 2050. The report identifies states and districts that are climate hotpots and flags states like Madhya Pradesh and Chhattisgarh as being especially vulnerable.

The report lays out two scenarios of warming—climate sensitive and climate intensive. Under the climate-intensive scenario, India's living standards would be worse by 1.5 percentage points by 2030 and 2.8 points by 2050. However, even the so-called climate-sensitive scenario isn't rosy. Under this scenario, India's living standard would decline by 1.3 and 2 percentage points by 2030 and 2050, respectively, relative to a historical baseline established by the report. In summary, we are talking about a decline in living standards under both the pessimistic and optimistic scenarios. Worse, averages hide interstate disparities. The decline in some states will be much worse than in other states.

When the World Bank published its report in 2018, the Indian economy was still growing at 7 per cent per year. Since then, the economy has been growing more slowly and, like the rest of the global economy, was hit by COVID-19. Many reputed economists believe that India's potential growth rate is in the 5 per cent range rather than in the 8–10 per cent that many in India may like to believe. That means India's current trajectory is slower and will also run into an increasingly stubborn climate-change wall. That is what makes it imperative for policymakers to put climate change at the heart of a new development paradigm.

Victims called to sacrifice

India and other developing countries have for long maintained that they are victims of policies pursued in the industrialized world. Countries like the US became wealthy by using polluting fossil fuels for their development. Now that global warming is threatening the planet, the US and other rich countries want everyone to make sacrifices by reducing their dependence on fossil fuels, which have been cheaper than other sources of energy. From 1701–2018, the US was responsible for cumulatively emitting 405 billion tons of carbon dioxide (25 per cent of the global total) while India emitted only 51 billion tons (3 per cent of the total). Canada, a country of less than 40 million compared to India's 1.4 billion, emitted 2 per cent of the total.[33]

In recent years, China has emerged as the biggest emitter, even though on a per capita basis, the US and Europe continue to lead the world. India is the third-biggest emitter of GHGs in absolute terms (figure 16.1).[34] But in per capita terms, India is not even in the top twenty.[35] Just twenty firms linked to the fossil fuel industry are behind a third of all carbon emissions. Infuriatingly, the cheap-fuel-powered economies of the world have created a situation that imperils the lives of people living in the poorest countries, those who did little to create the problem.

Figure 16.1: Top ten carbon emissions (in absolute terms, per capita)

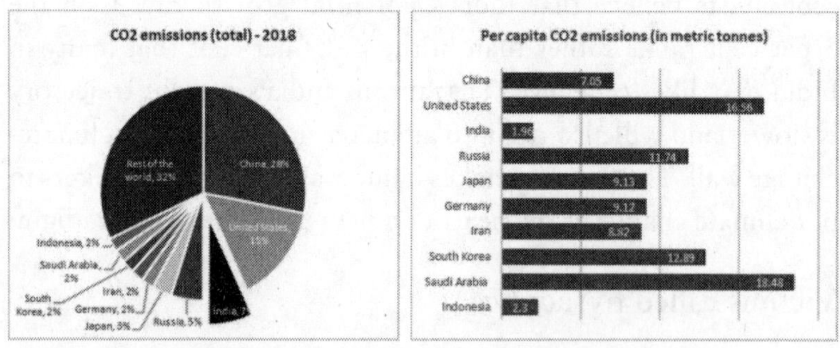

Source: Union of Concerned Scientists; IEA Atlas of Energy.

Developing countries had ensured the inclusion of the principle of 'common but differentiated responsibilities' in the Rio Declaration at the first Rio Earth Summit in 1992. The declaration states: 'In view of the different contributions to global environmental degradation, States have common but differentiated responsibilities. The developed countries acknowledge the responsibility that they bear in the international pursuit of sustainable development in view of the pressures their societies place on the global environment and of the technologies and financial resources they command.'[36] For Indian policymakers, seeking climate justice has been an article of faith. During the Kyoto negotiations, Prof. Saifuddin Soz, the leader of the Indian delegation, staked out the position that '... per capita basis is the most important criteria for deciding the rights to environmental space. This is a direct measure of human welfare. Since the atmosphere is a common heritage of humankind, equity has to be the fundamental basis for its management.'[37] Basically, the more developed world should be helping clean up the mess they have created.

While climate justice is important, it is equally true that without global cooperation, the climate crisis threatens countries like India disproportionately. India's climate negotiations strategy evolved over time for a variety of reasons. Foreign policy became an important driver, as did India's increased role at the high table of climate politics.[38] It is for this reason that India joined the Paris Agreement and is seen as one of its key signatories.

How the world is responding

Experts believe that the Paris commitments are neither ambitious enough nor will they take root fast enough to limit global warming to 1.5–2°C.[39] According to the Climate Action Tracker (CAT), current pledges and targets by countries imply that there is a 50 per cent chance that warming will exceed 2.6°C by 2100 with a range of 2.1– 3.3°C.[40] We already know that even 2°C warming is terrible for poor countries like India. This likely path would be catastrophic.

The Paris Agreement calls for a global target of net-zero emissions in the second half of the twenty-first century. This basically means that the world as a whole emits less GHGs into the atmosphere than it takes out. The European Union, Japan and South Korea are among 110 countries that have pledged carbon neutrality by 2050. China has pledged to be carbon neutral by 2060.[41] India has not yet pledged carbon neutrality and there isn't any consensus on the desirability of such a pledge. Jyoti and Kirit Parikh argue that putting pressure on India to quickly become net zero is 'not equitable to India', given where India is in its development trajectory and how critical fuel taxes are to government revenues.[42] Also, pledges are not the same as outcomes.

Time will tell if net-zero countries, and perhaps others, follow through on their commitments. Currently, many are well behind on their commitments. According to the CAT, the US, Russia, Japan, China and Argentina are making highly or critically insufficient progress on their commitments. Australia, Brazil, Canada and the EU are making insufficient progress. However, India is on track to meet its 2°C commitments.[43] But, as is the case with most countries, India faces a tricky balancing act as it deals with more immediate needs and troubling future prospects.

Still, there is progress and with improving knowledge, innovation, technology and institutional capacity, there is no telling how dramatically different the climate future could be. According to the World Resources Institute (WRI), there are several hopeful signs. Over 1,000 big companies have pledged major emission reductions. These companies account for $3.6 trillion in revenue and their combined emissions are equivalent to that of France. Microsoft, one of the biggest global corporations, could be carbon negative by 2030. Furthermore, around 400 cities worldwide have committed to net-zero emissions by 2050. In the US, cities are part of a coalition that is committed to fulfilling the Paris Agreement target. This coalition represents 70 per cent of the American economy.

Financial institutions are also beginning to defund fossil fuel investments and many countries, especially in Europe, are backing a 'green recovery' from the impact of COVID-19. Technological advances mean that renewable energy and other solutions are more attainable (figure 16.2). Solar energy prices have dropped 90 per cent between 2010 and 2019, while wind energy is cheaper than natural gas in some regions. There is also greater social pressure as stakeholders begin to absorb the implications of climate change to their own well-being.[44]

Figure 16.2: Growth in global wind and solar energy generation

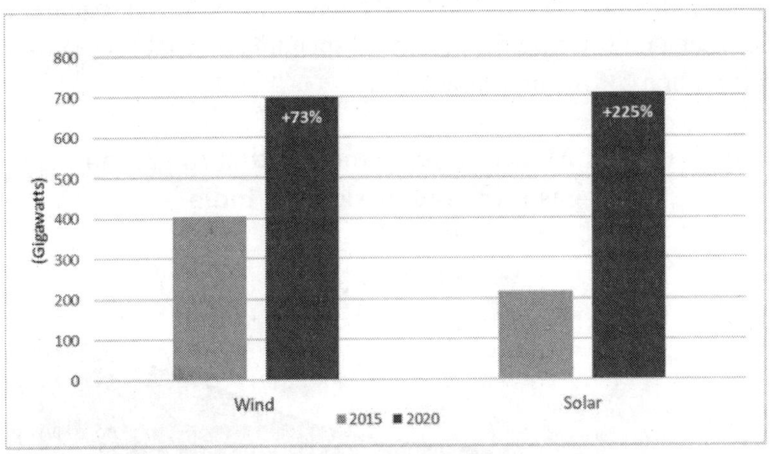

Source: *'Trends in Renewable Energy'*, International Renewable Energy Agency. https://www.irena.org/Statistics/View-Data-by-Topic/Capacity-and-Generation/Statistics-Time-Series

India must lead on climate change ... for its own sake

In recent decades, India's energy consumption has increased dramatically with fossil fuels like coal and gas being the main sources. India is the second-largest consumer of coal, after China. In 2017, coal accounted for 76 per cent of India's electricity. India is also the second-biggest producer of coal, with Coal India the reigning global champion (figure 16.3). India's Paris pledge is for a 33–35 per cent reduction in the energy intensity of its economic output by 2030, relative to 2005 levels. While this is a positive commitment, an analysis found that India's emissions could increase by 90 per cent between 2014 and 2030, even if the pledge is met.

India has also set a target of obtaining 40 per cent of its electricity from renewable sources by 2030.[45] India's leadership on climate change is welcomed by global leaders. In August 2020, the UN Secretary-General António Guterres praised India's efforts noting, 'Since 2015, the number of people working in renewable energy in India has increased five-fold. Last year, the country's spending on solar energy surpassed spending on coal-fired power generation for the first time.'

Figure 16.3: Major sectors contributing to greenhouse gas (GHG) emissions in India

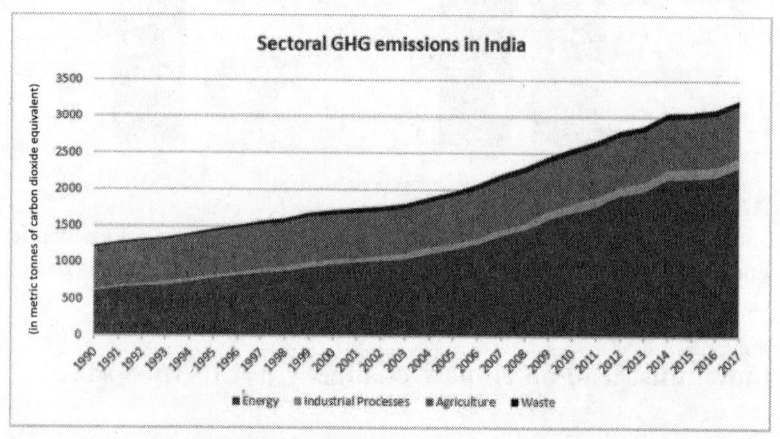

Source: *4 Charts Explain Greenhouse Gas Emissions by Countries and Sectors*, World Resources Institute (2020).

A Climate Assessment Tool (CAT) calculation shows that India's efforts could pay off. The adoption of the National Electricity Plan in 2018 could help India 'overachieve' its Paris targets. The

40 per cent non-fossil-fuel power capacity target could be met a decade early. CAT projects that India's energy intensity of output would be 50 per cent below 2005 levels, far ahead of the targeted 33–35 per cent. However, not everyone shares this optimism. Climate Transparency, an NGO, points out that while India's NDC is compatible with its below-2°C warming commitment, the current policy framework falls short.[46]

Researchers at Brookings Institution, a think tank, appear to support this view. They argue that coal will remain India's dominant fuel beyond 2030 and that 'Indian coal industry still faces structural and financial challenges'. Furthermore, they argue, 'The Indian power system is riddled with inefficiencies and distortions, from coal mining through final power sales to consumers.'[47] This suggests India has a far steeper hill to climb than what policy pronouncements might indicate (figure 16.4). It is not uncommon for India to have good policy intentions fail at the hurdle of bumbling implementation.

Figure 16.4: Electricity mix—India and China, October 2020

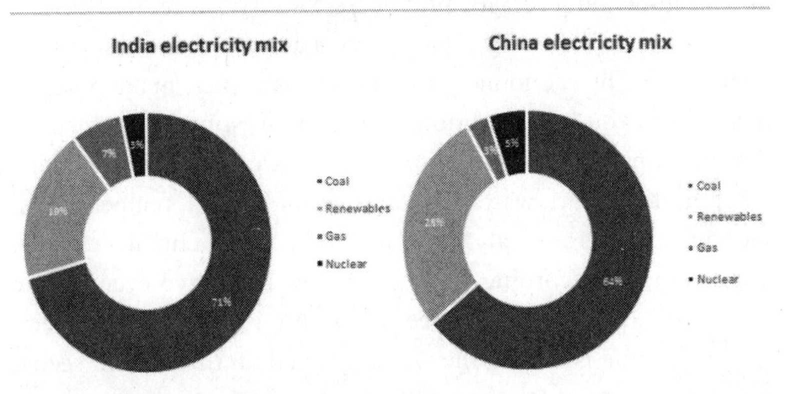

Source: International Energy Agency.

Beyond the standard discussion of energy mix, India must transcend one other hurdle. That has to do with the way the country thinks about the economic growth–climate action trade-off. Imagine you reduce coal consumption drastically and invest in renewables in a big way. India would be renouncing the use of an energy source that it has in abundance while having to invest in technologies that are developed elsewhere. India may also have to adapt in a variety of sectors. All this can be prohibitively expensive and that is why countries around the world have been unable to fully come to terms with climate change. Just to meets its 2030 Paris NDCs, India requires $2.5 trillion.[48] That is equivalent to almost its entire GDP in 2020.

In this context, what is the cost of climate inaction or insufficient action? In 1974, William Nordhaus wrote a landmark paper, 'Resources as a Constraint on Growth'. In this paper, Nordhaus argues that air, water and natural beauty should no longer be treated as free goods but as scarce resources. This was, Nordhaus argued, because excessive energy use and exploitation of environmental resources was creating a greenhouse effect and he worried about melting polar ice caps and an impending catastrophe.[49]

Burning fossil fuels is not a zero-cost activity as far as society is concerned. The economic growth that fossil fuels make possible has costs beyond the traditional costs of investing in production, distribution and consumption. There are costs like horrific air pollution and water contamination, rising temperatures, melting glaciers and all the other impacts of climate change. For example, according to *The Lancet*, heatwave events have led to the loss of almost three billion hours of labour capacity globally. India is among the worst affected on this count, 'seeing losses of potential labour capacity equivalent to 4–6 per cent of annual gross domestic product'.[50] Another study published in

The Lancet estimated that 1.24 million Indians died prematurely in 2017 due to factors attributable to air pollution.[51] Those costs need to become part of our climate vocabulary and our cost-benefit analyses. The more we think along those lines, the clearer it becomes that the level of ambition for countries like India needs to be at another level altogether.

Mind you, it isn't as if India's current growth trajectory is phenomenal. As discussed previously, many economists argue that the country's growth potential has dropped to about 5 per cent per year. At that rate, India is unlikely to hit upper-middle-income-country status before 2050. That means, India will not only remain in lower-middle-income status and have hundreds of millions of poor people, it will also suffer from many of the terrible impacts that a warming planet has in store for us. We propose a radically different agenda that not only sets much higher ambitions for India but also enables India to push the rest of the world to put up a bigger fight against climate change. After all, the wealthy countries will be able to weather this crisis much better than countries like India. It is imperative that through its actions, India highlights the urgency of securing deeper and more rapid cuts in GHGs.

The COVID-19 crisis has already dealt a massive blow to India's immediate economic prospects. However, COVID-19 is still a one-off crisis. Climate change impacts will feel like a series of crises that simply won't go away. It is for this reason that India must start to rethink development and use the post-pandemic period as a staging ground for a transformation of the economy. A key element of this transformation should include a far bigger push on renewable energy and a rapid pullback from fossil fuels. The latter imperil the future. Why would India not head in the other direction and quickly? The same goes for public transportation. Electric is the way to go. There appears to be no credible scenario in which gas-guzzling vehicles remain the preferred option in the future. China already has over 4,20,000 electric buses. By March 2020, India had added only about 1,031 electric buses, with close to 7,000 additional buses in the pipeline by 2022.[52] Why not cut future losses and invest heavily in that direction? It isn't even a gamble because we know the world is headed in that direction.

Not many in India may have heard of NextEra, Iberdrola, or Enel. However, we are certain many Indians know about Exxon and BP. What may surprise you is that NextEra and the others are green energy giants whose market valuations rival those of fossil fuel giants such as Exxon and BP. But even the green energy giants are likely to face competitive pressure as fossil fuel companies begin to transition to renewable energy. Should India not be thinking of transitioning Coal India away from coal, rebranding it as CI and start investing its considerable resources in renewable energy? The Indian government is always too happy to collect dividends from state-owned enterprises such as Coal India or ONGC or others. How about retooling these companies for the future? If Exxon can do it, why shouldn't Indian companies?

India must also focus on improving the energy efficiency of its industries. Ejaz Ghani believes that efforts towards greater energy efficiency alone could make a huge dent in reaching India's climate goals. Ghani notes that, '70% of the climate change agenda can be achieved by simply improving energy efficiency'.[53] Industries such as iron and steel, fertilizer, petroleum refining, cement and pulp and paper are among the most energy intensive and have improved efficiency standards over time. However, Ghani argues, much more needs to be done to improve energy efficiency to international standards. In this context, he points out, 'There is substantial potential for energy savings in many industries—it is

46-88% in textiles, 43-94% in pulp and paper, and 51-92% in iron and steel industry.'[54]

Of course, everything is not just about energy. There are so many sectors that require transformation. If you look at key sectors through the prism of climate change, life as we know it needs changing. Agriculture has to adapt and investing in that process now rather than in fighting old battles is perhaps the way to go. In construction, new codes are needed for climate resilience. Building standards have to evolve just as the use of light bulbs is evolving. Urban planning will require a greater focus on green infrastructure rather than the usual concrete-heavy methods that make cities vulnerable to heat island effects.

Transformation requires transformative thinking. It requires enabling institutions. It requires the human capital that can drive those institutions of change, that transformative thinking and that vision for a very different India. We keep coming back to the idea of investing more, much more in people, in their education and health. There must be greater investment in R&D and there has to be a retooling of public institutions with greater collaboration with the private sector. The twenty-first century is one in which India can dramatically alter its development trajectory and in the process alter the trajectory of climate change. We have forever lamented the missed opportunities of the past. It is time to engineer a whole new reality.

17

Preserving Progress

We cannot stop natural disasters, but we can arm ourselves with knowledge: so many lives wouldn't have to be lost if there was enough disaster preparedness.

—Petra Nemcova, Czech model and UNDRR World Tsunami Awareness Advocate

More frequently than not, we can predict that a disaster is coming. This is not only the case with approaching cyclones or a killer heatwave. This applies to most categories of disasters. It applies to pandemics too. Michael Osterholm, a top infectious diseases expert, once wrote that 'the arrival of a pandemic influenza would trigger a reaction that would change the world overnight. A vaccine would not be available for a number of months after the pandemic started …' He wrote further, 'Foreign trade and travel would be reduced or even ended in an attempt to stop the virus from entering new countries—even though such efforts would probably fail given the infectiousness of influenza and the volume of illegal crossings that occur at most borders.' Osterholm's prophetic words are from his 2005 essay in *Foreign Affairs* magazine.[1]

This warning is just one example among so many that are in the public domain and often presented formally to policymakers. Such warnings should ordinarily help prepare for emergencies that are likely to become reality. They can help mitigate the damage that a disaster may cause, reduce the time to recover from a disaster and possibly adapt to the underlying causes of future disasters. All this can ultimately lower the costs to society—countries and communities can save money by losing less to disaster impacts, as long as they are prepared. The old adage, 'money saved is money earned', applies to managing disaster risk. When disasters strike, governments sing paeans to the importance of disaster resilience. Once disaster impacts subside, so does the enthusiasm for ex-ante preparedness. India is no stranger to this failing. The COVID-19 pandemic is the latest example of an unwillingness to heed common-sense advice on preserving the gains of hard-earned progress.

India was unprepared for COVID-19. So were many other countries. The question really is what costs such unpreparedness imposes. If the costs are significant, then any sensible long-term development strategy should include a focus on preserving the gains of progress. It is self-serving to point to the failures of others to excuse our own. It is unacceptable to suggest that COVID-19 was an unpredictable 'black swan' event that caught India and the world by surprise. Nassim Nicholas Talib, who wrote the bestselling book *The Black Swan*, coined the term to describe an 'unpredictable, rare, catastrophic event'. COVID-19 was not such an event, as Talib explained in an interview with Bloomberg TV. Irritated by people calling COVID-19 a black swan event,

Talib told Bloomberg TV in March 2020 that 'we issued our warning that, effectively, you should kill it in the egg' and that governments 'did not want to spend pennies in January; now they are going to spend trillions'.[2]

Talib was referring to a paper from January 2020 that he co-authored with others. At that time, the virus was still largely confined to China.[3] In this paper, the authors argued that due to increased global connectivity, the spread of the virus would be 'nonlinear'. Taleb ruefully notes, 'Had we used masks then'—in late January—'we could have saved ourselves the stimulus'.[4] The stimulus Taleb referred to is the $2 trillion economic stimulus passed by the US Congress in March 2020. It is debatable if the entire stimulus would have been saved but a policy response that was ready for the pandemic would have helped the US save enormous resources. For reference, that stimulus was roughly equal to two-thirds of India's entire GDP in 2019. The bumbling response in the US led to need for a further infusion of resources to counteract the impact of the virus. Almost 6,00,000 Americans have died as of the writing of this book, millions have been infected and the economy has taken a massive hit.

It did not have to be this way, as experience in other countries has shown. South Korea, Taiwan, Singapore, China, New Zealand, Australia and some others avoided the worst impacts of the crisis.[5] Their success is often linked to lessons learnt after past crises. Some of China's neighbours strengthened their preparedness for future pandemics after the experience of the SARS crisis in 2003. After some initial stumbles, South Korea's response to the pandemic attracted global headlines. In March 2020, when the US, a country six times the size of South Korea, had tested a total of about 10,000 people, Korea had ramped up testing capacity to 10,000 per day.[6] A national emergency-alert system announced new confirmed cases on mobile phones, using a contact tracing system developed earlier. Drive-through testing facilities were rapidly established across the country. Those who were either infected or had come in contact with an infected person were isolated. The government supplied them with sanitizers, masks and groceries. In October 2020, when the IMF came out with its World Economic Outlook report, it projected that South Korea's growth in 2020 would contract by only 1.9 per cent. Compare that with India's 10.3 per cent and the 4.3 per cent contraction in the US.

While South Korea was rolling out a national testing plan, India was attempting to recruit epidemiologists in the middle of the pandemic. It emerged that more than a quarter of India's districts had no district-level epidemiologist. Worse, eleven states had no state-level epidemiologist.[7] India is a chaotic country, but one that has a rich tradition of institution-building. To be recruiting experts after the crisis had struck was akin to closing the stable door after the horse has bolted. COVID-19 laid bare the deficiencies in India's emergency preparedness as well as the deeply shambolic state of its health system.

In mid-March, the country of 1.3 billion people had tested only about 6,500 samples. The testing capacity was only 1,400 samples per day.[8] When the prime minister announced a fourteen-hour 'Janata (people's) Curfew' as a test run for a longer lockdown, the feeling in the country was that the pandemic would be subdued within weeks. This trial run saw millions of people respond positively to the prime minister's call to bang utensils as a way of showing solidarity with first responders and also warding off the evil virus. Scenes of crazed citizens banging on utensils and shouting, 'Go, Corona, go!' went viral on social media around the world. The prime minister himself stoked misperceptions about the pandemic. While announcing the first lockdown on 24 March, he told the country the 'Mahabharata war was won in eighteen days, but the battle which the entire country is fighting against coronavirus will take twenty-one days. Our aim is to win this war in twenty-one days.'[9]

The lockdown had devastating consequences because it had not been fully thought through. Millions of migrant workers, who are often daily wagers, were caught in no man's land. Their jobs were gone and they had no support systems in the cities they were living in. There was no transportation available to take them home to their villages. They quickly plunged into food insecurity and panic set in. Scenes of hundreds of thousands of workers desperately walking hundreds of miles to their homes became a regular feature of media coverage. It wasn't until May that the government got its act together and organized trains to take these workers home.

By early 2021, the government was declaring victory over COVID-19 after cases fell to less than 15,000 a day. That euphoria was short-lived and India was hit by a massive second wave that drove up reported cases to over 4,00,000 a day and deaths to over 4,000 a day (both vast undercounts). Scenes of thousands of dead bodies buried along riverbanks and frantic calls for help on social media underscored how the lessons of the first wave had been promptly forgotten by the government. India was totally unprepared, again.

Disasters impose costs and reverse progress

It will take time to fully assess the impact of COVID-19. Given wide disparities in data availability across countries, it is doubtful we will ever know the full cost in terms of the number of total infections, the number of lives lost or the overall economic costs. However, experts can help come up with more accurate estimates over time. For example, we could learn from the experience of the H1N1 flu pandemic, which started in the US in April 2009. Eventually, over 214 countries and territories reported H1N1 cases. By August 2010, the WHO declared the pandemic over.

There were 18,500 confirmed deaths between April 2009 and August 2010. However, researchers at the US Centers for Disease Control and Prevention (CDC) argued that 'an improved modelling approach' resulted in an 'estimated range of deaths from between 151,700 and 575,400 people who perished worldwide from 2009 H1N1 virus infection during the first year the virus circulated'. A study of reports from nineteen countries, including India, put the infection rate at 24 per cent of the population.[10] All this suggests that when the COVID-19 pandemic ends, the actual number of cases and deaths is likely to be much higher than reported data indicate.

The calculation of economic costs is similar. For now, we are focused on the contraction of economic output, loss of employment, business closures, fiscal and monetary policy responses, etc. Using these to assess losses, while legitimate, may still end up underestimating actual losses. There are several estimates of impacts on the global economy as a result of COVID-19. They vary widely but all point to deep economic pain. Using World Bank data, *The Economist* estimates that the world lost $5.6 trillion in GDP in 2020 compared to the previous year. However, the magazine notes, this number does not fully capture the cost of the pandemic. To do that we also need to see where the output would have been had there been no pandemic. Adding that difference in output to the earlier number makes the loss in global output $10.3 trillion. Only two countries, China and the US, have a bigger GDP than that number. Even so, *The Economist* notes that even this massive loss estimate does not present the full picture. The reason is that the World Bank expects global output in 2020 to be 4.4 per cent below its pre-pandemic projections.[11] But the crisis has continued in 2021 and it is unclear how long it will last, given the cross-country disparities in vaccine availability.

COVID-19 will leave deep scars on most economies. An analysis of economic vulnerabilities by Oxford Economics, a global forecasting consultancy, finds that long-term economic scarring in India could be among the deepest in the world.[12] Limited fiscal support for the recovery, structural rigidities, imbalances in the financial sector and other reasons will cause the economy to take longer to reach its pre-pandemic trajectory. This is not unusual. A decade after the Great Recession (2007–09), the US economy was 'significantly smaller' than it should have been, based on its pre-crisis growth trend.[13] Economists at the IMF have extensively studied the impact of recessions on economic output. They assert that 'all types of recessions, on average, lead to permanent output losses'.[14] But not all countries are the same and they don't all have the resources to weather recessions effectively. Oxford Economics estimates that by 2025, 'the long-term economic damage from the pandemic will be twice as severe in emerging markets compared with wealthy countries'.[15] With India's 2020 economic activity expected to contract by over 7 per cent, it faces a long-term struggle to get back to its pre-pandemic trajectory.

The growing toll of natural disasters

To better follow the rest of this chapter, it is important to understand the technical meaning of natural disasters (versus natural hazards). The United Nations Office for Disaster Risk Reduction (UNDRR) uses the definition of disaster that is followed by the Emergency Events Database (EM-DAT), a comprehensive disaster database. The EM-DAT database includes those disaster events that have one of the following four characteristics: (i) ten or more people reported killed; (ii) 100 or more people reported affected; (iii) declaration of a state of emergency; and (iv) call for international assistance. Furthermore, UNDRR distinguishes between natural hazards and natural disasters. According to UNDRR, the term hazard refers to a severe or extreme event such as a flood, storm, cold spell or heatwave, etc., which occurs naturally anywhere in the world. Hazards only become disasters when human lives are lost, and livelihoods are damaged or destroyed. Figure 17.1 shows various categories of natural hazards.

Figure 17.1: Different types of natural hazards

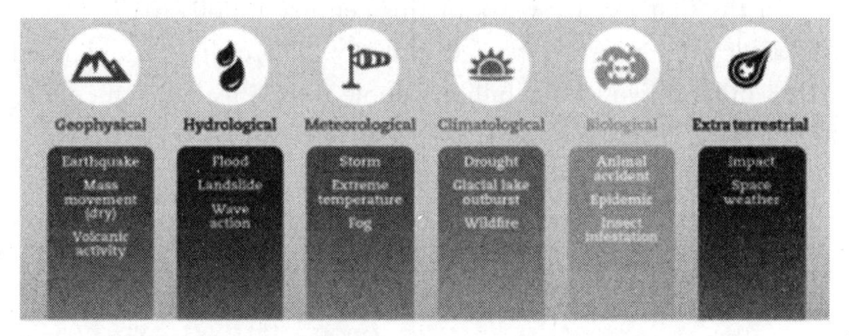

Source: United Nations Office for Disaster Risk Reduction.

Before COVID-19, experts had been warning about the growing costs of natural disasters. While the focus has been less on pandemics and more on the 'usual' geophysical and hydrometeorological disasters, there is growing evidence of the rising toll of natural disasters, and substantial literature on managing disaster risk. The focus here is mostly on economic losses but we will begin with the deadly impact of disasters. COVID-19's reported global death toll currently stands at over 3.5 million. Pandemics can have extremely high death tolls, as was the case with the Spanish Flu, which killed tens of millions of people around the world. Historically, plagues, flu pandemics, and other contagions have killed millions.[16,17]

However, non-pandemic disasters can be just as deadly and expensive. The table below presents the deadliest natural (non-pandemic) disasters in history. With more than two million deaths, China's Yangtze River floods in 1931 were of truly epic proportions (table 17.1). Melting snow and heavy rainfall combined to inundate 180,000 square kilometres, an area 3,000 times the size of Manhattan.[18] Imagine the ferocious Bhola cyclone with wind speeds of 205 kilometres per hour and a 35-foot storm surge that inundated low-lying areas and killed hundreds of thousands of people who had not been evacuated to safety.[19]

In the first twenty years of this century (2000–2019), 7,348 disaster events were reported globally. These disasters claimed 1.23 million lives. Four billion people were affected, some more than once. Total economic losses as a result of these disasters stood at about $3 trillion. Of these disaster events, 6,681 were climate-related, killing 510,837 people and affecting 3.9 billion people. That means other types of disasters (e.g., earthquakes, mass movements, etc.) affected fewer people overall.

Table 17.1: Top ten deadliest natural disasters in history

Rank	Disaster Event	Country	Year	Death Toll
1	Yangtze River floods	China	1931	2,000,000–3,7000,000
2	1887 Yellow River flood	China	1887	9,00,000–2,000,000
3	1556 Shaanxi	China	1556	830,000
4	Bhola cyclone	East Pakistan (now Bangladesh)	1970	3,00,000–3,16,000
5	Haiti earthquake	Haiti	2010	2,30,000–3,16,000
6	Haiphong typhoon	Vietnam	1881	3,000,000
7	Coringa cyclone	India	1839	3,000,000
8	526 Antioch earthquake	Byzantine Empire (now Turkey)	AD 526	250,000
9	Tangshan earthquake	China	1976	2,40,000–7,00,00
10	Aleppo earthquake	China	1138	2,30,000

Source: Top ten deadliest natural disasters in history, LiveScience

In the twenty years prior to 2000, the number of reported disaster events was 4,212, with 1.19 million lives lost and 3 billion people affected. Of these, 3,656 climate-related events killed almost 1 million people. The significant rise in the number of disasters and their human cost could have multiple explanations. For example, reporting mechanisms for disasters are now better and estimating losses is becoming more scientific. Another explanation could be that with greater urbanization, dense population centres are more vulnerable to hazards and the chances of higher human and economic losses are greater.

India recorded 321 disasters during 2000–19, the third-highest worldwide. Only China and the US had more. The Gujarat earthquake in 2001 and the floods in Kashmir in 2014 left behind a trail of destruction. The Gujarat earthquake is listed by the UNDRR as one of the top ten mega-disasters of the twenty-first century, killing 20,005 people and inflicting economic losses of over $1 billion.[20] The Kashmir floods in 2014 became the most expensive disaster globally that year. Of the twenty-seven natural disasters worldwide that cost over $1 billion that year, the Kashmir floods proved to be the most expensive with a price tag of $18 billion.[21] Initial government estimates put the cost of Kashmir's floods at $7 billion, which amounted to 50 per cent of Jammu and Kashmir's annual gross state domestic product (GSDP).[22] The revised $18 billion is well above 100 per cent of GSDP.

Natural disasters can inflict the kinds of losses that can cripple economies and it is imperative that policymakers and other stakeholders do more to internalize the recommendations of experts. Prevention is better than cure. If you can't prevent something, reduce the risk of it happening. If a risk is realized, be prepared to deal with the consequences. The faster you act, the less the pain and the duration of the after-effects of disasters.

Status of India's disaster risk management (DRM) framework

India's disaster risk management (DRM) framework mainly derives from the Disaster Management Act, 2005. Prompted by the 2004 Indian Ocean tsunami, this law established the National Disaster Management Authority (NDMA), which is the apex institution for disaster management in India. The NDMA presides over the institutional architecture, which includes state- and local-level DRM agencies. The NDMA 'is mandated to lay down the policies, plans and guidelines for Disaster Management' and 'envisions the development of an ethos of Prevention, Mitigation, Preparedness and Response'.[23] The prime minister is the chairperson of the NDMA, which can have nine additional members as part of its governance structure. The prime minister can appoint a vice chairperson to act as the executive head of the NDMA.

India's legal and institutional framework correctly emphasizes the need to move away from disaster response to prevention, mitigation, preparedness and response. This is consistent with the evolution of DRM frameworks around the world. India was a signatory to the Hyogo Framework for Action (HFA), which provided the global blueprint for efforts to reduce disaster risk between 2005 and 2015. After Hyogo, India signed the Sendai Framework, which establishes four priority areas of action and seven targets for all signatories (see table 17.2).

Undoubtedly, India has improved in some aspects of disaster management. The state of Odisha is a great example of improvements in preparing for disasters. In October 1999, a super-cyclone struck Odisha's coastal areas. The cyclone packed maximum wind speeds of 170–185 miles per hour. Torrential rains and a massive storm surge inundated large parts of the state. About 10,000 people were killed and hundreds of thousands displaced. Economic devastation ensued.[24] Fast forward to 2013 when Cyclone Phalin struck Odisha, the death toll was 0.5 per cent and the economic loss was about one-third of that in 1999.[25] In 2019, when Cyclone Fani struck Odisha, 64 people died. While 64 is not an insignificant number, it is a far cry from the devastating losses in 1999.

Table 17.2: Evolution of global disaster risk reduction networks

Hyogo Framework for Action (2005–15)	Sendai Framework (2015–30)
Five priorities for action	**Four priorities for action**
Ensure that disaster risk reduction (DRR) is a national and a local priority with a strong institutional basis for implementation	Understanding disaster risk
Identify, assess and monitor disaster risks, and enhance early warning	Strengthening disaster risk governance to manage disaster risk
Use knowledge, innovation and education to build a culture of safety and resilience at all levels	Investing in disaster reduction for resilience
Reduce the underlying risk factors	Enhancingdisaster preparedness for effective response, and to 'Build Back Better' in recovery, rehabilitation and reconstruction
Strengthen disaster preparedness for effective response at all levels	

Source: United Nations Office for Disaster Risk Reduction.

Accounts from the 1999 tragedy indicate that there was little attention paid to the dangers of natural disasters. Coordination between government agencies was weak and people did not have adequate warning of the impending calamity. By 2013 and 2019, the Odisha government had learnt key lessons from the 1999 experience. Over time, Odisha has built a vast community outreach network, built 450 cyclone shelters and trained people in search and rescue, first aid and early warning systems. During both Fani and Phalin, more than a million people were evacuated from the path of the cyclones. That is no mean feat for a poor state that gets pummelled regularly by such storms. Despite this progress, Odisha 'suffered major losses in terms of infrastructure, particularly electrical infrastructure, housing, public buildings, transport infrastructure, including airports and railway stations, and also port and harbor areas'.[26]

Commendable as Odisha's progress is, it is not representative of India as a whole. You only have to review the total communications breakdown during the 2014 Kashmir floods or the continued havoc wreaked by the Kosi River in Bihar to see that India has a long way to go to have a more effective and modern DRM system. Signing international agreements or putting in place legal frameworks or institutions is not sufficient. There is a lot more that must happen for real change to be visible on the ground. For India to be able to reduce the impact of an inevitable rise in the burden of natural disasters, a comprehensive agenda merits attention.

A post-COVID-19 agenda

Legal and institutional. The 2005 Disaster Management Act should be amended to make it more inclusive. COVID-19 has exposed the limitations of this law and also highlighted the confusion surrounding the term 'disaster'. When we think of disasters, earthquakes and floods come readily to mind. However, pandemics are disasters too. We need to have a common definition of natural hazards and disasters. The NDMA must also be reformed and it should have a full-time chief executive and a proper administrative team. The NDMA has not had a vice-chairperson for the last seven years. Imagine the United States Federal Emergency Management Agency (FEMA) without its administrator for seven years. The PM is the chairperson but cannot be expected to lead this agency when s/he has to lead the country. This structure should be replicated across the country, at different levels. The NDMA also has to link up with local-level DRM agencies as well as other agencies that need to be part of the DRM framework. It is a massive undertaking and one that requires constant fine-tuning. Imagine reforming land-use policies to help reduce disaster risk. India's DRM agencies are in no position to address such issues because of capacity challenges as well as jurisdictional constraints. Until such time that DRM is mainstreamed in a manner consistent with the letter and spirit of international frameworks and lessons and practices, India will be playing catch up to more advanced countries.

More focus on social impacts. There is a need to pay much more attention to the indirect impacts of disasters. For instance, the risk of an outbreak of diseases following natural disasters is very high, due to overcrowding, displacement, sanitation issues and lack of drinking water.[27] However, these types of issues are often dealt with on an ad hoc basis rather than as part of a coherent framework. Similarly, disasters leave lasting legacies that endure far beyond a visit to a disaster site by a high-profile dignitary or the announcement of immediate relief by a government. For example, one study found that the economic shock from the 2008 Kosi floods in Bihar was linked to an increase in child marriages.

There were more child marriages in districts that experienced greater destruction of property. For families of male children, such marriages can fetch dowries to help smooth consumption.[28] To modernize India's DRM framework, such social dimensions deserve to be included.

More green infrastructure. As India urbanizes, there is likely to be greater concentration of economic activity. This will magnify the risks of major disasters. Climate change is likely to add fuel to this fire. India is no stranger to unplanned development, competition for space and environmental degradation. This often results in the choking of floodplains and natural catchment areas of rivers and coastal zones. The focus often is on hard engineering or 'grey' solutions such as dams and levees to address the risk of floods. These solutions remain important as part of a broad DRM framework. However, with the growing threat of climate-related disasters, especially floods and heat island effects, there is now more interest in developing green infrastructure (GI) solutions such as wetlands, bioshields, buffer zones, green roofing, street side swales, porous pavements, wetlands, mangroves, etc. As India's rural–urban transition continues, this should become a more important element of urban DRM.[29]

Systematize lifesaving measures. Whether it is protection from storms, floods, or earthquakes, there are many measures that governments can take. We have seen in the case of Odisha that cyclone shelters save lives. However, this is not done systematically in India. Governments at different levels should invest in shelters to protect especially vulnerable populations from severe disaster events. Of course, a key method would be to ensure that people live in homes that are built to modern specifications or at least minimum specifications to offer protection against disaster events.

Disaster management should be more proactive. Despite efforts to create early warning systems, surveillance systems, etc., disaster management agencies still seem to be more reactive than truly prepared.[30] The burden of post-disaster rehabilitation remains on states and only a few states, such as Andhra Pradesh, Odisha and Kerala, have department-level disaster management plans in place.[31] Similarly, an analysis of India's response to COVID-19 and previous outbreaks of infectious diseases reveals that rather than developing national legislation to tackle infectious diseases, India mostly relies on ad hoc notifications and guidelines. Despite the fact that the 2005 Disaster Management Act is not geared towards pandemics, it became the legal basis for the government's response. This highlights the lack of readiness in combating infectious diseases.[32] This must change urgently.

Strengthen coordination, data harmonization and communication. Improved coordination and communication between agencies at various levels of government should be at the top of the agenda. For instance, when it comes to pandemic preparedness, multiple bodies at different levels (local, state and national) are responsible for the collection of data on the same disease. The use of different methods, standards and definitions with 'little or no coordination' creates weak surveillance and detection infrastructure.[33] Often there is also a duplication of efforts and financial allocation. For example, the National Action Plan on Climate Change does not take into consideration state-level risk assessments, and state-level action plans do not take into account national-level risk assessments, at the planning or implementation stage.[34]

In line with the Sendai Framework, India must standardize methodologies to collect data on fatalities, injuries and economic losses due to disasters. This data is necessary to improve our understanding of disaster impacts and help us analyse data in a disaggregated manner. This is how policymakers can prioritize interventions to safeguard against future disasters as well as reduce recovery and reconstruction efforts post disasters. There is also a need to better understand the pattern of communication during disaster events. Studying these patterns can help refine communication strategies that can save lives, reduce damage and help relief and recovery efforts. In this context, it is also important to ensure the physical preservation of lines of communication between different agencies and the general public.

Greater insurance penetration and social protection. Natural disasters can disproportionately impact poor and vulnerable populations. For poor and vulnerable populations, the damage to their meagre assets can be devastating. Given the low levels of insurance penetration, most households have to use their savings or borrow to cover their losses.[35] A study of the 2005 Mumbai floods found that families living below the poverty line lost more than a year's income (1,480 per cent of their average monthly income) due to the disaster. Those classified as poor lost five months of income and other income groups lost between one to two months' income. The largest share of this money was spent on house repair. Similarly, most small businesses did not have insurance coverage and covered their losses with their own resources. For those involved in global supply chains, shutting down their businesses for weeks resulted in a loss of international clients.[36] The full spectrum of insurance options must become part of India's DRM framework and India can gain much from global experience in this area.

Tech solutions. As with other aspects of modern societies, technology is also revolutionizing disaster management. From using drones in support of relief and rescue missions to big data analytics, technology can transform disaster management capabilities. For example, the World Food Programme (WFP) deploys a mobile technology in over thirty countries to conduct 20,000 surveys per month. This helps save millions of dollars and a lot of time in collecting and compiling survey data. In a different vein, Cisco uses mobile networking technology to establish connectivity when disasters strike. Cisco is often faster at doing this than local governments.[37] Digital communications systems and social media can play a hugely important role in disaster management. The goal for policymakers should be to make technology an integral part of India's national and sub-national DRM frameworks.

Given how sophisticated DRM has become, it is not possible to highlight all the advances that India must take notice of. However, the reader should be left with one key message: disasters can wipe out development gains of years in a matter of hours. They can leave lasting damage and can have a disproportionate impact on the poor and vulnerable. By investing in risk reduction, preparedness, early warning capabilities as well as in relief, rescue and recovery infrastructure and by utilizing modern technology, the worst impacts of disasters can be mitigated. Lives can be saved and losses can be curtailed. A rupee saved is a rupee earned.

18

Technology: Disruption, Inclusion and Governance

If you always do what you always did, you will always get what you always got.

—Albert Einstein, American theoretical physicist and mathematician

American military planners are coming to terms with a grim new reality. Its famed aircraft carriers, which have been synonymous with the projection of American military might around the world, may be on their way out. More than a century since they were originally conceived, aircraft carriers remain a mainstay of the US military. They are truly behemoths, can cost billions of dollars to manufacture and require hundreds of sailors to man them. It is no wonder that only a handful of countries operate aircraft carriers. The US has eleven, while China and the Uk have two each. Russia and India operate one each. (India is about to commission its second carrier.)[1]

The costs and logistics of operating these carriers can be immense. Commissioned in 2017, the USS *Gerald Ford* cost $13 billion. It can house seventy-five fighter aircrafts. These are deployed as part of a fleet of ships with extensive logistical networks. They are almost invincible, given that the last American carrier to be sunk was the USS *Bismarck* in 1945.[2] But that may be about to change in an unexpected way.

Just because an aircraft carrier has not been sunk in decades does not mean they are invulnerable. They are big targets with tremendous military and symbolic value for adversaries. Unsurprisingly, now there are new weapon systems in development that can immobilize or even destroy these carriers. In 2018, the Chinese military deployed the DF-26, a 'manoeuvring missile' that has gained the nickname of 'carrier killer'. Basically, this missile can alter its course just before its final approach towards its target, making it a potent weapon to disrupt an aircraft carrier. Imagine a missile that can be lugged around in a lorry and fired at a multi-billion-dollar aircraft carrier sitting like a duck, hundreds of kilometres away. It is perhaps for this reason that the US keeps its aircraft carriers about 1,600 km from the Chinese coastline.[3]

To deal with this threat, the Americans are now contemplating a countermeasure that involves aircraft carriers in the sky. The idea, which, according to *The Economist*, dates to 1917, involves a large cargo plane carrying drones that would be deployed for reconnaissance, communication disruption, actual combat and missile strikes.[4] The aircraft carrier is likely being re-engineered in ways that may have not occurred to planners just a few decades back. Perhaps it is for such reasons that the

Indian navy recommended to the government in March 2021 to not go ahead with a third aircraft carrier. The Indian navy has instead opted for six nuclear-powered attack submarines.[5] While the choice between a carrier and submarines must be a result of strategic planning, it is inconceivable that evolving technologies, including in China, had no role to play in this decision.

Riding the technology wave

The implications of technological evolution for India are far-reaching, well beyond the narrow scope of our military example above. Technology has become so interwoven with our existence that it is natural to imagine the immense strides a country can make in this era. In many respects, the potential for emerging and developing economies to leapfrog outdated technologies to maximize their development gains is tantalizingly close. The question before policymakers is to see how best to harness technology and innovation for growth and development, how to balance regulation with ease of doing business and how to close the technology divide that is already opening up in India. This chapter focuses on these issues.

Technology is too vast a topic to be prescriptive about. To keep the growth of technology in check is a fool's errand. We are not about to recommend the adoption of one innovation over another. That is far beyond the scope of this book or, for that matter, the abilities of the authors. However, our more limited task is to provide a sense of the potential for technology to do good and to discuss emerging regulatory practices. Since we believe that India's future prospects are best served by more inclusive policies, we also share here some of our concerns about the evolution of technology in India and ways in which those concerns can be mitigated.

Beyond modern manufacturing, discussed in depth in Chapter 12, technology has had a profound impact on India. In some ways, we are still in the early stages of the Fourth Industrial Revolution and the digital transformation that we expect will dramatically transform lives around the world and in India. Some of it is already happening. Visit a railway station and you will find people peering into their mobile phones, perhaps catching their favourite sporting event or listening to music or messaging friends.[6]

In 2018, Indians accounted for 1.2 billion mobile phone subscriptions and twelve billion app downloads. There were 560 million internet subscribers. Only China had more. Indian mobile data users consume 8.3 gigabytes (GB) of data each month on average, more than that in China and comparable to that in South Korea.[7] An analysis of seventeen countries by the McKinsey Global Institute (MGI) found that India was digitizing faster than all other countries except Indonesia. At the time, with only 40 per cent of the population having an internet connection, there was quite a bit of room to grow.[8]

Technology for development

Both the government and private players are helping drive technology adoption. The government deployed the Aadhaar unique digital identity programme, enrolling over 1.2 billion residents. Besides acting as an ID, Aadhaar also facilitates government transfers to citizens (e.g., pension or subsidy payments), and enables a variety of transactions affecting everyday life. In addition, starting in 2017, the government also enrolled about ten million businesses in the GST structure. This too has major implications for India going forward. But while Aadhaar and GST are more well known, there is a broader technology platform underpinning India's push towards digital transformation.

Starting in 2009, the government set up a payments infrastructure (National Payments Corporation of India or NPCI) to go along with Aadhaar, to create what we today call the IndiaStack.[9] As part of this platform, the United Payments Infrastructure (UPI) enables people to use their mobile phones to transfer money using biometric inputs of Aadhaar. And at zero cost! Think of Venmo, but much, much bigger. PwC, a consultancy, reported that UPI processed 12.5 trillion transactions valued at Rs 21 trillion ($281 billion) in 2020. Between 2017 and 2020, UPI's compound annual growth rate was 785 per cent in volume and 570 per cent in value.[10]

The private sector has also stepped up but technology adoption, especially in the digital sphere, has been uneven. McKinsey reports that in its survey of 600 firms, 'Digital leaders in the top quartile of adopters are two to three times more likely to use software for customer relationship management, enterprise resource planning or search engine optimization than firms in the bottom quartile, and are almost fifteen times more likely to centralize digital management.' McKinsey believes that digital applications are likely to proliferate across sectors and that by 2025, 'core digital sectors, such as IT-BPM, digital communication services and electronics manufacturing, could double their GDP level to $355 billion–$435 billion'.[11]

Beyond these core sectors, 'newly digitizing' sectors such as education, healthcare and agriculture could add tens or hundreds of billions of dollars to India's GDP. All this would help take India closer to the government's ambition of creating a $1 trillion digital economy by 2025.[12] This goal is an extension of the Digital India initiative launched in 2015, which aims to transform India into 'a digitally empowered society and knowledge economy'.[13]

In key sectors, such as agriculture, education, health, energy, public sector, etc., technology will likely transform the landscape in powerful ways. In agriculture, the Digital India programme focuses on three themes: (i) digital financing and insurance payouts; (ii) precision agriculture using data analytics; (iii) introduction of online marketplaces.[14] These changes would be part of a transformation in global agriculture that is currently taking place. AI, data analytics, connected sensors and other technologies are likely to increase yields, improve the use of water and build farm resilience. The MGI estimates that new technologies in the agriculture sector will help add $500 billion to annual global GDP by 2030.[15]

Healthcare is an obvious area in which technology has shown great promise. The COVID-19 pandemic has hastened the spread of telemedicine in India and around the world. Earlier in this book, we have recounted the immense challenges facing Indian healthcare. Without much greater use of technology, providing universal healthcare in a vast country like India is impossible. There isn't enough of anything—physicians, hospital beds, equipment, trained paramedical staff, etc. However, technology and innovation give India an opportunity to surmount many existing challenges. This is not to suggest that India will suddenly leapfrog other countries on health parameters. After all, technology solutions are available to other countries as well. However, if fifty million Indians could access online health services since March 2020 (almost half of them in non-metropolitan areas), that shows a possible pathway to improve health service delivery.[16] By even making some of the most basic strides in technology-driven health services—think primary health consultations, medical records management and prescription services—India's health outcomes could see vast improvements. Of course, innovations will go far beyond these basic changes. AI, interoperable data and sophisticated robotics will increasingly become part of modern healthcare. Before India gets there, the focus should be on getting the basics right even as innovators at the leading edge keep pushing the envelope further.

In education as well, technology can play a very helpful role. During the pandemic, online education has expanded around the world. However, its limits are also becoming clearer. The need for social interactions as well as the unavailability of childcare at home makes it difficult to conceive of an 'online-only' system of education. However, online education as a complement to 'in-person' education is going to continue to grow. BYJU'S, one of India's most successful unicorns, delivers online lessons and content, and has millions of paying subscribers.[17] In 2020, it was valued at $12 billion, making it similar in size to the venerable Tata Steel and the public sector giant Coal India.[18] It isn't just BYJU'S; more than 4,000 EdTech start-ups have come up in India and attracted over $2 billion in funding in the last few years.[19] There is likely to be a proliferation of EdTech solutions as one part of the response to the big learning outcome gaps in India and similar countries.

Our examples of agriculture, health and education are just the tip of the iceberg. Innovation will drive massive changes across the entire economy. And all of this may happen more rapidly than most of us imagine. Truly amazing technologies are in the works and, in many cases, science fiction will become a reality. Instead of using 3D teaching aids to explain molecular structures, teachers can use holograms to do the same. With more flexible and arguably cost-efficient methods, learning outcomes and spending efficiency can improve. Similarly, advances in water desalination could open up a lifeline for water-stressed regions; energy storage solutions could help drive the solar market; and data analytics could improve public service delivery.

There is so much more that the world is already working on. In 2012, Jennifer Doudna and Emmanuelle Charpentier discovered that an ancient bacterial immune system could help edit the genetic sequences of living things.[20] Doudna and Charpentier pioneered CRISPR technology (the succinct acronym stands for 'clustered regularly interspaced short palindromic repeats'), which is based on a family of DNA sequences, and is helping engineer thousands of organisms. Scientists believe CRISPR could help cure heritable diseases, increase food security and counter the impacts of climate change.[21] Imagine using CRISPR to eliminate a threat posed by a virus like the coronavirus that is ravaging our world today.[22] The possibilities of technological innovation appear limitless.

Technological disruption—a mixed blessing?

Technology and innovation are leading to socio-economic benefits, enhanced efficiency and improved productivity across sectors and across the world. However, these advances will also have disruptive consequences and not all of these will be risk-free or even positive. Inequality could rise, employment could decline, public safety and national security risks could grow, or the risks and consequences of systemic failures could rise exponentially in a globally networked environment. Before anyone accuses us of being Luddites, a bit of historical context is necessary.

We generally think of Luddites as those who oppose technological advances because of the potential for machines to replace human labour. However, the more than 200-year-old protests connected to Luddites were less about machines replacing human labour than their complaint against manufacturers who used machines in 'a fraudulent and deceitful manner'. Research indicates that the protesters who spawned the

Luddite movement wanted '... machines to be run by workers who had gone through an apprenticeship and got paid decent wages'.[23] Therefore, Luddites we definitely are not. However, Luddism, in its contemporary avatar of technology scepticism, has its benefits. There are those who believe that Luddism is an important counterbalance to 'smart-tech utopianism' because it '... enables critical reflection and evaluation of the world we have built and are building'.[24]

And it isn't as if technology-related fears are a preserve of people only in developing countries. In the 1980s, when computers began to proliferate, the term 'computerphobia' was coined. When the telephone was invented, people worried about the machine being used for communicating with the dead. Technology and anxieties go hand in hand.[25] In 2015, the Survey of American Fears quantified these anxieties. And what did Americans find scary at that time? Of the five scariest things, three were related to advances in technology—cyberterrorism, corporate tracking of personal information and government tracking of personal information. In fact, death did not strike as much fear in Americans.[26]

It is perfectly fine to be anxious or sceptical about technology-driven changes. In that spirit, three overarching concerns should animate Indian policymaking and public discourse. The approach to these issues will go a long way in managing risks, as India tries to leverage technology to advance socio-economic goals. First, advances in technology threaten to create a digital divide, exacerbating already sharp inequality within and between countries. Second, there are genuine concerns about privacy, data security and the power that technology can give to governments and corporations. Third, technologies such as AI are creating anxieties around the future of work. For countries like India, which struggle mightily to create decent jobs, labour-substituting technologies pose a serious threat to social stability. If India can develop robust and progressive governance and policy frameworks for these three issues, that would be quite an achievement.

A widening chasm

In 2005, *The Economist* acknowledged the emergence of a digital divide between richer and poorer nations and communities.[27] This divide was a result of broader problems such as incomes, development and literacy. The magazine argued that there was no magic wand that could simply erase this divide. Even if you put a computer in every home, the divide would remain. After all, what good is a computer if you don't have enough to eat or if you don't have electricity or if you cannot read? These were sensible observations. Instead of swishing a magic wand, *The Economist* suggested that mobile phones could have a much bigger impact on development. Quoting a paper, the magazine asserted that 'mobile phones raise long-term growth rates, that their impact is twice as big in developing nations as in developed ones, and that an extra ten phones per 100 people in a typical developing country increases GDP growth by 0.6 percentage points'.[28] The real divide then was about access to the internet and the World Bank had found that 77 per cent of the world's population already lived close to a mobile network.[29]

Over fifteen years later, we are still talking about a stubborn digital divide that not only is not going away but threatens to widen over time. As the cost of data has tumbled (95 per cent since 2013) and smartphone use has picked up, the use of the internet has substantially increased in recent years.[30] Estimates on the number of internet users in India vary between 500–700 million. In November 2019, Nielsen estimated that India has 504 million active internet users who are five years and above.

Just between March 2019 and November 2019, India added 53 million new internet users.[31] However, less than 40 per cent of the population has internet connectivity. Of these, only 33 per cent are female.[32] For many, internet connectivity remains patchy. One survey found, 'Among respondents who use home broadband, over 3 per cent face cable cuts, 53 per cent face poor connectivity and 32 per cent face signal issues. In case of mobile data, 40 per cent face poor connectivity and 57 per cent face signal issues.'[33]

Nobel Prize winner, and former president of Costa Rica, Oscar Arias suggests that IT access be added to food, shelter, clothing, education and health as a vital part of a basic needs package. IT access is now considered a vital part of infrastructure in the developed world. India has a lot of catching up to do. International Telecommunication Union (ITU) data shows that India lags behind others on IT access—and despite it being touted as an IT powerhouse—IT access in India is at about the same level as in Pakistan (table 18.1). While mobile telephony has expanded, data download speeds remain very low—again the same level as Pakistan and well behind India's competitors.

Table 18.1 India's IT access is low

Country	Percentage with internet access	Mobile download speed (Mbit/second)
Australia	87	89.4
Japan	91	49.3
Sweden	96	29.7
Germany	95	28.7
United States	96	26.7
Vietnam	70	20.6
Malaysia	80	11

Country	Percentage with internet access	Mobile download speed (Mbit/second)
Indonesia	80	9.9
Pakistan	47	8.4
India	55	8.1

Source: International Telecommunication Union.

Data privacy and security versus legitimate government–business needs

In 2017, a nine-member bench of India's Supreme Court unanimously declared individual privacy to be a fundamental right. The Union government had argued that the Constitution does not have a provision for the right to privacy. The Supreme Court, while overturning two previous judgments ruled that privacy was 'an intrinsic part of the right to life and liberty' and part of the freedoms guaranteed by the Constitution.[34] At the time, many felt that this judgement would lead to better data protection and adherence to personal privacy norms. A debate was raging about the ubiquitous nature of Aadhaar. It was a setback for Aadhaar, according to some. However, some years removed from that judgement, the use of Aadhaar is more widespread, individual privacy appears less guaranteed and technology appears to be increasingly used as a tool of surveillance by governments in India.[35]

India needs a legal framework that balances the right of individuals to protect their personal data with the need to ensure innovation for growth and progress. The Indian Data Protection Bill hopes to achieve that balance. However, it is increasingly clear that on this issue there is an asymmetry of power between individual citizens and the government and businesses. There are serious concerns that this legislation strengthens the government's increasingly intrusive powers and is less supportive of citizen rights.[36] When mass protests against a controversial citizenship law erupted in 2019, the police used facial recognition software in Delhi to screen protesters while drones surveilled them in Chennai.[37] It has now become routine for police to use facial recognition and fingerprinting on 'suspicious' individuals.[38] The combination of Aadhaar and new surveillance technologies, without adequate safeguards, has serious ramifications for India's democracy and its economy. In 2019, a UK-based research firm ranked India among the top three surveillance states (behind Russia and China).[39]

In India, as elsewhere, citizens, businesses and governments are all concerned about cybersecurity. Data breaches that impact millions of people are rising. Meanwhile, businesses and governments are also grappling with threats to their systems, including from foreign adversaries. In 2020, India saw a 37 per cent rise in data breaches and cyber threats compared to the previous year. Just in one instance, private details of 20 million customers of BigBasket, an online grocer, were sold on the dark web.[40] As we write, details of a massive breach emerged at Mobikwik, a payments firm. Details of 100 million users, including names, email addresses and phone numbers were put on sale.[41] Government systems have been targeted as well, including attacks on transportation systems, electricity grids and government websites. India's National Cyber Security Coordinator estimated that cyberattacks cost almost $17 billion in 2019.[42]

Governments and businesses have legitimate data needs. Without data sharing, how could vaccines against COVID-19 be developed so quickly?[43] However, societies must ensure strong data protection and individual rights, even as governments and businesses pursue goals from which societies can benefit. While data privacy and cybersecurity issues affect all countries, strengthening the legal and regulatory frameworks to ensure trust and security will become increasingly important in India.

Technology and the future of work in India

Does technology threaten India's demographic dividend? Just when India should be benefiting hugely, as its working-age population grows before peaking in 2041, will advances in technology reduce demand for labour?[44] Countries around the world are grappling with this worry. As technologies like AI gather speed, there are growing concerns about what all this will mean for countries that had pinned their hopes on growing with the help of cheap labour. Certainly, for India, with its vast reservoir of young people, the implications of labour-substituting technologies could not be more worrying. In a country where labour force participation has been stagnant or declining, especially for women, rapid advances in technology add to existing problems of relatively weak employment opportunities.

If we leave aside the issue of more inclusive growth and focus simply on economic growth, there are three main drivers to look at—labour, capital and productivity. Globally, all three are facing challenges. Productivity growth has been the biggest contributor to economic growth in recent decades. And technology has helped drive this growth. However, it appears that despite more technological advances, productivity growth in wealthier countries has slowed in the last decade or so.[45] How can that be, when we are constantly hearing about one amazing company after another? It turns out that companies at the leading edge of technological innovation appear to be doing really well. However, the productivity gains in these top companies are not seen more widely. Technology appears to be creating a 'winner-takes-all' environment.[46] The slowdown in productivity is mirrored in a slowdown in investments, despite low interest rates. Worried economists fear the risk of 'secular stagnation', which is as bad as it sounds.[47]

But it is the impact of technology on labour markets that worries us most because of its implications for countries like India, where the pool of unskilled and low-skilled labour is huge. On the one hand, AI and other advanced technologies could replace such labour; on the other, we appear unable to radically reorient the labour force to take on roles that may be less amenable to automation.[48] While technology helped raise worker productivity and enabled massive poverty reduction, we cannot assume that the process will continue. It is conceivable that the kind of inclusive growth that India and other emerging economies need could face significant challenges in the AI era. After all, in the initial decades after the Industrial Revolution, life expectancy decreased. It was only after some time that shared progress ensued and inequality declined.[49]

Replicating the East Asian Miracle appears increasingly difficult, as new technologies could possibly reduce the overall demand for labour.[50] This could have devastating consequences for unskilled and low-skilled labour. Such views find resonance in Indian government assessments. In 2017, the Ministry of Labour and Employment said that 69 per cent of jobs in India are susceptible to automation.[51] Meanwhile, an August 2020 McKinsey report estimates that India needs to create 'gainful (non-farm) jobs for 90 million workers by 2030'.[52] It is because of these types of concerns that the World Bank warns that developing countries will have to 'take rapid action to ensure they can compete in the economy of the future' and 'blunt the worst disruptions' of technological change.[53]

Preparing for an uncertain opportunity

Harnessing the power of technological innovation is not simple. There is no textbook way to do it. Technology evolves with time, and some countries are better able to latch on to evolving trends or adapting technology to development needs. However, given India's particular circumstances, there are things that can help India prepare for a more technology-driven future. Four areas, in particular, come to mind. First, investment in physical infrastructure and ongoing improvements to that infrastructure are important. Second, expanding access to digital technologies, especially for women, is critical. Third, India needs to focus on digital literacy and skill development to prepare for future work environments. Finally, India must develop a modern, progressive governance framework that protects the rights of citizens, and enables the responsible generation and use of data by the private and public sectors.[54]

India has much to be proud of in terms of progress on adopting digital technology. However, the COVID-19 pandemic has exposed serious shortcomings, which need to be addressed. Researchers at Tufts University assessed the readiness for remote work of forty-two countries. They scored these countries on 'several crucial dimensions: the robustness of key platforms essential to business continuity (technology-mediated remote work, e-commerce, digital media, and digital foundations); the proliferation of digital payments to facilitate transactions; and the resilience of internet infrastructure to traffic surges.'[55] India ranked last in this list of forty-two countries. The report argues that while digital infrastructure, especially IndiaStack, has improved, much more needs to be done. The Confederation of Indian Industry (CII), an industry association, believes that India should invest more in the broadband network, building digital highways and satellite technologies.[56] In addition, digitizing government operations can expand the market for digital solutions, encourage more start-up activity and greatly improve citizen services.[57]

To avoid the prospects of an entrenched digital divide, which could fuel further inequality, policymakers should focus on expanding access to new technologies. Women, in particular, are at risk of falling behind, as they have in contemporary labour markets. Can technology help bridge the labour market gap by enabling women to compete for jobs that pose fewer barriers to entry? Time will tell, but first, some serious gaps need bridging. In India, only 21 per cent of women are internet users while men are online at double that rate. In rural areas, access to the internet is generally worse with only 25 per cent of the population online.[58] Attention to this emerging divide could make a big difference in the future.

Along with access, it is important that Indians be well-versed in using new technologies. Digital literacy is critical for meeting needs in a variety of areas—accessing health and education services, political participation, work opportunities, commerce, etc.[59] The government's 'Digital India' programme includes digital literacy initiatives. However, despite efforts to strengthen digital literacy, serious deficiencies remain. A 2018 report found that 90 per cent of Indians were digitally illiterate,[60] while a parliamentary committee found that the government's three digital literacy schemes had barely touched 1.6 per cent of the population—well below targets.[61] The main complaint against the government's approach is that it uses outdated parameters for assessing digital literacy needs (e.g., access to computers as opposed to mobile phones). A flexible and long-term approach to digital literacy would probably serve citizens far better.[62]

A related area is that of investing in skills. Since the nature of work is undergoing changes and, as COVID-19 has shown, many jobs will move online, there is a need 'to equip workers with nonroutine, creative and higher-level skills that the new technologies demand, and to support workers during the adjustment process'.[63] This directly hinges on increasing access to quality education and training, opportunities for mid-career reskilling/readjusting and upgrading skills, adult learning, etc. Without this, people will remain trapped in low-productivity jobs that are at risk of being automated. Furthermore, this may be critical for helping women participate in greater numbers in the job market.

India is generating vast amounts of user data. Data is 'an increasingly important source of competitive advantage' for firms.[64] Meanwhile, the Indian government has increasingly used new technologies and citizen data in ways that would make any social democracy uncomfortable. For instance, the use of the Aarogya Setu app for contact tracing during COVID-19 caused much disquiet in the country. The linking of Aadhaar to all sorts of platforms creates a digital footprint that unscrupulous elements within government or outside of it could leverage for nefarious ends. These fears are growing in tandem with declines in India's standing on a variety of global indices that track freedom and democracy.

It is important, therefore, to ensure trust in digital technologies. A good way to start would be to give citizens comfort about the safety of their digital identities as well as transparency in how their data is stored and used. Perhaps India could adapt Europe's 2018 General Data Protection Regulation (GDPR), which has led the way on this important topic. But governance is not only about data. It is much broader than that. India must create an environment in which new technologies are assessed with greater openness. Ethical aspects, for example in bioengineering, should not be swept under the carpet. At the same time, businesses should be assured that their innovations will be protected and that governments (central or state) will not create the kinds of compliance burdens that reduce incentives and increase rent-seeking.

Getting the governance framework right is not going to be easy. It will evolve, perhaps incrementally. But a modern and progressive governance framework is critical to India's future, as we look ahead with hope but also some trepidation.

19

Conclusion: The Economy India Deserves

The future depends on what we do in the present.

—Mahatma Gandhi

In every crisis lies an opportunity.

—Albert Einstein

On 15 August 1947, at the stroke of midnight, Pandit Jawaharlal Nehru, independent India's first prime minister, gave his famous 'Tryst with Destiny' speech to the Constituent Assembly of India. But a tryst simply means a dalliance, an assignation or a date. It is time, some seventy-five years later, to aim higher and try to 'consummate' that destiny. Between now and 2047, some twenty-five years from now, India must strive to cross the so-called 'middle-income trap' and become an advanced, developed country. With a pandemic-ravaged economy and society, that path will not be an easy one, especially in a country with such huge diversity.

The venerable industrialist Jamsetji Tata said, 'I do not want India to be an economic superpower. I want India to be a happy country.' He was both right and wrong. India can be both or neither. It cannot be happy unless it achieves a certain level of sustainable prosperity, and it cannot prosper unless its development is more inclusive and removes disparities in income, gender, caste, religion and is sustainable. As countries around the world are learning, you cannot grow and clean up later; you cannot grow with huge disparities as social strife sets in and when populist politicians can spread hatred and fear. Balance is needed. The two go together—a certain level of prosperity is needed to be happy. But just being a richer country does not make India a happier nation.

If India reaches an average yearly per capita income level of $12,500 by 2047—considered to be the cut-off to move from middle-income status to high-income status—roughly where Mauritius or Romania is today, with a projected population of 1.6 billion, it will be a $20 trillion economy close to the size of the US today. It will be an economic superpower. Even if it achieves a level of income of $10,000, roughly where Mexico or Argentina are today, India will be a $16 trillion economy—the third largest in the world—but by no means will it be a happy country if it has their level of income inequality and, most likely, just like them, will be stuck in a middle-income trap. The point is that, given its size, India is likely to be the world's third-largest economy by 2047—but whether it will be a happy country, more inclusive, less unequal or go by way of Latin America remains to be seen.

In this book, we have tried to show how India needs to be reshaped to become not just a more prosperous but also a happier nation. A nation that takes its rightful place in the world but is also a beacon to others in becoming a more inclusive, democratic, sustainable society, which provides a better life for its girls and marginalized communities. A genuinely secular and caring society, with a state that belongs to the people and not an overbearing state that stifles innovation, ingenuity and initiative.

But in any look forward, we must factor in the ravages of the pandemic. India's GDP will not recover to FY19-20 levels well into FY22-23. The second wave has ensured that, and a third wave may also hit India well before much of the population has been vaccinated. The seventy-fifth anniversary of independent India in 2022 will not be a reason for a full-hearted celebration. But, as the famous scientist Albert Einstein said, every crisis presents an opportunity as well. What trajectory India's economy will take post-pandemic, will depend on our actions. It could recover and go back to its past growth trajectory of 6-7 per cent growth that we have seen since 2000, it could take a hit and slump along at 3-4 per cent growth—the kind of growth India saw in the period 1960–80—or it could be transformed in significant ways to accelerate growth to 8-9 per cent—but more inclusive and sustainable—the growth India needs to utilize its demographic dividend. We could have a metamorphosis—a huge transformation that this book has tried to chart out. It is not predetermined. As the Mahatma aptly said, 'The future depends on what we do now.'

An economy or, for that matter, the broader society is a mix of moving parts. When they grind together at the right gear, the economy can move ahead and if all are on board, society can prosper in an inclusive manner. If not, social strife sets in and does further damage to the economy. Think of an economy as a bus. If the bus's gearbox is impaired, the best that is achievable is maybe second gear. To get it to move faster at fourth or fifth gear, the gearbox must be fixed. If the bus is overloaded, then, too, it cannot move fast. If different parts do not work, the exhaust system or the steering wheel, then the bus moves in fits and starts or veers off in the wrong direction. And if the lights are not working, the bus can only be used during daylight. If any of the parts malfunction, the bus is not travel worthy.

It is the same for the economy: if some parts are not working, the country cannot compete and slows down. If you neglect health and education, you cannot move up the development ladder. If you neglect infrastructure, your economy cannot compete. If you neglect its defences, it can be taken over. If you neglect its finances, it will be unable to deliver the credit without which no modern economy can thrive. The many parts must come together to make the economy function at top gear. So, what are the key areas for reform that our book has highlighted?

1. Reduce the scope and reach of the state and strengthen its capability

In Part I of the book, we argued that India needs a new social contract between the state and citizens. The Modi government has a slogan, 'Maximum Governance, Minimum Government', which has not yet been seriously addressed. India needs to be unshackled from an overbearing state trying to do too much and doing much of it badly. The scope of the state must be reduced to focus on doing the basics much better and in keeping regulations simpler, more transparent and less subject to discretion. Predictability matters. Unburdening the economy from excessive, overbearing government is the need of the hour.

India must focus much more on basic education, primary healthcare as well as on irrigation, drinking water and sanitation, internal security and national defence. These are vital state functions, which do not have adequate resources devoted to them. Another important state function is R&D that has huge benefits not only to society but also to private businesses who typically underinvest in it, as there are innovation benefits that they cannot capture entirely. There are also huge benefits to collective action on climate finance, since the market will not deliver there as well.

In most other areas, the state's role should be regulator, not provider. Roads, railway lines and electricity transmission can also be, for now, considered state functions but could be corporatized—with state companies rather than departments run on commercial principles. Power distribution, generation, airports, ports, air travel, telecommunications, tertiary education, tertiary healthcare, could all be areas where the state sells its PSUs and becomes a regulator. In Part I, we make the case for privatization. But how it is done will also matter. Selling to cronies and oligarchs, as was the case in Latin America or Russia, will not work.

Light-touch industrial policy is what has worked well in India, not heavy-handed state intervention. India's welfare system is evolving. SSNs are slowly being introduced, such as in health, where OOP expenditures are very high and one major illness can drop people back into poverty. Poverty has declined but remains sufficiently high (about 25 per cent of the population), so social assistance will be needed for some time to come. But India needs to overhaul its social assistance system from product-focused subsidies to people-focused subsidies. DBTs are a better way than a slew of subsidies on food, fertilizers, electricity, which cause huge market distortions and breed corruption. The PM Kisan scheme must be expanded and a new cash transfer programme in lieu of the PDS should be introduced—starting with urban areas—and once it is functioning, expanded to rural areas. Migrant labour should be provided cash transfers rather than the One Nation One Ration Card scheme, which will breed even more corruption and leakages.

But, as the pandemic has shown, India has the largest share of population (77 per cent), among countries at its level of development, who are in vulnerable employment. Their employment does not have any defined social security. They have no immediate access to social protection. More than 200 million people are estimated to have fallen back into poverty—as many as came out of poverty in the previous two decades. MGNREGA forms the only employment guarantee scheme that much of the rural population and returning migrants could fall back on during the pandemic. It shows how desperate the situation must be for returning migrants to have lived in urban areas for many years, and yet be willing to take on back-breaking rural works programmes originally designed for famine-stricken people. This is where the state must focus as well.

Reducing the scope of state intervention is one part of the strategy to make the state more effective. The other part is improving its capability to do what it does better. Reforming government is not easy—especially as it takes time—and is therefore not easy to do for a democratic government subject to a five-year electoral cycle. As we showed earlier, one part of it is administrative reform. India has too few teachers, doctors, judges, police personnel and foreign service officers. It appears to have too many clerical and support staff. Go to any government office and you find many people hanging about, occasionally serving tea, waiting to carry the boss's bag to their car, carrying files.

Ironically, despite the appearance of so many people hanging around in government offices, the total number is quite small—

smaller than what India needs and smaller than most other countries per capita. But India's government is expensive because the lower 90 per cent of government staff are overpaid relative to the private sector—a tendency pushed by various Pay Commissions—especially the last one. Were it not for the sloppy appearance of most government offices, we could well describe it as a boutique government: small but very expensive. A major reform would be to drastically reduce the support staff in the Central government and shift that money to hire more technical people.

But instead of hiring these people at the central level, it would be better to hire them at the state or, better yet, at the local government level, where salaries are much lower. India flouts every principle of subsidiarity—that the location of a service should be at the lowest level possible. In China, almost 50 per cent of government spending is at the local level, compared to less than 5 per cent in India. The Central government, on the recommendations of successive Finance Commissions, has shifted more and more resources to the state (provincial) level but there is very little further devolution to the local level.

Giving local government much greater authority to raise revenues through property taxes and user fees is also necessary, as without control over their own resources they are left to the mercy of state governments willing to transfer more resources to them. Some argue that their capacity to deliver services and manage funds is weak—but this excuse has gone on long enough. Most Indian states are the size of major countries, so just devolving to that level is not enough. At some point, India must also think of a union of about fifty states by breaking up large states into numerous smaller ones.

Corruption remains a huge bane in India. There are claims that corruption has improved in India since the BJP came to power, based on the perceptions of businesspeople. But if citizens are surveyed, India emerges as the most corrupt country in Asia. There is no quick fix here: a multi-pronged approach will be needed, including greater transparency, greater competition, more IT based services, harsher penalties and reform of the police and the judiciary. Electoral bonds give the facade of less corruption, but it just hides huge political corruption.

2. Greater focus on learning, skilling and health outcomes—including nutrition

The foundations of India's development—education and health—remain weak. Education has expanded—including for girls—but enrolment is not learning and, as repeated ASER surveys show, there are huge learning gaps in India. In the twenty-first century, with huge technological advances already underway, from AI to space exploration to biotechnology, India will fall behind unless it fixes its yawning learning gap. India pulled out of the PISA rankings because it scored so poorly. Running away from the problem will not solve the issue; confronting it squarely will be needed.

Pratham, which does the ASER surveys, thinks the solution lies in fixing public schools. Others think the government should fund education but allow civil society to run the schools. What everyone seems to agree on is that learning problems are being caused by unprepared learners, ineffective teaching, inputs that do not reach the classroom and terrible governance. One important factor often missed is that cognitive abilities are most affected by early childhood nutrition and education. How the Anganwadis are run will determine to a large extent the future development of children, especially in the rural areas of India. Repairing school education development will not be enough, if those entering schools are already deprived in their ability to learn.

The governance issues in education mirror what we see more broadly in the public sector: too much centralized spending, with the Central government providing top-down funding and a set model unsuited to local conditions, too-high salary scales that make public school education more expensive than private schools, with lower learning outcomes. The new NEP 2020 tries to address some of these deficiencies by focusing on early childhood education, learning outcomes and more funding, but it does not adequately address the top-down structure and the resultant governance problems, and may end up remaining a vision. Allowing greater experimentation at the state and local levels must be the way forward to find what works best and why.

India must also build up world-class universities and research centres. It must allow greater freedom and involvement of the private sector to build and run these freely while using public funds to support not supplant them. In line with the NEP's push for higher GERs in the tertiary education sector, India must also learn from others. In 1980, China had a GER of a little over 1 per cent. India's GER was nearly five times more. But China soon overtook India. Reforms that included increased public spending, cheap tuition, an emphasis on applied fields, research incentives, frequent changes to respond to market needs, etc., helped China improve its enrolment rates (53.6 per cent in 2020) and the quality of its institutes and graduates.[1,2] More recently, China has brought home Chinese-born PhDs from abroad 'with dollar salaries and monetary incentives for published research'.[3] India could explore the adoption of similar steps.

When Indians look to East Asia for solutions, they focus on industrial policy, export-led growth and infrastructure, but they forget that the bedrock of East Asian growth was education and health. India has seen improvements in child and maternal mortality, but the latest health surveys show that stunting is increasing despite all the improvements in overall income and food production. This is a shocking trend and suggests that health outcomes are dependent on not just what we do on health but on a host of factors that determine health outcomes.

Poor maternal nutrition is a key factor in causing LBW, which then leads to stunting. Maternal nutrition is, in turn, dependent on mothers' education, gender disparities in food intake and, more broadly, income inequalities. Then, water quality, sanitation and air quality matter as well. DBT-based schemes to ensure children are fed better and using Anganwadis to supplement diet in the first three years will have huge pay offs for India at multiple levels, as will special diet supplements for pregnant mothers.

India also greatly underspends on health: spending is only around 3.54 per cent of GDP, of which public spending is only 1.3 per cent of GDP. OOP spending remains very high, at 63 per cent of total spend. The Ayushman Bharat health insurance scheme has been introduced to reduce OOP expenses and ensure that people do not fall into poverty due to a severe illness in the family. It started well but has run into problems due to COVID-19. The government hopes to increase public health spending to 2.5 per cent of GDP but even if it were to reach that number it will not be enough. India needs to spend overall at least 6 per cent of GDP on health to match other emerging economies.

And as with all other sectors, a top-down approach plagues the health sector as well. Local and community-based systems are better suited to solve many of India's health sector woes, with Kerala showing the way forward. Tamil Nadu and Himachal Pradesh also run good health systems, with a heavy focus on local administration with state monitoring. Addressing huge inequalities in access to health and education are also a key factor holding back India's development. The UNDP's inequality-adjusted HDI pushes India from a medium-development country category to a low-development country category—in the same group as many African countries.

3. End women's exploitation: Economic, legal, political and gender violence

While women have made progress on health and education indicators since independence, their economic contribution to India's development remains hugely unfulfilled. With a declining sex ratio of 918 in the 2011 Census, female infanticide has been on the rise in India—especially in the so-called heartland states of Haryana, Punjab, Uttar Pradesh, Bihar, Madhya Pradesh, Rajasthan and Gujarat. It shows that the value parents attach to girls has been declining. Since 2015, the government has launched the 'Beti Bachao, Beti Padhao' programme (Save the girl child, educate the girl child), but only the 2021 census will tell us if it has reversed the trend in female infanticide. The maternal mortality ratio has declined but remains too high at around 130. Much greater focus on ensuring that births take place in health centres, maternal nutrition and better education are key factors in making progress on this issue.

While primary school enrolment has increased both in urban and rural areas, women's economic empowerment has declined. The FLFP rate, which was already one of the lowest in the world, has declined further to around 0.20. The decline is largely due to rural FLFP, as women find no suitable paid employment and, unlike other countries such as Bangladesh, where girls with secondary education find jobs in the garment industry, no such options exist in India. Of course, women do a large amount of unpaid work and if this were counted, their FLFP would be 87 per cent. As a result of lack of paid work, girls also drop out of school at twice the rate than boys do. According to Agarwal et al. (2021), women's ownership of assets also remains low, averaging 14 per cent of landowners and 11 per cent of the land. Despite the Succession Act, which gives girls equal rights to family assets, widows are more likely to inherit land than daughters, as there is the fear that land inherited by them will transfer to the families they marry into.

Gender violence is a major issue in India—beyond infanticide. There have been improvements in laws to prevent this, but it has made no dent in incidence. Within-family violence is also a major problem in India. If women own land and other assets, this gets reduced. Employment does not seem to have much influence on its incidence. Much broader societal change will be needed to reduce this. Without land, access to credit and other benefits is also reduced. Political power for women is also very unequal and the law providing one-quarter reservations to seats in Parliament for women has languished for over a decade. Currently, only 13.5 per cent of Lok Sabha members are women. Reservations have been brought in at the panchayat (local government) level and have been shown to make a difference in many cases towards better governance.

Women also suffer more during natural disasters than men, as they are more vulnerable. Gender issues do not figure in policymaking as much as they should. For example, women's interest in forest products (mainly firewood and fruits) is very different from men's (timber). Gender budgeting is a tool that India should start to use in a much more significant way to allocate resources with a gender lens.

The better half of India's population is either killed at birth or exploited in ways that deny them an opportunity to contribute economically in ways that would empower them. India's GDP would be at least 25 per cent higher if the FLFP rate was equal to men. What a waste! While there may not be easy solutions to this issue, preferential affirmative action may be the only solution—in jobs, political power, access to credit, education and health, as was done for making progress on caste discrimination. Educating children on women's rights, feminizing the police and creating greater awareness of property rights issues must be given the highest priority.

4. Re-engineer the economy for more inclusive growth

While the world has changed, India's farm policy is stuck in a fifty-year-old mindset. India's response to food shortages in the 1960s was to establish a mix of price (procurement, ration and MSPs) and non-price policies (irrigation, high-yielding seed, subsidized fertilizer), which led to a green revolution in cereals and a complex system of procuring and selling this grain through the FCI and the PDS. This system has outlived its usefulness for India but changing it is not easy, as those whose livelihoods depend on it are unwilling to risk any changes, as the farm protests show.

The solutions to problems in India's agriculture sector lie partly in the farm sector, but also in what happens in manufacturing and services. Unlike in East Asia, India did well in the service sector but failed to create the low-skilled manufacturing that pulled millions out of poverty in China, South Korea, Malaysia, Thailand and Vietnam, and now, increasingly in Bangladesh. As a result, in India the share of agriculture in output has fallen to 15 per cent of GDP. But over 42 per cent of the workforce still toils away on the farm. The average farm size in India is about

1 hectare, and 86 per cent of farms are under 2 hectares, with limited surplus to sell.

In the farm sector, India needs to expand PM Kisan and MGNREGA and reduce input subsidies—such as free electricity and wasteful fertilizer subsidies that disproportionately benefit the larger farms. The shift to PM Kisan, which is a broader production-based subsidy, could also be used to reduce MSPs for specific commodities. This shift could be designed to be budget neutral. It would enhance productivity, as farmers would be able to take greater risks in their crop mix and would increase rural demand and thereby help recovery. It would put more income in the hands of farmers and landless labour, boost rural demand and give farmers greater choice in cropping patterns. It would also ensure that less paddy and sugar cane are grown, especially in parts of the country where water is scarce. Groundwater depletion would be curtailed, and land productivity would increase.

Instead of wasteful subsidies, the priority should be more funds for irrigation, rural roads, expanding the online e-NAM and credit. Group farming is also an obvious solution when farm size has become so small, especially for commercial crops. Partial reforms of the system have led to huge protests, as farmers see one part of the system being taken away with a lack of clarity of what may follow. Expanding PM Kisan and *then* opening the farm system to greater market forces would be the better solution. Only then can the FCI—where huge sums are wasted on the inefficient storage of cereals for which there is no demand—be gradually dismantled: something that needs to be done.

The reforms in farming must be preceded by changes in the PDS, the FPS system set up during the period of food shortages. Some argue that the PDS has proven its usefulness during the COVID-19 pandemic when some 80 million were provided free rations. But cash transfer systems have done even better in the rest of the world, including neighbouring Pakistan. If India is not yet ready for a full-scale switch to cash transfers, a partial shift, starting with urban areas, would be the first step. India's food consumption pattern has changed with less demand for cereals and more for protein (pulses, poultry, fish), vegetables, fruits and oils, where India must ramp up production—not in more cereals. India needs a second green revolution but one quite different from the first one.

India's structural transformation has missed the bus on industrialization. Some argue that with India's service sector growth, India does not need industrialization. But this has created a distorted structural transformation and jobless growth. The service sector had added to the GDP but does not create as many jobs, especially for low-skilled workers leaving agriculture. India has, in fact, been 'prematurely de-industrializing'.[4] India industrialized substantially until 1980 due to heavy public investment in PSUs, which grew to capture the commanding heights of the economy. Large public sector companies in steel, oil and gas, heavy machinery, power, aeronautics, aluminium, shipping, electronics, mining and construction were set up. But after the 1991 liberalization, their growth slowed down, some smaller companies were privatized, and asset sales (partial privatization) were pursued, mainly to raise revenue for the budget.

After 1991, there was no active industrial policy, as in the case of East Asian tiger economies of South Korea, Taiwan, Singapore and China. Instead, a more laissez-faire approach was followed, and tariffs were cut drastically from a weighted average tariff of 57 per cent in 1991 to 7.3 per cent in 2015 and on to 4.88 per cent in 2018. India's trade deficit with China and ASEAN widened and India's industrialization reversed. A few industries, where the government provided a helping hand, flourished, such as pharmaceuticals, automobile and auto parts manufacturing and aircraft parts, but traditional labour-intensive industries, such as textiles, leather and brassware, languished under the onslaught of cheaper imports from China.

An inverted duty structure, where tariffs on intermediate products in some cases remained higher than on final products, made India's industry even less competitive. And FTAs were pursued aggressively, with India agreeing to concessions in industry with ASEAN, in the hope that in the second stage the FTA would be expanded to services, which never materialized.

In 2015, the government announced a new 'Make in India' initiative to try and reverse deindustrialization. But it remained just an announcement and between 2009 and 2019, over a ten-year period, industry share in GDP fell from over 31 per cent of GDP to around 25 per cent of GDP. India has focused on improving its rank on the World Bank's EBDI, which has risen from 142 in 2014 to 63 in 2019. But the costs of doing business have remained high and Indian industry has not been able to compete with China and ASEAN on a range of products. In 2018, the government changed course and began to increase tariffs to protect industry and by 2019 the weighted average tariff rate was above 10 per cent. India has also begun to review its policy on FTAs. But this reversal risks going back to the old protectionist model for India, which did not serve it well.

To attract industry, especially firms leaving China, India has announced a new PLI scheme. The ten sectors covered under the PLI schemes are pharmaceuticals, automobiles and auto components, telecom and networking products, advanced chemistry cell batteries, textiles, food products, solar modules, white goods and specialty steel. The scheme envisages new investments leading to higher production would get cash incentives at the rate of 4–6 per cent of incremental sales. If the scheme is to succeed it must be handled in a smart unbureaucratic manner—something India is not easily able to do. But it does signal the recognition that laissez-faire will not work in a fiercely competitive global market where everyone else, especially China, aggressively uses industrial policy.

In contrast to its poor showing in industry, India was hugely successful in services, especially IT services, healthcare and now increasingly in e-commerce. This was because, unlike in industry, the costs of doing business, which come from poor infrastructure, and weak education and health systems, were not so debilitating. In fact, India had sufficient, well-trained, English-speaking IT engineers to give it a competitive advantage in grabbing the outsourcing of chunks of business out of developed high-wage countries to low-wage India. India became the back office for many services.

Competition has emerged in these areas, but India continues as a leader in back-office outsourcing, which may grow even further due to the pandemic. Nevertheless, India remains a back office and has not yet been able to become a formidable leader in IT because it spends very little on R&D. On the other hand, while services have provided jobs to thousands of IT engineers and have spawned a supporting ecosystem, they are not able to provide mass employment to lower-skilled workers with secondary education, which lifted millions out of poverty in East Asia.

Tourism remains another low-hanging fruit that India has not yet exploited to employ its underemployed. Despite its vast coastline, huge historical and religious heritage and varied geography, India gets fewer foreign tourists than the islands of Hawaii or Macau. India needs a concerted effort post-COVID-19 to rectify this gap, as tourism and related mobility services generate huge employment for relatively lower-skilled workers.

India's exports grew rapidly after the first wave of liberalization and India's trade GDP ratio grew hugely. But India remains a small player in international trade, with its exports forming only 2 per cent of global exports. Some feel India has missed the bus on export-led growth; but as we have shown, India's shares in many major markets are so low that even if global trade slows down, India could capture a much larger market share if it made a concerted effort. A more competitive exchange rate policy, more focus on back-of-the-border measures to reduce cost of exporting, EPZs run by established global companies, a greater effort to enter GVCs must be given the highest priority.

With signs of global economic recovery, India's exports have again started to rise. But others such as China, Japan, South Korea and Vietnam are doing even better because they remain more competitive not only in manufacturing but even in agriculture. As India remains uncompetitive, it has raised tariffs hugely and dropped out of the RCEP. But this will not make Indian industry more competitive globally—in fact even less so. A $30-billion-PLI scheme has been designed to help attract new investment in twelve-odd industries—but whether this will be sufficient to overcome the more fundamental costs of doing business remains to be seen. Picking winners with expensive subsidies, alone, may not work unless the reasons behind India's lack of competitiveness are addressed.

5. Pursue next-generation reforms for realizing demographic dividend

India has over forty different laws which apply to various sizes of firms. What that has done is to push firms to hire more daily wage workers called 'casual labour' instead of contract labour. India has the world's largest share of casual labour. Some believe that the restrictions on hiring and firing for firms with above

100 workers has led to a 'missing middle' section among Indian firms, of the size hiring 100–500 workers. But that is not the case. However, most of India's firms are below ten workers as a myriad of labour legislation does not apply at all below that level. India does not have a missing-middle problem but a small-firm size problem.

Many large firms have outsourced some of their functions to mid-sized firms so that, over time, in manufacturing, the mid-sized firms have increased employment at the expense of larger firms. India has now reformed its labour laws and put two-thirds of them into four codes. Now firms with above 300 workers will only need permission before laying off workers, and various other laws have been harmonized. But it is not clear if these changes will have any effect at all on employment, firm size and labour productivity. Further experimentation will no doubt be needed, and more state-level flexibility may be the answer for a country of India's size on these issues to see what works best.

Some believe that India's land market is even more distorted than labour, and that it has more significant effects on productivity because land is used as collateral to borrow capital. Land distortions then create capital market distortions and have a negative effect on the overall productivity and competitiveness of the economy. Land grab and exploitation of poor landowners—especially in tribal areas by mining and energy companies—as well as badly managed labour displacement in public projects, created a huge political brouhaha.

A new land act passed in 2014 has made the acquisition of land even more costly and slow due to myriads of clearances and social and environmental assessments. All this has rightly been done to avoid the exploitation of landowners, especially in rural and tribal areas. But it has led to a slowdown in public infrastructure projects as well and led to a rise in NPAs in the banking system due to delays in project completion. Some 11 states have now passed legislation to bypass the 2014 Land Acquisition Act. Land-lease has been tried in some cases and maybe a better solution. But without better solutions, India's long-term development will suffer.

It is amazing that with land so scarce, India has one of the lowest FARs in the world so that land becomes even more scarce and costly in the cities. It has also resulted in urban sprawl, and huge increases in costs of city transport and municipal infrastructure. Massive and unchecked migration has also meant that most cities have grown in an unplanned manner, with slums coming up in peri-urban areas, which eventually get formalized as their dwellers become vote banks for politicians, who are open to regularizing these. India neglected urban development for a long time, and a slew of top-down central schemes after 2000, lacking flexibility and without strong local government, have not really solved India's urbanization problems. Increasing the FAR and providing greater empowerment to local government seems to be the way forward.

India is gradually improving its infrastructure, but much remains to be done. Rail tariff rationalization and expediting commissioning of DFCs; seamless and efficient road transport experience—introduce a One Nation, One Permit, One Tax System; establish a National Council of Logistics and Trade Facilitation with private sector and trade stakeholders represented; fully automated paperless trade environment with minimum face-to-face interactions; target cargo dwell time to reach levels comparable to the successful Southeast Asian countries and encourage the growth of river transport to open landlocked areas for commerce and tourism, especially along the Ganges and its tributaries.

India's financial markets remain the most inefficient and non-inclusive in the world. Without reform, it is like trying to run a marathon with a weak heart with clogged arteries—the surest way to a cardiac arrest (financial crisis). What got us here is like an Agatha Christie whodunnit with bankers, politicians, borrowers all equally to blame. The credit-to-GDP ratio is at 50 per cent and must be at least doubled in the coming decade. The intermediation cost of India's commercial banks is around 500 basis points—amongst the highest in the world. Other issues to be addressed are NPAs, directed lending requirements for rural and MSMEs, a 20 per cent SLR to help finance the government's borrowing needs at low cost and the general inefficiencies of PSBs. India's financial system, despite efforts to open bank accounts for the poor, remains hugely exclusive with access to credit, usage of bank accounts amongst the lowest in the world despite directed lending.

Major reform of the financial system is needed, starting with partial reprivatization of the banking system. After consolidation, India now has twelve PSBs—these could be reduced to, at best, four PSBs to ensure regional coverage, and the remaining privatized. Remove directed lending from commercial banks and establish or designate one or two banks to perform priority sector lending. For MSMEs, a MUDRA bank to provide non-collateralized lending has already been set up and NBFCs are a major source of credit for MSMEs, and their growth should be encouraged. Jan Dhan accounts could be transferred to the newly established Indian Post Payments Bank, a more suitable entity for such accounts than a scheduled commercial bank.

The clean-up of the existing NPAs—now slated to rise further—should be swift. The IBC process was not designed for system-wide problems. An asset resolution agency will be needed to remove the NPAs from the banks for separate resolution. In any case, no privatization of PSBs will be possible without removing their NPAs. Promoters whose NPAs are transferred must lose their equity.

The RBI should be given full supervisory powers over PSBs, and officials of the former should not sit on the boards of these banks. The RBI should not be the debt manager for the government—this function should be with a treasury department in the finance ministry and removed from the RBI. SLR requirements should be eliminated to encourage fiscal discipline. SLR requirements are a rarity and have been eliminated in most modern emerging economies. Such a move will also encourage the development of a corporate bond market and an asset quality review of the NBFCs should be performed; weaker ones should be closed, and stronger ones encouraged, particularly for priority sectors such as housing, exports and MSMEs, especially as banks are released from directed lending to them.

6. Prepare to leave behind a better country for our children

India needs to focus less on its contentious history and its various divisive interpretations and focus much more on the future India we want to leave for our children and grandchildren. The COVID-19 has shown us how unprepared we are for shocks, whether they come from natural disasters or economic crises or health pandemics. We are unprepared because we have not built the resilience that is needed. Health is seen as a cost, not an investment, which is why it is given such a low priority in the government's spending. The same goes for education. The basics have been ignored and money is spent on wasteful schemes. India does not even spend enough on defence, despite threats from two major neighbours, China and Pakistan.

The biggest threat looming ahead for India and the world is climate change. As we see in Chapter 16, India will be one of the worst-affected countries but until recently it took the position that since India did not create the problem, it must not be part of the solution. But that is like 'cutting off your nose to spite your face'. India's per capita emissions remain well below global averages and, as a result, the latest planetary pressures-adjusted HDI shows India has moved up eight places in the ranks. It could move up much more if the energy efficiency of its GDP could improve. India emits 0.3 kg of carbon dioxide for every dollar of gross domestic product based on purchasing power parity or $GDP (PPP)—about the same as Australia, Canada and the US—three energy-intensive countries, and well above Europe where it is 0.1 kg for every $GDP (PPP). It is below China and Russia, which produce 0.5 kg for every $GDP (PPP), but now India, as the world's third-largest emitter, must become part of the solution. All that is changing now, with India signing the Paris Agreement, helping establish the Global Solar Alliance.

India is also creating huge amounts of local pollution, which may not have a global impact but leaves India's air and water heavily polluted, with huge costs to health, life expectancy and productivity, as it increases vulnerability to diseases. India must not go China's way—a model described as 'pollute now and clean up later'. China has made huge progress in renewables but continues to invest heavily in coal-based energy as well, the effects of which will be with the world for decades. India also has vast reserves of coal but until we find better technology to capture carbon dioxide, it is best left in the ground. India must also avoid seeing action on climate change and local pollution as a cost to growth. The pollute-now-and-pay-later model is not the path to emulate. Instead, seeing climate action investments as improved infrastructure and job creation and a better future for our children is the right way forward. Jobs, infrastructure and climate action must be viewed as the synergistic path to a new India.

India is investing aggressively in renewables but is forced to import much of the equipment for those investments, as local production is insufficient or too costly. China has taken the lead in the production of equipment for renewable use, from solar panels and wind turbines to electric cars and buses. India must also incentivize such production in the country.

Climate change and the heavy human ecological footprint have led to changes that are in many cases irreversible. But nature will react in ways that are unpredictable: heavy rain and flooding in areas unforeseen, increased storm and cyclonic activity, drought and forest fires and health pandemics, and some that are predictable and already well underway, such as ice melt in the polar regions and glaciers. As Chapter 17 shows, India has seen its share of such events, from floods in Mumbai, Chennai and Kashmir, to glacial lake outbursts in Uttarakhand, to droughts elsewhere. The predictions for India for the effects of climate change, such as on agricultural production and coastal flooding leading to people falling back into poverty, are dire indeed.

While India may be a victim of global climate change, it can do a lot more to prepare and build its future in a more resilient manner. With glacial lake outbursts likely to increase, building more dams in the upper reaches of the Himalayas seems like a bad investment. Over-building cities and affecting natural water flows so they are constantly prone to flooding must be avoided. Avoiding building in harm's way is one way to reduce vulnerability. But getting better prepared to handle disasters when they do arise is another. India has a disaster management authority at national and state levels, but keeping them prepared and ready is always a challenge. But government capacity is not enough and must be buttressed more broadly by resilient systems in the economy and community.

Generally, loss of life is much lower in developed countries than in developing ones, because people live and work in better infrastructure. Building codes exist but are often not enforced in developing countries—India is a great example of that problem. India must introduce compulsory building insurance—like third-party car insurance. This not only helps build up forced savings for disasters, but also helps better enforcement of building codes. India also has one of the world's highest shares of vulnerable employment in the world at 77 per cent. If you factor in vulnerability, India should be classified as a less developed country, not a middle-income country. The COVID-19 pandemic has exposed that vulnerability conclusively. A health insurance scheme—Ayushman Bharat—had been introduced and was making progress with about ten million beneficiaries but has now languished due to the pandemic. Community disaster support systems are also important, as they can be triggered quickly and help save lives till more comprehensive help can arrive.

With the world going through huge technological change, AI, and new ways of doing business (and more to come), some argue that it is difficult to predict change. That is true. The only thing we can predict for sure is that 'change is inevitable': change in the way we will learn, in healthcare, in transport and travel, in the way we will work and live. Since it is hard to predict when and where the next biological, IT or material technologies will come from, it is best we prepare our children for the ability to adapt to and thrive with change. Some fear new technologies will take away people's livelihoods. But such predictions were also made for previous technologies such as the automobile, the telegraph, the mobile phone, the railroad. In the end, it meant higher and higher productivity on average. But yes, it did mean some benefited and some were left behind.

We need to, therefore, build a new India where we do not resist change but ensure that all can participate, as we argue in

Chapter 18. This means ensuring digital skills for all and digital access for all, a well-balanced education that prepares people for learning for life in whatever field they choose and a comprehensive health system that ensures healthy and energetic citizens. With India likely to be one-fifth of humanity by 2047 at our 100th year of independence, we must build a base where India's youth contribute to innovation and technological change, and are not just passive consumers of that change. If data is the new oil, with over 1.5 billion points of data, India will be the Saudi Arabia of the next phase of global development. As India builds the new regulatory architecture for data protection, let us not err on the side of overbearing regulation and government, which has hobbled us for the last seventy-five years, whether it is our labour, land or capital market-related laws. But if regulatory capture leads to overly protective data regulations, a few connected cronies will benefit but India will lose out.

7. Metamorphosis: Reshaping India's economic and social trajectory

Will India make the change for a better future? Yes, it will. But at what pace and for whom?

On 15 August 1947, Prime Minister Nehru declared India's independence with his famous 'tryst with destiny' speech. As India enters the 75th year of independence, ravaged by the pandemic, the question on everyone's mind is will India ever consummate that destiny?

In a muddled-through, somewhat haphazard manner, India has, of course, made progress since the end of the British rule—certainly far better than the previous hundred years of that colonization. Most villages have been electrified; most of our children are going to primary schools in villages and urban slums, most people now use mobile phones, and road and highway construction, airports and ports have expanded to increase mobility across the country. Poverty, which had fallen by over 250 million, has risen again sharply due to COVID-19, but this reversal is hopefully temporary as was the case during the GFC.

India's ranking in global GDP rose, on the back of the 1991 reforms, as its GDP grew more than five times since then and a middle class of around 300 million emerged—about 25 per cent of India's population—but so did inequality. The share of income going to the top 1 per cent doubled from just over 10 per cent in 1990 to over 20 per cent in 2019 and the Gini coefficient, which was around 0.32 in 2000 and shot up to 0.48 in 2019, making India the second-most unequal country in the world after Russia. And COVID-19 has increased inequality—even further.

India has held together as a ramshackle, rambunctious democracy. But even that designation is under question by many inside and outside India, who feel it's better termed an 'electocracy'—where elections are held but is not a genuine democracy. The Indian growth model had run out of steam, even before the pandemic. GDP growth had slumped back to Raj Krishna's 'Hindu growth rate' of 4 per cent. Over 77 per cent of its workforce was in vulnerable employment—with no work benefits and no social security—as was cruelly exposed during the pandemic. Its demographic dividend is beginning to look like a demographic disaster.

Some argue that India genuinely and comprehensively reforms only when it faces a crisis. The politicians then act, as they fear losing it all. The crisis focuses the mind. The 1991 reforms, put off by at least a decade, were surely triggered by a massive balance of payments crisis. But the 2008-09 GFC which hit India, did not trigger reforms—instead, India opened the fiscal and monetary spigots and spent its way out of that crisis. And that high fiscal spending and loose monetary policy generated massive inflation and a huge rise in bad loans in the banking sector—which India is still grappling with.

The Modi government's recent reforms include an IBC and GST. The IBC is now frozen due to the pandemic—but was struggling even before the pandemic, as its resolutions were challenged in courts. The GST remains bogged down with implementation issues and the half-baked farm and labour laws are being strongly opposed. And rising protectionism from 2018 onwards is even reversing the reforms that India benefited from since 1991 and is potentially cutting itself off from GVCs.

India's political class must broaden its goals and create a new economic and social vision, instead of weakening institutions to serve narrow political goals, and creating divisions in society to pit one group or religion against another. Unshackling India from its interventionist state, allowing young, aspirational India's innovativeness, flair and talent to be nurtured through better education and health systems, and building resilience with better preparedness for threats from climate change, natural disasters and pandemics, with robust social assistance and insurance systems must be the way forward.

But how to motivate the country to get all this done?

Many countries have used external threats to spur reforms. Over 150 years ago, the US used the threat from England to spur reforms. Japan and Germany used the need to rebuild after suffering enormous devastation after World War II. China used humiliation from the Western colonial powers as a unifying sentiment to sustain development and South Korea and Taiwan used existential threats from North Korea and China to modernize and develop. What can motivate India in the twenty-first century to rise after this devastating pandemic?

What India needs is an aspirational goal. GDP targets—$5 trillion or even $10 trillion—do not inspire the broader citizenry. China is a huge threat, so catching up with China could be one motivation. While China's economy has done well—its social and political development hardly warrants emulation. For India, becoming a developed country—in all aspects, economic, social and political—by 2047, the 100th year of its independence, could be such a goal. 'Samriddh aur Sajit Bharat @100' (Prosperous and Inclusive India @100) is a slogan all political parties could sign up to. India Inc. should aim to grow at home and abroad instead of looking for tweaks in tariffs and regulations to serve very narrow short-term interests.

India has many individual inspiring stories—soldiers who fought bravely, sportsmen and women who persevered despite adversity and entrepreneurs who have built businesses despite all odds. But to become a developed country, India's institutions need bolstering so that collectively India can propel its individual genius and strength into countrywide progress and prosperity. French Emperor Napoleon said it best: 'Institutions determine the destinies of nations.'

Bending the arc of India's trajectory over the next twenty-five years—when India will celebrate 100 years of independence—will surely make India an economic power of the twenty-first century—but also a much happier country that all Indians deserve. Let the pandemic wake up the country to make a resolute change for that much-needed metamorphosis if India is to consummate its destiny that started with a tryst on 15 August 1947.

Notes

Chapter 1

1 Socrates is a fictional character in *Way of the Peaceful Warrior: A Book That Changes Lives* by Dan Millman.
2 Gideon Rachman, 'Narendra Modi and the perils of Covid hubris', *Financial Times* (26 April 2021). https://www.ft.com/content/fa3096ff-4325-4a02-97fd-89095e44d5c1
3 International Monetary Fund, *World Economic Outlook* (April 2021).
4 United Nations Development Programme (UNDP), *Support to Vaccine Equity | Beyond Recovery: Towards 2030* (UNDP). undp.org
5 Ibid.
6 Thomas Piketty, *Capital and Ideology*, (Harvard University Press, 2020).
7 Sudipto Mundle, 'Covid's aftershocks: Why we need wide-ranging reforms now', *Mint* (16 July 2021). livemint.com/opinion/online-views/potential-long-term-economic-consequences-of-the-pandemic-11626366362188.html
8 Ibid.

9 Regis Barnichon, Christian Matthes and Alexander Ziegenbein, 'The Financial Crisis at 10: Will We Ever Recover?' *FRBSF Economic Letter*, Federal Reserve Bank of San Francisco (13 August 2018).
10 Valerie Cerra and Sweta C. Saxena, 'The Economic Scars of Crises and Recessions' (International Monetary [IMF], 21 March 2018).
11 Ajay Chhibber, Jayati Ghosh and Thangavel Palanivel, *The Global Financial Crisis and the Asia-Pacific Region: A Synthesis Study Incorporating Evidence from Country Case Studies* (UNDP Regional Centre).
12 India carried out substantial first generation reforms from 1991 onwards, which liberalized its product markets and trade, although agriculture remained controlled.
13 'World Bank Group to Discontinue Doing Business Report', The World Bank (16 September 2021). https://www.worldbank.org/en/news/statement/2021/09/16/world-bank-group-to-discontinue-doing-business-report
14 '230 million Indians pushed into poverty amid Covid-19 pandemic: Report', *Business Standard* (6 May 2021). business-standard.com
15 'Can India become stronger than China? Yes, it can'—Kishore Mahbubani.

Chapter 2

1 India's official numbers on incidence and deaths are probably a substantial undercount.
2 Devesh Kapur (2020) says it's too small—but he looks at tax receipts, not at total receipts, and when we add large fiscal deficits, the total government spend is not too low by India's level of GDP. Devesh Kapur, 'Why Does the Indian State Both Fail and Succeed?' *Journal of Economic Perspectives* 34, no. 1 (2020): 31–54.
3 Lant Pritchett, 'Is India a Flailing State? Detours on the Four Lane Highway to Modernization', HKS Faculty Research Working Paper Series RWP09-013 (John F. Kennedy School of Government, Harvard University, 2009).
4 Gurcharan Das, *India Grows at Night: A Liberal Case for a Strong State* (Penguin Global, 2012).
5 Peter B. Evans, 'Predatory, Developmental, and Other Apparatuses: A Comparative Political Economy Perspective on the Third World State', *Sociological Forum* 4, no. 4 (1989): 561–587.

6 Pratap Bhanu Mehta and Michael Walton, 'Ideas, Interests and the Politics of Development Change in India: Capitalism, Inclusion and the State', ESID Working Paper No. 36 (2014).
7 See also Bardhan (1996) for a review of the role of the state. Pranab Bardhan, 'State and Development: The Need for a Reappraisal of the Current Literature', *Journal of Economic Literature* 54, no. 3 (2016): 862–92. doi:10.1257/jel.20151239
8 Ravinder Kaur, *Brand New Nation: Capitalist Dreams and Nationalist Designs in Twenty-First Century India* (Stanford University Press, 2020).
9 Devesh Kapur (2020) shows that British India spent even less than other colonial administrations. Perhaps that was good as it meant less taxation and had it spent more it would probably have not been to help India's development but to meet colonial interests.
10 In fact, as brought out by Tharoor (2016), under Churchill's orders grain was moved from India to southern Europe for troops fighting there while millions starved. Shashi Tharoor, *An Era of Darkness: The British Empire in India* (Aleph Book Company, 2016).
11 Manmohan Singh, 'Of Oxford, Economics, Empire, and Freedom', *The Hindu* (2 October 2005). hindu.com/2005/07/10/stories/2005071002301000.htm
12 World Bank, *World Development Report: The State in a Changing World* (Oxford University Press, 1997).
13 See also Kelkar and Shah (2019) for numerous examples of where the Indian state intervenes far beyond justified reasons for intervention such as addressing market failure, provision of public goods and asymmetric information. Vijay Kelkar and Ajay Shah, *In Service of the Republic: The Art and Science of Economic Policy* (Allen Lane, Penguin Random House India, 2019).
14 See Mohan and Aggarwal (1990) for a detailed description and its history of India's licence-raj regime. Rakesh Mohan and Vandana Aggarwal, 'Commands and Controls: Planning for Indian Industrial Development, 1951–1990', *Journal of Comparative Economics* 14, no. 4 (1990): 681–712. doi:10.1016/0147-5967(90)90048-e
15 Ajay Chhibber (2018) in a chapter published in a book on the Bombay Plan, edited by Sanjaya Baru and Meghnad Desai, shows that '... the parenthood of India's shift to State Planning is hard to pin on Prime Minister Nehru alone. Even the top industrialists of that time, JRD Tata and GD Birla, were pushing for State control and planning as

co-authors of the Bombay Plan.' Sanjaya Baru and Meghnad Desai, eds., *The Bombay Plan: Blueprint for Economic Resurgence* (Rupa Publications, 2018).

16 This was, of course, faster than growth in the period 1900–50, but well below what other developing countries in East Asia and Latin America were able to achieve, especially after 1965.

17 As Kelkar and Shah (2019) point out, it would have been better to have started with a single-rate GST with additional revenue collected in the form of luxury or sin taxes and introduce complexity once the implementation was well established. Vijay Kelkar and Ajay Shah, *In Service of the Republic: The Art and Science of Economic Policy* (Allen Lane, Penguin Random House India, 2019).

18 Reserve Bank of India (RBI), *Handbook of Statistics on the Indian Economy*, RBI, various issues.

19 Organisation for Economic Co-operation and Development (OECD), 'General Government Revenues as a Percentage of GDP: 2007, 2017 and 2018', *Government at a Glance 2019* (OECD Publishing, 2019).

20 OECD, 'General Government Expenditures as a Percentage of GDP: 2007, 2017 and 2018', *Government at a Glance 2019* (OECD Publishing, 2019).

21 We prefer the term capability to capacity—capability means capacity plus the ability to use that capacity.

22 See Akram and Rath (2020) for evidence of state size and effectiveness. Vaseem Akram and Badri Narayan Rath, 'Optimum Government Size and Economic Growth in Case of Indian States: Evidence from Panel Threshold Model', *Economic Modelling*, 88 (2020): 151–62.

23 World Bank, *World Development Report: The State in a Changing World* (Oxford University Press, 1997).

24 An administrative reforms commission (the second one after 1956) was established under Veerappa Moily in 2005 and it submitted a comprehensive report with over 1,600 recommendations, but very little was done.

25 National Council of Applied Economic Research (NCAER) 2008.

26 NCAER, *Role of the Public Distribution System in Shaping Household Food and Nutritional Security in India*, NCAER Report (2016).

27 This could be considered a quasi-UBI (universal basic income) system, a means-tested income transfer not a universal UBI.

28 Based on authors' calculations using data on accounts of MGNREGA.

Chapter 3

1 Ajay Chhibber and Swati Gupta, 'Public Sector Undertakings: Bharat's Other Ratnas', *The International Journal of Public Sector Management* 31, no. 2 (2018): 113–127.
2 The PSUs which have shown biggest improvements in value added in the last three years are: Bharat Electronics Ltd, Bharat Petroleum Corporation Ltd, Chennai Petroleum Corporation Ltd, Hindustan Petroleum Corporation Ltd, Indian Oil Corporation Ltd, Numaligarh Refinery Ltd, Rashtriya Chemicals & Fertilizers Ltd, and Steel Authority of India Ltd.
3 These figures do not include the contribution of the state-level PSUs for which a centralized data base does not exist. Their contribution varies widely. In 2015-16, for example, sales in Assam were just over 2 per cent of state GDP, whereas in Punjab they were around 13 per cent of state GDP.
4 This does not include SLPEs, but given their much poorer performance, and lack of any established skills-development and training programmes, their growth in labour productivity is likely to be even lower.
5 The main issue is whether land owned by these PSUs is entered at book value or market value. In the latter case, the picture on their financial performance could look different.
6 Arpita Mukherjee, 'Services Sector in India: Trends, Issues, and the Way Forward', *Eurasian Geography and Economics* 56, no. 6 (2015): 635–655. doi:10.1080/15387216.2016.1151371
7 Earlier it was a department of the finance ministry. The subsequent UPA government once again abolished the ministry and the NDA government under Modi has pushed privatization but has not created a separate ministry to carry it out, presumably because there was so much opposition to that ministry when it was created by PM Vajpayee and headed by Arun Shourie.
8 Holger Muhlenkamp, *From State to Market Revisited: More Empirical Evidence on the Efficiency of Public (and Privately Owned) Enterprises*, Munich Personal RePEc Archive (MPRA) (2013).
9 In India we call a performance contract between the government and a PSU a Memorandum of Understanding (MOU).
10 Mary M. Shirley and Lixun Colin Xu, 'Information, Incentives, and Commitment: An Empirical Analysis of Contracts Between Government

and State Enterprises', *Journal of Law, Economics, and Organization* 14, no. 2 (1998): 358–378

11 T.G. Arun and F.I. Nixson, 'The Disinvestment of Public Sector Enterprises: The Indian Experience', *Oxford Development Studies* 28, no. 1 (2000): 19–32. doi:10.1080/713688302

12 B.L. Mathur and Reeta Mathur, 'Accountability and Autonomy Relationship in Central Public Sector Enterprises (CPSEs) in India through Memorandum of Understanding (MOUs)', International Conference on Applied Economics (ICOAE) – (2010): 495.

13 R. Nagaraj, 'Disinvestment and Privatization in India: Assessment and Options', Asian Development Bank Policy Networking Project (2005).

14 Prajapati Trivedi, 'Lack of Understanding on Memorandum of Understanding', *Economic and Political Weekly* 25, no. 47 (1990): M175-M182.

15 Ritika Jain, 'Do Political Factors Influence Performance of Public Sector Enterprises? The Indian Disinvestment Experience', 12th Annual Conference on Economic Growth and Development (ISI, 2016).

16 Nandini Gupta, 'Partial Privatization and Firm Performance', *The Journal of Finance* 60, no. 2 (2005): 987–1015. doi:10.1111/j.1540-6261.2005.00753.x

17 Nandini Gupta, *Selling the Family Silver to Pay the Grocer's Bill? The Case of Privatization in India* (2005). host.kelley.iu.edu/NAGUPTA/gupta_mar2011.pdf

18 Sangeetha Gunasekar and Jayati Sarkar, 'Does Autonomy Matter in State Owned Enterprises? Evidence from Performance Contracts in India' (working paper, Indira Gandhi Institute of Development Research, 2014).

19 Ajay Chhibber and Swati Gupta, 'Public Sector Undertakings—Bharat's Other Ratnas', National Institute of Public Finance and Policy (NIPFP) Working Paper No. 186 (2017).

20 Ajay Chhibber and Swati Gupta, 'Bolder Disinvestment or Better Performance Contracts? Which Way Forward for India's State-Owned Enterprises', *Public Enterprise Half-Yearly Journal* 1, no. 24 (2019): 1–22.

21 The model used ensures correction for self-selection by estimating the results with and without MOUs, and with and without disinvestment, creating six different samples of firms. The results are therefore done separately for firms without MOU or disinvestment, with disinvestment only, with MOU only, and with firms that have both MOU and disinvestment.

22 It is, of course, possible that there was a selection bias, in that better performing CPSUs were selected for strategic disinvestment (privatization).
23 There is a strong risk that in India's 'Billionaire Raj', privatization will allow large corporate interests to grab these assets.
24 Vijay Kelkar, *Report of the Committee on Revisiting and Revitalizing the PPP Model of Infrastructure Development*, Government of India (2015).

Chapter 4

1 Matt Andrews, Lant Pritchett and Michael Woolcock (2017) changed the Israel terminology from specificity to discretion. But here we stick to the Israel terminology and use specificity. Kelkar and Shah (2019) add two other elements to this terminology—stake and secrecy. These may be relevant as well in some circumstances but broadly the two elements identified by Israel suffice.
2 Matt Andrews, Lant Pritchett and Michael Woolcock, *Building State Capability: Evidence, Analysis, Action* (Oxford University Press, 2017).
3 Vijay Kelkar and Ajay Shah, *In Service of the Republic: The Art and Science of Economic Policy* (Allen Lane, Penguin Random House India, 2019).
4 Arturo Israel, *Institutional Development: Incentives to Performance* (Johns Hopkins University Press, 1987).
5 Ibid.
6 The RBI has a specific task—setting its interest rates—which is now done through the Monetary Policy Committee (MPC). Whether it does this well is a matter of judgement but it is very specific. Less specific is its regulation of the banking system; it is not easy to decide how to judge its performance, what yardstick to use. India has not had a full-blown banking crisis but rising numbers of NPAs and scams have indicated a growing problem in the banking system.
7 See Anand, Dimble and Subramanian (2021) for a discussion on this new welfarism. But this type of welfarism has prevailed in India in the past as well. In many states, local leaders have distributed such welfarism to win elections. What may be new is that India's Central government has now made it more widespread and national.
Abhishek Anand, Vikas Dimble and Arvind Subramanian, 'New Welfarism and the Child in India: New Evidence from the NFHS',

Centre for Economic Data and Analysis (CEDA) (Ashoka University, 2021).

8 Centre for the Study of Developing Societies, Politics and Society between Elections, Survey Report by CSDS (Lokniti and Azim Premji University, 2019).

9 Political parties are completely in the doghouse as per this survey and the new laws that allow donors to buy electoral bonds without divulging their identity allows electoral funding to be used to buy favours legally without any scrutiny from the Election Commission.

10 Given how difficult an election funding reform would be.

11 Devesh Kapur, 'Why Does the Indian State Both Fail and Succeed?', *Journal of Economic Perspectives* 34, no. 1 (2020): 31–54. doi:10.1257/jep.34.1.31

12 Salvatore Schiavo-Campo, Giulio de Tommaso and Amitabha Mukherjee, *Government Employment and Pay in Global Perspective: A Selective Synthesis of International Facts, Policies and Experience* (World Bank, 1996). doi:10.1596/1813-9450-1771

13 Desai shows that at every level, public sector wages in India are higher than in the private sector. She writes, 'The CPC found that compensation to Group C and D employees in government was higher than that in the private sector; for Group B it was similar and only for Group A was it lower. Group A employees form less than 5 per cent of the total Central government workforce; Group C and D are about 90 per cent.' Sonalde Desai, 'An Unjustified Pay-Hike', *The Hindu* (15 October 2015). https://www.thehindu.com/opinion/op-ed/is-the-seventh-pay-commissionmandated-hikes-necessary/article7819275.ece

14 Hyung-Ki Kim, 'The Japanese Civil Service and Economic Development: Lessons for Policy Makers from Other Countries', The Japanese Civil Service and Economic Development Catalysts of Change, Hyung-Ki Kim et al., eds. (Clarendon Press, Oxford University Press, 1995).

15 Kapur (2020) makes the case that India's civil administration is not based on patronage because there are so many vacancies. Many of those exist because of lack of funds. The main issue is lack of motivation and stagnation, as there is no performance-based evaluation system. People are promoted based on years of service, except at the very end.
Devesh Kapur, 'Why Does the Indian State Both Fail and Succeed?', *Journal of Economic Perspectives* 34, no. 1 (2020): 31–54.

16 The Telecom Regulatory Authority of India (TRAI) started well but is now perceived as being captured by one large promoter. The RBI is now considering allowing corporates to own banks.

17 Devesh Kapur, 'Why Does the Indian State Both Fail and Succeed?', *Journal of Economic Perspectives* 34, no. 1 (2020): 31–54. doi:10.1257/jep.34.1.31
18 Tea estates in the Northeast have shifted their clocks by an hour to increase daylight savings.
19 Maulik Jagnani, 'Poor Sleep: Sunset Time and Human Capital Production' (Cornell University, 2019).
20 Drawing conclusions from these across time and countries is subject to some debate, as these are perceptions. Also, a score can improve yet a rank may decline as other countries might have done better.
21 Transparency International, 'Corruption Perceptions Index 2020' (Transparency International, 2021). transparency.org/en/cpi/2020/index/nzl
22 Transparency International, 'Global Corruption Barometer: Asia 2020', (Transparency International, 2021). transparency.org/en/publications/gcb-asia-2020
23 Even former chief justice of India Ranjan Gogoi admitted to the judicial system's failure when he said he would not go to court if he had a dispute.
24 Meaning the number of things, it gets involved in.

Chapter 5

1 Associated Press, 'India: 600 Expelled for Test Cheating', *The New York Times* (20 March 2015). nytimes.com/2015/03/21/world/asia/india-600-expelled-for-test-cheating.html
2 Ankit Vyas, 'Status Report—Government and Private Schools During COVID-19: Findings of Rapid Surveys by Oxfam India' (Oxfam India, 2020).
3 Richard Pérez-Peña, 'Futures in Peril: The Rise of Child Labor in the Pandemic', *The New York Times* (27 September 2020). nytimes.com/2020/09/27/world/asia/coronavirus-education-child-labor.html
4 World Bank, *Beaten or Broken: Informality and Covid-19 in South Asia* (World Bank Group, 2020): 14. openknowledge.worldbank.org/handle/10986/34517
5 UNDP, *Human Development Report 1990: Concept and Measurement of Human Development* (UNDP, 1990). hdr.undp.org/en/reports/global/hdr1990
6 Ibid.

7 World Bank, *World Development Report 1978 (English)* (World Bank Group, 1978). documents.worldbank.org/en/publication/documents-reports/documentdetail/297241468339565863/world-development-report-1978
8 World Bank, *World Development Report 2018: Learning to Realize Education's Promise (English)* (World Bank Group, 2018). worldbank.org/en/publication/wdr2018
9 World Bank, 'Median Percentage Increase in Wages with Each Additional Year of Schooling, by Country, Group, and Gender', *World Development Report 2018: Learning to Realize Education's Promise (English)* (World Bank Group, 2018). bit/do/WDR2018-Fig_1-1
10 Jean Drèze and Amartya Sen, 'The Centrality of Education', *An Uncertain Glory: India and its Contradictions* (Allen Lane, Penguin Books, 2013): 107–142.
11 Urvashi Sahni, 'Reframing Girls' Education in India', Brookings Institution (Brookings) (2017). brookings.edu/blog/education-plus-development/2017/09/13/reframing-girls-education-in-india/
12 World Bank, 'Girls' Education'. worldbank.org/en/topic/girlseducation
13 World Bank, *World Development Report 2018: Learning to Realize Education's Promise (English)* (World Bank Group, 2018).
14 Ibid.
15 '260 Million Children Miss Out Education: UNESCO', *DW* (23 June 2020). dw.com/en/260-million-children-miss-out-education-unesco/a-53908881#
16 Salman Anees Soz, *The Great Disappointment: How Narendra Modi Squandered a Unique Opportunity to Transform the Indian Economy* (Ebury Press, Penguin Random House India, 2019).
17 Sophie Edwards, 'India's Re-entry to PISA Triggers Mixed Response', *Devex* (20 February 2019). devex.com/news/india-s-re-entry-to-pisa-triggers-mixed-response-94286
18 Salman Anees Soz, *The Great Disappointment.*
19 Barbara Bruns and Javier Luque, *Great Teachers: How to Raise Student Learning in Latin America and the Caribbean* (World Bank, 2015).
20 World Bank, *World Development Report 2018: Learning to Realize Education's Promise (English)* (World Bank Group, 2018). worldbank.org/en/publication/wdr2018
21 James J. Heckman, 'Invest in Early Childhood Development: Reduce Deficits, Strengthen the Economy'. heckmanequation.org/resource/

invest-in-early-childhood-development-reduce-deficits-strengthen-the-economy/

22 Marie Lall, *The Challenges for India's Education System* (Asia Programme, Chatham House, 2005).

23 Ibid.

24 Ibid.

25 Ibid.

26 Avani Kapur, Mridusmita Bordoloi and Ritwik Shukla, 'Budget Brief 2018-19: Sarva Shiksha Abhiyan (SSA)', *Budget Briefs* 10, no. 1 (Centre for Policy Research, 2018). cprindia.org/research/reports/budget-brief-2018-19-sarva-shiksha-abhiyan-ssa

27 Chirantan Chatterjee, Eric Hanushek and Shreekanth Mahendiran, 'Unintended Consequences to Education for All: India's Right to Education Act', CEPR (2020). voxeu.org/article/unintended-consequences-education-all-india-s-right-education-act

28 National Sample Survey (NSS), *Household Social Consumption in India: NSS 75th Round (July 2017–June 2018)* (Ministry of Statistics and Programme Implementation, Government of India, 2020).

29 Pratham, 'Annual Status of Education Report (Rural) 2018 (Provisional)' (ASER Centre, 2019). img.asercentre.org/docs/ASER%202018/Release%20Material/aserreport2018.pdf

30 Ibid.

31 Karthik Muralidharan, 'Reforming the Indian School Education System', *What the Economy Needs Now*, Abhijit Banerjee et al., eds. (Juggernaut, 2019). econweb.ucsd.edu/~kamurali/papers/Published_Book_Chapters/Muralidharan%20-%20School%20Education%20Reforms%20in%20India%20(February%202019).pdf

32 Lant Pritchett, 'India: Massive Expansion in Schooling, Too Little Learning, Now What?', Center for Global Development (5 February 2018). cgdev.org/blog/india-massive-expansion-schooling-too-little-learning-now-what

33 Ibid.

34 Ibid.

35 Karthik Muralidharan, 'Reforming the Indian School Education System', *What the Economy Needs Now*, Abhijit Banerjee et al., eds. (Juggernaut, 2019).

36 Yamini Aiyar, 'Schooling is Not Learning', *Policy Challenges 2019–2024: Charting a New Course for India and Navigating Policy Challenges in the 21st Century* (Centre for Policy Research, 2019):

95–99. cprindia.org/policy-challenge/7864/economy-%26-the-welfare-state

37 Lant Pritchett and Yamini Aiyar, *Value Subtraction in Public Sector Production: Accounting Versus Economic Cost of Primary Schooling in India*, Center for Global Development Working Paper No. 391 (2015). doi:10.2139/ssrn.2623073

38 Mridusmita Bordoloi, Sharad Pandey, Vatsav Irava and Ruchi Junnarkar, *State Education Finances: A Deep Dive into School Education Finances in Eight States* (Centre for Policy Research, 2020). cprindia.org/research/reports/state-education-finances-deep-dive-school-education-finances-eight-states

39 Ibid.

40 Lant Pritchett, *The Risks of Dangerous Dashboards in Basic Education*, CGD Notes, Center for Global Development. cgdev.org/publication/risks-dangerous-dashboards-in-basic-education

41 Yamini Aiyar, 'Schooling Is Not Learning', *Policy Challenges 2019–2024: Charting a New Course for India and Navigating Policy Challenges in the 21st Century* (Centre for Policy Research, 2019): 95–99. cprindia.org/policy-challenge/7864/economy-%26-the-welfare-state

42 Amarnath Tewary, 'The Rot in India's Primary Education', *BBC News* (15 July 2015). bbc.com/news/world-asia-india-28190261

43 'Why the World's Biggest School System Is Failing Its Pupils', *The Economist* (8 June 2017). economist.com/asia/2017/06/08/why-the-worlds-biggest-school-system-is-failing-its-pupils

44 'Teacher Absenteeism Common: Report', GovernanceNow (24 October 2017). governancenow.com/news/regular-story/teacher-absenteeism-common-report

45 World Bank, *World Development Report 2018: Learning to Realize Education's Promise (English)* (World Bank Group, 2018). worldbank.org/en/publication/wdr2018

46 Karthik Muralidharan et al., 'Fiscal Cost of Weak Governance: Evidence from Teacher Absence in India', *Journal of Public Economics* 145 (2016): 116–135. doi:10.1016/j.jpubeco.2016.11.005

47 'India School Teacher "Absent for 23 Years"', *BBC News* (7 August 2014). www.bbc.com/news/world-asia-india-28684751

48 'Why the World's Biggest School System Is Failing Its Pupils', *The Economist* (8 June 2017).

49 Government of India, 'All India Survey on Higher Education (AISHE) 2018-19' (Ministry of Education, Government of India, 2019). aishe.gov.in/aishe/home.
50 Nandini Sundar, 'India's Higher Education Troubles', *The New York Times* (3 August 2018). nytimes.com/2018/08/03/opinion/india-higher-education-modi-ambani-rss-trouble.html
51 Ibid.
52 Mohini Bishnoi, 'The Many Structural Flaws in India's Higher Education System', *The Hindu* (5 December 2019). thehindu.com/opinion/op-ed/the-many-structural-flaws-in-indias-higher-education-system/article30169923.ece
53 Government of India, *National Education Policy 2020* (Ministry of Human Resource Development, Government of India).
54 Urvashi Sahini, 'India's National Education Policy 2020: A Reformist Step Forward?', Brookings (2 October 2020). www.brookings.edu/blog/education-plus-development/2020/10/02/indias-national-education-policy-2020-a-reformist-step-forward/
55 Karthik Muralidharan and Abhijeet Singh, 'India's new National Education Policy: Evidence and challenges', *Science* (2 April 2021). https://science.sciencemag.org/content/372/6537/36.full?ijkey=6%2FGAB.U7eq%2FSs
56 Ibid.
57 Michelle Kaffenberger, 'How Much Learning May Be Lost in the Long-run From COVID-19 and How Can Mitigation Strategies Help?', Brookings (15 June 2020). www.brookings.edu/blog/education-plus-development/2020/06/15/how-much-learning-may-be-lost-in-the-long-run-from-covid-19-and-how-can-mitigation-strategies-help/
58 'Education Technology is Coming of Age During the Pandemic', *The Economist* (11 November 2020). www.economist.com/international/2020/11/11/educational-technology-is-coming-of-age-during-the-pandemic
59 Yamini Aiyar, 'Schooling Is Not Learning', *Policy Challenges 2019–2024: Charting a New Course for India and Navigating Policy Challenges in the 21st Century* (Centre for Policy Research, 2019): 95–99. cprindia.org/policy-challenge/7864/economy-%26-the-welfare-state
60 Mike Colagrossi, '10 Reasons Why Finland's Education System Is the Best in the World', World Economic Forum (10 September 2018). weforum.org/agenda/2018/09/10-reasons-why-finlands-education-system-is-the-best-in-the-world

61 Cristian Aedo, Hanna Alasuutari and Jouni Välijärvi, 'Finland: A Miracle of Education?', *World Bank Blogs* (26 June 2017). blogs.worldbank.org/education/finland-miracle-education

Chapter 6

1 Jeffrey Gettleman and Suhasini Raj, '8 Hospitals in 15 Hours: A Pregnant Woman's Crisis in the Pandemic', *The New York Times* (12 July 2020). nytimes.com/2020/06/21/world/asia/coronavirus-india-hospitals-pregnant.html
2 M.A. Bashar and Sonu Goel, 'Are Our Subcenters Equipped Enough to Provide Primary Health Care to the Community: A Study to Explore the Gaps in Workforce and Infrastructure in the Subcenters from North India', *Journal of Family Medicine and Primary Care* 6, no. 2 (2017): 208–210. doi:10.4103/2249-4863.220027
3 Sonali Campion and Taryana Odayar, '"India is the Only Country Trying to Become a Global Economic Power with an Uneducated and Unhealthy Labour Force"—Amartya Sen', *LSE Blogs* (LSE South Asia Centre, 15 November 2015). blogs.lse.ac.uk/southasia/2015/11/19/india-is-the-only-country-in-the-world-trying-to-become-a-global-economic-power-with-an-uneducated-and-unhealthy-labour-force-amartya-sen/
4 Sanam Roder-Dewan, Francisca Ayodeji Akala and Jeremy Veillard, 'Human Capital and Health', *World Bank Blogs* (10 June 2019). blogs.worldbank.org/health/human-capital-and-health
5 Puja Mehra, 'India's Economy Needs a Big Dose of Health Spending', *Mint* (8 April 2020). livemint.com/news/india/india-s-economy-needs-big-dose-of-health-spending-11586365603651.html
6 Suchit Arora, 'Health, Human Productivity and Long-Term Economic Growth', *The Journal of Economic History* 61, no. 3 (2001): 699–749. JSTOR, jstor.org/stable/2698133
7 Jaana Remes et al., *Prioritizing Health: A Prescription for Prosperity* (McKinsey Global Institute, 2020). mckinsey.com/industries/healthcare-systems-and-services/our-insights/prioritizing-health-a-prescription-for-prosperity
8 Ibid.
9 World Health Organization (WHO), 'Universal Health Coverage', WHO. who.int/health-topics/universal-health-coverage

10 Ibid.
11 World Bank, 'Universal Health Coverage', World Bank. worldbank.org/en/topic/universalhealthcoverage
12 WHO, 'Universal Health Coverage (UHC)', WHO (1 April 2021). who.int/news-room/fact-sheets/detail/universal-health-coverage-(uhc)
13 GBD 2019 Universal Health Coverage Collaborators, 'Measuring Universal Health Coverage Based on an Index of Effective Coverage of Health Services in 204 Countries and Territories, 1990–2019: A Systematic Analysis for the Global Burden of Disease Study 2019', *The Lancet* 396 no. 10258 (2020): 1250–1284.
14 'India: How Well Is This Country or Territory Providing Effective, Essential Health Services?', Institute for Health Metrics and Evaluation. healthdata.org/india
15 Sneha Alexander, 'How Caste Affects Public Health Services', *Mint* (9 October 2019). livemint.com/news/india/how-caste-affects-public-health-services-11570609511853.html
16 'Frugal Innovation in Healthcare | The Economist', YouTube, uploaded by *The Economist* (24 November 2015). youtube.com/watch?v=hmqaW4VSSHI
17 Praveen Kumar and Nalini Singhal, 'Mapping Neonatal and Under-5 Mortality in India', *The Lancet* 395, no. 10237 (2020): 1591–93. doi:10.1016/s0140-6736(20)31050-3
18 Indrani Gupta and Nishali Patel, 'International Health Care System Profiles: India', *International Profiles of Health Care Systems*, Roosa Tikkanen et al., eds. (The Commonwealth Fund). commonwealthfund.org/international-health-policy-center/countries/india
19 Sadia Ali, 'Healthcare in the Remote Developing World: Why Healthcare Is Inaccessible and Strategies towards Improving Current Healthcare Models', *Harvard Health Policy Review* (14 August 2016). hhpronline.org/articles/2016/11/10/healthcare-in-the-remote-developing-world-why-healthcare-is-inaccessible-and-strategies-towards-improving-current-healthcare-models
20 Indo-Asian News Service (IANS), 'India's Most Populous State Uttar Pradesh Spends the Least on Health', *Every Life Counts,* NDTV (23 March 2017). everylifecounts.ndtv.com/indias-most-populous-state-uttar-pradesh-spends-the-least-on-health-9626
21 National Health Mission, *Rural Health Statistics (2018-19)* (Ministry of Health and Family Welfare, Government of India, 2019).

22 V. Raman Kutty, 'Historical analysis of the development of health care facilities in Kerala State, India', *Health Policy and Planning* 15, no. 1 (2000): 103–109.
23 V.R. Muraleedharan, Umakant Dash and Lucy Gilson, 'Tamil Nadu 1980s-2005: A Success in Story in India. From 'Good Health at Low Cost,' 25 Years On: What Makes A Successful Health System? (2011).
24 Statista Research Department, 'Estimated number of public and private hospitals across India as of 2019, by state' (2020). Statista.com/statistics/1128739/india-number-of-public-and-private-hospitals-by-state-estimated/
25 The Primary Health Care Performance Initiative, 'Kerala, India: Decentralized governance and community engagement strengthen primary care'. improvingphc.org/promising-practices/kerala
26 Press Trust of India (PTI), 'India Facing Shortage of 600,000 Doctors, 2 Million Nurses: Study', ET Healthworld.com, *The Economic Times* (14 April 2019). health.economictimes.indiatimes.com/news/industry/india-facing-shortage-of-600000-doctors-2-million-nurses-study/68876861
27 WHO, 'Medical Doctors (per 10,000 Population)', *The Global Health Observatory* (WHO). who.int/data/gho/data/indicators/indicator-details/GHO/medical-doctors-(per-10-000-population)
28 PTI, 'India's Doctor-Patient Ratio Still Behind WHO-Prescribed 1:1,000: Govt', *Business Standard* (19 November 2019). business-standard.com/article/pti-stories/doctor-patient-ratio-in-india-less-than-who-prescribed-norm-of-1-1000-govt-119111901421_1.html
29 Amy Kazmin, 'Doctors Are Scapegoats for India's Failing Health System', *Financial Times* (8 May 2017). https://www.ft.com/content/8053cef2-33d5-11e7-bce4-9023f8c0fd2e
30 Richard Mahapatra, 'Over 80% Indians Not Covered Under Health Insurance: NSSO Survey', *DownToEarth* (21 July 2020). downtoearth.org.in/news/health/over-80-indians-not-covered-under-health-insurance-nsso-survey-72394
31 Amy Kazmin, 'India's Healthcare: Does Modi Have the Right Cure?', *Financial Times* (8 May 2018). ft.com/content/a37648b0-4e00-11e8-8a8e-22951a2d8493
32 Richard Mahapatra, 'Over 80% Indians Not Covered Under Health Insurance: NSSO Survey', *DownToEarth* (21 July 2020). downtoearth.org.in/news/health/over-80-indians-not-covered-under-health-insurance-nsso-survey-72394

33 Global Health Expenditure Database, *World Health Organization.*
34 Hai Fang, 'International Health Care System Profiles: China', *International Profiles of Health Care Systems*, Roosa Tikkanen et al., eds. (The Commonwealth Fund, 2020). commonwealthfund.org/international-health-policy-center/countries/china
35 Elizabeth Armstrong Moore, 'How Can We Improve Access to Healthcare in Emerging Countries?', World Economic Forum (26 November 2015). weforum.org/agenda/2015/11/how-can-we-improve-access-to-healthcare-in-emerging-countries
36 Lawrence C. Loh, Cesar Ugarte-Gil and Kwame Darko, 'Private Sector Contributions and Their Effect on Physician Emigration in the Developing World', *Bulletin of the World Health Organization* 91, no. 3 (March 2013): 227–233. doi:10.2471/BLT.12.110791
37 'Domestic Private Health Expenditure (% of Current Health Expenditure)-India', *World Development Indicators* (World Bank). data.worldbank.org/indicator/SH.XPD.CHEX.GD.ZS?locations=IN
38 'Literacy Rate, Adult Total (% of People Ages 15 and Above)—India', *World Development Indicators* (World Bank). data.worldbank.org/indicator/SE.ADT.LITR.ZS?locations=IN
39 Global Health Expenditure Database, WHO.
40 Ibid.
41 Sadhika Tiwari, 'India Spent 1% Of GDP On Public Health For 15 Years. Result Is Vulnerability to Crises', IndiaSpend (26 June 2020). indiaspend.com/india-spent-1-of-gdp-on-public-health-for-15-years-result-is-vulnerability-to-crises/
42 PTI, 'The Common Minimum Programme: The Complete Document', *The Economic Times* (27 May 2004). economictimes.indiatimes.com/news/economy/policy/the-common-minimum-programme-the-complete-document/articleshow/703712.cms?from=mdr
43 IANS, 'Committed to Raise Health Expenditure to 2.5% of GDP: Harsh Vardhan', *Business Standard* (28 September 2020). business-standard.com/article/health/committed-to-raise-health-expenditure-to-2-5-of-gdp-harsh-vardhan-120092701027_1.html
44 Tarun Khanna, Nachiket Mor and Sandhya Venkateswaran, 'Transition paths towards better health outcomes in India: Optimizing the use of existing pooled government funds', Brookings (29 June 2021). brookings.edu/blog/up-front/2021/06/29/transition-paths-towards-better-health-outcomes-in-india-optimizing-the-use-of-existing-pooled-government-funds/

45 Ibid.
46 Ibid.
47 Richard Mahapatra, 'Over 80% Indians Not Covered Under Health Insurance: NSSO Survey', *DownToEarth* (21 July 2020). downtoearth.org.in/news/health/over-80-indians-not-covered-under-health-insurance-nsso-survey-72394
48 Manish Sabharwal and Rajiv Mehrishi, 'Covid is an opportunity to make structural changes to our largest health insurance and pension schemes', *The Indian Express* (21 April 2021). indianexpress.com/article/opinion/columns/covid-india-pension-scheme-health-insurance-7282123/
49 Rukmini S., IndiaSpend, 'Child Undernutrition May Be on a Rise in India, Reversing Decades of Gains', Scroll.in (15 December 2020). scroll.in/article/981197/child-undernutrition-may-be-on-a-rise-in-india-reversing-decades-of-gains
50 International Institute for Population Sciences, 'State Fact Sheet: West Bengal', *National Family Health Survey-5 2019-20* (Ministry of Health and Family Welfare, Government of India). rchiips.org/nfhs/NFHS-5_FCTS/FactSheet_WB.pdf
51 International Institute for Population Sciences, 'State Fact Sheet: Maharashtra', *National Family Health Survey-5 2019-20* (Ministry of Health and Family Welfare, Government of India). rchiips.org/nfhs/NFHS-5_FCTS/FactSheet_MH.pdf
52 International Institute for Population Sciences, 'State Fact Sheet: Bihar', *National Family Health Survey-5 2019-20* (Ministry of Health and Family Welfare, Government of India). rchiips.org/nfhs/NFHS-5_FCTS/FactSheet_BR.pdf
53 Natalia Agapitova, Cristina Navarrete Moreno and Rahul Barkataky, *Waterlife: Improving Access to Safe Drinking Water in India* (World Bank, 2017). openknowledge.worldbank.org/handle/10986/27664
54 Shishir Gupta and Rishita Sachdeva, *Revisiting the role of funding: Lessons from expenditure and performance on cleanliness in Indian cities,* Centre for Social and Economic Progress (2021). csep.org/working-paper/revisiting-the-role-of-funding-lessons-from-expenditure-and-performance-on-cleanliness-in-indian-cities/
55 Ibid.
56 India | WaterAid US.
57 Luis Andres et al., 'A Multiple-Arm, Cluster-Randomized Impact Evaluation of the Clean India (Swachh Bharat) Mission Program in Rural

Punjab, India', World Bank Policy Research Working Paper No. 9249 (World Bank). openknowledge.worldbank.org/handle/10986/33796

58 Pragya Akhilesh, 'The pandemic has exposed India's dirty truth: a broken sanitation system', *The Indian Express* (29 April 2021). indianexpress.com/article/opinion/columns/the-pandemic-has-exposed-indias-dirty-truth-a-broken-sanitation-system-7292937/

59 Soonman Kwon, 'Thirty Years of National Health Insurance in South Korea: Lessons for Achieving Universal Health Care Coverage', *Health Policy and Planning* 24, no. 1 (2009): 63–71. doi:10.1093/heapol/czn037

60 Manfred Huber, 'Health Expenditure Trends in OECD Countries, 1970–1997', *Health Care Financing Review* 21, no. 2 (1999): 99–117. ncbi.nlm.nih.gov/pmc/articles/PMC4194642/

61 Soonman Kwon, 'Thirty Years of National Health Insurance in South Korea: Lessons for Achieving Universal Health Care Coverage', *Health Policy and Planning* 24, no. 1 (2009): 63–71.

62 'COVID-19: Coronavirus Pandemic Reported Cases and Deaths by Country or Territory', Worldometer. worldometers.info/coronavirus/#countries

63 Tsung-Mei Cheng, 'Universal Health Coverage: An Overview and Lessons From Asia', Health Care, *Harvard Public Health Review* 5 (Spring 2015). harvardpublichealthreview.org/universal-health-coverage-an-overview-and-lessons-from-asia

64 Dave A. Chokshi, '4 Principles for Improving Health Care Around the World', *Harvard Business Review* (22 October 2019). hbr.org/2019/10/4-principles-for-improving-health-care-around-the-world

65 Ibid.

66 'Kerala, India: Decentralized Governance and Community Engagement', *PHCPI*, (23 October 2018). improvingphc.org/kerala-india-decentralized-governance-and-community-engagement-strengthen-primary-care

67 Udit Misra, 2020. 'ExplainSpeaking: Economics Behind India's Rising Child Malnutrition', *The Indian Express* (21 December 2020). indianexpress.com/article/explained/explainspeaking-economics-behind-indias-rising-child-malnutrition-7112946

68 Ibid.

69 Peter Svedberg, 'Child Malnutrition in India and China', *2020 Focus Brief on the World's Poor and Hungry People* (International Food Policy Research Institute [IFPRI], 2007).

70 'India: How Much Is Spent on Health—Now, and in the Future—And from Which Sources?', Institute for Health Metrics and Evaluation. healthdata.org/india
71 WHO, OECD and International Bank for Reconstruction and Development (IBRD), *Delivering Health Services: A Global Imperative for Universal Health Coverage* (World Health Organization, 2018): 29. apps.who.int/iris/handle/10665/272465
72 Dave A Chokshi, '4 Principles for Improving Health Care Around the World', *Harvard Business Review* (22 October 2019). hbr.org/2019/10/4-principles-for-improving-health-care-around-the-world
73 Rakhi Dandona and Rajesh Sagar, 'COVID-19 Offers an Opportunity to Reform Mental Health in India', *The Lancet Psychiatry* 8, no. 1 (2021): 9–11. doi:10.1016/S2215-0366(20)30493-4
74 Anamika Gulati, 'Time to end the battle of Indian pharmaceutical players and Chinese key ingredients', Observer Research Foundation (8 July 2021). https://www.orfonline.org/expert-speak/time-to-end-the-battle-of-indian-pharmaceutical-players-and-chinese-key-ingredients/
75 'The Dawn of Digital Medicine', *The Economist* (7 December 2020). economist.com/business/2020/12/02/the-dawn-of-digital-medicine

Chapter 7

1 Nandini Ramnath, 'Single Woman Seeking a House in Mumbai? "Bachelor Girls" Tells You Why It's Like Hell', Scroll.in (13 September 2016). scroll.in/reel/816356/single-woman-seeking-a-house-in-mumbai-bachelor-girls-tells-you-why-its-like-hell
2 'Budget debut: Nirmala Sitharaman bats for women-led initiatives, empowerment; wants AI, VR, big data-driven economy', *The Economic Times* (5 July 2019).
3 Lourdes Benería and Gita Sen, 'Accumulation, Reproduction and "Women's Role in Economic Development": Boserup Revisited', *Signs: Journal of Women in Culture and Society* 7, no. 2 (The University of Chicago Press, 1981): 279–298. doi:10.1086/493882
4 Alberto Alesina, Paola Giuliano and Nathan Nunn, 'On the Origins of Gender Roles: Women and the Plough', *Quarterly Journal of Economics* 128, no. 2 (2013): 469–530.
5 WHO, *The Health and Well-Being of Men in the WHO European Region: Better Health Through a Gender Approach (2018)* (WHO,

2018). euro.who.int/en/publications/abstracts/the-health-and-well-being-of-men-in-the-who-european-region-better-health-through-a-gender-approach-2018

6 Ana Revenga and Sudhir Shetty, 'Empowering Women Is Smart Economics', *Finance and Development* 49, no. 1 (International Monetary Fund, 2012): 40–43. imf.org/external/pubs/ft/fandd/2012/03/revenga.htm

7 Jonathan Woetzel et al., *The Power of Parity: Advancing Women's Equality in Asia Pacific* (McKinsey Global Institute, 2018). mckinsey.com/featured-insights/gender-equality/the-power-of-parity-advancing-womens-equality-in-asia-pacific

8 Katrin Elborgh-Woytek et al., 'Women, Work, and the Economy: Macroeconomic Gains from Gender Equity', IMF Staff Discussion Note, International Monetary Fund (2013). imf.org/external/pubs/ft/sdn/2013/sdn1310.pdf

9 'Why India Needs Women to Work', *The Economist* (5 July 2018). economist.com/leaders/2018/07/05/why-india-needs-women-to-work.

10 'Culture and the Labour Market Keep India's Women at Home', *The Economist* (24 July 2018).

11 Torben Iversen and Frances Rosenbluth, 'Work and Power: The Connection Between Female Labor Force Participation and Female Political Representation', *Annual Review of Political Science* 11, no. 1 (2008): 479–495. doi:10.1146/annurev.polisci.11.053106.151342

12 Ruchika Chaudhary and Sher Verick, 'Female Labour Force Participation in India and Beyond', ILO Asia-Pacific Working Paper Series (International Labour Organization [ILO], 2014).

13 International Labour Organization (ILO), 'Labour Force Participation Rate', *Key Indicators of the Labour Market 2015 (KILM)* (ILO, 2016).

14 Salman Anees Soz, 'Without Women, India Cannot Progress', *The New Indian Express* (24 October 2020). newindianexpress.com/opinions/2020/oct/24/without-women-india-cannot-progress-2214366.html

15 Soumya Kapoor Mehta, 'Do Indian Women Hold up Half the Sky? A Historical Perspective', CNBC TV18 (22 August 2020). cnbctv18.com/india/do-indian-women-hold-up-half-the-sky-a-historical-perspective-6700231.htm

16 Angel Mohan, IndiaSpend, 'Here's How Institutional Births in India Have Doubled in Last 10 Years', *Business Standard* (2018). business-

standard.com/article/current-affairs/institutional-births-have-doubled-in-10-years-118011300163_1.html

17 Neelanjan Sircar, 'Female Labour Force Participation: Asking Better Questions', Centre for Policy Research (2019). cprindia.org/news/7917

18 Sneha Menon, Dona Tomy and Anita Kumar, *Female Work and Labour Force Participation in India—A Meta-study* (UNDP, Sattva, 2019).

19 Mitali Nikore, 'Where Are India's Working Women? The Fall and Fall of India's Female Labour Participation Rate', *LSE Blogs* (LSE South Asia Centre, 22 October 2019). blogs.lse.ac.uk/southasia/2019/10/22/where-are-indias-working-women-the-fall-and-fall-of-indias-female-labour-participation-rate

20 Sunita Sanghi, A. Srija and Shirke Shrinivas Vijay, 'Decline in Rural Female Labour Force Participation in India: A Relook into the Causes', *Vikalpa* 40, no. 3 (2015): 255–268. doi:10.1177/0256090915598264

21 Ruchika Chaudhary and Sher Verick, 'Female Labour Force Participation in India and Beyond', ILO Asia-Pacific Working Paper Series (ILO, 2014).

22 Farzana Afridi, Taryn Dinkelman and Kanika Mahajan, 'Why Are Fewer Married Women Joining the Work Force in Rural India? A Decomposition Analysis Over Two Decades', *Journal of Population Economics* 31 (2018): 783–818. doi:10.1007/s00148-017-0671-y

23 Ibid.

24 National Sample Survey Office (NSSO), *Key Indicators of Employment and Unemployment in India—NSS 68th Round (July 2011–June 2012)* (Ministry of Statistics and Programme Implementation, Government of India, 2013). mospi.nic.in/sites/default/files/publication_reports/KI-68th-E%26U-PDF.pdf

25 Mitali Nikore, 'Where Are India's Working Women? The Fall and Fall of India's Female Labour Participation Rate', *LSE Blogs* (LSE South Asia Centre, 22 October 2019). blogs.lse.ac.uk/southasia/2019/10/22/where-are-indias-working-women-the-fall-and-fall-of-indias-female-labour-participation-rate

26 Sameer Khatiwada and Mia Kim Maceda Veloso, 'New Technology and Emerging Occupations: Evidence from Asia', Asian Development Bank (ADB) Economics Working Paper Series No. 576 (Asian Development Bank, 2019): 20. doi:10.22617/WPS190087-2

27 Mitali Nikore, 'Where Are India's Working Women? The Fall and Fall of India's Female Labour Participation Rate', *LSE Blogs* (LSE South Asia Centre, 22 October 2019). blogs.lse.ac.uk/southasia/2019/10/22/

where-are-indias-working-women-the-fall-and-fall-of-indias-female-labour-participation-rate

28 Seema Jayachandran, 'Social Norms as a Barrier to Women's Employment in Developing Countries', World Institute for Development Economics Research (WIDER) Working Paper No. 2019/74 (Helsinki: UNU-WIDER, 2020).

29 Ibid.

30 Ministry of Statistics and Programme Implementation, *Periodic Labour Force Survey Report (2018-19)* (Government of India, 2020). mospi.nic.in/sites/default/files/publication_reports/Annual_Report_PLFS_2018_19_HL.pdf

31 This is according to 2019 national estimates, which report a higher FLFP average (24.5 per cent) than the modelled ILO figures (20.52 per cent).

32 Kashif Mansoor, 'Post-Lockdown, Bihar's Labour Market Needs a Long-Overdue Shot in the Arm', The Wire (8 July 2020). thewire.in/labour/bihar-covid-19-labour-workers

33 Mitali Nikore, 'Where Are India's Working Women? The Fall and Fall of India's Female Labour Participation Rate', *LSE Blogs* (LSE South Asia Centre, 22 October 2019). blogs.lse.ac.uk/southasia/2019/10/22/where-are-indias-working-women-the-fall-and-fall-of-indias-female-labour-participation-rate

34 Tish Sanghera, IndiaSpend, 'Rural Employment: As Opportunities Drop, Women Pay the Highest Price', Scroll.in (21 April 2019). scroll.in/article/920373/rural-employment-as-opportunities-drop-women-pay-the-highest-price

35 Gerhard Peters and John T. Woolley, 'Relationship Between Female Labor Force Participation Rates and GDP', The American Presidency Project. presidency.ucsb.edu/node/334830

36 Sameer Khatiwada and Mia Kim Maceda Veloso, 'New Technology and Emerging Occupations: Evidence from Asia', ADB Economics Working Paper Series No. 576 (Asian Development Bank, 2019): 20. doi:10.22617/WPS190087-2

37 Mitali Nikore, 'Where Are India's Working Women? The Fall and Fall of India's Female Labour Participation Rate', *LSE Blogs* (LSE South Asia Centre, 22 October 2019). blogs.lse.ac.uk/southasia/2019/10/22/where-are-indias-working-women-the-fall-and-fall-of-indias-female-labour-participation-rate

38 Ibid.

39 Ruchika Chaudhary and Sher Verick, 'Female Labour Force Participation in India and Beyond', ILO Asia-Pacific Working Paper Series (ILO, 2014).
40 Seema Jayachandran, 'Social Norms as a Barrier to Women's Employment in Developing Countries', WIDER Working Paper No. 2019/74 (Helsinki: UNU-WIDER, 2020).
41 Ibid.
42 Saundarya Rajesh, Karthik Ekambaram and Anju Rakesh, 'Second Careers of Women Professionals: The India Story', (AVTAR Group, 2019). avtarinc.com/resources/second-careers-of-women-professionals.pdf
43 Swati Narayan, 'India is no country for women. Could the pandemic help change that?', *The Indian Express* (28 April 2021). indianexpress.com/article/opinion/columns/india-gender-gap-women-empowerment-pandemic-7291648/
44 Girija Borker, 'Safety First: Perceived Risk of Street Harassment and Educational Choices of Women' (2020). girijaborker.files.wordpress.com/2020/11/borker_2020_safetyfirst-1.pdf
45 Ibid.
46 Zahara Siddique, 'Violence and Female Labor Supply', IZA Discussion Paper No. 11874 (IZA Institute of Labor Economics, 2018).
47 Sneha Alexander and Vishnu Padmanabhan, 'How Much Does the Indian Government Spend on Women?', *Mint* (8 March 2020). livemint.com/news/india/how-much-does-the-indian-government-spend-on-women-11583662675936.html
48 Rohini Pande and Charity Troyer Moore, 'The Budget Relegated Women's Economic Participation to Secondary Importance', *The Indian Express* (14 February 2020). indianexpress.com/article/opinion/columns/women-work-gender-equality-india-6266947
49 Rukmini S., 'India's Post-Covid "Recovery" in Employment Has Not Been Equal for Men and Women', *Mint* (17 November 2020). livemint.com/news/india/india-s-post-covid-recovery-in-employment-has-not-been-equal-for-men-and-women-11605509801472.html
50 Madhura Swaminathan, 'Reset Rural Job Policies, Recognise Women's Work', *The Hindu* (3 July 2020). thehindu.com/opinion/lead/reset-rural-job-policies-recognise-womens-work/article31984168.ece
51 Renu Kohli, 'Women & Banking: India's Financial Inclusion Suffers from a Gender Gap', *The Financial Express* (19 May 2018). financialexpress.

com/opinion/women-banking-indias-financial-inclusion-suffers-from-a-gender-gap/1173467

52 Ibid.

53 'The Law of the Land and the Case for Women's Land Rights', Landesa Rural Development Institute. cdn.landesa.org/wp-content/uploads/Women_Land_print.pdf

54 Chris Jochnick, 'Closing the Gap Between Policy and Practice on Women's Land Rights', *World Bank Blogs* (19 March 2018). blogs.worldbank.org/developmenttalk/closing-gap-between-policy-and-practice-women-s-land-rights

55 Bina Agarwal, Pervesh Anthwal and Malvika Mahesh, 'How Many and Which Women Own Land in India? Inter-gender and Intra-gender Gaps', *The Journal of Development Studies* (2021). doi:10.1080/00220388.2021.1887478

56 Council of Economic Advisors, 'Relationship Between Female Labor Force Participation Rates and GDP' (2019). trumpwhitehouse.archives.gov/articles/relationship-female-labor-force-participation-rates-gdp/

57 Claudia Goldin, 'The U-Shaped Female Labor Force Function in Economic Development and Economic History', National Bureau of Economic Research (NBER) Working Paper No. w4707 (1994). ssrn.com/abstract=233692

58 Seema Jayachandran, 'Social Norms as a Barrier to Women's Employment in Developing Countries', WIDER Working Paper No. 2019/74 (Helsinki: UNU-WIDER, 2020).

59 *Global Gender Gap Report 2020* (World Economic Forum, 2019):12. http://www3.weforum.org/docs/WEF_GGGR_2020.pdf

60 Ruchika Chaudhary and Sher Verick, 'Female Labour Force Participation in India and Beyond', ILO Asia-Pacific Working Paper Series (ILO, 2014).

61 Nepalese women have taken over traditional rural employment opportunities as the men have moved out of villages to look for livelihoods.

62 World Bank, 'Labor Force Participation Rate, Female (% of Female Population Ages 15+) (Modeled ILO Estimate)—India, World, Sri Lanka, Bangladesh, Nepal, Pakistan, South Asia', *World Development Indicators* (World Bank). data.worldbank.org/indicator/SL.TLF.CACT.FE.ZS?locations=IN-1W-NP-PK-BD-LK-8S

63 Rohini Pande and Charity Troyer Moore, 'Why Aren't India's Women Working?', *The New York Times* (23 August 2015). www.nytimes.com/2015/08/24/opinion/why-arent-indias-women-working.html
64 Saman Amir et al., *Female Labor Force Participation in Pakistan: What Do We Know?* (World Bank, 2018). openknowledge.worldbank.org/handle/10986/30197
65 Ibid.
66 Jay Shambaugh, Ryan Nunn and Becca Portman, 'Lessons from the Rise of Women's Labor Force Participation in Japan', Brookings (1 November 2017). brookings.edu/research/lessons-from-the-rise-of-womens-labor-force-participation-in-japan
67 Kathy Matsui, '"Womenomics" Continues as a Work in Progress', *The Japan Times* (25 May 2016). japantimes.co.jp/news/2016/05/25/business/economy-business/womenomics-continues-work-progress/
68 Sigbjørn Johnsen, 'Women in Work: The Norwegian Experience', *The OECD Observer* 293, Fourth Quarter (2012): 6-7
69 Ann-Zofie Duvander et al., 'Parental Leave Policies and Continued Childbearing in Iceland, Norway and Sweden', *Demographic Research* 40, no. 51 (2019): 1501–1528. doi:10.4054/DemRes.2019.40.51
70 Luciana Etcheverry, *Work Half-time, Receive Full-time pay: Effect of Novel Family Policy on Female Labor Market Outcomes* (2020). lucianaetcheverry.com/research/Etcheverry_jmp_draft.pdf.
71 Manavi Kapur, 'India's Maternity Leave Policy Benefits Only 1% Working Women', Quartz (25 September 2019). qz.com/india/1715618/indias-maternity-leave-policy-benefits-only-1-percent-working-women
72 Medhavi Arora, 'India's Generous Maternity Leave May Be Bad for Women', *CNN Money* (30 March 2017). money.cnn.com/2017/03/30/news/economy/india-maternity-leave-law-employment-hiring
73 Divya Arya, 'Why Motherhood Makes Indian Women Quit Their Jobs', *BBC News* (23 April 2015). bbc.com/news/world-asia-india-32377275
74 Motoko Rich, and Hisako Ueno, 'Shinzo Abe Vowed Japan Would Help Women "Shine." They're Still Waiting', *The New York Times* (13 September 2020). nytimes.com/2020/09/13/world/asia/japan-women-abe.html
75 Bina Agarwal, Pervesh Anthwal and Malvika Mahesh, 'How Many and Which Women Own Land in India? Inter-gender and Intra-gender Gaps', *The Journal of Development Studies* (2021). doi:10.1080/00220388.2021.1887478

76 Emma Fulu, *Born to be Free: A Regional Study of Interventions to Enhance Women and Girls' Safety and Mobility in Public Spaces, Asia and the Pacific Region* (UN Women, 2016). asiapacific.unwomen.org/en/digital-library/publications/2016/09/born-to-be-free
77 'NCERT Textbooks Riddled with Gender Stereotypes: Study', *The Hindu* (27 June 2017). thehindu.com/news/national/karnataka/ncert-textbooks-riddled-with-gender-stereotypes-study/article19157408.ece
78 PTI, 'Women Under Represented in School Textbooks, Shown Mostly in Traditional Roles: UNESCO Report', *The Indian Express* (29 June 2020). indianexpress.com/article/world/women-under-represented-in-school-textbooks-shown-mostly-in-traditional-roles-unesco-report
79 'Move Over "Sons of the Soil": Why You Need to Know the Female Farmers that Are Revolutionizing Agriculture in India', Oxfam India (15 November 2018). oxfamindia.org/women-empowerment-india-farmers
80 Alice Newton, 'How Can Policy Makers Increase Women's Labor Force Participation?', *Private Sector Development Blog, World Bank Blogs* (13 January 2012). blogs.worldbank.org/psd/how-can-policy-makers-increase-women-s-labour-force-participation
81 'India's Maternity Benefits Law Will Do More Bad Than Good—Here Is Why', *The Financial Express* (29 June 2018). financialexpress.com/opinion/indias-maternity-benefits-law-will-do-more-bad-than-good-here-is-why/1225954
82 Yogima Seth, 'Govt to Pay Half of Extended Maternity Leave Benefit', *The Economic Times* (31 January 2019). economictimes.indiatimes.com/news/politics-and-nation/govt-to-pay-half-of-extended-maternity-leave-benefit/articleshow/67767241.cms
83 Sarika Panda, 'How to Make Our Cities Safer for Women', The Wire (8 March 2019). thewire.in/women/how-to-make-our-cities-safer-for-women
84 Bureau on Police Research and Development, *Data on Police Organisations 2019 (As on January 01, 2019)* (Ministry of Home Affairs, Government of India, 2019): 38. bprd.nic.in/WriteReadData/userfiles/file/202001301028101694907BPRDData2019-19forweb-2.pdf
85 Pankaj Khurana and Jyoti Bhasin, 'India's New Age of Policing to Improve Women's Safety', PwC. https://www.pwc.com/gx/en/industries/government-public-services/public-sector-research-centre/

agile-policing-networks-policing-in-a-networked-world/indias-policing-to-improve-womens-safety.html

86 Torben Iversen and Frances Rosenbluth, 'Work and Power: The Connection Between Female Labor Force Participation and Female Political Representation', *The Annual Review of Political Science* 11 (2008): 479–495. doi: 10.1146/annurev.polisci.11.053106.151342
87 Ibid.
88 Philipp Hessel et al., 'Increases In Women's Political Representation Associated With Reductions In Child Mortality In Brazil', *Health Affairs* 39, no. 7, 1166-1174 (2020). doi:10.1377/hlthaff.2019.01125
89 'Proportion of women parliamentarians worldwide reaches "all-time high"', *UN News* (5 March 2021). news.un.org/en/story/2021/03/1086582
90 Geetika Dang, 'Women's Reservation Bill: What can India learn from other countries?', Brookings (2019). brookings.edu/blog/up-front/2019/10/18/womens-reservation-bill-what-can-india-learn-from-other-countries/

Chapter 8

1 Ashwaq Masoodi, 'Inside Jharkhand's Singhbhum, the Worst Constituency in India', *Mint* (26 March 2019). livemint.com/news/india/inside-jharkhand-s-singhbhum-the-worst-constituency-in-india-1553561625193.html
2 Sadhika Tiwari, IndiaSpend, 'The Fallout of India's Lockdown on Child Malnutrition Will Be Felt Long After the Covid-19 Crisis', Scroll.in (8 June 2020). scroll.in/article/964033/the-fallout-of-indias-lockdown-on-child-malnutrition-will-be-felt-long-after-the-covid-19-crisis
3 Sadhika Tiwari and Shrinkhala Pandey, IndiaSpend, 'Covid-19 Undoing Decades of Progress in Reducing Malnutrition Among Kids', *Business Standard* (2020). business-standard.com/article/current-affairs/malnutrition-could-cost-children-s-health-lives-for-years-after-pandemic-120060600192_1.html
4 Prabhu Pingali, Anaka Aiyar, Mathew Abraham and Andaleeb Rahman, 'Reimagining Safety Net Programs', *Transforming Food Systems for a Rising India*, Palgrave Studies in Agricultural Economics and Food Policy (Palgrave Macmillan, 2019): 135–164. doi:10.1007/978-3-030-14409-8_6

5 World Bank, *World Development Report 1990: Poverty* (World Bank Group, 1990).
6 Prabhu Pingali, Anaka Aiyar, Mathew Abraham and Andaleeb Rahman, 'Reimagining Safety Net Programs', *Transforming Food Systems for a Rising India*, Palgrave Studies in Agricultural Economics and Food Policy (Palgrave Macmillan, 2019): 135–164
7 World Bank, *Resilience, Equity, and Opportunity: The World Bank's Social Protection and Labor Strategy 2012–2022 (English)* (World Bank Group).
8 World Bank, *The State of Social Safety Nets 2018* (World Bank, 2018). openknowledge.worldbank.org/handle/10986/29115
9 Ibid.
10 Prabhu Pingali, Anaka Aiyar, Mathew Abraham and Andaleeb Rahman, 'Reimagining Safety Net Programs', *Transforming Food Systems for a Rising India*, Palgrave Studies in Agricultural Economics and Food Policy (Palgrave Macmillan, 2019): 135–164.
11 Jean Drèze, 'On the Mythology of Social Policy', *The Hindu* (8 July 2014). thehindu.com/opinion/lead/on-the-mythology-of-social-policy/article6186895.ece
12 United Nations Economic and Social Commission for Asia and the Pacific (UNESCAP) and ILO, *The Protection We Want: Social Outlook for Asia and the Pacific* (Bangkok: United Nations, 2020). unescap.org/sites/default/files/publications/RC5_Social_Outlook-Report.pdf
13 Ibid., 8.
14 PTI, 'India Lifted 271 Million People Out of Poverty in 10 Years: UN', *The Hindu* (12 July 2019). thehindu.com/news/national/india-lifted-271-million-people-out-of-poverty-in-10-years-un/article28397694.ece
15 Vaishali Bansal, 'More Evidence of India's Food Insecurity', *The Hindu* (23 August 2020). thehindu.com/opinion/lead/more-evidence-of-indias-food-insecurity/article32424037.ece
16 Jean Drèze and Anmol Somanchi, *The Covid-19 Crisis and People's Right to Food* (2021).
17 Ankit Kumar, 'Covid-19 Could Push 12 Million Indians Into Extreme Poverty: World Bank', *India Today* (6 May 2020). indiatoday.in/india/story/covid-19-could-push-12-million-indians-into-extreme-poverty-world-bank-1675173-2020-05-07
18 Archana Chaudhary, 'Hunger crisis forces even middle-class Indians to line up for rations', *The Economic Times* (15 July 2021). economictimes.

indiatimes.com/news/india/hunger-crisis-forces-even-middle-class-indians-to-line-up-for-rations/articleshow/84396184.cms

19 Devesh Kapur and Prakirti Nangia, 'A Targeted Approach: India's Expanding Social Safety Net', *World Politics Review* (24 September 2013). worldpoliticsreview.com/articles/13244/a-targeted-approach-indias-expanding-social-safety-net

20 Ibid.

21 Food and Agriculture Organization (FAO) et al., *The State of Food Security and Nutrition in the World 2020: Transforming Food Systems for Affordable Healthy Diets* (Rome: FAO, 2020): 155.

22 Shrayana Bhattacharya, Vanita Leah Falcao and Raghav Puri, 'The Public Distribution System in India: Policy Evolution and Program Delivery Trends', *The 1.5 Billion People Question: Food, Vouchers, or Cash Transfers?* (World Bank, 2017): 43-105.

23 Yamini Aiyar and Michael Walton, 'Rights, Accountability and Citizenship: Examining India's Emerging Welfare State', Engaging Accountability: Working Paper Series, Accountability Initiative (2014).

24 Prabhu Pingali, Anaka Aiyar, Mathew Abraham and Andaleeb Rahman, 'Reimagining Safety Net Programs', *Transforming Food Systems for a Rising India*, Palgrave Studies in Agricultural Economics and Food Policy (Palgrave Macmillan, 2019): 135–164.

25 World Bank, *India Development Update (July 2020)* (World Bank, 2020). openknowledge.worldbank.org/handle/10986/34367

26 PTI, 'Narendra Modi Launches PM Kisan Scheme, 12 Crore Farmers Will Be Benefited', *Mint* (24 February 2019). livemint.com/politics/policy/narendra-modi-launches-pm-kisan-scheme-12-crore-farmers-will-be-benefited-1550995773911.html

27 'Pradhan Mantri Kisan Samman Nidhi: New List 2020—How to Check?' Sarkari Yojanas.

28 Tarun Khanna, Nachiket Mor and Sandhya Venkateswaran, 'Transition paths towards better health outcomes in India: Optimizing the use of existing pooled government funds', Brookings (29 June 2021). brookings.edu/blog/up-front/2021/06/29/transition-paths-towards-better-health-outcomes-in-india-optimizing-the-use-of-existing-pooled-government-funds/

29 World Bank, *India Development Update (July 2020)* (World Bank, 2020). openknowledge.worldbank.org/handle/10986/34367

30 Department of Economic Affairs, *India Public Finance Statistics 2017-2018* (Ministry of Finance, Government of India, 2019).

dea.gov.in/sites/default/files/INDIAN%20PUBLIC%20FINANCE%20 STATISTICS%202017-18.pdf

31 PTI, 'GDP Growth Rate for 2017-18 Revised Upwards to 7.2 %', *The Economic Times* (31 January 2019). economictimes.indiatimes.com/news/economy/indicators/gdp-growth-rate-for-2017-18-revised-upwards-to-7-2-/articleshow/67775487.cms

32 While India spends more than its neighbours in South Asia on social protection, it still performs poorly (ADB estimates). Even Afghanistan does better than India (in terms of ASPIRE adequacy and spending).

33 World Bank, *The Atlas of Social Protection Indicators of Resilience and Equity (ASPIRE)*, World Bank Group.

34 Ibid.

35 PTI, '60% of India's Population to Live in Cities by 2050: Government', *Mint* (27 July 2016). livemint.com/Politics/CyaMfUg L7r9dEAPKIRYMkI/60-of-Indias-population-to-live-in-cities-by-2050-governm.html

36 Shrayana Bhattacharya, John Blomquist and Rinku Murgai, 'Schemes to Systems | Rebalancing Social Protection in India', *World Bank* (5 March 2019). worldbank.org/en/news/feature/2019/11/22/schemes-to-systems-rebalancing-social-protection-india

37 World Bank, *India Development Update (July 2020)* (World Bank, 2020): 74. openknowledge.worldbank.org/handle/10986/34367

38 Harikishan Sharma, 'NREGS Surge: Ministry Spends 72% of Budget in First Quarter', *The Indian Express* (5 August 2020). indianexpress.com/article/india/nregs-surge-ministry-spends-72-of-budget-in-first-quarter-6539622

39 PTI, 'Wages Under MGNREGA Delayed, Urgent Need to Release Additional Funds: PAEG', *Outlook* (10 September 2020). outlookindia.com/newsscroll/wages-under-mgnrega-delayed-urgent-need-to-release-additional-funds-paeg/1933449

40 Jean Drèze, 'Budget 2020: Giving NREGA Workers Their Due', BloombergQuint (17 January 2020). bloombergquint.com/union-budget-2020/budget-2020-giving-nrega-workers-their-due-by-jean-dreze

41 'Of 42 'Hunger-Related' Deaths Since 2017, 25 "Linked to Aadhaar Issues"', The Wire (21 September 2018). thewire.in/rights/of-42-hunger-related-deaths-since-2017-25-linked-to-aadhaar-issues

42 Rajendra Sharma, 'MP CM Shivraj Singh Chouhan Puts Egg Debate to Rest, Says Milk Is a Better Option', *The Times of India* (16 September

2020). timesofindia.indiatimes.com/city/bhopal/cm-puts-egg-debate-to-rest-says-milk-is-a-better-option/articleshow/78136251.cms

43 'As Per the National Family Health Survey (NFHS)-4 (2015-16), 35.7 Per Cent Children Below Five Years Are Underweight', *Business Standard* (12 August 2017). business-standard.com/article/news-cm/as-per-the-national-family-health-survey-nfhs-4-2015-16-35-7-per-cent-children-below-five-years-are-underweight-117081101085_1.html

44 'More than 100mn Excluded from PDS as Govt Uses Outdated Census 2011 Data', IndiaSpend (12 August 2017). indiaspend.com/more-than-100mn-excluded-from-pds-as-govt-uses-outdated-census-2011-data/

45 Devesh Kapur and Prakirti Nangia, 'A Targeted Approach: India's Expanding Social Safety Net', *World Politics Review* (24 September 2013).

46 Ruth Alexander, 'Dollar Benchmark: The Rise of the $1-a-Day Statistic', *BBC News* (9 March 2012). bbc.com/news/magazine-17312819

47 Simon Maxwell, 'Heaven or Hubris: Reflections on the New "New Poverty Agenda"', *Development Policy Review* 21, no. 1 (2003): 5–25. doi:10.1111/1467-7679.00196

48 World Bank, *World Development Report 1990: Poverty* (World Bank Group, 1990): 3.

49 Ruth Alexander, 'Dollar Benchmark: The Rise of the $1-a-Day Statistic', *BBC News* (9 March 2012). bbc.com/news/magazine-17312819

50 Prabhu Pingali, Anaka Aiyar, Mathew Abraham and Andaleeb Rahman, 'Reimagining Safety Net Programs', *Transforming Food Systems for a Rising India*, Palgrave Studies in Agricultural Economics and Food Policy (Palgrave Macmillan, 2019): 135–164.

51 SDG 1.3: 'Implement nationally appropriate social protection systems and measures for all, including floors, and by 2030 achieve substantial coverage of the poor and the vulnerable.'

52 ILO, *World Social Protection Report 2017–19: Universal Social Protection to Achieve the Sustainable Development Goals*, International Labour Office (ILO, 2017).

53 Ibid.

54 Ibid., 20.

55 Pinaki Chakraborty, 'Implementation of the National Rural Employment Guarantee Act in India: Spatial Dimensions and Fiscal Implications', The Levy Economics Institute of Bard College, Working Paper No. 505 (2007).

56 'Centre Replicates Telangana's Rythu Bandhu Scheme to Give Income Support to Farmers', The News Minute (1 February 2019). thenewsminute.com/article/centre-replicates-telanganas-rythu-bandhu-scheme-give-income-support-farmers-96057
57 'Survivor's Pension in Sweden', Nordic Co-operation. norden.org/en/info-norden/survivors-pension-sweden
58 'COVID-19: Coronavirus Pandemic Reported Cases and Deaths by Country or Territory', *Worldomete* worldometers.info/coronavirus/#countries
59 Jae-Jin Yang, 'South Korea's Social Safety Net Wasn't Prepared for Coronavirus', *The National Interest* (4 October 2020). nationalinterest.org/blog/korea-watch/south-koreas-social-safety-net-wasnt-prepared-coronavirus-169993
60 Swati Dhingra, 'Protecting Informal Workers in Urban India', VOX, CEPR Policy Portal (2 May 2020). voxeu.org/article/protecting-informal-workers-urban-india
61 Surbhi Bhatia and Vishnu Padmanabhan, 'Can UBI Reignite the Economy?' *Mint* (29 January 2020). livemint.com/news/india/can-ubi-reignite-the-economy-11580293689566.html
62 Maitreesh Ghatak and Karthik Muralidharan, 'An Inclusive Growth Dividend: Reframing the Role of Income Transfers in India's Anti-Poverty Strategy', India Policy Forum 2020 (2019). econweb.ucsd.edu/~kamurali/papers/Working%20Papers/IGD%20(Current%20WP).pdf
63 Junaid Ahmad, 'Schemes to Systems: The Future of Social Protection in India', World Bank (20 February 2019). worldbank.org/en/news/feature/2019/11/20/schemes-to-systems-future-social-protection-india
64 Jean Drèze, 'Budget 2020: Giving NREGA Workers Their Due', BloombergQuint (17 January 2020). bloombergquint.com/union-budget-2020/budget-2020-giving-nrega-workers-their-due-by-jean-dreze
65 Shrayana Bhattacharya, John Blomquist and Rinku Murgai, 'Schemes to Systems: Rebalancing Social Protection in India', World Bank (5 March 2019). worldbank.org/en/news/feature/2019/11/22/schemes-to-systems-rebalancing-social-protection-india
66 Swati Dhingra, 'Protecting Informal Workers in Urban India', VOX, CEPR Policy Portal (2 May 2020).
67 PTI, '60% of India's Population to Live in Cities by 2050: Government', *Mint* (27 July 2016). livemint.com/Politics/CyaMfUg

L7r9dEAPKIRYMkI/60-of-Indias-population-to-live-in-cities-by-2050-governm.html

68 World Bank, *India Development Update (July 2020)* (World Bank, 2020). openknowledge.worldbank.org/handle/10986/34367

69 Gautam Bhardwaj and Robert Palacios, 'Schemes to Systems: Mind the Gap: Ageing and Pensions', World Bank (21 February 2019). worldbank.org/en/news/feature/2019/11/25/schemes-to-systems-mind-gap-ageing-pensions

70 Jean Drèze and Reetika Khera, 'Recent Social Security Initiatives in India', *World Development, Elsevier* 98(C) (2017): 555–572. doi: 10.1016/j.worlddev.2017.05.035

71 Gautam Bhardwaj and Robert Palacios, 'Schemes to Systems: Mind the Gap: Ageing and Pensions', World Bank (21 February 2019). worldbank.org/en/news/feature/2019/11/25/schemes-to-systems-mind-gap-ageing-pensions

72 Shrayana Bhattacharya, John Blomquist and Rinku Murgai, 'Schemes to Systems: Rebalancing Social Protection in India', World Bank (5 March 2019). worldbank.org/en/news/feature/2019/11/22/schemes-to-systems-rebalancing-social-protection-india

73 *Public Goods for Economic Development* (Vienna United Nations Industrial Development Organization, 2008).

74 Shruti Rajagopalan, 'India Should Fix Its Warped State-Citizen Relationship', *Mint* (12 October 2020). livemint.com/opinion/columns/india-should-fix-its-warped-state-citizen-relationship-11602513627251.html

Chapter 9

1 India's southern states have seen a rapid slowdown in population growth and are ageing as well.

2 W. Arthur Lewis, 'Economic Development with Unlimited Supplies of Labour', *The Manchester School* 22, no. 2 (1954): 139–191.

3 Douglas Gollin, 'The Lewis Model: A 60-Year Retrospective', *Journal of Economic Perspectives* 28, no. 3 (2014): 71–88.

4 Carmel U. Chiswick, 'Modelling Economic Development: The Lewis Model Updated', International Institute of Educational Planning (UNESCO) Working Paper-2018-5 (George Washington University, 2018).

5 If you add unpaid work, the female LFPR jumps to 87 per cent.
6 World Bank, *South Asia Economic Focus, Spring 2018: Jobless Growth?* (World Bank, 2018). https://openknowledge.worldbank.org/handle/10986/29650 License: CC BY 3.0 IGO
7 Total factor productivity measures how productively have the factors of labour and capital been used to generate output.
8 Reema Nayar et al., 'More and Better Jobs in South Asia', South Asia Development Matters (World Bank, 2012). openknowledge.worldbank.org/handle/10986/2391
9 India did not adequately expand low-skilled employment in apparel, textiles and electronics, where women with secondary-level education find jobs in countries like Bangladesh, Cambodia, Malaysia, Thailand and Vietnam.
10 Centre for Economic Data and Analysis (CEDA), 'Manufacturing Employment Halves in 5 Years', CEDA-CMIE Bulletin. ashoka.edu.in.
11 'Share of agriculture sector in employment sees steady increase: CMIE'. *The Economic Times* (indiatimes.com)
12 Reema Nayar et al., 'More and Better Jobs in South Asia', South Asia Development Matters (World Bank, 2012). openknowledge.worldbank.org/handle/10986/2391
13 Ministry of Statistics and Programme Implementation, *Periodic Labour Force Survey Report (2018-19)* (Government of India, 2020). mospi.nic.in/sites/default/files/publication_reports/Annual_Report_PLFS_2018_19_HL.pdf
14 W. Li, T. Mengistae and L.C. Xu, 'Diagnosing Development Bottlenecks China and India,' World Bank Policy Research Working Paper No. 5641 (World Bank, 2011).
15 Mariya Aleksynska and Angelika Muller, 'The Regulation of Collective Dismissal: Economic Rationale and Legal Practice', ILO Working Paper No. 4 (International Labour Organization, 2020). ilo.org/wcmsp5/groups/public/---ed_protect/---protrav/---travail/documents/publication/wcms_745125.pdf
16 This limit can be increased under the law.
17 Ministry of Finance, 'Reorienting Policies for MSME Growth', *Economic Survey 2018-19, Vol. 1* (Government of India, July 2019). indiabudget.gov.in/budget2019-20/economicsurvey/doc/echapter.pdf.
18 A. Maira and P. Mehta, 'View: Labour Laws Are Not the Only Villain Hampering Growth as They Are Made Out to Be', *The Economic Times*, 20 February 2020).

19 'Why the New Labor Law Reforms Make India Fertile for Jobs'. upenn.edu
20 It also provides for automatic absorption of contract workers into the establishment of the principal employer where they are engaged through an unlicensed contractor.
21 In its absence a negotiating council may be formed.
22 Rajesh Shukla, Megha Shree and P. Geetha Rani, 'Explained: Gap Between Skill India Goals and Current Status', *The Financial Express* (19 March 2019). financialexpress.com/opinion/skill-india-why-there-is-a-gap-between-current-status-and-goals-explained/1520633
23 Wheebox, PeopleStrong, Confederation of Indian Industry, *India Skills Report 2019: Say Hello to the Future of Work* (2019). aicte-india.org/sites/default/files/India%20Skill%20Report-2019.pdf
24 Ministry of Finance, *Economic Survey 2018-19, Vol. 1* (Government of India, 2019). indiabudget.gov.in/budget2019-20/economicsurvey/doc/echapter.pdf

Chapter 10

1 W. Arthur Lewis, 'Economic Development with Unlimited Supplies of Labour', *The Manchester School* 22, no. 2 (1954): 139–191. doi:10.1111/j.1467-9957.1954.tb00021.x
2 Ejaz Ghani, 'Opinion: The Problems with India's Land Market Distortions', *Mint* (10 September 2018). livemint.com/Leisure/EH1dfluTX13RpcWziGBhUJ/The-problems-with-Indias-land-market-distortions.html
3 Gilles Duranton et al., 'A Detailed Anatomy of Factor Misallocation in India', World Bank Policy Research Working Paper No. 7547 (World Bank, 2016). openknowledge.worldbank.org/handle/10986/23720 License: CC BY 3.0 IGO
4 Ajay Chibber and Akshata Kalloor, '*Reviving Private Investment in India: Determinants and Policy Levers*', IIEP-WP-2017-5, Institute for International Economic Policy (George Washington University, 2017). www2.gwu.edu/~iiep/assets/docs/papers/2017WP/ChhibberIIEPWP2017-5.pdf
5 Abhishek Dangra, 'The Missing Piece in India's Economic Growth Story: Robust Infrastructure', *S&P Global* (2 August 2016).

6 Ramakrishna Nallathiga et al., 'Factors Affecting the Success/Failure of Road Infrastructure Projects Under PPP in India', *Journal of Construction Engineering and Project Management* 7, no. 4 (2018): 1–12.

7 Suraj K. Patil et al., 'Causes of Delay in Indian Transportation Infrastructure Projects', *IJRET: International Journal of Research in Engineering and Technology* 2, no. 11 (2013): 71–80.

8 Eleven states have changed land ceiling laws meant to benefit poor farmers in favour of industries. scroll.in

9 Abhiman Das et al., *Infrastructure and Finance: Evidence from India's GQ Highway Network*. Harvard Business School Entrepreneurial Management Working Paper No. 19–121 (2019).

10 Vibhuti Garg and Kashish Shah, *The Curious Case of India's Discoms: How Renewable Energy Could Reduce Their Financial Distress* (Institute of Energy Economics and Financial Analysis, 2020).

11 'Electricity Prices', GlobalPetrolPrices.com (2021). globalpetrolprices.com/electricity_prices/

12 Ministry of Finance, *Economic Survey 2018-19: Vol. 1* (Government of India, 2019). indiabudget.gov.in/budget2019-20/economicsurvey/doc/echapter.pdf

13 'Gasoline Prices', GlobalPetrolPrices.com (November 2020). globalpetrolprices.com/gasoline_prices/

14 'Diesel Prices', GlobalPetrolPrices.com (November 2020). globalpetrolprices.com/diesel_prices/

15 Sarah Colenbrander, 'Cities as Engines of Economic Growth: The Case for Providing Basic Infrastructure and Services in Urban Areas' (International Institute for Environment and Development, 2016). pubs.iied.org/sites/default/files/pdfs/migrate/10801IIED.pdf

16 Stephen Adams, 'Global Cities: The Outlook for the World's Leading Urban Economies Amid the Global Slowdown' (Oxford Economics, 2019).

17 World Bank, *Urbanization beyond Municipal Boundaries: Nurturing Metropolitan Economies and Connecting Peri-Urban Areas in India* (World Bank, 2013).

18 Amit Kapoor and Harshula Sinha, 'View: India's Urbanisation Challenges and the Way Forward', *The Economic Times* (27 November 2020). economictimes.indiatimes.com/news/economy/policy/view-indias-urbanisation-challenges-and-the-way-forward/articleshow/79443872.cms

19 Abdul Shaban, Karima Kourtit and Peter Nijkamp, 'India's Urban System: Sustainability and Imbalanced Growth of Cities', *Sustainability* 12, no. 7 (2020): 2941. doi.org/10.3390/su12072941
20 Mariaflavia Harari, *Cities in Bad Shape: Urban Geometry in India*, The Wharton School (University of Pennsylvania, 2016). faculty.wharton.upenn.edu/wp-content/uploads/2016/02/CityShape26Dec2016.pdf
21 Apoorva Shenvi and Ron H. Slangen, 'Enabling Smart Urban Redevelopment in India through Floor Area Ratio Incentives', ADB South Asia Working Paper Series No. 58 (Asian Development Bank, 2018). adb.org/sites/default/files/publication/435936/swp-058-smart-urban-redevelopment-india.pdf
22 Alain Bertaud, 'The Economic Impact of Land and Urban Planning Regulations in India' (2002). alainbertaud.com/wp-content/uploads/2013/06/AB_-India_-Urban_Land_Reform.pdf
23 Prottoy Aman Akbar et al., 'Mobility and Congestion in Urban India', World Bank Policy Research Working Paper No. 8546 (World Bank, 2018). doi:10.1596/1813-9450-8546

Chapter 11

1 Serious recognition started only in 2015 and peaked in 2017-18—at which time they were over 11 per cent of all advances.
2 RBI's *Financial Stability Report (*FSR) 2021 now states 'Macro stress tests indicate that the gross non-performing asset (GNPA) ratio of SCBs may increase from 7.48 per cent in March 2021 to 9.80 per cent by March 2022 under the baseline scenario; and to 11.22 per cent under a severe stress scenario, although SCBs have sufficient capital, both at the aggregate and individual level, even under stress'. The previous RBI FSR showed that under the severe stress test scenario, GNPAs might rise to 14 per cent. *Financial Stability Report*. rbi.org.in
3 World Bank, 'Domestic Credit to Private Sector (% of GDP)', *World Development Indicators* (World Bank, October 2020).
4 Liaquat Ahamed made this point in a talk at the Envisioning India series at IIEP, George Washington University. 'Fiscal Dominance: A Theory of Everything in India (Webinar)', *Envisioning India*, Institute for International Economic Policy (George Washington University, 2020). iiep.gwu.edu/2020/08/04/fiscal-dominance-a-theory-of-everything-in-india/

5 Sengupta, R. and H. Vardhan, 'Productivity growth in Indian banking: Who did the gains accrue to?', Indira Gandhi Institute of Development Research (IGIDR) Working Paper Series, 2020-024; http://www.igidr.ac.in/working-paper-productivity-growth-indian-banking-gains-accrue/
6 The first farm loan waiver was introduced in 1990 by the V.P. Singh government. A second large one was introduced in 2008 for small and marginal farmers well before the GFC but in preparation of upcoming elections. Waivers of state-level loans have been done in 2014 in Telangana and Andhra Pradesh, and lately in 2017 in Uttar Pradesh, Punjab, Karnataka and Maharashtra.
7 Raghuram Rajan, 'Has Financial Development Made the World Riskier?', NBER Working Paper No. 11728 (2005).
8 'Economic Survey: From Crony Socialism to Stigmatised Capitalism', BloombergQuint (29 January 2018). bloombergquint.com/business/economic-survey-from-crony-socialism-to-stigmatised-capitalism
9 A decade of credit collapse in India (ideasforindia.in).
10 Both the CEA Subramaniam and Deputy Governor Viral Acharya initially favoured such a approach but eventually backed off as it became clear the government was going with the slower IBC process. But with rising NPAs, the government maybe forced to rethink its approach as the revival of the IBC process may be difficult.
11 The Banks issued bonds which were bought by the government and used to recapitalize the banks—so that only the interest cost of the bonds shows up as a fiscal cost in the year when interest is to be paid.
12 Saner Writing: A Post-Pandemic Assessment of the Insolvency and Bankruptcy Code (sanerlog.blogspot.com)
13 They are liquid assets, as they can be transacted in the market, but their value can fluctuate depending on the yield. Calculated as liquid reserves divided by time and demand liabilities.
14 Calculated as liquid reserves divided by time and demand liabilities.
15 Viral Acharya (2020) believes this fiscal dominance explains many of the problems of India's banking system. Viral Acharya, *Quest for Restoring Financial Stability in India*, (SAGE Publications, 2020).
16 Niranjan Rajadhyaksha writes in *Mint* in July 2019, 'Banks were asked to push funds towards sectors that the government wanted to target for growth. Indira Gandhi told the Lok Sabha on 29 July 1969 that the "purpose of nationalization is to promote rapid growth in agriculture, small industries and export, to encourage new entrepreneurs and to

develop all backward areas"'. Niranjan Rajadhyaksha, 'The 1969 Bank Nationalization Did India More Harm Than Good', *Mint* (16 July 2019). livemint.com/opinion/columns/opinion-the-1969-bank-nationalization-did-india-more-harm-than-good-1563295097940.html

17 Morarji Desai, then finance minister, resigned over the decision and Mrs Gandhi took over the finance ministry.

18 A respected chair of BBB, the former Comptroller and Auditor General of India resigned as its chairman when he was often not consulted on major issues.

19 Asli Demirgüç-Kunt et al., *The Global Findex Database 2017* (World Bank, 2017).

20 ICFI - BC Network - White Paper.pdf

21 RBI, Press Releases. rbi.org.in

22 For a good description of India's financial system and the role of NBFCs, see Rashmi U. Arora and Quanda Zhang, 'Banking in the Shadows: A Comparative Study of China and India', *Australian Economic History Review* 59, no. 1 (2018): 103–131.

23 In recent years, two RBI governors and one deputy governor has been at public loggerheads with the government and have either resigned or left.

24 They turned out to be too independent and openly expressed disagreement.

25 In India, deposit insurance was only ₹1,00,000 per bank per depositor. It has been raised to ₹5,00,000 in the 2020 budget after the collapse of a cooperative bank.

26 Viral Acharya, *Quest for Restoring Financial Stability in India* (SAGE Publications, 2020).

27 This was the argument made by Mrs Gandhi in 1969 to nationalize the banking sector; that banks were under corporates who cornered the bulk of the credit to their own in-house companies.

28 'Government set up "bad bank" to clear the NPA mess', *The Hindu* (16 September 2021). https://www.thehindu.com/business/Economy/government-sets-up-bad-bank-to-clear-the-npa-mess/article36495756.ece

Chapter 12

1 C. Rangarajan and S. Mahendra Dev, 'How FPOs Can Help Small and Marginal Farmers', *The Indian Express* (11 March 2021).

indianexpress.com/article/opinion/columns/nabard-agrarian-distress-farmers-protest-farm-laws-7222830/

2 CSDS-Lokniti, 'State of Indian Farmers: A Report' (CSDS-Lokniti, 2018).

3 For a more detailed discussion, see Ajay Chhibber, 'The Aggregate Supply Response: A Survey', *Structural Adjustment and Agriculture: Theory and Practice in Africa and Latin America,* Simon Commander, ed. (Heinemann, 1989).

4 Norman Borlaug, a Nobel Prize-winning American economist played a huge role in bringing the Green Revolution to India and M.S. Swaminathan, often called 'the father of the Green Revolution', was the key scientist behind the revolution in India, but the Indian government played a huge role in providing the funding and organizational support as well.

5 Yujiro Hayami and Vernon W. Ruttan, *Agricultural Development: An International Perspective* (Johns Hopkins University Press, 1971).

6 Bina Agarwal, 'Diffusion of Rural Innovations: Some Analytical Issues and Application to Wood Burning Stoves', *World Development* 11, no. 4 (1983): 359–376. doi: 10.1016/0305-750X(83)90047-5

7 Directorate of Economics and Statistics, *Agricultural Statistics at a Glance 2019* (Ministry of Agriculture and Farmers Welfare, Government of India, 2020). eands.dacnet.nic.in/PDF/At%20a%20Glance%202019%20Eng.pdf

8 Sandip Mitra et al., 'Asymmetric Information and Middleman Margins: An Experiment with Indian Potato Farmers'. *The Review of Economics and Statistics* 100, no. 1, (2018):1–13. doi:10.1162/REST_a_00699

9 Binod B. Bhoi et al., 'Supply Chain Dynamics and Food Inflation in India', *RBI Bulletin* (Reserve Bank of India, 11 October 2019). rbi.org.in/scripts/BS_ViewBulletin.aspx?Id=18527#CH1

10 Rudrani Bhattacharya and Sabarni Chowdhury, 'How Effective is e-NAM in Integrating Food Commodity Prices in India? Evidence from Onion', NIPFP Working Paper No. 336 (2021).

11 Hitesh Bhatt, 'National Milk Day: Dr. Kurien's Lessons from Building India's Largest Rural Industry', *Outlook Magazine* (2019). outlookindia.com/website/story/india-news-national-milk-day-dr-kuriens-lessons-from-building-indias-largest-rural-industry/343081.

12 Richa Singh, 'Remembering Charan Singh, the Man Who Brought Peasant Issues into India's Electoral Politics', The Wire (23 December 2017). thewire.in/government/remembering-chaudhary-charan-singh-man-brought-peasant-issues-indias-electoral-politics

13 Bina Agarwal, 'Does Group Farming Empower Rural Women? Lessons from India's Experiments', *The Journal of Peasant Studies* 47, no. 4 (2020): 841–872. doi: 10.1080/03066150.2019.1628020
14 C. Rangarajan and S. Mahendra Dev, 'How FPOs Can Help Small and Marginal Farmers', *The Indian Express* (11 March 2021). indianexpress.com/article/opinion/columns/nabard-agrarian-distress-farmers-protest-farm-laws-7222830/
15 Smriti Verma et al., 'Are Farmer Producer Organizations a Boon to Farmers? The Evidence from Bihar, India', *Agricultural Economics Research Review* 32 (Conference) (2019): 123–137. doi:0.5958/0974-0279.2019.00022.3
16 OECD and the Indian Council for Research on International Economic Relations (ICRIER), *Agricultural Policies in India*, OECD Food and Agricultural Reviews (OECD Publishing, 2018). doi:10.1787/9789264302334-en
17 Raj Krishna and Ajay Chhibber. 1983. *Policy Modeling of a Dual Grain Market: The Case of Wheat in India*. Research Reports 38, International Food Policy Research Institute (IFPRI) (1983).
18 Shanta Kumar Committee Report, *Report of the High-Level Committee on restructuring of the Food Corporation of India* (Government of India, 2016).
19 webinarAbstract20210719.pdf (igidr.ac.in)
20 Kyle Frankel Davis et al., 'Assessing the sustainability of post-Green Revolution cereals in India'. https://www.pnas.org/content/116/50/25034
21 The number is even higher if you include forestry and animal husbandry.
22 Sardara Singh Johl, *Diversification of Agriculture in Punjab*, Report of Expert Committee (Government of Punjab, 1986).
23 Sardara Singh Johl, *Agricultural Production Pattern Adjustment Programme in Punjab for Productivity and Growth* (Government of Punjab, 2002).
24 Johl is reported to have said, 'Either the Swaminathan Committee did not have an economist on it, or if they had one, he wasn't a very good one.'
25 Uma Lele, 'Growing Water Scarcities: Responses of India and China', *Applied Economic Perspectives and Policies* (2020). doi:10.1002/aepp.13146

Chapter 13

1 Kalpana Sunder, 'RoboDoc: How India's Robots Are Taking On Covid Patient Care', *The Guardian* (2 December 2020). theguardian.com/global-development/2020/dec/02/robodoc-how-india-robots-are-taking-on-covid-patient-care-mitra
2 Abhijit Ahaskar, 'Hospitals Turn to Robots to Clear Backlog of Elective Surgeries Amid Covid-19', *Mint* (12 September 2020). livemint.com/news/india/hospitals-turn-to-robots-to-clear-backlog-of-elective-surgeries-11599913639699.html
3 P.B. Jayakumar, 'Coronavirus Scare: Demand for Cleaning Robots to Grow 4,000% in 5 Years', *Business Today* (12 June 2020). businesstoday.in/technology/news/coronavirus-scare-demand-for-cleaning-robots-to-grow-4000-in-5-years/story/406776.html
4 Kazuya Manabe and Yuki Fukumoto, 'China Dominates World Export Markets Despite US Trade War', *Nikkei Asia* (29 November 2020). asia.nikkei.com/Spotlight/Datawatch/China-dominates-world-export-markets-despite-US-trade-war
5 Tania Branigan, 'China's Great Famine: The True Story', *The Guardian* (1 January 2013). theguardian.com/world/2013/jan/01/china-great-famine-book-tombstone
6 Donald S. Zagoria, 'China's Quiet Revolution', *Foreign Affairs* (Spring 1984). foreignaffairs.com/articles/asia/1984-03-01/chinas-quiet-revolution
7 Alexander Eckstein, *China's Economic Revolution* (Cambridge University Press, 1977). doi:10.1017/cbo9780511571732
8 Ibid.
9 Yi Wen, 'China's Rapid Rise: From Backward Agrarian Society to Industrial Powerhouse in Just 35 Years', *Regional Economist* (Federal Reserve Bank of St. Louis, April 2016). stlouisfed.org/publications/regional-economist/april-2016/chinas-rapid-rise-from-backward-agrarian-society-to-industrial-powerhouse-in-just-35-years
10 Ibid.
11 Department of Industrial Policy and Promotion, *National Manufacturing Policy* (Government of India). https://www.meity.gov.in/writereaddata/files/National%20Manufacturing%20Policy%20(2011)%20(167%20KB).pdf
12 Stratfor, 'The Difficulties of Retooling the Indian Economy' (2018). stratfor.com/analysis/difficulties-retooling-indian-economy

13 Dani Rodrik, 'Premature Deindustrialization', NBER Working Paper No. 20935 (NBER, 2015). doi:10.3386/w20935
14 Sukti Dasgupta and Ajit Singh, 'Manufacturing, Services and Premature Deindustrialization in Developing Countries: A Kaldorian Analysis', *Advancing Development: Core Themes in Global Economics (Studies in Development Economics and Policy)* George Mavrotas and Anthony Shorrocks, eds. (Palgrave Macmillan, 2006). doi:10.1057/9780230801462_23
15 Dani Rodrik, 'Premature Deindustrialization', NBER Working Paper No. 20935 (NBER, 2015). doi:10.3386/w20935
16 Ibid.
17 Mary Hallward-Driemeier and Gaurav Nayyar, *Trouble in the Making? The Future of Manufacturing-Led Development* (World Bank Group, 2017). doi:10.1596/978-1-4648-1174-6
18 Ibid.
19 M. Suresh Babu, 'Why 'Make in India' Has Failed', *The Hindu* (20 January 2020). thehindu.com/opinion/op-ed/why-make-in-india-has-failed/article30601269.ece
20 Elizabeth Paton, 'After Factory Disaster, Bangladesh Made Big Safety Strides. Are the Bad Days Coming Back?', *The New York Times* (1 March 2020). nytimes.com/2020/03/01/world/asia/rana-plaza-bangladesh-garment-industry.html
21 Kaushik Basu, 'Why Is Bangladesh Booming?', Brookings (1 May 2018). brookings.edu/opinions/why-is-bangladesh-booming
22 Ibid.
23 Shirish Sankhe et al., *India's Turning Point: An Economic Agenda to Spur Growth and Jobs* (McKinsey Global Institute, 2020).
24 International Organization of Motor Vehicle Manufacturers, '2019 Production Statistics'. oica.net/category/production-statistics/2019-statistics/
25 IEA, *Global EV Outlook 2020* (IEA, 2020). iea.org/reports/global-ev-outlook-2020
26 Mary Hallward-Driemeier and Gaurav Nayyar, *Trouble in the Making? The Future of Manufacturing-Led Development* (World Bank Group, 2017). doi:10.1596/978-1-4648-1174-6
27 Cristian Alonso, Siddharth Kothari and Sidra Rehman, 'How Artificial Intelligence Could Widen the Gap Between Rich and Poor Nations', *IMF Blog* (2 December 2020). blogs.imf.org/2020/12/02/how-artificial-intelligence-could-widen-the-gap-between-rich-and-poor-nations

28 Rajat Dhawan and Suvojoy Sengupta, 'A New Growth Formula for Manufacturing in India', McKinsey & Company (30 October 2020). mckinsey.com/industries/advanced-electronics/our-insights/a-new-growth-formula-for-manufacturing-in-india

29 World Bank, 'Research and Development Expenditure (% of GDP)—India, China, United States', *World Development Indicators* (World Bank). data.worldbank.org/indicator/GB.XPD.RSDV.GD.ZS?locations=IN-CN-US

Chapter 14

1 Geethanjali Nataraj and Rishika Singh, 'Service Sector, Driver of India's Growth, Has Been Left Out of Centre's Relief Package', *The Indian Express* (27 August 2020). indianexpress.com/article/opinion/columns/service-sector-jobs-economy-covidan-unserviced-sector-6571279

2 Stephen Broadberry and Bishnupriya Gupta, 'The Historical Roots of India's Booming Service Economy', VOX, CEPR Policy Portal (9 May 2008). voxeu.org/article/historical-roots-india-s-booming-service-economy

3 Nandita Mathur, 'India's IT Workforce May Become Obsolete Unless Govt Supports Reskilling Program: NASSCOM', *Mint* (29 January 2020). livemint.com/news/india/india-s-it-workforce-may-become-obsolete-unless-govt-supports-reskilling-program-nasscom-11580302213042.html

4 Ejaz Ghani and Stephen D. O'Connell, 'Can Service Be a Growth Escalator in Low-Income Countries?', World Bank Policy Research Working Paper No. 6971, (World Bank Group, 2014). openknowledge.worldbank.org/handle/10986/19352

5 Robert Koopman, 'Services Are the Next—and Fast Approaching—Frontier of Global Trade and Financial Services Is a Sector Leading the Way', Société Universitaire Européenne de Recherches Financières/The European Money and Finance Forum (SUERF) Policy Notes, No. 167 (2020). suerf.org/policynotes/13093/services-are-the-next-and-fast-approaching-frontier-of-global-trade-and-financial-services-is-a-sector-leading-the-way

6 Ibid.

7 World Bank, 'Services, Value Added (Annual % Growth)', *World Development Indicators* (World Bank). data.worldbank.org/indicator/NV.SRV.TOTL.KD.ZG?locations=BD

8 Ejaz Ghani and Stephen D. O'Connell, 'Can Service Be a Growth Escalator in Low-Income Countries?', World Bank Policy Research Working Paper No. 6971 (World Bank Group, 2014). openknowledge.worldbank.org/handle/10986/19352
9 Donghyun Park and Marcus Noland, *Developing the Service Sector: As an Engine of Growth for Asia* (Asian Development Bank, 2013). adb.org/publications/developing-service-sector-engine-growth-asia
10 Rashmi Banga, 'Critical Issues in India's Services-led Growth', Working Paper No. 171 (ICRIER, 2005). icrier.org/pdf/WP171.pdf
11 Jens Arnold et al., 'Services Sector Reform and the Indian Manufacturing Miracle', VOX, CEPR Policy Portal (12 October 2010). voxeu.org/article/services-sector-reform-and-indian-manufacturing-miracle
12 Ibid.
13 Abhishek Chatterjee, 'India's Mobile Revolution Turns 25: Tracking the High and Low Points', *The Hindu* (22 October 2020). thehindu.com/sci-tech/technology/indias-mobile-revolution-turns-25-tracking-the-high-and-low-points/article32916145.ece
14 Jens Arnold et al., 'Services Sector Reform and the Indian Manufacturing Miracle', VOX, CEPR Policy Portal (12 October 2010). voxeu.org/article/services-sector-reform-and-indian-manufacturing-miracle
15 Ejaz Ghani and Stephen D. O'Connell, 'Can Service Be a Growth Escalator in Low-Income Countries?', World Bank Policy Research Working Paper No. 6971 (World Bank Group, 2014). openknowledge.worldbank.org/handle/10986/19352
16 Sanjoy Hazarika, 'In Southern India, a Glimpse of Asia's High-Tech Future', *The New York Times* (6 October 1991). nytimes.com/1991/10/06/business/in-southern-india-a-glimpse-of-asia-s-high-tech-future.html?searchResultPosition=36
17 Ministry of Finance, 'Services', *Economic Survey 2020-21, Vol. 2* (Government of India, 2021). indiabudget.gov.in/economicsurvey/doc/vol2chapter/echap09_vol2.pdf
18 Abhijit Das, Rashmi Banga and Dinesh Kumar, *Global Economic Crisis: Impact and Restructuring of the Services Sector in India* (Asian Development Bank, 2011). hdl.handle.net/11540/3899
19 Jens Arnold et al., 'Services Sector Reform and the Indian Manufacturing Miracle', VOX, CEPR Policy Portal (12 October 2012). voxeu.org/article/services-sector-reform-and-indian-manufacturing-miracle
20 Rashmi Banga, 'Critical Issues in India's Services-led Growth', Integrated Natural Resources Management (INRM) Policy Brief

No. 2 (Asian Development Bank, 2005). adb.org/sites/default/files/publication/29420/inrm2.pdf

21 The Indian government pegs this difference in contribution and employment as even larger—services employ only 25 per cent of the labour force who create 54 per cent of the GDP (*Economic Survey of India 2021-22*). For uniformity, we use ILO data in this chapter.

22 Ministry of Finance, 'Services', *Economic Survey 2020-21, Vol. 2* (Government of India, 2021). indiabudget.gov.in/economicsurvey/doc/vol2chapter/echap09_vol2.pdf

23 Rashmi Banga, 'Critical Issues in India's Services-led Growth', INRM Policy Brief No. 2 (Asian Development Bank, 2005). adb.org/sites/default/files/publication/29420/inrm2.pdf

24 Ibid.

25 Shirish Sankhe et al., *India's Turning Point: An Economic Agenda to Spur Growth and Jobs* (McKinsey Global Institute, 2020). mckinsey.com/featured-insights/india/indias-turning-point-an-economic-agenda-to-spur-growth-and-jobs

26 Mahesh Vyas, 'Migration from factories to farms', Centre for Monitoring Indian Economy (CMIE), (9 August 2021). https://www.cmie.com/kommon/bin/sr.php?kall=warticle&dt=20210809122441&msec=850

27 Jun Hou, Stephen Gelb and Linda Calabrese, *The Shift in Manufacturing Employment in China* (Overseas Development Institute, 2017). set.odi.org/wp-content/uploads/2017/08/SET-China_Shift-of-Manufacturing-Employment-1.pdf

28 Ibid.

29 Mary Hallward-Driemeier and Gaurav Nayyar, *Trouble in the Making? The Future of Manufacturing-Led Development* (World Bank Group, 2017). doi:10.1596/978-1-4648-1174-6

30 Prachi Salve, IndiaSpend, 'Data Check: 90% of Jobs Created in India After Liberalisation Were in the Informal Sector', Scroll.in (10 May 2019). scroll.in/article/922863/data-check-90-of-jobs-created-in-india-after-liberalisation-were-in-the-informal-sector

31 Nalini Gulati, 'I4I Panel Discussion: The Challenge of Job Creation', Ideas for India (30 January 2018). ideasforindia.in/topics/macroeconomics/i4i-panel-discussion-the-challenge-of-job-creation.html

32 Donghyun Park and Marcus Noland, *Developing the Service Sector as an Engine of Growth for Asia* (Asian Development Bank, 2013). adb.org/publications/developing-service-sector-engine-growth-asia
33 Prashant K. Nanda, 'Construction Fuels Jobs Revival in Rural India, Cities Struggle', *Mint* (7 February 2021). livemint.com/industry/infrastructure/construction-fuels-jobs-revival-in-rural-india-cities-struggle-11612718038800.html
34 Govindan Raveendran and Joann Vanek, 'Informal Workers in India: A Statistical Profile', Statistical Brief No. 24 (Women in Informal Employment: Globalizing and Organizing [WIEGO], 2020). wiego.org/publications/home-based-workers-india-statistical-profile
35 Ministry of Finance, 'State of the Economy 2020-21: A Macro View', *Economic Survey 2020-21, Vol. 2* (Government of India, 2021). indiabudget.gov.in/economicsurvey/doc/vol2chapter/echap01_vol2.pdf
36 Govindan Raveendran and Joann Vanek, 'Informal Workers in India: A Statistical Profile', Statistical Brief No. 24 (WIEGO, 2020). wiego.org/publications/home-based-workers-india-statistical-profile
37 *Counting the World's Informal Workers: A Global Snapshot* (WIEGO, 2019). wiego.org/statistics-global-snapshot
38 Salman Anees Soz, 'Demonetisation and the Cash-Dependent Informal Sector', *The Hindu* (9 November 2020). thehindu.com/opinion/op-ed/informal-is-normal/article20005296.ece.
39 Shreya Raman and Rizvi Saif, IndiaSpend, 'Gender Pay Gap and Occupational Segregation Have Followed Indian Women Into Gig Economy', Scroll.in (12 January 2021). scroll.in/article/983727/gender-pay-gap-and-occupational-segregation-have-followed-indian-women-into-gig-economy
40 Manishii Pathak and Natasha Sahni, 'India: Gig Economy—Legal Developments', Mondaq (19 June 2020). mondaq.com/india/employment-and-workforce-wellbeing/955662/gig-economy-legal-developments
41 Gautam Bhatia, 'Devise a New Labour Law Regime for Gig Economy Workers', *Hindustan Times* (22 September 2020). hindustantimes.com/analysis/devise-a-new-labour-law-regime-for-gig-economy-workers/story-eUgPxsALs8kokE40MddbGN.html
42 Patricia Buckley and Rumki Majumdar, 'The Services Powerhouse: Increasingly Vital to World Economic Growth', *Deloitte Insights*

(12 July 2018). deloitte.com/us/en/insights/economy/issues-by-the-numbers/trade-in-services-economy-growth.html

43 World Bank, 'Trade in Services: Helping Countries Optimize Services in Trade', World Bank. worldbank.org/en/topic/trade-in-services

44 Mary Hallward-Driemeier and Gaurav Nayyar, *Trouble in the Making? The Future of Manufacturing-Led Development* (World Bank Group, 2017). doi:10.1596/978-1-4648-1174-6

45 Ibid.

46 Ram Mudambi, 'Location, Control and Innovation in Knowledge-Intensive Industries', *Journal of Economic Geography* 8, no. 5 (2008): 699-725. doi:10.1093/jeg/lbn024

47 Jason Dedrick, Greg Linden and Kenneth L. Kraemer, 'We Estimate China Only Makes $8.46 from an iPhone—and That's Why Trump's Trade War Is Futile', The Conversation (7 July 2018). theconversation.com/we-estimate-china-only-makes-8-46-from-an-iphone-and-thats-why-trumps-trade-war-is-futile-99258

48 Edd Gent, 'Why Automation Could Be a Threat to India's Growth', BBC Future (19 May 2017). bbc.com/future/article/20170510-why-automation-could-be-a-threat-to-indias-growth

49 Nalini Gulati, 'I4I Panel Discussion: The Challenge of Job Creation', Ideas for India (30 January 2018). ideasforindia.in/topics/macroeconomics/i4i-panel-discussion-the-challenge-of-job-creation.html

50 PTI, 'Up to 6 Lakh IT Staff May Lose Jobs', *The Hindu* (14 May 2017). thehindu.com/business/Industry/up-to-6-lakh-it-staff-may-lose-jobs/article18451843.ece

51 Ayushman Baruah, 'Mass Layoffs Brewing in IT Sector Amid Uncertainties', *Mint* (8 July 2020). livemint.com/companies/news/mass-layoffs-brewing-in-it-sector-amid-uncertainties-11594174446353.html

52 Edward A. Gargan, 'India Booming as a Leader in Software for Computers', *The New York Times* (29 December 1993). nytimes.com/1993/12/29/world/india-booming-as-a-leader-in-software-for-computers.html?searchResultPosition=9

53 Dorcas Wong, 'China's Services Industry Expansion: How Beijing Is Playing a Pivotal Role', China Briefing News (22 September 2020). china-briefing.com/news/chinas-services-sector-expansion-beijing-9-industry-reforms

54 Bloomberg, 'China Aims Stronger 2020; Monetary Settings, Free Trade and Other Measures on Govt's Agenda', *The Financial Express* (25

December 2019). financialexpress.com/economy/china-aims-stronger-2020-monetary-settings-free-trade-and-other-measures-on-govts-agenda/1803708

55 Rush Doshi, Emily de La Bruyère, Nathan Picarsic and John Ferguson, 'China as a 'cyber great power': Beijing's two voices in telecommunications', Brookings (2021). brookings.edu/research/china-as-a-cyber-great-power-beijings-two-voices-in-telecommunications/

56 PTI, 'India Faces Rising Competition from China, Brazil in ICT: Economic Survey', *The Economic Times* (29 January 2018). economictimes.indiatimes.com/tech/ites/india-faces-rising-competition-from-china-brazil-in-ict-economic-survey/articleshow/62695008.cms?from=mdr

57 Ministry of Finance, 'Services'. In *Economic Survey 2020-21, Vol. 2* (Government of India, 2021). indiabudget.gov.in/economicsurvey/doc/vol2chapter/echap09_vol2.pdf

58 Geethanjali Nataraj and Rishika Singh, 'Service Sector, Driver of India's Growth, Has Been Left Out of Centre's Relief Package', *The Indian Express* (27 August 2020). indianexpress.com/article/opinion/columns/service-sector-jobs-economy-covidan-unserviced-sector-6571279

59 Deepa Kurup, 'Bangalore: The Success Story of ICT Industry', *The Hindu* (28 September 2010). thehindu.com/books/Bangalore-the-success-story-of-ICT-industry/article16050731.ece

60 Aditi Dey and Anish Pendharkar, 'Map: How Bangalore's IT Sector Flowered from a Princely State Diwan's Industrial Dream in 1911', Scroll.in (12 October 2019). scroll.in/article/938388/map-how-bangalores-it-sector-flowered-from-a-princely-state-diwans-industrial-dream-in-1911

61 Arpita Mukherjee, 'The Service Sector in India', Asian Development Bank Economics Working Paper Series No. 352 (2013). doi: 10.2139/ssrn.2282311

62 Ibid.

Chapter 15

1 *Economic Survey 2020-21*.

2 Sajjid Z. Chinoy and Toshi Jain, 2019. 'What Drives India's Exports and What Explains the Recent Slowdown? New Evidence and Policy Implications', *India Policy Forum* 15, no. 1 (NCAER, 2019): 217–256.

3 Federation of Indian Chambers of Commerce and Industry (FICCI), *Envisioning India 2030* (FICCI, 2018).
4 FICCI, *Envisioning India 2030* (FICCI, 2018). ficci.in/spdocument/23058/Envisioning-India-2030_Foreword-Overview-and-Executive-Summary.pdf
5 Jens Matthias Arnold, Beata Javorcik, Molly Lipscomb, Aaditya Mattoo, 'Services Reform and Manufacturing Performance: Evidence from India', *The Economic Journal*, 29 October 2014 (first published).
6 Ministry of Electronics and Information Technology, 'Production Linked Incentive Scheme (PLI) for Large Scale Electronics Manufacturing' (Government of India). meity.gov.in
7 Petia Topalova and Amit Khandelwal, 'Trade Liberalization and Firm Productivity: The Case of India', *The Review of Economics and Statistics* 93, no. 3 (2011): 995–1009.
8 Pinelopi Koujianou Goldberg, Amit Kumar Khandelwal, Nina Pavcnik, Petia Topalova, 'Imported Intermediate Inputs and Domestic Product Growth: Evidence from India, *The Quarterly Journal of Economics* 125, no. 4 (November 2010): 1727–1767.
9 PTI, 'PLI Scheme Likely to Boost India's Manufacturing Output by $520 Billion in 5 Years: PM Modi', *The Hindu* (5 March 2021). thehindu.com/news/national/pli-scheme-likely-to-boost-indias-manufacturing-output-by-520-billion-in-5-years-pm-modi/article33995487.ece
10 India has announced an initial funding for such an institution in the FY21-22 Budget.

Chapter 16

1 'India Climate Stories', Climate Stories Project. climatestoriesproject.org/india-climate-stories.html
2 David Eckstein et al., *Global Climate Risk Index 2020: Who Suffers the Most from Extreme Weather Events? Weather-Related Loss Events in 2018 and 1999 to 2018* (Germanwatch). germanwatch.org/en/17307
3 Bill Gates, 'COVID-19 Is Awful. Climate Change Could Be Worse', *GatesNotes* (4 August 2020). gatesnotes.com/Energy/Climate-and-COVID-19.
4 Intergovernmental Panel on Climate Change (IPCC), *Climate Change 2021: The Physical Science Basis*. IPCC VI Assessment Report, Working Group I, (2021). ipcc.ch/report/ar6/wg1/#SPM

5 Tamma A. Carleton et al., 'Valuing the Global Mortality Consequences of Climate Change Accounting for Adaptation Costs and Benefits', National Bureau of Economics Working Paper No. 27599 (2020). doi:10.3386/w27599
6 Spencer Weart, 'The Discovery of Global Warming [Excerpt]', *Scientific American* (17 August 2012). scientificamerican.com/article/discovery-of-global-warming
7 Charles Mann, 'Meet the Amateur Scientist Who Discovered Climate Change', *WIRED* (23 January 2018). wired.com/story/meet-the-amateur-scientist-who-discovered-climate-change
8 Elizabeth Kolbert, 'Three Scenarios for the Future of Climate Change', *The New Yorker* (5 October 2020). newyorker.com/news/annals-of-a-warming-planet/three-scenarios-for-the-future-of-climate-change
9 Ibid.
10 Ibid.
11 Ibid.
12 IPCC, *IPCC Special Report: Emissions Scenarios: Summary for Policymakers* (IPCC, 2000). ipcc.ch/site/assets/uploads/2018/03/sres-en.pdf
13 David Wallace-Wells, 'Intelligencer: Global Warming Is Melting Our Sense of Time', *New York Magazine* (27 June 2020). nymag.com/intelligencer/2020/06/global-warming-is-melting-our-sense-of-time.html
14 William Nordhaus, 'Projections and Uncertainties about Climate Change in an Era of Minimal Climate Policies', *American Economic Journal: Economic Policy* 10, no. 3 (2018): 333–360. doi:10.1257/pol.20170046
15 Ibid.
16 Joseph Stiglitz, 'Are We Overreacting on Climate Change?' *The New York Times* (16 July 2020). nytimes.com/2020/07/16/books/review/bjorn-lomborg-false-alarm-joseph-stiglitz.html
17 'The Paris Agreement', United Nations Climate Change. unfccc.int/process-and-meetings/the-paris-agreement/the-paris-agreement
18 Nicola Jones, 'How the World Passed a Carbon Threshold and Why It Matters', *Yale Environment 360* (26 January 2017). e360.yale.edu/features/how-the-world-passed-a-carbon-threshold-400ppm-and-why-it-matters
19 David Wallace-Wells, 'Intelligencer: The Paris Climate Accords Are Looking More and More Like Fantasy', *New York Magazine* (25

March 2020). nymag.com/intelligencer/2018/03/the-paris-climate-accords-are-starting-to-look-like-fantasy.html

20 Zeke Hausfather, 'State of the Climate: How the World Warmed in 2018', Carbon Brief (17 January 2019). carbonbrief.org/state-of-the-climate-how-world-warmed-2018

21 Zeke Hausfather, 'State of the Climate: How the World Warmed in 2019', Carbon Brief (20 January 2020). carbonbrief.org/state-of-the-climate-how-the-world-warmed-in-2019

22 Zeke Hausfather, 'Climate Change: 2020 Is Set to Be the Warmest Year on Record', World Economic Forum (26 October 2020). weforum.org/agenda/2020/10/climate-change-environment-earth-temperature-global-warming-heat

23 NASA, 'Greenland, Antarctica Melting Six Times Faster Than in the 1990s', NASA Global Climate Change (16 March 2020). climate.nasa.gov/news/2958/greenland-antarctica-melting-six-times-faster-than-in-the-1990s

24 'Heatwave Shatters September Records in Western Europe', Euronews (16 September 2020). euronews.com/2020/09/16/heatwave-shatters-september-records-in-western-europe

25 Nithin Coca, 'Flooded Asia: Climate Change Hits Region the Hardest', *Financial Times* (16 October 2020). ft.com/content/471c9e50-5921-4a49-bc36-a913adb64797

26 Holly Yan, 'Creek Fire: California Sets New Record for Land Torched by Wildfires as 224 People Escape by Air From a 'hellish' Inferno', CNN (6 September 2020). edition.cnn.com/2020/09/05/us/california-mammoth-pool-reservoir-camp-fire/index.html

27 Bibek Bhattacharya, 'Is Extreme Heat Making India Unlivable?', *Mint* (26 September 2020). livemint.com/mint-lounge/features/is-extreme-heat-making-india-unlivable-11601034638011.html

28 Katy Daigle, 'India's Rising Temperatures Are Already Deadly, Study Shows', AP News (8 June 2017). apnews.com/article/cd86d634c5e54902b5fbe4a1404c6beb

29 '2018 Was Sixth Warmest Year in India's Recorded History: IMD', The Wire (17 January 2019). thewire.in/environment/2018-was-sixth-warmest-year-in-indias-recorded-history-imd

30 Disha Shetty, IndiaSpend, 'Mumbai, Chennai, Kolkata among cities that may be submerged by 2050: Report', *Business Standard* (1 November 2019). business-standard.com/article/current-affairs/

mumbai-chennai-kolkata-among-cities-that-may-be-submerged-by-2050-report-119110100146_1.html

31 David Wallace-Wells, *The Uninhabitable Earth: Life After Warming* (Tim Dugan Books, 2019).

32 Muthukumara Mani, 'South Asia's Hotspots: The Impact of Temperature and Precipitation Changes on Living Standards', *South Asia Development Matters* (World Bank, 2018). openknowledge.worldbank.org/handle/10986/28723

33 Hannah Ritchie, 'Who Has Contributed Most to Global CO2 Emissions?', Our World in Data (1 October 2019). ourworldindata.org/contributed-most-global-co2

34 'Each Country's Share of CO2 Emissions', Union of Concerned Scientists (12 August 2020).

35 Ibid.

36 Youssef Nassef, *NAPAs in the Context of the UNFCCC Process* (United Nations Framework Convention on Climate Change [UNFCCC] Secretariat, 2020). unfccc.int/files/adaptation/napas/application/pdf/03_unfccc.pdf

37 R. Ramachandran, 'Yielding Ground', *Frontline* (26 March 2010). frontline.thehindu.com/science-and-technology/article30179700.ece

38 Aniruddh Mohan, 'From Rio to Paris: India in Global Climate Politics', ORF Occasional Papers No. 130 (Occasional Research Foundation, 2017). orfonline.org/research/rio-to-paris-india-global-climate-politics

39 Lindsay Maizland, 'Global Climate Agreements: Successes and Failures', Council on Foreign Relations (25 January 2021). cfr.org/backgrounder/paris-global-climate-change-agreements

40 'The CAT Thermometer', Climate Action Tracker. climateactiontracker.org/global/cat-thermometer/

41 'The Race to Zero Emissions, and Why the World Depends on It', *UN News* (4 December 2020). news.un.org/en/story/2020/12/1078612

42 Kapil Subramanian, 'Is India on track to meet its Paris Commitments', *DownToEarth* (1 October 2019). downtoearth.org.in/blog/climate-change/is-india-on-track-to-meet-its-paris-commitments-67345

43 Jyoti Parikh and Kirit Parikh, 'Weighing our net zero challenge: It's not just about energy. India has to assess technological, economic and societal transitions', *The Times of India* (29 April 2021). timesofindia.indiatimes.com/blogs/toi-edit-page/weighing-our-net-zero-challenge-

its-not-just-about-energy-india-has-to-assess-technological-economic-and-societal-transitions/

44 Molly Bergen and Helen Mountford, '6 Signs of Progress Since the Adoption of the Paris Agreement', World Resources Institute (8 December 2020). wri.org/insights/6-signs-progress-adoption-paris-agreement

45 Jocelyn Timperley, 'The Carbon Brief Profile: India', *Carbon Brief* (14 March 2019). carbonbrief.org/the-carbon-brief-profile-india.

46 Ibid.

47 Samantha Gross, 'Coal Is King in India—And Will Likely Remain So', Brookings (8 March 2019). brookings.edu/blog/planetpolicy/2019/03/08/coal-is-king-in-india-and-will-likely-remain-so

48 PTI, 'India Needs $2.5 Trillion to Meet its 2030 Climate Change Targets: Centre', *Business Standard* (16 March 2018). business-standard.com/article/pti-stories/india-needs-usd-2-5-trillion-to-meet-its-2030-climate-change-targets-govt-118031601090_1.html

49 Carolyn Kormann, 'The False Choice Between Economic Growth and Combatting Climate Change', *The New Yorker* (4 February 2019). newyorker.com/news/news-desk/the-false-choice-between-economic-growth-and-combatting-climate-change

50 Nick Watts et al., 'The 2020 Report of the Lancet Countdown on Health and Climate Change: Responding to Converging Crises', *The Lancet* 397, no. 10269 (2021): 129–170. doi:10.1016/s0140-6736(20)32290-x

51 Kalpana Balakrishnan et al., 'The Impact of Air Pollution on Deaths, Disease Burden, and Life Expectancy Across the States of India: The Global Burden of Disease Study 2017', *The Lancet Planetary Health* 3, no. 1 (2019): e26–39. doi:10.1016/s2542-5196(18)30261-4

52 Uma Gupta, 'India Could Add 6,490 Electric Buses in Next Two Years', *PV Magazine* (11 September 2020). pv-magazine-india.com/2020/09/11/india-could-add-6490-electric-buses-in-next-two-years

53 Ejaz Ghani, 'India's promising green growth', *The Financial Express* (8 April 2021). financialexpress.com/opinion/indias-promising-green-growth/2228971/.

54 Ibid.

Chapter 17

1 Michael Osterholm, 'Preparing for the Next Pandemic', *Foreign Affairs* (July/August 2005). foreignaffairs.com/articles/2005-07-01/preparing-next-pandemic
2 Bernard Avishai, 'The Pandemic Isn't a Black Swan but a Portent of a More Fragile Global System', *The New Yorker* (21 April 2020). newyorker.com/news/daily-comment/the-pandemic-isnt-a-black-swan-but-a-portent-of-a-more-fragile-global-system
3 Joseph Norman, Yaneer Bar-Yam and Nassim Nicholas Taleb, 'Systemic Risk of Pandemic Via Novel Pathogens—Coronavirus: A Note', New England Complex Systems Institute (26 January 2020).
4 Bernard Avishai, 'The Pandemic Isn't a Black Swan but a Portent of a More Fragile Global System', *The New Yorker* (21 April 2020). newyorker.com/news/daily-comment/the-pandemic-isnt-a-black-swan-but-a-portent-of-a-more-fragile-global-system
5 Ian Bremmer, 'The Best Global Responses to the COVID-19 Pandemic, 1 Year Later', *Time* (12 June 2020). time.com/5851633/best-global-responses-covid-19
6 Anne Applebaum, 'Coronavirus Showed That America Wasn't Up to the Task', *The Atlantic* (15 March 2020). theatlantic.com/ideas/archive/2020/03/coronavirus-showed-america-wasnt-task/608023
7 Anoo Bhuyan, 'India Tries to Hire 227 Epidemiologists in the Middle of COVID-19 Pandemic', IndiaSpend (20 April 2020). indiaspend.com/india-tries-to-hire-227-epidemiologists-in-the-middle-of-covid-19-pandemic/
8 Ipchita Bharali, Preeti Kumar and Sakthivel Selvaraj, 'How Well Is India Responding to COVID-19?', Brookings (2 July 2020). brookings.edu/blog/future-development/2020/07/02/how-well-is-india-responding-to-covid-19
9 Neelam Pandey, 'Mahabharata War Won in 18 Days, but Fight Against Coronavirus Will Take 21 Days, Says Modi', The Print (25 March 2020). theprint.in/india/mahabharata-war-won-in-18-days-but-fight-against-coronavirus-will-take-21-days-says-modi/388267
10 Salman Anees Soz, 'Making Sense of COVID-19 Data and Why It Is Too Early to Jump to Conclusions', The Wire (1 April 2020). thewire.in/health/covid-19-data-early-jump-conclusions

11 'What Is the Economic Cost of Covid-19?', *The Economist* (7 January 2021). economist.com/finance-and-economics/2021/01/09/what-is-the-economic-cost-of-covid-19
12 'Which Economies Are Most Vulnerable to Covid-19's Long-Term Effects?', *The Economist* (15 December 2020). economist.com/graphic-detail/2020/12/15/which-economies-are-most-vulnerable-to-covid-19s-long-term-effects
13 Regis Barnichon, Christian Matthes and Alexander Ziegenbein, 'The Financial Crisis at 10: Will We Ever Recover?', *FRBSF Economic Letter* (Federal Reserve Bank of San Francisco, 2018). frbsf.org/economic-research/publications/economic-letter/2018/august/financial-crisis-at-10-years-will-we-ever-recover
14 Valerie Cerra and Sweta C. Saxena, 'The Economic Scars of Crises and Recessions', *IMF Blog* (21 March 2018). blogs.imf.org/2018/03/21/the-economic-scars-of-crises-and-recessions
15 Peter Goodman, 'One Vaccine Side Effect: Global Economic Inequality', *The New York Times* (25 December 2020). nytimes.com/2020/12/25/business/coronavirus-vaccines-global-economy.html
16 Owen Jarus, '20 of the Worst Epidemics and Pandemics in History', Live Science (20 March 2020). livescience.com/worst-epidemics-and-pandemics-in-history.html
17 Ensheng Dong, Hongru Du and Lauren Gardner, 'An Interactive Web-based Dashboard to Track COVID-19 in Real Time', *The Lancet Infectious Diseases* 20, no. 5 (2020): 533-534. doi:10.1016/S1473-3099(20)30120-1
18 Stephanie Pappas and Tiffany Means, 'Top 10 Deadliest Natural Disasters in History', Live Science (17 December 2020). livescience.com/33316-top-10-deadliest-natural-disasters.html
19 Ibid.
20 Anil Kkumar Sinha, *The Gujarat Earthquake 2001* (Asian Disaster Reduction Centre). drc.asia/publications/recovery_reports/pdf/Gujarat.pdf
21 Aon Benfield, *2014 Annual Global Climate and Catastrophe Report: Impact Forecasting*. thoughtleadership.aonbenfield.com/Documents/20150113_ab_if_annual_climate_catastrophe_report.pdf
22 Salman Anees Soz, 'After the Deluge, What?', *The Hindu* (28 March 2016). thehindu.com/opinion/op-ed/jammu-and-kashmir-floods-after-the-deluge-what/article7612336.ece

23 National Disaster Management Authority, Government of India. ndma.gov.in/
24 Nibedita S. Ray-Bennett, 'Learning from Deaths in Disasters: The Case of Odisha, India', Middle East Institute (9 June 2016). mei.edu/publications/learning-deaths-disasters-case-odisha-india
25 Ayan Jha, Rivu Basu and Atreyee Basu, 'Studying Policy Changes in Disaster Management in India: A Tale of Two Cyclones', *Disaster Medicine and Public Health Preparedness* 10, no. 1 (2015): 42–46. doi:10.1017/dmp.2015.116
26 World Bank, 'What States Can Learn from Odisha in Disaster Preparedness and Mitigation', World Bank (14 June 2019). worldbank.org/en/news/speech/2019/06/14/odisha-fani-disaster-preparedness
27 Nikunj Makwana, 'Public Health Care System's Preparedness to Combat Epidemics After Natural Disasters', *Journal of Family Medicine and Primary Care* 9, no. 10 (2020): 5107–5112. doi:10.4103/jfmpc.jfmpc_895_19
28 Madhulika Khanna and Nishtha Kochhar, 'Natural Disasters and Child Marriages: A Case Study from Bihar', Center for the Advanced Study of India (CASI) (21 December 2020). casi.sas.upenn.edu/iit/madhulikakhanna-nishthakochhar
29 Salman Anees Soz, Jolanta Kryspin-Watson and Zuzana Stanton-Geddes, *The Role of Green Infrastructure Solutions in Urban Flood Risk Management* (World Bank, 2016). openknowledge.worldbank.org/handle/10986/25112
30 Eilia Jafar, 'Disaster Management: India Is Not Completely Ready', *Hindustan Times* (3 September 2018). hindustantimes.com/analysis/disaster-management-india-is-not-completely-ready/story-WQ7TEVdfWibfohDQXSCnzO.html
31 Ibid.
32 Shruti Sharma, 'Biological Risks in India: Perspectives and Analysis', Carnegie Endowment for International Peace (9 December 2020). carnegieendowment.org/2020/12/09/biological-risks-in-india-perspectives-and-analysis-pub-83399
33 Shruti Sharma, 'India's Pandemic Preparedness and Response', Carnegie India (6 December 2019). carnegieindia.org/2019/12/06/india-s-pandemic-preparedness-and-response-event-7276
34 Vineetha Nalla and Nihal Ranjit, 'Beyond Preparedness', *The Hindu* (4 February 2020). thehindu.com/opinion/op-ed/beyond-preparedness/article30735985.ece

35 Archana Patankar, 'Impacts of Natural Disasters on Households and Small Businesses in India', ADB Economics Working Paper Series (2019). doi:10.22617/wps190617-2
36 Ibid.
37 Tae Yoo, '4 Ways Technology Can Help Us Respond to Disasters', World Economic Forum (8 January 2018). weforum.org/agenda/2018/01/4-ways-technology-can-play-a-critical-role-in-disaster-response

Chapter 18

1 Kyle Mizokami, 'Here's Every Aircraft Carrier in the World', *Popular Mechanics* (16 December 2020). popularmechanics.com/military/navy-ships/g2412/a-global-roundup-of-aircraft-carriers
2 Blake Stilwell, 'The USS Bismarck Sea Was the Last Commissioned US Aircraft Carrier Sunk by an Enemy', Military.com (18 February 2021). military.com/history/uss-bismarck-sea-was-last-commissioned-us-aircraft-carrier-sunk-enemy.html
3 'Aircraft-Carriers Take to the Air', *The Economist* (25 March 2021). economist.com/science-and-technology/2021/03/25/aircraft-carriers-take-to-the-air
4 Ibid.
5 'Indian Navy Planning to Dump its Plan to Acquire Third Aircraft Carrier—Reports', The EurAsian Times (24 March 2021). eurasiantimes.com/has-indian-navy-changed-its-priority-from-third-carrier-to-more-nuclear-submarines
6 Vijay Mahajan, 'How Indian Companies Are Using Technology to Reach New Consumers', *Harvard Business Review* (15 October 2020). hbr.org/2020/10/how-indian-companies-are-using-technology-to-reach-new-consumers
7 Noshir Kaka et al., *Digital India: Technology to Transform a Connected Nation* (McKinsey Global Institute, 2019). mckinsey.com/business-functions/mckinsey-digital/our-insights/digital-india-technology-to-transform-a-connected-nation
8 Ibid.
9 'What Is the India Stack? Nandan Nilekani Explains', Digital Finance (28 July 2020). digfingroup.com/what-is-india-stack
10 Ibid.
11 Ibid.

12 Ministry of Electronics and Information Technology, *India's Trillion Dollar Digital Opportunity* (Government of India, 2019). meity.gov.in/writereaddata/files/india_trillion-dollar_digital_opportunity.pdf
13 Ibid.
14 Ibid.
15 Lutz Goedde et al., 'Agriculture's Connected Future: How Technology Can Yield New Growth', McKinsey & Company (9 October 2020). mckinsey.com/industries/agriculture/our-insights/agricultures-connected-future-how-technology-can-yield-new-growth
16 Nivruti Rai, 'Reimagining India's Digital Transformation in Vital Sectors', *Mint* (24 November 2020). livemint.com/opinion/online-views/opinion-reimagining-india-s-digital-transformation-in-vital-sectors-11606199247553.html
17 Akira Hayakawa, 'Indian Startup Byju's Set to Buy Test-Prep Tutor for up to $1bn', Nikkei Asia (27 January 2021). asia.nikkei.com/Business/Education/Indian-startup-Byju-s-set-to-buy-test-prep-tutor-for-up-to-1bn
18 'Valued at $12 Billion, Byju's a Class Apart', *The Financial Express* (22 November 2020). financialexpress.com/industry/sme/valued-at-12-billion-byjus-a-class-apart/2134159
19 'Technology Is Coming of Age During the Pandemic', *The Economist* (11 November 2020). economist.com/international/2020/11/11/educational-technology-is-coming-of-age-during-the-pandemic
20 Natalie Kofler, 'Timely Book Tells the CRISPR Story so Far'. *Nature* 587, no. 7832 (2020): 31–33. doi:10.1038/d41586-020-03071-0
21 Ibid.
22 Jennifer Straiton, 'CRISPR Vs COVID-19: How Can Gene Editing Help Beat a Virus?', *BioTechniques* 69, no. 5 (2020): 327–329. doi:10.2144/btn-2020-0145
23 Richard Conniff, 'What the Luddites Really Fought Against', *Smithsonian Magazine* (March 2011). smithsonianmag.com/history/what-the-luddites-really-fought-against-264412
24 Brett Frischmann, 'There's Nothing Wrong with Being a Luddite', *Scientific American Blog Network* (20 September 2018). blogs.scientificamerican.com/observations/theres-nothing-wrong-with-being-a-luddite
25 Adrienne LaFrance, 'When People Feared Computers', *The Atlantic* (30 March 2015). theatlantic.com/technology/archive/2015/03/when-people-feared-computers/388919

26 Cari Romm, 'Americans Fear Technology More Than Dying', *The Atlantic* (17 October 2015). theatlantic.com/technology/archive/2015/10/americans-are-more-afraid-of-robots-than-death/410929
27 'The Real Digital Divide', *The Economist* (10 March 2005). economist.com/leaders/2005/03/10/the-real-digital-divide
28 Ibid.
29 Ibid.
30 Noshir Kaka et al., *Digital India: Technology to Transform a Connected Nation* (McKinsey Global Institute, 2019). mckinsey.com/business-functions/mckinsey-digital/our-insights/digital-india-technology-to-transform-a-connected-nation
31 Nielsen, and Internet and Mobile Association of India, *Digital in India 2019—Round 2 Report* (2019). cms.iamai.in/Content/ResearchPapers/2286f4d7-424f-4bde-be88-6415fe5021d5.pdf
32 Nielsen, and Internet and Mobile Association of India, *India Internet 2019* (2019). cms.iamai.in/Content/ResearchPapers/d3654bcc-002f-4fc7-ab39-e1fbeb00005d.pdf
33 Protiva Kundu, 'Indian Education Can't Go Online—Only 8% of Homes with Young Members Have Computer with Net Link', Scroll.in (5 May 2020). scroll.in/article/960939/indian-education-cant-go-online-only-8-of-homes-with-school-children-have-computer-with-net-link
34 Suchitra Mohanty and Rahul Bhatia, 'Indian Court's Privacy Ruling Is Blow to Government', Reuters (24 August 2017). reuters.com/article/us-india-court-privacy/indian-courts-privacy-ruling-is-blow-to-government-idUSKCN1B40CE
35 Gautam Bhatia, 'India's Growing Surveillance State', *Foreign Affairs* (19 February 2020). foreignaffairs.com/articles/india/2020-02-19/indias-growing-surveillance-state
36 Anirudh Burman, *Will India's Proposed Data Protection Law Protect Privacy and Promote Growth?* (Carnegie India, 2020). carnegieindia.org/2020/03/09/will-india-s-proposed-data-protection-law-protect-privacy-and-promote-growth-pub-81217
37 Gautam Bhatia, 'India's Growing Surveillance State', *Foreign Affairs* (19 February 2020).
38 Ibid.
39 Niharika Sharma, 'India's Among the World's Top Three Surveillance States', Quartz (16 October 2019). qz.com/india/1728927/indias-among-the-worlds-top-three-surveillance-states

40 Abhinav Singh, 'India Sees 37% Increase in Data Breaches, Cyber Attacks This Year', *The Week* (17 November 2020). theweek.in/news/biz-tech/2020/11/17/india-sees-37-increase-in-data-breaches-cyber-attacks-this-year.html
41 Aashish Aryan, 'As Data Leak Claims Resurface, MobiKwik Plans Forensic Audit', *The Indian Express* (31 March 2021). indianexpress.com/article/business/companies/as-data-leak-claims-resurface-mobikwik-plans-forensic-audit-7251966
42 'Significant Cyber Incidents', Center for Strategic and International Studies. csis.org/programs/strategic-technologies-program/significant-cyber-incidents
43 David Deming, 'Balancing Privacy with Data Sharing for the Public Good', *The New York Times* (19 February 2021). nytimes.com/2021/02/19/business/privacy-open-data-public.html
44 Suneera Tandon, 'Economic Survey Warns of India's Ageing Population, Says Retirement Age Should Rise', *Mint* (4 July 2019). www.livemint.com/budget/economic-survey/eco-survey-warns-of-india-s-ageing-population-says-retirement-age-should-rise-1562248716749.html
45 Zia Qureshi, 'Technology and the Future of Growth: Challenges of Change', Brookings (25 February 2020). brookings.edu/blog/up-front/2020/02/25/technology-and-the-future-of-growth-challenges-of-change
46 Ibid.
47 Ibid.
48 Ibid.
49 Anton Korinek and Joe Stiglitz, 'Artificial Intelligence Could Mean Large Increases in Prosperity—But Only for a Privileged Few', Institute for New Economic Thinking (18 February 2021). ineteconomics.org/perspectives/blog/artificial-intelligence-could-mean-technological-advancement-but-only-for-a-privileged-few
50 Ibid.
51 Ministry of Labour and Employment, 'Loksabha Unstarred Question No. 3991: Automation Impact on Jobs', *Lok Sabha* (Government of India, 27 March 2017). 164.100.47.194/Loksabha/Questions/QResult15.aspx?qref=50404&lsno=16
52 Shirish Sankhe et al., *India's Turning Point: An Economic Agenda to Spur Growth and Jobs* (McKinsey Global Institute, 2020). mckinsey.com/featured-insights/india/indias-turning-point-an-economic-agenda-to-spur-growth-and-jobs

53 World Bank, *World Development Report 2018: The Changing Nature of Work* (World Bank Group, 2019). worldbank.org/en/publication/wdr2019
54 Bhaskar Chakravorti, 'Dear Sundar Pichai: There's a Lot You Take on When You Take on the Task of Digitising India. Here Are a Few Pointers', *The Indian Express* (8 August 2020). indianexpress.com/article/opinion/columns/sundar-pichai-google-education-digital-india-6544793
55 Bhaskar Chakravorti et al., 'Digital Light at the End of the COVID Tunnel for India? How to Translate Digital Momentum into Job Creation and Recovery Beyond the Pandemic', The Fletcher School (Tufts University, 2020).
56 'Digital Infrastructure—Backbone of an Economy', Confederation of Indian Industry (CII) (24 June 2020). ciiblog.in/technology/digital-infrastructure-backbone-of-an-economy/
57 Prashant Singhal, 'A Policy Roadmap for India's Digital Transformation', *Mint* (2 July 2020). livemint.com/opinion/online-views/a-policy-roadmap-for-india-s-digital-transformation-11593685812184.html
58 Bhaskar Chakravorti, 'Dear Sundar Pichai: There's a Lot You Take on When You Take on the Task of Digitising India. Here Are a Few Pointers', *The Indian Express* (8 August 2020).
59 Sumeysh Srivastava, 'International Literacy Day: Bridging India's Digital Divide', BloombergQuint (8 September 2020). bloombergquint.com/technology/international-literacy-day-bridging-indias-digital-divide
60 'National Digital Literacy Mission', Digital Empowerment Foundation. defindia.org/national-digital-literacy-mission/
61 IANS, 'Digital Literacy Drive Barely Touched 1.6 Percent of the Population: Parliamentary Committee Report', *News18* (6 February 2019). news18.com/news/india/digital-literacy-drive-barely-touched-1-6-percent-of-the-population-parliamentary-committee-report-2026819.html
62 Sumeysh Srivastava, 'International Literacy Day: Bridging India's Digital Divide', BloombergQuint (8 September 2020). bloombergquint.com/technology/international-literacy-day-bridging-indias-digital-divide
63 Zia Qureshi, 'Inequality in the Digital Era', *Work in the Age of Data* (Banco Bilbao Vizcaya Argentaria, 2019). brookings.edu/wp-content/

uploads/2020/02/BBVA-OpenMind-Zia-Qureshi-Inequality-in-the-digital-era.pdf

64 Ibid.

Chapter 19

1 Suzanne Pepper, *China's Education Reform in the 1980s: Policies, Issues, Historical Perspectives* (University of California, 1990).
2 Wan-Hua Ma, *Economic Reform and Higher Education in China*, Center for International and Development Education (CIDE) Occasional Papers Series: Higher Education (2003). usp.br/feafuturo/assets/files/China.pdf
3 Mohini Bishnoi, 'The Many Structural Flaws in India's Higher Education System', *The Hindu* (5 December 2019). thehindu.com/opinion/op-ed/the-many-structural-flaws-in-indias-higher-education-system/article30169923.ece
4 The well-known economist Dani Rodrik coined this phrase.

Index

Acknowledgements

I wish to acknowledge my research assistant Kayla Malcy, who provided invaluable support in preparing this book. Her services were provided to me by the Institute of International Economic Policy (IIEP), Elliott School of International Affairs, George Washington University, to whom I am very grateful. Thanks, Kayla!

At IIEP, the Envisioning India series which I helped put together with James Foster, Jay Shambaugh and Kyle Renner and his excellent team, was also very helpful in writing this book. The series ran through the academic year 2020-21 and had some of the best minds on the Indian economy speak on various topics which helped shape my thinking for this book. They are of course not responsible for any of what I took away from their remarks, but they may find hints of it in the book.

I owe a deep intellectual debt to my favourite professor at the Delhi School of Economics, Professor Raj Krishna, with whom I wrote a paper on India's food policy at IFPRI and worked under at the Planning Commission in the late 1990s. Many of my views on India's farm policy were shaped during that period of working with Professor Raj Krishna. At DSE, I also learnt a lot from A.L. Nagar, Pranab Mukherjee, Mrinal Dutta-Choudhary and Dharma Kumar. At Stanford University, I remember very fondly the teachings of Ben Bernanke (macroeconomics) and Michael Boskin (public finance). Their foundational teachings set me up to understand economics much better.

At the World Bank, I learnt a lot from many people—but especially, Michael Bruno (who selected me to lead the 1997 World Development Report on the Role of the State) and Joseph Stiglitz, with whom I finished that report after Michael's untimely demise. I also wish to thank Stanley Fischer (with whom I worked for two years when he was Chief Economist) and Lyn Squire and the WDR 1997 team from whom I learnt a lot—especially about the role of the state in shaping a country's economic destiny.

I also want to acknowledge Kemal Dervis, who was Turkey's Economic Czar after the 2001 financial crisis and with whom I worked closely as World Bank Director to Turkey in the subsequent recovery, learning closely how the art of economic policymaking is as important as the science. He also, subsequently, brought me to head the Asia Department of UNDP where I learnt a lot about the region, its dynamism and India's place in it—which has filtered through in many parts of this book.

On my return to India in 2013 to become the first Director-General of an Independent Evaluation Office at the invitation of the government, I immersed myself deeply into India's challenges and options. That one year also told me why I had been so disillusioned with Indian planning and government in general when I had worked at the Planning Commission in 1977-78. When the UPA government of Dr Manmohan Singh was voted out in 2014, my father—not an economist, but an avid reader—said to me, 'Why don't you write a book on the Indian economy? But write it in such a style that even I can understand.' Several publishers were after me to write such a book, but, as is my usual style, I procrastinated.

Vijay Kelkar and Rathin Roy at NIPFP gave me a two-year appointment as Distinguished Visiting Professor and the opportunity to do a detailed study of India's state-owned enterprises, which is summarized in Chapter 3 of the book. I am grateful to them and to my colleague Swati Gupta who worked with me on that giant exercise. She is the first Swati I must thank.

FICCI, where I served as Chief Economic Advisor from 2017-20, and now CII, where I have recently joined the Economic Advisory Council, have given me a good idea of how India Inc. thinks (or does not) on various issues affecting the Indian economy.

I was fortunate to meet Salman and we found that not only were we from the same college in Delhi, but that a lot of our thinking was also very compatible. We also complemented each other—in that I was interested in some matters, and he in others. And so over some badly played golf rounds, we decided to write this book together—a process which worked very well. Salaam, Salman!

I also want to thank another Swati. Our publisher Swati Chopra of HarperCollins India, who I did not know as well as Salman did, but have been very impressed with her professionalism, despite her own personal tragedies. Many thanks, Swati for holding us steadfast to the completion of this book, and for your many contributions to help us pull all this together.

The onset of COVID-19, in a way, has given me the opportunity to fulfill my father's wish and write the book he wanted me to write. And as I said earlier, I was always reminded of his request to write it shorn of jargon and in a language he would understand. He was a constant presence as I wrote the book. A sort of conscience on my shoulder that urged me on to finish the book. My children Aparna and Siddartha—having flown the coop—nevertheless, also kept encouraging me. They are the future we hope will inherit a better, more prosperous and caring India we wish for.

Last, but by no means the least, I owe a deep debt of gratitude to my wife Rita Jalali, who has been the light of my life in more than forty-two years of our married life. She has helped shape my thinking on social issues tremendously and with her deep knowledge and academic rigour in sociology, she has constantly reminded me of the limitations of just focusing on economist's logic and thinking. Thanks to our friends, I married her again on our twenty-fifth wedding anniversary—this time in a proper Indian ceremony, as against our court wedding the first time around at Stanford University, where we were both pursuing our PhDs. Thank you, Rita, for being by my side all these years and for your social conscience and generosity towards those less fortunate. I owe you much more than I can ever repay.

Ajay Chhibber

As was the case with my first book, I want to begin by thanking Swati Chopra at HarperCollins India. Swati is a consummate professional who persevered through personal struggles to make sure we delivered this book, largely on schedule, and in spite of the uncertainty caused by COVID-19. Thank you, Swati!

I benefited enormously by the excellent research assistance provided by Simar Singh. Simar prepared exceptionally good, well-researched background material that helped me stay focused on the ideas I wanted to convey through this book. I am grateful for Simar's many reviews of the book, which can become tedious after a while. But she was a thorough professional throughout. If she puts her mind to it, Simar can and must write a book of her own in the not-so-distant future. Thank you, Simar!

The ideas I have tried to convey are a reflection of the person I have become over the years. So many have contributed in so many ways. It is impossible to name all here but I do want to mention the late Vinod Chowdhury at St. Stephen's College, whose comparative economic history course was most interesting. Professor Stephen L. Parente helped me learn macroeconomics at Northeastern University, and the late David Cromwell at Yale School of Management helped me understand the importance of writing purposefully. Thank you, teachers!

I understood the importance of research at the World Bank and the person I have to thank for that is Jayati Datta-Mitra. She took a chance by hiring me and that started my World Bank career. Many colleagues and friends at the World Bank have helped shape my views. However, my former boss Shigeo Katsu is perhaps most responsible for making me think more broadly about development, especially its social dimensions. It was also at the World Bank that I met one of my best friends, Julius Gwyer. Since 1995, Jules has been a source of wisdom and encouragement for my writing projects. Thank you, friends and colleagues!

It was wonderful to write this book with Ajay Chhibber. Over the last few years, Ajay and I have become friends, often exchanging notes about India, its economy and politics. We remain connected to our roots in international development and that is one reason we came together to write this book. One of the unexpected benefits of writing this book has been to hear amusing anecdotes from Ajay's time at the World Bank and the UNDP. Ajay has much to offer India and the world of economic development. He can also be a terrific companion on the golf course. It has been a pleasure collaborating with him. Thank you, Ajay!

I want to thank my parents for remaining patient at a time of great difficulty in Kashmir. Politics and the pandemic prevented us from seeing each other for a long time. Despite that, they did not burden me with their considerable challenges and, in some ways, enabled my focus on this book. I am proud to be the son of Saifuddin Soz and Mumtaz Soz and I know they will be beaming when they hold their copy of this book in their hands. Thank you, Mummy and Daddy!

My amazing children, Asmara and Zaydan, are my biggest fans even though writing this book has meant less 'daddy time' for them than usual. I think they are very excited about this book even though they know it is not like a J.K. Rowling bestseller. Their eyes sparkled when I presented them with a copy of my first book. It is that sparkle I want to recapture again and again. Clearly, they make me want to do more and better. Thank you, Asmara and Zaydan! As usual, Soola, our gentle and loving Havanese, kept me company while I wrote. I am so glad he is part of our family.

Finally, I'd like to thank my wife, Asia. I am not really sure what to write. Even though this book bears my name, it is also Asia's book. Writing takes a lot of time and effort. There are practical things in life that can't wait for the completion of manuscripts. Someone has to plug the deficit. This is especially hard if you are moving continents, as we did in the middle of the writing of this book. It simply could not have happened without Asia. She puts up with a lot because she loves me and she knows I love her and that we are good together. She is my biggest supporter and enabler and for that I thank her with all my heart. Thank you, my love!

Salman Anees Soz

About the Authors

Ajay Chhibber is Distinguished Visiting Scholar at the Institute of International Economic Policy, George Washington University, and Non-Resident Senior Fellow at the Atlantic Council. He was Distinguished Visiting Professor at the National Institute for Public Finance and Policy and India's first Director General of Independent Evaluation with the status of Minister of State in 2013–14. From 2008–13 he was UN Assistant Secretary-General, Assistant Administrator at UNDP. He served as the World Bank's Country Director in Turkey and Vietnam and led the 1997 World Development Report on the role of the state. He has published five books on economic development and many articles in international journals and major newspapers. He has a PhD from Stanford University, a master's degree from the Delhi School of Economics, and has done advanced management programmes at Harvard University and at INSEAD, France. He won the David Rajaram Prize as best all-rounder at St. Stephen's College, New Delhi.

Salman Anees Soz is an economic development consultant, author and commentator. He has extensive experience across a range of economic development issues in Eastern Europe and Central Asia, Middle East and North Africa, Sub-Saharan Africa, and South Asia. He serves as a consultant to multiple World Bank teams and was previously a consultant at the Asian Development Bank. He is a recipient of the World Bank President's Award for Excellence. His commentaries appear in a variety of media outlets. He also speaks on politics, economics and international affairs at universities, think tanks and conferences. He is Deputy Chairman of the All India Professionals' Congress and serves as an advisor to other institutions. He holds a master's degree in business administration from Yale University, a master's degree in economics from Northeastern University, and a BA (Hons) in economics from St. Stephen's College, where he was the president of the Students' Union Society.